D0615585

ALL THE
BABE'S MEN

Joe —
Wishing you much continued
long ball success with
Home Run Inn Pizza.
Enjoy!

07-12-13

Related Titles from Potomac Books

Baseball's Most Wanted™: The Top 10 Book of the National Pastime's Outrageous Offenders, Lucky Bounces, and Other Oddities
—Floyd Conner

Home Run's Most Wanted™: The Top 10 Book of Monumental Dingers, Prodigious Swingers, and Everything Long-Ball
—David Vincent

Pull Up a Chair: The Vin Scully Story
—Curt Smith

ALL THE BABE'S MEN

☆

Baseball's Greatest Home Run Seasons and
How They Changed America

ELDON L. HAM

Potomac Books
Washington, D.C.

Copyright © 2013 Potomac Books, Inc.

Published in the United States by Potomac Books, Inc. All rights reserved. No part of this book may be reproduced in any manner whatsoever without written permission from the publisher, except in the case of brief quotations embodied in critical articles and reviews.

Library of Congress Cataloging-in-Publication Data
Ham, Eldon L., 1952–
    All the Babe's men : baseball's greatest home run seasons and how they changed America / Eldon L. Ham.—1st ed.
        pages cm
    Includes bibliographical references and index.
    ISBN 978-1-59797-938-2 (hardcover : alk. paper)
    ISBN 978-1-59797-939-9 (electronic)
    1. Home runs (Baseball) 2. Baseball—United States—History. 3. Baseball players—United States. I. Title.
    GV868.4.H36 2013
    796.357'26—dc23

                                                                                2012047587

Printed in the United States of America on acid-free paper that meets the American National Standards Institute Z39-48 Standard.

Potomac Books
22841 Quicksilver Drive
Dulles, Virginia 20166

First Edition

10 9 8 7 6 5 4 3 2 1

CONTENTS

ACKNOWLEDGMENTS

Chicago-Kent College of Law took a chance on a new student more decades ago than seems possible and in 1994 took another flier on me when I began teaching sports law as an adjunct professor. As a result, a good deal of whatever success and credibility I have garnered while establishing my author's platform, as they say, has been enhanced by my long affiliation with the law school, and for that I am grateful.

This book would not have been possible without its publisher, Potomac Books, Inc.; my dedicated editors, Elizabeth Demers, Aryana Hendrawan, and Vicki Chamlee; and my literary agent, Mike Farris, a colleague and dependable compatriot in the worlds of law and literature. I also owe a debt of gratitude to my assistant Cassie, who tirelessly compiled the bibliography, then audited the footnotes and made them work. Also to my administrative right hand, Meghan, who keeps my work and me in line, and to my student and fact-checker Lee Oliff. Many thanks both to my photograph researcher and archivist, Joan, who found a plethora of historic photos that give life to Babe Ruth and the men who followed, and to the National Baseball Hall of Fame and Museum in Cooperstown, New York. The museum supplied legions of photos from which to choose, and a select few are featured in this final work.

Many thanks are in order for all my supportive friends and family but in particular to my wife, Nan, whose beloved Chicago White Sox have produced their share of baseball posterity, and to our children, Carla and Brandon, who represent the best hopes of the next generations of America, our land of proverbial opportunity that was shaped, in no small part, by the immortal sluggers of baseball.

Finally, although my researchers and editors have been invaluable, all the facts, opinions, and errors in this book are my own responsibility.

INTRODUCTION

I don't believe what I just saw. I don't believe what I just saw!
—JACK BUCK, 1988 WORLD SERIES

On August 25, 2011, the powerful Hurricane Irene bore down on the Eastern Seaboard with New York City looming in its sights. Irene was daunting, to be sure (although not as devastating as Sandy would be a year later), but the most remarkable national headlines that August day featured a much different form of wonder, one that has become the iconic American symbol of strength, success, and glamour: the almighty home run. One team in the same game that day launched three home runs, in fact—all grand slams—setting a major-league record and a standard of long-ball prowess that not even George Herman "Babe" Ruth, Lou Gehrig, Willie Mays, Hank Aaron, Mickey Mantle, or Barry Bonds had ever experienced.

Home runs are the stuff of American legends, four to five seconds of baseball glory that are savored or scorned as they sail over the walls of long-ball immortality. The great ones are remembered for decades. Some are never forgotten because they changed the course of baseball, such as Bobby Thomson's 1951 "shot heard round the world," Bill Mazeroski's miracle 1960 World Series winner for the Pirates, or Kirk Gibson's pinch-hit "limp-off" home run on two bad legs to steal Game 1 of the 1988 World Series. But some home runs even affected America, such as the immortal record setters from Babe Ruth, who went deep so prodigiously that the term "Ruthian" still connotes great magnitude; those from fair-haired Mickey Mantle, who emulated the charismatic president John F. Kennedy and invented the tape measure blast that has become a part of the game and the American lexicon itself; or those from Roger Maris, a sullen hero who was baseball's version of the introspective Richard Nixon. Fittingly, Kennedy's National Aeronautics and Space Administration space program would propel an actual "moon shot" skyward in 1969, the same year that Mickey Mantle retired from baseball. Or consider the irascible Ted Williams, fierce competitor and genuine American war hero; the ill-tempered Barry Bonds, who tainted his own image with performance enhancers, apparently in an ill-fated quest for baseball immortality reminiscent of the fictional Charles Foster Kane (from *Citizen Kane*); or the trailblazing missiles of Jackie Robinson, the flashy Willie Mays, and that easygoing pillar of consistency, Hank Aaron.

The modern-day home run is the marquee attraction in baseball, and the grand slam is a special feat made of long-ball power and baseball proclivity. "Grand slam" is a term that transcends baseball, since golf, tennis, and big business all have their own grand slam moments. Conversely, no one ever described a baseball home run as being a hole in one or a touchdown, yet plenty of home runs have rocked the world of golf and football, business, science, and even politics.

The diminutive Ross Barnes, a 145-pound infielder for the Chicago White Stockings, the team that would eventually be known as the Chicago Cubs, hit the first official major-league home run on May 2, 1876. Other home runs, even quantifiable ones as the longest home run, are the topic of much debate. Even so, the longest-recognized home run is generally regarded to be Mickey Mantle's reputed 565-foot monster that left Washington's Griffith Stadium on April 17, 1953, a blast that clanked off a stadium sign 460 away and kept going. The ball went so far that it inspired a tape measure calculation and become the first literal tape measure shot.

Anointing the most impressive homers is fodder for even more controversy, but the following four candidates, listed in no particular order, stand out. Mantle's towering shot on May 22, 1963—a line drive that struck the 102-foot-high right-field facade and nearly left Yankee Stadium altogether—may have been the most visually impressive. The magical pinch-hit game winner that Dodger Kirk Gibson crushed to open the 1988 World Series may have been the most improbable, evoking announcer Jack Buck's "I don't believe" exclamation. Since the injured Gibson could not run at all and barely could limp to the plate on two bad legs, he needed either to coax a walk from one of the game's greatest closers or do the unthinkable and hit a miracle walk-off home run. The third candidate may have been the most stunning: Bobby Thomson's walk-off "shot heard round the world" took all of four seconds to snatch the 1951 pennant from the Dodgers. The fourth would perhaps be Bill Mazeroski's World Series winner, which wrested a title for the Pirates from the 1960 Yankees and cost the aging New York manager Charles "Casey" Stengel his job.

And then there is Ruth's record. One could argue that all 714 of Ruth's career home runs made their marks on baseball, if not America itself, since all contributed to baseball posterity and some even made their mark on history. But the one Babe Ruth home run that will never be forgotten, an unprecedented sixtieth home run, came on September 30, 1927, and set the baseball record for the ages. It haunted the greatest hitters for decades until Roger Maris squeaked past with sixty-one runs in an elongated season, after which Ruth's ghost has continued to bait history and dare the greatest sluggers, some to the point of self-destruction.

And so it was. Then, in the wake of Gehrig, Mantle, Aaron, Williams, Mays, Jimmie Foxx, Hank Greenberg, and the immortal Ruth himself, and with a hurricane threatening, the Yankees' Curtis Granderson stepped to the plate during the dog days of August 2011 and one-upped them all when he cracked a 1-2 pitch from Athletics reliever Bruce Billings into the right-field seats. The veteran slugger had already clubbed thirty-five round-trippers on the season, but when this one cleared the right-field stands, it was historic.

This singular blast of home run dominance was a particularly remarkable feat, since home runs are no stranger to either the old or new Yankee Stadium, where both right-field porches were left intentionally short to exploit the left-handed home run power of the Babe and all those lefty sluggers who followed Ruth onto the Big Apple stage.

No team in major-league history had smacked three grand slams in one game until Granderson's eighth-inning ball cleared the right-field stands at Yankee Stadium, scoring four of New York's twenty-two runs on the day and leading an awesome come-from-behind demolition of the Oakland Athletics. Robinson Cano had already slammed starter Rich Harden for four runs in the fifth inning, and Russell Martin had smashed a second grand slam courtesy of reliever Fautino De Los Santos in the sixth. When it was Granderson's turn in the eighth, he completed the grand slam hat trick, to mix sports metaphors.

The Yankees had clocked two grand slams in one game on three other occasions, the first time by Tony Lazzeri, who smacked two himself on May 24, 1936. Among the all-time major-league records that may never be broken are Lou Gehrig's twenty-three career grand slams *for one team*, the Yankees. On June 12, 2012, Alex Rodriguez actually tied Gehrig for career slams at twenty-three, but only thirteen of the former's had come while wearing a Yankees uniform. The second-most slams in Yankees pinstripes came from the great Joe DiMaggio with thirteen, which Rodriguez equaled. Babe Ruth had sixteen slams, but four of those were in 1919 for the Boston Red Sox. Ted Williams slugged seventeen, all for Boston, and Willie McCovey had sixteen for the Giants. But with the modern era of free agency, surpassing Lou Gehrig's legendary twenty-three grand slams for one team would take a superhuman effort.

The great home run sluggers and their long-ball drives have a special place, not only in baseball history, but also in American lore itself. The home run hitters before the one-man epiphany named Ruth, such as John Franklin "Home Run" Baker or Walter "Wally" Pipp, had led the league by clubbing perhaps ten or twelve round-trippers per year. But then came Ruth. Pushing the power records of America's game not by a few runs but by orders of magnitude, he hit his twenty-ninth in 1919, his fifty-fourth in 1920, and his fifty-ninth in 1921. When he eventually slugged the elusive sixtieth, it defined not only the 1927 Murderers' Row Yankees but also personified American dominance in industry, politics, and military muscle. It still does.

The reasons for Ruth's long-ball dominance are many. He was bigger and stronger than most players of his era were, and as a pitcher in the early years, he wasn't expected by many to perform at the plate. As a result, the irascible Ruth could ignore many of the prevailing baseball strategies of the era, and he decided to swing for the fences instead of spraying singles around the field. He had nothing to lose, so he invented the idea of turning on the ball the way modern sluggers now do, rather than simply slapping flat-footed for singles and doubles. Ruth did not invent home runs, but he did learn how to hit them in bunches. Evoking the grit of American innovation, Ruth, baseball, and all the sluggers to follow soon discovered the marquee value of mammoth home runs. Legions of power hitters from Gehrig and DiMaggio to Greenberg, Foxx, and Williams, and to those who followed, such as Mays, Ralph Kiner, Mantle, Ernie Banks, Aaron, Sammy Sosa, Mark McGwire, Bonds, Rodriguez, and all the rest—all are descendents of the original. They are the personification of long-ball prowess, the legend of Ruth, and all the Babe's men who followed in the shoot-for-the-stars image of America.

Sometimes it takes a whole career to achieve greatness, but sometimes it emerges in a flash, as when Mazeroski won the 1960 World Series or when Thomson launched the 1951 Giants to a pennant with one swing. St. Louis Cardinals slugger Albert Pujols was already on his way to a lifetime of baseball achievement, averaging forty-one home runs and 121 RBIs through the 2011 regular season, but then baseball lightning struck, suddenly immortalizing Pujols on the World Series' stage. Before the sparks faded, Pujols had slammed three home runs in one World Series game, the third contest of the 2011 fall classic. Beforehand, only Babe Ruth and Reggie Jackson had ever accomplished such a Ruthian feat. And Ruth did it twice.

This book tells the story of great home run seasons, singular home runs, and history's most prodigious home run hitters—and how they personified and even transformed America itself.

> *My name is Ted F—king Williams and*
> *I'm the greatest hitter in baseball.*
> **—TED WILLIAMS, BOSTON RED SOX LEFT FIELDER**

★ 1 ★

THE HOME RUN MYSTIQUE

I didn't have evil intentions, but I guess I did have power.
—HARMON KILLEBREW[1]

Cadillacs are down at the end of the bat.
—RALPH KINER[2]

Open the window, Aunt Minnie, here it comes!
—ROSEY ROWSWELL[3]

Baseball has long been considered the American pastime, and for many decades it was the consummate American sport. Baseball, however, was not on top until home runs put it there. Championship boxing was actually king long before the emergence of baseball's George Herman "Babe" Ruth in 1914. Sports evolution does not always come easily, and baseball has fought its share of headwinds. College football ruled the gridiron and sports pages before and even after Harold "Red" Grange put the Chicago Bears and the fledgling National Football League (NFL) on the map in the early 1920s, and track and field was a global sport for generations, influencing politics and world events through Jesse Owens's triumph in the 1936

Olympics and President Jimmy Carter's boycott of the Olympics in 1980.

Baseball eventually surpassed these other sports partly because it is unique. The game, at heart, is a paradox, a complex game of simple axioms, suggesting that baseball is an enigma much as America itself is. The fundamental concept of baseball is homogeneous, yet the game is difficult to explain. "How can you think and hit at the same time?" asked Yogi Berra,[4] symbolizing the complexity of the backward game. Indeed, baseball is the only major team sport where the defense, not the offense, controls the ball.

"Aunt Minnie" did not really live beyond the Pirates' walls at venerable Forbes Field, but she did exist in the hearts and minds of anxious Pittsburgh fans as they hung on the play-by-play of one-time announcer Rosey Rowswell, who called Pirates games for nineteen years and had conjured Minnie and her open window as his trademark home run call. As a result, Aunt Minnie *was* the soul of the fans from 1936 to 1954 if not beyond, and her expectant window was always open to the game, to the legions of radio listeners, and, of course, to the home runs launched by Ralph Kiner and other Pirates sluggers. Even Babe Ruth got into the act.

Known for his long-ball legacy, Yankee pinstripes, and jaded Red Sox history, Ruth had returned to his Boston roots in 1935 to close a storied career while playing for the National League Braves, where, in true Ruthian fashion, he even made history on his way out. On May 25, 1935, against the Pirates in Pittsburgh, Ruth slammed a two-run shot in the first inning and another two-run homer in the third. He then capped a long-ball hat trick with a third home run in the seventh inning.[5] This last run proved to be the mystical 714th four-bagger that cemented his baseball record for the ages, a mark that in some ways still sets the standard for baseball prowess. Aside from its obvious place in history, this last blast was itself no ordinary home run. It was, in fact, a towering moon shot that actually cleared the roof in right field before leaving the park altogether, perhaps setting the stage for Aunt Minnie's open window in the years to come. Some say Ruth's ball traveled more than 600 feet, a mystical distance that evokes images of the fictional ballplayer Roy Hobbs who dramatically eclipsed the grandstand's lights in the enduring baseball film *The Natural*. Physics suggests that such

600-footers are more legend than fact, but no one disputes that Ruth's last shot was the longest home run ever launched in the storied Forbes Field while hosting Major League Baseball from 1909 to 1970. The Pirates' pitcher Guy Bush, who gave up the homer, could only shake his head. "I never saw a ball hit so hard before or since," he lamented.

Aunt Minnie may have been the symbol of the Pirates' long-ball prowess, but she was not real, at least in the literal sense. The Cadillacs that Pirates left fielder Ralph Kiner talked about, though, were both symbolic *and* real, and he knew they came from the sweet spot of a long-ball swing. Kiner was an authority on home runs: he led the league in home runs for each of his first seven seasons in the major leagues, including 1951 when he slugged forty-two and led the league in runs scored (124), walks (137), on-base percentage (.452), and slugging average (.627).[6] In 1951 Bobby Thomson slugged what might be the most famous home run in the annals of the game, but it was Kiner who scored the home run paycheck, becoming the highest-paid player in the National League while another long ball slugger, Ted Williams, only the year before had become the highest paid in baseball history. During Kiner's era, and for years thereafter, those Cadillacs symbolized more than baseball and Kiner's success; they stood for the image of America itself in the 1950s, with their tail fins, confidence, and gaudy charisma.

Started in 1902 and acquired by General Motors in 1909, Cadillac had captured the domestic luxury car market not only with innovations of comfort and style but also with engineering feats like the V-12 and V-16 engines. It became the car of choice for Elvis Presley and Gen. Dwight "Ike" Eisenhower, who rode in a Cadillac for his 1953 presidential inauguration.[7] Cadillac connoted quality and style to such a high degree that it became a perpetual metaphor for "the best," as in "the Cadillac" of television sets— or of sluggers, like Ralph Kiner.

But baseball, with its home runs and impressive paychecks, was more than just gaudy; it was irreverent and sometimes even surly. In the late nineteenth century a Pittsburgh judge, discouraged by baseball's appeal for gamblers and other knaves of the day, once proclaimed baseball "the evil game."

Harmon Killebrew's quip about not having evil intentions in playing the game suggests that he knew baseball is somehow different, that it harbors a darker side that paradoxically haunts both pitchers and hitters. Killebrew was highly respected around the league, having jacked a combined 573 homers for the Washington Senators, Minnesota Twins, and Kansas City Royals. He also appreciated the dark side of the game that originally attracted game-rigging gamblers and more recently tempted the players with steroids, and that has always embraced the unique on-field gamesmanship of spit-balls, hidden balls, corked bats, and phantom tags at second. The brood-ing slugger Roger Maris saw that side, too, claiming, "I never wanted all this hoopla." Victimized by his own success, Maris was destined to taste mostly the malevolent side of home run Karma after he dethroned the icon Babe Ruth. Likewise, stunned hurler Ralph ("Why me?") Branca was a victim of insult and history when Bobby Thomson's 1951 blast left the stadium, stage left field, crashing down to earth as perhaps the most famous walk-off home run in all of baseball history. Curiously, when Thomson acknowledged decades later that the Giants had been stealing signs much of the season— including on the day of his historic homer, although not the actual pitch he hit for the game winner—the aura of that home run did not diminish; indeed, the legend of Branca and Thomson grew larger. That a hint of larceny could actually enhance the Thomson moment, rather than diminish it, sug-gests a part of the game's darker, more mischievous side. After all, baseball is a game that personifies the hip-shooting, tobacco-spitting, no-holds-barred personality of industrial America, which matured as baseball was finding its long-ball roots.

The Thomson blast still rings through American culture. Nothing could be more American than its descriptive moniker, "the shot heard round the world"—particularly given baseball's possible roots in Valley Forge and the Ralph Waldo Emerson 1836 poem "Concord Hymn" about the beginnings of the Revolutionary War, from which the moniker was taken:

> *By the rude bridge that arched the flood,*
> *Their flag to April's breeze unfurled,*

Here once the embattled farmer's stood,
And fired the shot heard round the world.

The home run is a dramatic exclamation point to what was already becoming the quintessential American game. Baseball, the country's dominant professional team sport, had already earned a long history by the turn of the twentieth century when the NFL, National Basketball Association (NBA), and National Hockey League (NHL) were not yet fledgling ideas. In W. P. Kinsella's novel *Shoeless Joe*, a romantic labor of baseball sentiment, baseball is virtually painted like a portrait: "Colors can change, lives can alter, anything is possible in this gentle, flawless, loving game."[8] But that era was before the thunder of home runs and the roar of ravenous home crowds, both of which would transform the game from "gentle" to explosive.

The only major team sport without a clock, baseball is potentially a game without end. But the game's indifference to time is only one of its many distinctions that range from the silly, beer-gut managers stuffed into tight uniforms to the sublime. Baseball, for example, shunned instant replay for years, stubbornly avoiding it long after other team sports embraced it. Steadfastly refusing the hindsight accuracy of replay is a trait of defiance that baseball shares with mostly non-team sports that stress individual effort, more like golf or boxing. Such ties to those non-team sports may be more than mere coincidence, for baseball is really a one-on-one contest disguised as a team sport. This distinction is also important in the context of America because the game's celebration of individual effort has a uniquely capitalist quality. It partially explains why its heroes have historically been larger-than-life figures, since the players are pitted against each other in carefully defined mini-dramas of personal confrontation, success, and failure. Just like boxing, baseball ultimately becomes a zero-sum team game where every single play highlights one player's success and another's failure.

Irregularity is another important quirk that helps define the game's singular personality. By contrast, when the NFL's Dallas Cowboys travel to Philadelphia to play the rival Eagles, no one asks what size the football field is or how high the goal posts are. But in the game of baseball the players actually expect those kinds of distinctions. Each park is not only different but also wildly and intentionally so, thus linking the game again to golf: each sport is played on irregular fields and predicated on the solitary efforts of the individual in striking the ball and navigating the terrain.

Some baseball parks are deep and others are shallow. Some outfield walls are high, some are short, some are hidden by vines, and some, like in Houston, are marked by a mere yellow stripe that indicates where the stadium ends and the home runs begin. But those differences pale in comparison to the foul lines. Take the left-field line at Boston's Fenway Park that leads directly to a mammoth obstacle of fame and history affectionately known as the Green Monster, and the line at the original New York Yankee Stadium, which was built for Ruth and the massive crowds he and his home runs would likely bring. And this point is not only suggested by Ruth's home run on April 18, 1923—Opening Day in the "house that Ruth built"—but also corroborated by a 1923 *Literary Digest* article on the impressive new Yankee Stadium:

Travelers approaching New York from the sea are greeted by the lofty torch of the Statue of Liberty. Visitors arriving from the north over the tracks of the New York Central or New Haven Railroads are confronted by the imposing pile of the new Yankee Stadium. The approaches to the world's metropolis are appropriate in either case. To the sojourner from Europe, New York means opportunity. To the visitor from other parts of America, New York is the amusement center of the continent. And that spirit of diversion find fitting expression in the colossal monument of athletic sport.[9]

Some sources vary by a few feet, but most agree that when Yankee Stadium debuted, the old left-field wall was a distance of 281 to 285 feet and the original right field at 295 feet, even though the center field wall was planted a staggering 490 feet from home plate.[10] These dimensions would change over the years, with the foul lines growing slightly, and the deep outfield creeping in until it finally hit 399 feet.

Fenway Park is so irregular that a full description defies imagination, if not physics. For starters, its right-field foul pole rises from the shortest fence in the major leagues at barely 3 feet high, while in left field the Green Monster looms 37 feet from top to turf. Until 1934, Boston's left field also offered a 10-foot rise in the grass leading up to the Monster, a nightmare incline for visiting outfielders that is mimicked in the new millennium by a 30-degree deep center-field incline at the Houston Astros' Minute Maid Park.[11]

Unique stadiums, odd dimensions, and quirky outfields not only contribute to the romance and personality of the game, but they also offer a distinctly naughty temptation that frequently is related, directly or indirectly, to home runs. The Green Monster is listed as 315 feet from home plate, but many sources suggest that that distance is a fabrication. Some argue that the true distance is a blade short of 300 feet, a foreboding blend of mystery and reality that intimidates pitchers, fielders, and batters alike. Even so, the specter of the Green Monster pales when compared to the shenanigans in Fenway's right field, where the bullpens were installed in 1940 unabashedly to shorten the right-field power alley for Boston superstar slugger Ted Williams. Those pens were soon dubbed Williamsburg for obvious reasons.

Likewise, the short foul lines in Yankee Stadium, especially the 295-foot porch in right field, were almost certainly designed to enhance the home run power of those left-handed sluggers who played there. Although the so-called house that Ruth built opened in 1923, the Babe had already played three full seasons at the Yankees' famed Polo Grounds, which also brandished a bizarrely deep center field and strangely shallow foul lines. Ruth had jerked thirty-two homers there in one season, a pace that mathematically would have translated to a sixty-four-homer year, home and away, hinting of greater seasons to come. The marquee value of those gopher ball shots was not lost on the Yankees, whose management then mimicked the Polo Grounds in their new park with a distant center field complemented by inviting foul lines. The tempting right-field fence would prove especially friendly to the Babe and legions of lefty sluggers to follow, including a fair-haired switch hitter who would capture the hearts of New York and America, Mickey Mantle.

Mantle and home runs became synonymous in the 1950s, and to this day "the Mick" is still somewhat officially credited with longest home run in the history of the major leagues thanks, in part, to a proactive Yankees public relations (PR) department. Mantle's effort became a literal tape measure shot that was pegged at a superhuman 565 feet, or almost two full football fields. Modern mathematicians have recalculated a more "down to earth" distance, however. Robert K. Adair, Sterling Professor Emeritus of Physics at Yale, suggested a reckoning of 506 feet, which still represents the longest legitimate home run shot in the annals of the game.[12] Interestingly, Mantle's memorable blast did not occur at homer-friendly Yankee Stadium at all but on the road against the Senators.

Griffith Stadium in Washington, D.C., featured a left-center power alley of 391 feet and an outfield wall that stood 50 feet high. On April 17, 1953, Mantle, batting right handed, not only reached that wall but also rocked a Chuck Stobbs fastball over the top with so much power that it cleared the stadium altogether, bounced, rolled down the street, and stopped at 434 Oakdale Street.[13] It was Mantle's second anniversary in the big leagues, and he celebrated with an explosive moon shot. With a light breeze blowing toward center field, Stobbs hurled a fastball that caught the middle of the plate in Mantle's wheelhouse, and the Mick launched the ball skyward past the sign 391 feet away in left field (some reports have the sign as far as 460 feet). It cleared the unusually high outfield wall, ricocheted off the edge of a distant beer sign, and kept going. A ten-year-old boy retrieved the ball more than 600 feet from home plate and exchanged it for a new one that Mantle signed and reputedly augmented with a little cash, the exact amount having been long lost to history. The most common explanation for the discrepancy between 565 feet and the more modest 510-foot distance or fewer that likely happened concerns the roll of the ball—that is, where the boy found it versus where it landed.

When the Yankees took a tape measure reading and concluded the ball had landed 565 feet from home, the concept of the "tape measure" home run was born. Before Mantle, baseball had no such thing as tape measure shots; after Mantle, they are what make legends.

Named for the Senators' owner, Clark Griffith, the stadium was used from 1911 to 1961 before it was eventually demolished in 1965. Of course, the Mick is gone now as well, taken in 1995 at only age sixty-three after a bout with liver cancer and other illnesses related, directly or indirectly, to a lifetime of drinking, perhaps Mantle's greatest shortcoming. He was the consummate ballplayer, though, an affable towhead with a mischievous twinkle who played eighteen years in the majors, much of it in pain owing to bad knees and a host of injuries. Perhaps because he played in the Big Apple or sported such a boyish grin or had such speed and prodigious power—or most likely because of all of those reasons—Mantle became synonymous with baseball, home runs, and America. He was, after all, the all-American boy cut from the same homespun cloth as Lou Gehrig, Williams, Hank Greenberg, and, indeed, all of us in some mystical sense of America's youth. America embraced the Mick because he *was* us—or at least the "us" that many Americans in the 1950s wanted to be.

Mantle, along with a handful of other standouts like Willie Mays, Roberto Clemente, Ken Griffey Jr., and for a time Barry Bonds, was one of the ultimate five-tool ballplayers—that is, one who possessed baserunning speed, hitting for average, hitting for power, fielding, and throwing skills—but Mantle also sported a likable but naughty Huck Finn charm. Mantle's center-field speed and sterling defense were outstanding, too, but his home run power overshadowed them both. The Mick hit 536 runs in 2,401 games from 1951 to 1968, some of them rocket shots that not only cleared walls but often made history along the way. Although no player ever lofted a fair ball completely out of Yankee Stadium—not even a Hall of Fame list of sluggers like Ruth, Gehrig, Joe DiMaggio, Maris, Reggie Jackson, and Alex Rodriguez—on five separate occasions Mantle did manage to strike the wrought-iron facade hanging from the stadium roof. One blast in 1956 missed clearing the fabled summit by only eighteen inches. That shot clanked off the facade 115 feet up (some reports say from 102 to 117 feet) and 370 feet away from the plate, so far from home that some suggest the ball would have traveled a mind-bending 620 feet had it not struck iron.[14]

Yankee pitcher Tom Sturdivant, who had personally witnessed Mantle's Griffith Stadium tape measure blast, concluded years later that the five-foot-eleven Mantle was stronger than even the towering Mark McGwire. Frank Crosetti, who played seventeen years for the Yankees in the 1930s and 1940s and was the team's third base coach for twenty more seasons, witnessed the Mantle shot off the facade. Crosetti announced that the ball "got out so quick a lot of people didn't even see it, they couldn't follow it with their eyes—they just heard the crack of the ball and bat and another crack when it hit that facade."[15]

In a game against Detroit on May 13, 1955, Mantle hit two 400-footers in a 5–2 Yankee victory and became only the third player to club homers from both sides of the plate in the same game (Wally Schang did it for Philadelphia in 1916, and the St. Louis Browns' Johnny Lucadello was second in 1940). Days later, on June 5, Mantle rocketed a pitch completely over the upper deck's roof in left field at Chicago's Comiskey Park. Then, on June 21, 1955, Mantle became the first player ever to smash a home run to straightaway center at Yankee Stadium, a 486-foot bomb that cleared the 30-foot hitters' backdrop. And this stadium had already seen decades of homers from Ruth, Gehrig, and DiMaggio.

In 1960 Mantle slammed a ball over the right-field roof at Tiger Stadium, the third time he had done so, but this one sailed past Trumbell Avenue before landing in a parking lot outside. Years later, it was estimated that the ball had traveled 643 feet altogether. Perhaps it did, counting the distance it may have rolled.

But 1956 was Mantle's consummate year. It belonged to the Mick—and still belongs to him—the way 1927 is perpetually owned by Ruth, 1941 by DiMaggio, 1951 by Thomson, and 1961 by Maris. When Mantle won the elusive Triple Crown that year, batting .353 with fifty-two home runs and 130 runs batted in (RBIs), slugger Al Kaline could only shake his head. "I wish I was half the player he was," lamented the Detroit legend who would smash 399 jacks among his own 3,007 career hits.[16] On May 30, 1956, when the Mick clubbed one of his roof-bound shots at Yankee Stadium, sportscaster Bob Wolff was there: "The ball [was] rising when it hit the copper frieze."[17] Pitcher Pedro Ramos, who not only saw the missile but also was the last man to touch the ball (because he threw it), humbly noted, "Had it not hit the roof, it would have been in Brooklyn."[18]

At first Mantle gripped baseball, then he captivated America, and soon he even became part of the image of America itself. Fifties pop star Teresa Brewer released a single, "I Love Mickey," and his name turns up in pop music and television even today. Many still simply call him Number 7, as though he were the only 7 who ever played any sport, a tribute echoed and simultaneously spoofed in an episode of television's *Seinfeld* almost forty years after the magical 1956 season when the show's character George proposes using Seven for a baby's name. From the beginning Mantle benefited from the advent of television. The new medium defined itself and found baseball as Mantle emerged, showcasing the Mick's charisma in living rooms coast to coast. It helped that Mickey played on so many World Series teams, thus increasing both his national exposure and his growing legend by playing sixty-five World Series games in all. But all those championships were more than mere coincidence. Mantle did not simply ride the Yankee success; he propelled it.

Mickey Mantle's fifty-two jacks in 1956 beat Cleveland's Vic Wertz, the league's runner-up, by twenty. His .353 average was eight basis points above that of second-place Ted Williams, while the Mick's .705 slugging average bested the latter's .605 by a wide margin.[19] Mantle and Boston's Williams crossed paths numerous times, often making history, but perhaps no encounter was more entertaining than their game on August 7, 1956, when Williams botched a Mantle pop fly. The Red Sox faithful booed Williams, so Williams returned the scorn by spitting on them and received a $5,000 fine from the league. Such miscreant behavior added to the stuff of baseball legends and lore, then and now.

Evoking its emotional highs and lows, the home run spectacle has made and broken careers, hearts, and men. It has been part of the American cultural landscape since Ruth put it on the Big Apple stage in 1920, but one fundamental question is rarely asked: just what *is* a home run? With so much ado about the long ball from Ruth to Mantle to Bonds, it is remarkable that the official major league rules do not expressly include the home run among their many official definitions. Myriad circumscriptions are listed at Rule 2.00, which defines what a "home team" is yet fails to even mention "home run." The idea of the home run is ultimately found buried in the midst of Rule 6.09, which defines how a batter becomes a runner. Subpart d offers one way, when "a fair ball passes over the fence or into the stands at a distance from home base of 250 feet or more. Such hit entitles the batter to a home run when he shall have touched all bases legally. A fair fly ball that passes out of the playing field at a point less than 250 feet from home base shall entitle the batter to advance to second base only."[20]

That's it. But in practice, actually defining the home run has been anything but simple; the definition has not always been applied the same way or even, at times, logically. Until 1925, the minimum distance for a home run was 235 feet, suggesting much about the not-so-long balls of yesteryear. And before 1920, dramatic walk-off home runs did not count at all unless the batter's own run scored was necessary to win the game. In other words, if the batter's team was down by one run and he hit a three-run homer, the game was "over" when the second run crossed the plate. Thus, the batter was credited only with an extra base hit. This situation happened on thirty-seven different occasions. For a period Major League Baseball actually reversed the rule and credited those home runs, but then reversed itself again in 1969 and discredited those same homers. In so doing, the league reduced Ruth's career record by one and took away what would have been his record 715th shot, which was hit on July 8, 1918, in a victory against the Indians.[21] That blast now counts as a triple, and Ruth's career homer mark still stands at only 714. Remarkably, it seems to have happened again eight days later with another possible Ruth walk-off homer that was scored as a triple. (It is improbable that the plodding, aging Ruth could have clubbed both alleged triples on his own without extraordinary luck, and the run count rules may explain partly a handful of unlikely triples early in his career, including both of his suspect triples from July 1918.)

Regardless of how they are measured or defined, home runs are perceived as either an exuberant spectacle or a deflating dagger. Their importance is suggested by the many varied names they are called, with one website listing no fewer than fifty different iterations.[22] Some terms—homer, long ball, or four-bagger—are merely descriptive, while others are more colorful: jack, blast, or gopher (as in "go for") ball. Still others are energized metaphors: rocket, bomb, missile, yard, dinger, and moon shot. Some, like tater, are plain silly, though. Depending upon the mood, conditions, or level of drama in the game, numerous suggestive verbs describe how a home run is put into play, besides simply hitting one: slug, slam, clock, club, launch, cannon, crack, crank, blast, park one in the seats, and go deep.

Mantle went deep 536 times, still the all-time record for a switch hitter, and besides those famous fifty-two jacks in 1956, he launched another fifty-four more during his chase with Roger Maris five years later. He homered eighteen times in World Series play, setting a record, and he literally invented the tape measure home run with his Griffith Stadium blast and those Yankee facade shots. A rare Triple Crown winner, Mantle was the American League's most valuable player (MVP) three times, was an all-star sixteen times, led the league in home runs and in runs scored four times in six years from 1955 through 1960, and won seven World Series rings. When a youngster heckled the Tigers' Al Kaline, who slammed 399 career home runs, and said Kaline was not half as good as Mickey Mantle, the slugger's reply became legendary: "Son, nobody is half the player Mickey Mantle is."

With a nagging bad knee that he originally injured when his cleats stuck in an outfield drain at Yankee Stadium in 1951, Mantle achieved many feats virtually on one leg. "I always loved the game, but when my legs weren't hurting it was a lot easier to love," he conceded.[23] Still, what could Mantle have done without all those setbacks? Like his father and grandfather, the Mick was victim of a brittle bone disease called osteomyelitis. It did not stop his big-league career, but it did get in the way more than once and was enough to earn him a 4-F draft rating that kept him out of the armed forces during the Korean War and through much of the Vietnam era, when draft deferments were not highly regarded. For a time, some journalists called him unpatriotic, and opposing fans showered him with epithets like "draft dodger" and "Commie." But thanks to Mantle's on-field heroics, courage, and irresistible charm, those dark days did not last.

Mantle had begun his big-league career with little fanfare but under a great deal of pressure. A kid from small-town Commerce, Oklahoma, who had married his high school sweetheart, Mantle soon confronted towering Manhattan skyscrapers and the vultures of the New York media. Yankee insiders leaked such provocative accolades to the press as "the greatest natural hitter I ever saw" or "he'll make everyone forget DiMaggio." America did not forget Joe DiMaggio, but most have indeed forgotten that Mantle and DiMaggio played on the same team during one season, Mantle's rookie year, when the two of them made dubious history together in the 1951 World Series.

Days after Bobby Thomson blasted the Giants into the World Series with his "shot heard round the world" at the expense of pitcher Ralph Branca, the Giants were in the 1951 World Series. But they still had to face a Yankee juggernaut that featured such stars as DiMaggio, Yogi Berra, and Hank Bauer, plus a pair of twenty-one-game winners on the mound in Eddie Lopat and Vic Raschi. Berra would win the league MVP that year and DiMaggio would slug the last of his many World Series home runs. Remarkably, even though 1951 was Mantle's first season with the Yankees, he did not even beat out his own teammate Gil McDougald for American League Rookie of the Year honors. McDougald would rock a grand slam homer to lead a Game 5 Yankees win, while Mantle would tear ligaments in his right knee courtesy of that dubious outfield drain—an injury that would plague Mantle for most of his eighteen big-league seasons.

Those Giants were no pushovers. Managed by the irascible Leo Durocher, they were led by league RBI leader Monford "Monte" Irvin (121), Alvin Dark, Bobby Thomson (thirty-two homers, including the one that sailed into destiny), and two twenty-three-game winners in Larry Jansen and Sal Maglie. They also featured their own National League Rookie of the Year in a speedy, polite, and talented youngster named Willie Mays.

It was actually Mays who contributed to Mantle's infamous knee injury when he slapped a fly ball to right-center field in the fifth inning of World

Series Game 2. DiMaggio and Mantle quickly converged on the ball, with Mantle pulling up at the last second to defer to the Yankee Clipper. In so doing the kid caught his spikes on a drain (sometimes reported as a sprinkler) in right-center field at Yankee Stadium, rendering it perhaps the most infamous lawn care device in history. Mickey Mantle was only nineteen years old when he first injured that knee chasing down Mays's fly. Manager Casey Stengel had told Mantle to go hard for any ball hit between him and Joe DiMaggio, whose outfield range was not what it used to be. Mantle did charge but at the last second heard DiMaggio call for the ball. Mantle stopped hard, catching his spikes.[24] With torn knee ligaments, Mantle was out for the remainder of the Series, and his bad knee became a part of destiny. No one knew the full importance of that misstep at the time, including Thomson and the other players that day, but it would haunt Mantle the rest of his playing career. As it was, Mantle was one of the best ballplayers of any era with a career based on both speed and power, so one can only imagine what the Mick could have done with two healthy legs.

That game day would be an especially tragic one for the whole Mantle family. Mickey was rushed to Lenox Hill Hospital, taken there by his father, Elvin "Mutt" Mantle, in a cab immediately after the injury. When helping Mantle out of the cab, his father collapsed on the sidewalk and was also admitted to the same hospital, landing in a room with Mickey. The doctors soon discovered that Mick's father had something much more serious, Hodgkin's disease. Mutt Mantle would be dead by the following May, taken at only thirty-nine years of age, in a severe loss to Mickey.[25] His father had been an amateur ballplayer who loved the game and even named Mickey after his own favorite ballplayer, Detroit catcher Mickey Cochrane. His father's death haunted Mantle his whole life, for the Mick would perpetually fear his own early demise. In the end Mantle's concern was justified, his personal demons and insecurities had led to serious alcohol problems, and he eventually drank himself into a bout with liver cancer that took his life at age sixty-three, one year after receiving a last-ditch liver transplant.[26]

Five years after his big-league debut in 1951, Mantle would become the only Triple Crown winner of the decade. What about Gil McDougald, the

1951 Rookie of the Year? Indeed, his first season had outshined Mick's, the only year when that would happen, although McDougald was more than a journeyman in his ten years with the Yankees. McDougald's inaugural year had been much more "Mantle-like" than the rest of his career, however, as he slugged fourteen home runs and batted .306 during his regular season and added a grand slam in Game 5 of the World Series. He played several infield positions for the Yankees and was an all-star in 1952. Even though Mantle's 1956 season overshadowed everybody's, McDougald held his own, batting .311, and in 1957 he led the league in triples with nine. McDougald won the pennant eight times with the "Bronx Bombers," playing in fifty-three World Series games, but thanks to fate and Mantle, he is hardly remembered except by the New York faithful.[27]

Although he was a speedy player who could hit for average, McDougald could not compete with two of Mantle's best traits—charisma and tape measure home runs. When the Yankees signed Mantle straight from high school, the team was already looking for the "next DiMaggio." The marquee star had already told the team of his impending retirement. The Yankees had developed a tradition of superstar sluggers, for DiMaggio himself had been the "next Gehrig," who had been in turn a great second act for Ruth. Each of them, including Mantle, would hand the baton to the other in succession, with Ruth arriving in New York in 1920, then Gehrig replacing Wally Pipp in the Yankee lineup in 1925. The two would share star power and prodigious home runs until Ruth left the Yankees in 1934 as his career waned. Gehrig carried the marquee load until June 12, 1939, when the notorious disease amyotrophic lateral sclerosis (ALS) that now carries his name forced him into early retirement.

DiMaggio debuted for the Yankees on May 3, 1936, and played with the established icon Gehrig for barely more than three seasons, thus keeping the unbroken superstar string intact. On April 29, 1939, the young DiMaggio tore a leg muscle while navigating a muddy outfield at Griffith Stadium, causing him to miss five weeks of the season. Ironically, the next day the "Iron Horse," Lou Gehrig, played in his 2,130th consecutive game, setting the all-time record. Gehrig was worn down, however, not only from all those grueling games but also likely from his bout with ALS.

On June 6 DiMaggio returned to the lineup with a three-hit tear, clubbing a single, a double, and, of course, a home run against the White Sox. But the Gehrig-DiMaggio duo lasted only six more days, with Gehrig taking the field the last time for an exhibition night game in Kansas City. He checked into the Mayo Clinic the next day, and by July 4 Gehrig was at Yankee Stadium, where he delivered his immortal "luckiest man" farewell speech, probably the greatest baseball address ever given and one of the top speeches in U.S. history. In between, without their established hero on the field, the energized Yankees imposed their frustration against an unsuspecting league. In one doubleheader on June 28, they demolished the Philadelphia Athletics on the road by a combined score of 33–2, scoring twenty-three runs in the first game with eight home runs coming from six players: DiMaggio, who hit two; Gehrig's replacement, Babe Dahlgren, who also hit two; Bill Dickey; Joe Gordon; Tommy Henrich; and George Selkirk.

DiMaggio proceeded to log a career year in 1939, winning the American League's MVP, leading the league in batting at a stellar .381, and adding thirty home runs and 126 RBIs for good measure.[28] Gehrig remained as team captain, even though he would never again step into the batter's box. DiMaggio led this new Yankee wrecking crew to a four-game World Series sweep over the Cincinnati Reds, but 1939 is still remembered for Lou Gehrig, who ended his famous consecutive game streak, announced he had ALS, and retired from the game. The Yankees organization made history, too, by retiring Gehrig's number 4 on July 4, 1939, during Gehrig's Appreciation Day. It was the first time that any baseball player's number had been retired.

By June 2, 1941, Lou Gehrig was gone for good, finally succumbing to the final paralysis of ALS. His death occurred in the middle of the greatest hitting streak of all time, DiMaggio's fifty-six straight games. Both men held the two most famous streaks in the history of the game.

Although not recognized by any official record books, another streak was still very much in progress: the uninterrupted string of winning, charisma, and home run power provided by a succession of stellar players, beginning with Ruth's first Yankee homer on May 1, 1920, to Mantle's very last long ball on September 20, 1968. For forty-nine straight years, excepting DiMaggio's absence for military service, each Yankee season featured at least one home run from Ruth, Gehrig, DiMaggio, or Mantle, with each slugger handing his home run baton to the next. Other Yankee stars have been added to the list, of course, including such power hitters as Bob Meusel, Bill "Moose" Skowron, Reggie Jackson, Bernie Williams, Jason Giambi, and Alex Rodriguez, to name a few. Among them, Jackson was the biggest showman, though an overdose of hubris and a noticeable lack of charm diminished his charisma. Further, none of these sluggers made history at the expense of the others—except one: Roger Maris, who was not celebrated for his home runs but blamed for them because he broke Babe Ruth's record sixty-homer season instead of Mickey Mantle, the fan favorite.

And so it goes. Home runs are not only the shock-and-awe spectacle of baseball destiny but also a great enigma. The country seemed to demand an apology from Maris for his unpopular home run record in 1961, and exactly four decades later the public demanded more apologies of Barry Bonds, whose own home run records were tainted by the steroid era. Once again, baseball seems more like a one-on-one encounter. The only other sport in which the victors feel a need to be sorry is boxing, as when Muhammad Ali destroyed the popular Floyd Patterson or when Larry Holmes could barely avoid embarrassing Ali, his own idol, many years later. No NFL touchdown ever evoked an apology—except maybe one, when William "Refrigerator" Perry lumbered over the goal line in Super Bowl XX in lieu of the fabled Walter Payton at the latter's career twilight. Even that call was not Perry's fault, as his coach, Mike Ditka, shouldered the blame.

Ruth had invented the home run as we know it, but the subsequent record holders are mostly known for how many they hit. There are isolated exceptions, of course. For one, Reggie Jackson crushed an astonishing ball during the 1971 All-Star Game at Tiger Stadium that not only made it over the outfield wall but also clanked off the top of a 100-foot-high transformer.

Two other sluggers known for the sheer distance of their home runs—the powerful Ruth, who sometimes clubbed them over the roof, and Mickey Mantle, who invented the original tape measure shot—also helped seal baseball's fate as a slice of America itself.

There have been longer home runs than Mantle's bomb at Griffith Stadium, but none of them occurred in a regulation big-league game. Ruth reportedly banged a 600-footer at a 1919 exhibition game in Tampa, and in 1926 the Babe pounded a legitimate 500-foot shot at Navin Field in Detroit, though it was widely reported at the time as a 600-foot monster. In 1934 Josh Gibson of the storied Negro leagues, who probably hit more professional home runs than anyone (though we'll never know for sure because of faulty record books), struck a ball that clunked 2 feet from the Yankee Stadium roof, reportedly 580 feet from the plate. Some witnesses insist Gibson actually hit one over the original Yankee Stadium; if so, it would have been the only fair ball ever to clear that venerable roof.

These mammoth long balls not only counted for the distance they traveled but also for the drama that they elicited. Some evoked colorful slices of memorable lore. For instance, Cardinals trainer Gene Geiselmann drily commented when Juan Gonzalez knocked one out of the park, "The ball went further [sic] than I ever went on vacation as a kid."[29] The first time Casey Stengel saw Mickey Mantle hit a homer was in Arizona, and the hot, dry air helped inspire both the homer and the reaction from Stengel, who blurted something about the "stratmosphere." When Kevin Mitchell clubbed a ball in the upper-deck stratosphere at Joe Robbie Stadium in Miami, a Marlins publicist was also reduced to Stengelese: "There have been a plethora of guys to hit it up there, but that was the plethorest."[30] Probably the most colorful reaction was served up by Giants manager Leo Durocher when he witnessed the first home run of Willie Mays's career on May 28, 1951: "I never saw a fucking ball get out of a fucking ball park so fucking fast in my fucking life."[31]

Most tales about 500- and 600-foot shots, however, are little more than fiction. In 1982 IBM installed an electronic measuring device in a number of ballparks, and in seventeen subsequent seasons it detected only one ball hit more than 500 feet, the 502-footer that Detroit's Cecil Fielder clubbed at Milwaukee in 1991. Mantle's 506-foot homer at Griffith Stadium is still credited as the longest ever, and indeed he may have smacked the longest unofficial blast, too. On March 26, 1951, the Mick launched an exhibition homer at the University of Southern California–Los Angeles that left Bovard Field on the fly and allegedly cleared the width of a football practice field before landing an estimated 654 feet away.

According to Adair, the acclaimed physicist and published expert on baseball physics, a 600-foot homer on the fly is virtually impossible without wind. The IBM tracking system, called the Tale of the Tape and used in fifteen home parks in 1988 and nineteen in 1989, measured about two thousand home runs. Only two of those legitimately carried more than 470 feet, including a 478-footer by Dave Winfield and a 473-foot blast from Fred McGriff. Taking into consideration the actual wind conditions, probable pitch speed, and the height of the outfield wall, Adair calculates that Mantle's Griffith blast took six seconds to come down and likely carried a wind-aided 506 feet. He also calculates that 550 feet is the longest theoretical distance a baseball can be hit with a wooden bat, but in reality even distances of 450 feet or more are extremely rare. Only eight of the IBM-measured shots cleared the 450-foot mark.[32]

Measuring distance is one thing, but there is no clear-cut answer to the qualitative question of who may be the *greatest* home run hitter ever, be it Josh Gibson, Williams, Mays, Mantle, Bonds, or Ruth himself. There is less doubt, though, about who hit them very far the most often—and that player was Mickey Mantle. But Mantle was about more than distance, of course. Indeed, his combined career on-base percentage and slugging average computes to a higher level than his impressive contemporaries Willie Mays and Hank Aaron had, and his engaging personality remains unique among baseball's greatest sluggers.

It had all started with Ruth, though, whose prodigious jacks were a quantum leap beyond anything his predecessors could muster. After Ruth, the game's long-ball fever continued to flourish under the likes of Kiner, Jimmie Foxx, Aaron, Mays, Mantle, Maris, Gehrig, and all those who followed.

Together these men share the marquee home run glory of the game and collectively are indeed all the Babe's men, sluggers who have melded baseball and America into a long-ball marriage of legend and lore that not only reinvented baseball but also helped define who we are as a nation of heroes, hitting home runs on and off the baseball field.

OUR NATIONAL METAPHOR

If one weighty swing of hickory could ever redirect destiny, it did so during an early autumn day, September 30, 1927.

Babe Ruth's home run record that season created an epiphany, a cultural transformation so powerful that his record is sometimes referred to simply as 1927. With that swing came a new era, or an almost ecclesiastical reset in the annals of baseball lore that defined an *ante diem* of hardball posterity, where everything that had come before suddenly belonged to a different epoch. Thereafter, all things baseball would be defined, jaded, or qualified by that monolithic 1927 season of the Babe and the Murderers' Row Yankee juggernaut.

But more than baseball changed during that trenchant year, for America would never be quite the same. Not only was the American lexicon suddenly salted by new adjectives of grandeur like "Ruthian," but entirely new expressions also evolved, such as this enduring put-down: "Who do you think you are, the 1927 Yankees?"

History would partially repeat itself thirty-four years later in 1961, a year that is known more for witnessing baseball's ephemeral home run asterisk than for launching the first American into space, Alan Shepard. The United States had finally caught up to the Russian space program with Shepard's historic launch, but the final record-setting home run of 1961 punctuated an entire year of long-ball greatness as Mickey Mantle and Roger Maris blasted their own rips at destiny. Both of those milestones—the new single-season home run record and America's first manned space flight—were shown on television, yet only one is remembered as the threshold moment of 1961. And so it is that "1961" does not harken the Mercury space program but means instead "baseball." No wonder the term "moon shot" today does not refer to astronauts at all but instead means an impressive, towering home run.

Those two landmark seasons of 1927 and 1961 became forever bonded by the distinctly American mystique of the single-season home run record. Whether by fate or by Karma, but perhaps not by coincidence alone, those respective years occurred during two remarkably parallel decades of American history and, in the end, are defined by the distinct crack of big-league lumber.

When a Redstone booster rocket propelled Alan Shepard into his fifteen-minute ride from Cape Canaveral and through the fringes of outer space to the Atlantic Ocean on May 5, 1961, it echoed the legendary voyage of American hero Charles A. Lindbergh in 1927.[1] When Lindbergh completed his famed solo transatlantic flight, crossed over the coast of France, and followed the Seine River before landing the *Spirit of St. Louis* at Le Bourget Field in Paris, he secured an important place in history.[2] Lindbergh provided a lasting threshold moment in history, but his legacy did not supplant the bigger-than-life image of Ruth that remains today.

While 1927 and 1961 were both literal and figurative seasons in the sky, they were symbolic of much more as two baseball beacons that continue to illuminate the entire respective decades of the 1920s and 1960s. These two eras have much in common on and off the diamond. The 1960s call to mind classic rock and roll, hippies, marijuana, and the emerging drug culture, while the 1920s featured the emergence of jazz, flappers, illicit booze, Prohibition, and a "reefer" drug culture. Both decades experienced national prosperity at the cusp of economic downturns, with the Great Depression following the Roaring Twenties and then the severe recession of

1974 and its oil crisis occurring in the wake of the postwar boom. Each era also showcased one of history's most dominant heavyweight boxing figures: hard-punching Jack Dempsey, known the "Manassa Mauler," and later a young Cassius Clay who would morph into an even loftier place in sports history as Muhammad Ali, or "The Greatest."

Radio was widely commercialized during the 1920s, bringing Babe Ruth and baseball into millions of American living rooms by 1927, while television expanded during the 1960s and featured the landmark 1961 Maris-Mantle duel. In 1927 Chicago's Clarence Darrow was America's most famous trial lawyer, still known for the famous Scopes evolution trial of 1925 and the 1924 trial of the Nathan Leopold and Richard Loeb thrill killings of fourteen-year-old Bobby Franks. Later, criminal attorney F. Lee Bailey grabbed headlines for representing the Boston Strangler, Albert DeSalvo, who was tied to the murder of thirteen single women in the early sixties, and in 1966 for winning an appeal for Dr. Sam Sheppard, who had been accused of murdering his wife and inspired the television and Hollywood versions of *The Fugitive*.

The year 1927 is inexorably tied to baseball. The most famous personalities of the Roaring Twenties included Chicago gangster Al Capone, Darrow, Dempsey, Lindbergh, and actors Charlie Chaplin and Rudolph Valentino, but for most Americans, 1927 evokes Babe Ruth and Murderers' Row more than it does Capone, Lindbergh, or any of the others, who are all still famous but not necessarily defined by a single date. Many may remember or at least acknowledge that both Lindbergh's flight and Dempsey's famous "long count" also took place in 1927, but if pressed about the year itself, more Americans likely will associate it with Ruth and "the '27 Yankees" than they will peg the year to Jack Dempsey or even Charles Lindbergh. Likewise, the 1960s meant John F. Kennedy; Martin Luther King, Jr.; the Beatles; Woodstock; and astronaut Neil Armstrong and the moon landing. If only the year 1961 is singled out, however, it still connotes baseball more than it does politics, rock music, or the space program. Fittingly, in both 1927 and 1961, the vaunted New York Yankees won the World Series crown; and both baseball seasons influenced America and left indelible marks on those touched by the allure of the game and its home run spectacle.

One can only imagine the full extent of baseball's home run imprint on America, particularly on its young people, who would have been exposed to the unavoidable home run drama during both threshold seasons of 1927 and 1961. For instance, among those born in 1951 who would have been an impressionable ten years old when the Maris-Mantle home run chase was beamed across American television screens were political figures Al Franken, Jesse Ventura, Lawrence O'Donnell, and Rush Limbaugh. Born in 1917, and thus ten years old in 1927, were John F. Kennedy, business-man Kirk Kerkorian, and author Arthur C. Clarke, among other notables.

Perhaps the most dramatic impact of baseball on our youth can be found in the Oval Office. Ronald Reagan was sixteen years old when Ruth slammed number 60 in 1927. The future movie star and president soon found himself broadcasting Chicago Cubs games as an Iowa radio announcer in the 1930s. In fact, the broadcasting job first took Reagan to Hollywood when the Cubs traveled to play exhibitions in Southern California. Lured by the Hollywood mystique, Reagan took a detour in 1937 that led him to become an actor. Although known for numerous B-picture roles, two of Reagan's most recognized performances were in sports films—first playing George "the Gipper" Gipp in *Knute Rockne, All American* (1940), and then big-league pitcher Grover Cleveland Alexander in *The Winning Team* (1952). "Win one for the Gipper" is widely recognized as one of the top film quotes of all time, and Reagan even used it as a political campaign slogan. Reagan, like many Americans, also experienced the other milestone year in baseball, having recently turned fifty before the Maris-Mantle season of 1961. After Reagan played in an old-timers' game with former big leaguers in 1983, he observed that it was more fun than being president. He then wistfully hoped that an errant ball could sail through the window of the Oval Office once in a while. Fifty years after his stint with baseball and radio, Reagan changed history with his "Mister Gorbachev, tear down this wall" scolding of the Russian leader in June 1987.

When the Apollo 11 astronauts returned from their historic moon flight in July 1969, meanwhile, one of the first questions sitting president Richard M. Nixon asked them was whether they had learned how the All-Star Game turned out. Nixon, the thirty-seventh president, was aged fourteen and forty-eight, respectively, during those legendary home run seasons, both of which must have affected Nixon. Even during the dark hours of his presidency, Vietnam, Watergate, and social unrest could have overwhelmed the president's affinity for baseball in those days, but he remained a vocal fan of the game.

Among the many differences between the two home run eras, none was more obvious than the racial makeup of America and of baseball. Reflecting America's segregated population during both years—the Maris-Mantle chase of 1961 predated the Civil Rights Act of 1964 and the assassination of Martin Luther King, Jr., in 1968—the major leagues were completely segregated in 1927 and still largely so in 1961. It took twelve years after Jackie Robinson's debut for all major-league teams to have an African American on their rosters. The Red Sox were the last holdouts, with Elijah "Pumpsie" Green taking the field on July 21, 1959. The proportion of African Americans on major-league rosters peaked at 27 percent in 1975, then began a gradual decline into the single digits in the new millennium.

Baseball has seen many notable seasons in addition to 1927 and 1961, of course. Some are linked to single years, such as Joe DiMaggio's fifty-six-game hitting streak in 1941, the 1951 season when Bobby Thomson hit the "shot heard round the world," and the memorable 1956 season, with Mickey Mantle's stunning Triple Crown year, that is still revered as perhaps the best individual year for any baseball player in history. But no season was more important to baseball than 1947, the watershed year when Jackie Robinson and the Dodgers' general manager Branch Rickey desegregated Major League Baseball.

Their action changed more than baseball. Its front-page visibility influenced America's attitude toward integration, albeit with much resistance. Hollywood soon joined the act, releasing the feature-length film *The Jackie Robinson Story* in 1950. A well-received baseball biopic, the film starred Robinson himself.

Hollywood had discovered the marquee value of sports as drama, inspiration, biography, and even humor as early as 1925's acclaimed football
comedy *The Freshman* starring Harold Lloyd. It followed with *The Champ*
with Jackie Cooper, earning a nomination for best picture in 1931, and the
Marx Brothers' farce *Horse Feathers* in 1932. While some might not view the
Marx Brothers' romp as a sports movie at all, the Robinson film was more
than a mere sports movie, since it not only depicted an iconic moment of
American history but also starred the actual hero who made that history
happen.

Sports offer a convenient subject for storytelling, for they provide drama
packaged within a definable framework for a game, a career, or even an
entire sport. More celebrated films have featured baseball than any other
sport. In 2003 *Sports Illustrated* listed its version of the top fifty sports films
of all time, eleven of which were about baseball, nine were about football,
and seven featured boxing. Basketball accounted for a few, including the
acclaimed documentary *Hoop Dreams* at number 4 plus the film *Hoosiers*
starring Gene Hackman in the number 6 slot. Racing is a common topic,
too, whether powered by humans—for example, *Breaking Away* and
Chariots of Fire—racecars, or horses.[3]

Most credible listings of top sports films, including *Sports Illustrated*'s,
rank *Bull Durham,* Kevin Costner's provocative tribute to baseball and life
that was released in 1988 and also stars Tim Robbins and Susan Sarandon,
as the best sports film of all time. Many other sources rank Martin Scorsese's
award-winning 1980 masterpiece starring Robert De Niro, *Raging Bull*,
and its dramatic depiction of brutality as the greatest of all sports films,
again suggesting the similarities between baseball and boxing.

Both sports have more in common with each other than either one does
with football or basketball, for they are driven by explicit one-on-one confrontations. On the one hand, boxing provides a compelling platform for
individual competition and drama, as illustrated in the soul-numbing
Raging Bull, the sentimental *Rocky* series, the 1996 Muhammad Ali boxing
documentary *When We Were Kings* (number 10 on *Sports Illustrated*'s all-
time list), Clint Eastwood's *Million Dollar Baby* (2004*)*, or Ron Howard's

romantic period piece *Cinderella Man* (2005). The latter two films were too recent for the *Sports Illustrated* listing, but they are largely recognized today as top sports movies. No sports list recognizes the 2000 Academy Award winner *Gladiator*, Ridley Scott's Shakespearean-like tragedy about the days of the Roman Coliseum and those who battled there, but part of *Gladiator's* appeal stems from Russell Crowe's numerous one-on-one confrontations that mimic the drama of boxing films like *Raging Bull.*

Boxing, with its hand-to-hand combat, has a gladiator-like appeal. Its crowds of spectators in the early days are reminiscent of those in the ancient Coliseum in Rome, with more than 104,000 people assembling to watch such major fights as the Jack Dempsey–Gene Tunney rematch at Soldier Field in 1927. These bouts made good drama and entertainment, and they often had to take place in the largest stadiums available to handle the massive crowds.

Baseball, on the other hand, has an inherent dramatic advantage over other team sports, both on the field and as portrayed in films, because the game is played as a one-on-one confrontation disguised as a team sport. This feature gives baseball a distinctly American spin on both the competition and the romance that goes with rooting for the underdog as Americans are wont to do, especially in the movies. Once the ball is put into play, a necessary level of teamwork is set into motion, of course, but until that time the game is all pitcher versus hitter, or a mano a mano "hit it if you can" contest. The drama is easy to define, capture, and exploit. This advantage not only explains Hollywood's historic affinity for baseball, but given the game's symbolic role in the capitalistic, swing-for-the-fences image, it also helps explain why baseball became the original American pastime in the first place.

Fate also contributed to the emergence of baseball. The game was transforming itself into a home run spectacle with Ruth's 1920 exodus from Boston to New York. Other early sluggers, such as Lou Gehrig, Hank Greenberg, Jimmie Foxx, and Lewis "Hack" Wilson, soon followed the Babe's lead, swinging for home runs, glory, and money and evoking Ralph Kiner's quip about Cadillacs at the end of the bat. Ruth's journey to the

Big Apple and the subsequent emergence of baseball as a long-ball game accompanied by expanding crowds and Ruth's swollen pocketbook symbolized American capitalism and simultaneously took advantage of it.

But fate was only getting started. As baseball was beginning to exploit the power and drama of home runs in bunches, the newfangled radio "talking box" was first being commercialized. Because of baseball's deliberate pace, which is largely the product of its singular pitcher-batter drama, the game was especially suited to radio. The slower action allowed—even necessitated—a detailed verbal description over the airwaves. Such broadcasts brought baseball to millions of living rooms and parlors across America, where the game's announcers evolved as poetic ambassadors of the game, endearing themselves to listeners almost as much as the players themselves did. Add the drama of long-ball home runs, where four seconds unfold with the announcer's excited home run call delivered over the background roar of the exuberant hometown crowd, and the romantic marriage of baseball and radio became inevitable.

Another intangible element to baseball is probably a function of both the game's one-on-one mentality and its ultrafine line between success and failure. Hitting the ball safely twenty-five times out of a hundred at-bats over the course of a career makes for a forgettable .250 hitter, while only five more hits per hundred at-bats could be become a Hall of Fame career. In five hundred at-bats during a season, a .250 hitter will produce 125 hits and a .300 hitter only 25 more, or about one bloop, bunt, or infield hit per week. To the players, such fine lines between baseball success and failure can be daunting. No wonder the players become obsessed with such rituals as crossing themselves; nervously adjusting their helmets, gloves, or jock straps; stepping in and out of the box; wearing dirty socks; and all the rest. It all contributes to the unique mysticism of baseball, a game that many players and fans believe is impacted by ritual and superstition, if not magic.

With its rituals and mischievous personality, baseball can be an emotional game, too, which Hollywood finds inviting. In 2005, the fifty-fourth-ranked greatest quote in a hundred years of movie history, courtesy of the American Film Institute, was the inimitable "There is no crying in baseball." Tom

Hanks delivered this enduring line in 1992's *A League of Their Own*, which depicted the women's professional baseball league that sprang up during World War II.[4] A widely recognized admonition about baseball effort and etiquette, the "no crying" remark ranks ahead of famous lines from such classic films as *Psycho, The Graduate, Dr. Strangelove, Chinatown,* and even "win one for the Gipper" from *Knute Rockne, All American* (number 89), helping to confirm baseball's place in America's heart and lexicon.

Three noted baseball films unabashedly exploit America's romanticism about baseball: *The Natural, Field of Dreams,* and *Bull Durham*. Nowhere is that link more pronounced than Susan Sarandon's ecclesiastical soliloquy from the classic tribute to baseball, *Bull Durham*:

I believe in the Church of Baseball. I've tried all the major religions, and most of the minor ones. I've worshiped Buddha, Allah, Brahma, Vishnu, Siva, trees, mushrooms, and Isadora Duncan. I know things. For instance, there are 108 beads in a Catholic rosary and there are 108 stitches in a baseball. When I heard that, I gave Jesus a chance. But it just didn't work out between us. The Lord laid too much guilt on me. I prefer metaphysics to theology. You see, there's no guilt in baseball, and it's never boring . . . which makes it like sex. There's never been a ballplayer slept with me who didn't have the best year of his career. Making love is like hitting a baseball: you just gotta relax and concentrate. Besides, I'd never sleep with a player hitting under .250 . . . not unless he had a lot of RBIs and was a great glove man up the middle. You see, there's a certain amount of life wisdom I give these boys. I can expand their minds. Sometimes when I've got a ballplayer alone, I'll just read Emily Dickinson or Walt Whitman to him, and the guys are so sweet, they always stay and listen. 'Course, a guy'll listen to anything if he thinks it's foreplay. I make them feel confident, and they make me feel safe, and pretty. 'Course, what I give them lasts a lifetime; what they give me lasts 142 games. Sometimes it seems like a bad trade. But bad trades are a part of baseball—now who can forget Frank Robinson for Milt Pappas, for God's sake? It's a long season and you gotta trust it. I've tried 'em all, I really have, and the only church that truly feeds the soul, day in, day out, is the Church of Baseball.[5]

No wonder high school boys equate the ultimate sexual experience as a home run, or at least making it to home, not to mention the various symbolic steps in getting to the bases. Baseball has this effect on one's psyche. Delivered in character as baseball groupie and sage Annie Savoy, Sarandon's fictional speech was the opening narration for the 1988 film, yet its nonfictional message is quintessential baseball. The film's director, Ron Shelton, wrote the original screenplay, which was nominated for an Academy Award®. Shelton's effort lost to *Rain Man*, starring Tom Cruise and Dustin Hoffman; but, remarkably, Shelton's overall body of work includes no fewer than four of the best sports films in recent decades: *White Men Can't Jump* (1992, basketball), *Cobb* (1994, baseball), *Tin Cup* (1996, golf), and the top choice of many, *Bull Durham*.

The *Bull Durham* story is driven by the conflict between aging minor-league catcher Crash Davis and the raw pitching phenom, "Nuke" LaLoosh, Crash is assigned to mentor. Davis has been in the minors for a dozen years and once even had "a cup of coffee" in the big-league "show." Nuke knows only two pitches—hard and harder—and has virtually no control on the mound and little discipline off it. But because of baseball's singular zero-sum personality, the film is as much about hitting as it is about Nuke's pitching. When LaLoosh gives up a monster home run after Davis tips off the batter in order to teach LaLoosh a lesson, Davis rubs it in. "Man that ball got outta here in a hurry. I mean anything travels that far oughta have a damn stewardess on it, don't you think?"[6]

Ever since 1927, all things baseball, sooner or later, come back to home runs. The actual major-league home run leader in 1988, the same year that *Bull Durham* was released, was the Athletics' Jose Canseco, who slammed forty-two jacks that season while driving in 124 runs. Ten years later Canseco's 1988 teammate Mark McGwire would become the first man to slug seventy homers in a single season, and seven years after that Canseco would rock the baseball world with his autobiographical exposé of steroid use titled *Juiced*.

A daunting precursor to the coming steroid era, 1988 also featured Boston pitching sensation Roger Clemens, who led the American League in strikeouts with 291, only to find himself indicted in August 2010 for allegedly lying about steroids to a congressional panel in February 2008. (In 2012 Clemens was acquitted but only after a great deal of expense, damaging testimony, and relentless innuendo.) The year 1988 was also the season of Kirk Gibson's unbelievable walk-off home run that captured Game 1 of the Word Series for the Dodgers, as Gibson limped the bases on a bum leg. Fiction has nothing on the real-life drama of baseball, a game that supplies its own mystique.

Jose Canseco was born in Havana, Cuba, but grew up in Miami, where the Oakland Athletics drafted him. In 1986 he became a major-league star, winning Rookie of the Year and the American League MVP, and in 1989 took home a World Series ring. Competitive, charismatic, and sometimes nasty, Canseco launched home runs with abandon, stacking up 462 in all.[7] In 1988 he and teammate McGwire would slam 74 homers between them (42 for Canseco), or only one more than Barry Bonds would smash in 2001, a year that would soon blow the cover off a lurking steroid problem.

According to Canseco, he was already on steroids when he won Rookie of the Year for the 1986 season, the same year that Roger Clemens won both the Cy Young Award and league MVP honors. Canseco was an unabashed steroid advocate. "I was the godfather of steroids in baseball," he says of himself, admitting that he introduced steroids to the big leagues the year prior to his rookie season. "I single-handedly changed the game of baseball by introducing [steroids] into the game."

Canseco ties the steroid era to the 1994 labor action that shortened the season and canceled the World Series. The strike drove fans away, and its image needed a boost. Baseball found its excitement in the sky; unfortunately, the genesis of those moon shots lurked in the shadows of the game. Canseco fingers the game itself:

> Everyone in the game has been hoping the lie could last as long as possible. They wanted steroids in the game to make it more exciting, hoping

they would be able to build its popularity back up after the disastrous cancelation of the 1994 World Series. So when I taught other players how to use steroids, no one lifted a finger to stop me. When I educated trainers and others on how to inject players with steroids, there was nothing standing in my way. Directly or indirectly, nearly everyone in baseball was complicit.[8]

American capitalism is built on competition and sometimes winning at all costs. Whether exploiting antitrust laws, defeating unions, building new industries, making the better mousetrap, or, better yet, rendering the mousetrap unnecessary (as when the telephone replaced the telegraph), capitalism is an unstoppable force. Professional sports are part of the entertainment business. Fans buy tickets, listen to the radio, or watch games on television because they want to be entertained and are willing to pay for the experience.

Baseball has been in the entertainment business for so long that it has become a front-page example of American capitalism and a metaphor for America itself. Noted cultural historian Jacques Barzun substantiates the point when he says that anyone wishing to understand the heart and mind of America should study the sport of baseball.[9] Not only does baseball represent the images of competition, success, and winning, but also its personality and contributions to language and culture render it a symbol of the American experience.

Baseball also permeates American literature. As celebrated author Ernest Hemingway wrote in *The Old Man and the Sea*, the central character Santiago worships Joe DiMaggio: "But I must have the confidence and I must be worthy of the great DiMaggio who does all things perfectly even with the pain of the bone spur in his heel."[10] Thomas Wolfe also idolized spring and baseball, noting the romantic "sound of the ball smacking into the pocket of the big mitt. . . ." James T. Farrell wrote of baseball and family: "My grandmother . . . wanted to see a baseball game because I was so full of baseball in my boyhood." Roger Kahn romanticized the game in *The Boys of Summer*, and Doris Kearns Goodwin wrote of family, baseball, and posterity in *Wait Till Next Year*. Mark Twain recognized the game as integral to America itself in his widely quoted 1889 speech at a banquet honoring sporting goods magnate Albert (Al) Spalding's sponsorship of a worldwide major-league baseball tour: "Baseball is the very symbol, the outward and visible expression of the drive and push and rush and struggle of the raging, tearing, booming nineteenth century."[11] Twain's lofty comments about the impact of baseball were decades *before* Tyrus "Ty" Cobb, Ruth, Gehrig, and DiMaggio appeared.

In 2004, the Smithsonian Museum of Natural History debuted a "Baseball As America" tribute in conjunction with the National Baseball Hall of Fame, an exhibition that toured museums across the country. According to the Smithsonian, "Baseball As America" was a national celebration of America's romance with baseball that examined the game's rituals and myths, its ethnic integration and advancement, the business of baseball, the physics of the game from home runs to curveballs, and baseball's influence on American culture, literature, films, communications, art, and language. Perhaps no sport has permeated American language more than baseball has. While boxing has contributed its own litany of expressions, such as "throw in the towel" or "saved by the bell," baseball's influence on language is even more pervasive.

The study of language provides an intriguing window to human behavior and culture. Language as we know it is thought to have begun developing about six million years ago, although linguists debate both the origin and even the actual definition of "language." Famed linguist Noam Chomsky of the Massachusetts Institute of Technology, who was once named "the world's top intellectual," believes that some of the human development of language is innate; that is, some form of universal grammar rubric can be found inside the human brain, thus making language possible and also tying all languages together.[12] About five thousand distinct human languages exist (some sources say up to six thousand, with four hundred coming from Nigeria alone), and around two thousand of them have never been written down. Experts agree that two-year-old children typically have more than two hundred words in their vocabulary. After that, the level of understanding varies widely among children. While estimates are anything but certain, it seems that by age three the child's active vocabulary is more than two thousand words, and that number doubles again by age five. Once children learn to read, their exposure to words and their resultant vocabulary increase dramatically.[13]

Where baseball is concerned, the relevant part of language study involves the evolutionary process, particularly what linguists call borrowing. Vocabulary is dynamic; it changes with fashions and other trends, science, literature, and pop culture, all of which frequently add words to language. But anyone who has read works from Shakespeare, or even books published in the late 1800s, knows that words also disappear over time.[14] Although we still speak of "dialing the phone," even though rotary phones are largely extinct, no one talks about "buying a record" of a pop song recording anymore. We still sometimes refer to a compact disc (CD) as an "album," although electronic files of music are now replacing CDs. As evolution progresses, many new phrases are borrowed from other languages or other endeavors. Foreign languages are a prolific source of English words while also borrowing such American terms as "blue jeans" and even the exalted word "weekend." Largely because of the British Empire's global expansion in the 1800s, followed by the twentieth-century success of America and the frequent travels of its people, the English language has borrowed from others so extensively that it utilizes more foreign words than words of its original Germanic origins.[15] Experts note that English, in fact, has robbed from more than 350 other languages about 75 percent of all words now thought of as "English." (Think of constructions based on Latin words, for example, and all of their derivations.) This phenomenon has always worked both ways, with millions of immigrants coming to America through Ellis Island, bringing words from Italian, Swedish, French, Russian, and other languages to enrich our native English.

Words have also been borrowed from specific disciplines as science, contextual uses based on time and circumstances ("never look a gift horse in the mouth" or "beware of Greeks bearing gifts"), or special activities like singing, running, boxing, or baseball. Boxing was extremely popular in

America from the late 1800s to around Muhammad Ali's retirement in 1981, or a period of about a hundred years; so understandably boxing has added many terms to our lexicon. Baseball has been influential in numerous ways as well, adding scores of terms from "home runs" to "strikeouts" to "left field." Much of this language borrowing was a function of settings and circumstances—for example, the proliferation of home runs in Ruth's era and the development of such creative pitches as curveballs and screwballs to stop good hitting. As noted earlier, baseball also benefited from the phenomenon of radio, which spread the language of baseball at an accelerated pace during Ruth's explosive years with Murderers' Row and its expansion throughout the prosperous Roaring Twenties.

Pioneer radio station KDKA in Pittsburgh (then with the call letters 8ZZ) broadcast the winner of the 1920 presidential election in one of the first popular uses of the broadcasting media. Two years later nearly two million American homes had a radio, and, remarkably, more than five hundred licensed radio stations existed. Most of them were mere fledgling start-ups, although some would go on to dominate the airwaves and make significant imprints on the game of baseball.[16] Later owned by the *Chicago Tribune* media conglomerate, WGN Radio (which stands for "World's Greatest Newspaper") broadcast the 1925 Cubs' season opener in Chicago, thus following in the footsteps of KDKA, which began broadcasting Pirates games in August 1921.

In 1923, Sears, Roebuck and Company began selling radio receiver sets in its famed catalog. New York station WJZ, which had begun broadcasting in 1921, aired a musical offering from pianist Violet Pearch followed by soprano Elsa Rieffin and then the riveting "things to tell the Housewife about cooking a meal" on May 16, 1923, at 3 p.m. A second New York station, WJY, would offer 340 soprano solos and 205 bedtime stories in 1923, but it also experimented with sports programming, airing five boxing matches and six baseball games. Soon consortiums of stations sprang up to create the beginnings of radio networks.[17] Radio Corporation of America (RCA) began the National Broadcasting Company (NBC) as a subsidiary in 1926 to operate two networks of twenty-four stations. The Columbia

Broadcasting System (CBS) began with a network of sixteen stations in 1928. By the end of World War II, 95 percent of all American homes had at least one radio.

By the 1920s an industry specifically designed to spread the human word was in "full swing," but radio needed programming to fill the dead airwaves. It would take more than sopranos, pianists, and bedtime stories to keep America adequately entertained.

Soon radio discovered both boxing and baseball. Since baseball had many more meaningful contests, with each big-league team playing 154 games per year, baseball was soon broadcast to remote farms, city parlors, barbershops, hospitals, and even jails across the country. And with it came the language of baseball. Sometimes the evolution of words and meaning is contrived—for example, the intentional pop phrase "jump the shark"— or inspired, as in author Malcolm Gladwell's thoughtful new treatment of the term "tipping point." Often, however, it comes from cutting-edge grassroots necessity, which gives it a sense of fashion, if not coolness. Words such as "hippie" and "yuppie"; texting slang, such as "OMG," "LOL," and "WTF"; and the powerful, trademark-turned-verb "Google" come to mind. The same baseball terms have been around for more than a hundred years, and the game still makes new contributions to the English language, although perhaps not always in a flattering manner. Thanks to baseball's great steroid era and its front-page blunders, anything large or dominant these days is described as being on steroids. For instance, an epic novel is "a story on steroids."

Some of baseball's language contribution comes from futility, like the word "whiff," while specific teams, such as the Cubs, Giants, and Mets, also provided new terms. Indeed, the Mets organization gave us the term "Miracle Mets," but the original team represented futility with its staggering losses in its first years. The team's colorful manager Casey Stengel added to the American jargon with his unorthodox approach to baseball and language and spawned volumes of Stengelese with such phrases as "the amazin' Mets," "can't anybody here play this game," and "you can look it up." The Giants served up "Bonehead Merkle," referring to Fred Merkle, a young player who in 1908 strolled directly home too early instead of going to second base after his team seemed to have won its game against the rival Cubs during a tight pennant race. He thus made the third out and actually erased the third run, resulting in a tie. When the game had to be replayed, the Cubs won, and the whole mishap dominated the American lexicon for decades under the somewhat unfortunate reference to "Merkle's boner." More recently, the Cubs added to local legend, lore, and futility in October 2003 when the Cubs were only five outs away from their first World Series since 1945. As a young fan named Steve Bartman reached for a foul ball, he knocked it away from left fielder Moisés Alou, costing a third out and contributing to a Cubs slide that propelled the underdog Florida Marlins to the Series instead. Bartman was ostracized in headlines and elsewhere, and his likeness became the best-selling Halloween costume in the Chicago area that year. At the time, Florida governor Jeb Bush reportedly offered "asylum" to Bartman, but he apparently remained in the Chicago area and managed to keep a remarkably low profile. To this day in Chicago, and sometimes on national broadcasts, a major baseball blunder involving a fan is often referred to as "pulling a Bartman." Time will tell whether the Bartman reference will endure, but as of November 2012, a Google search of the term "Steve Bartman" yielded 1,280,000 results, one being Bartman's own Wikipedia entry (while a more targeted search of "Steve Bartman Cubs" produced 436,000 entries).

Ernest Thayer's "Casey at the Bat" is one of the most famous American poems, and Jack Norworth and Albert Von Tilzer's "Take Me Out to the Ballgame" is still a beloved song standard. Moreover, some say the most famous American comedy routine of all time is the Bud Abbott and Lou Costello classic "Who's on First?" The rapid-fire explosion of baseball double meanings debuted in vaudeville and may have first appeared on national radio during *The Kate Smith Hour* in March 1938. The phrase still is used in everyday language to describe a confusing, fast-paced situation in sports, business, or politics. (One of the more creative uses is found among the culinary listings for an Asian style restaurant in Winnipeg called Hu's on First.) In 1999, *Time* magazine designated "Who's on First?" as the best comedy sketch of the twentieth century. The routine is often parodied, as in an irreverent 2001 episode of television's *South Park*. The American Film Institute ranked the line itself, which derives its humor from the confusion over whether it is actually a question or a statement of fact, number 91 on its list of 100 memorable movie quotes as it was referenced in the 1945 film *The Naughty Nineties*.[18] The video sequence from that film continuously plays in the Baseball Hall of Fame in Cooperstown, New York, and a gold record version of "Who's on First?" has been featured in the hall since 1956.

Baseball dominates the American lexicon in ways that no other sport does. Everyday terms such as "blooper," "Bronx cheer," "heavy hitter," "screwball," "sweet spot," and legions of others all trace their beginnings to the game of baseball. Many are derived from the long-ball spectacle called the home run—for example, the business and political use of "swing for the fences"—or the lingering adjective of grandeur, "Ruthian." With fifty or more synonyms for the term "home run," the cultural importance of baseball's marquee run-scoring image is clear.

No lure in American sports is quite similar to that of baseball, the game that has dominated our culture, our language, and our history over the past 150 years. Further, no lure to the game is greater than that enduring symbol of American achievement, the home run. It brought crowds to the game in the 1920s, electrified a nation in 1927 and 1961, and pulled droves of fans back again in 1998 after the disappointing 1994 labor action and cancellation of the World Series. Perhaps nothing describes the allure of baseball more than the speech actor James Earl Jones gave in the motion picture *Field of Dreams* (1989), based on Kinsella's book *Shoeless Joe*:

> The one constant through all the years, Ray, has been baseball. America has rolled by like an army of steamrollers. It has been erased like a blackboard, rebuilt and erased again. But baseball has marked the time. This field, this game: it's a part of our past, Ray. It reminds of [*sic*] us of all that once was good and it could be again. Oh . . . people will come Ray. People will most definitely come.[19]

☆ **3** ☆

BASEBALL'S
ANTE DIEM

No one knows when baseball officially began, for the game, quite simply, did not "begin" at all; it evolved. It had no peach baskets, no Naismith rules, and no overnight epiphanies in a Massachusetts Young Men's Christian Association (YMCA) gymnasium as happened with basketball at definable moments in 1891 and 1892.

Before 1891, no game similar to basketball existed. James Naismith, a Canadian physical education instructor, was searching for a new game to provide students with indoor physical activity during the winter months. Then he experimented with a game to be played using a soccer ball and two peach baskets that were suspended from the ten-feet-high upper-level railing in the Springfield gym. Naismith wrote the first formal rules in 1892, and "basketball" was born.

Baseball's beginning has its romantic legends, of course. The stories surrounding Abner Doubleday, who reigned as the game's apparent inventor for more than 150 years, are now considered dubious. Although Doubleday might have written a set of rules defining a game of baseball around 1839, the evidence was based on hearsay; moreover, plentiful references to the game of baseball occurred well before then.[1] And, tellingly, although Doubleday kept copious diaries, not one mention of baseball is found in any of them. For decades even the Hall of Fame recognized both a different date, 1845, and a different inventor, Alexander Cartwright.[2]

Author David Block may have summed it up best in his book *Baseball Before We Knew It: A Search for the Roots of the Game*: "The age-old debate over baseball's ancestry has always been long on bluster and short on facts."[3] There is much disagreement about the roots of baseball, such as whether it started from the early British games of cricket or rounders or from an American boyhood game called two old cat or from elsewhere. The best explanation is that baseball continually borrowed from other games and experiences and was pushed along by necessity depending on the available equipment in the cities or countryside. It progressed much in the same ways that languages borrowed from others, species evolved, and America developed as a hodgepodge society. Nothing happens in a vacuum, and the progression of baseball is no different.

In 1991 the Hall of Fame learned about an edition of a small New York newspaper, the *Delhi Gazette*, dated July 13, 1825, that contained a written notice by nine men challenging others to a game of baseball for the grand stakes of a dollar per contest.[4] A schoolmate of Doubleday's claims that Doubleday had actually invented baseball in 1839, and on the strength of the classmate's letter describing rules for the game at that date, a panel convened more than a century ago recognized Doubleday as the inventor in Cooperstown, New York, one reason that the Baseball Hall of Fame is located there. But for many years the Hall of Fame itself continued to recognize Cartwright and the 1845 date, which is when Cartwright devised the written rules of baseball for the New York Knickerbocker team on which he played.

Notwithstanding the Doubleday legend or the Hall of Fame version, evidence shows organized clubs played a form of baseball in the New England area during the 1820s and 1830s. Moreover, American soldiers described playing a crude version of baseball in Gen. George Washington's army. One contemporaneous letter said they "played base" and recounted that the general himself played catch for hours as a diversion.[5] Most likely those activities at Valley Forge were a variation of rounders, a contest strikingly similar to baseball, since it was played with four bases (each being a stick in the ground), a ball, and batter. It also had nine players to a side and was played during five to seven innings. Scoring was similar to baseball's, too, although the fourth base was not at "home" but down the line to the left of home, resulting in a different shape than the perfect diamond of the baseball field. Nonetheless, making it to the fourth base was called hitting a rounder, and the game followed a process similar to the way baseball is played.

In 1846 a New York team called the Knickerbockers, in a one-sided contest against a group of cricket players, seems to have played the first official baseball game in a form that more closely resembles today's baseball. By 1857 at least one publication, the *Spirit of the Times*, referred to baseball as the national pastime. The game grew enough in popularity to justify charging admission when a crowd of about fifteen hundred people paid fifty cents each to watch an all-star game held at a Long Island race course in 1858.[6] By 1861 the nation was embroiled in the Civil War, but baseball remained a diversion for the beleaguered president, Abraham Lincoln. "Honest Abe" was a fan of the game and was known to quip about taking turns at bat, striking a fair ball, and even making home runs. He had a baseball field constructed behind the White House and was sometimes seen playing baseball with children on its front lawn.[7]

On May 15, 1862, the first enclosed park with an admission charge, the Union Baseball Grounds, opened in Brooklyn, and "The Star-Spangled Banner" was played before a baseball game for the first time. On Christmas Day that same year, as the Civil War raged, a crowd of perhaps forty thousand watched two Union Army teams play baseball at Hilton Head, South Carolina. In the fall of 1865, about six months after the Civil War ended, a Philadelphia Athletics team must have set some form of baseball record by scoring a combined 263 runs in a morning-afternoon doubleheader.[8]

In 1866, a group of Vassar College players fielded the first women's baseball team. Most accounts credit William "Candy" Cummings with throwing the first curveball in competition, but they differ as to whether he did so in 1866 or 1867. When the first all-professional team began play as the Cincinnati Red Stockings in 1869, the seeds of major-league baseball, as we one day would know it, were duly sown. Nine years later, the first black professional player took the field when John "Bud" Fowler, who happened to be from Cooperstown, appeared for the Lynn Live Oaks, an International League team from Massachusetts.

In 1875, pitching phenom Albert Spalding was induced to leave Boston to sign with Chicago, and by year's end Spalding and Chicago owner William A. Hulbert designed a constitution and bylaws for a new league, the National League of Professional Baseball Clubs, the forerunner of today's National League. In 1876, Spalding won a remarkable forty-seven games for Chicago's team, which at the time was called the White Stockings. (Not the forerunner of the Chicago White Sox, the team would later become the National League's Chicago Cubs.)

Home runs were not yet the baseball marquee they one day would become. In 1877 the National League's leader swatted only four. Pitcher Al Spalding, however, hit a home run of a different sort when he formed a company to manufacture baseballs. That company, which still bears his name, became a sports marketing juggernaut. He would only pitch one more year, winning a single game, but the A. G. Spalding & Bros. sporting goods company continued to flourish. Its baseball was the official ball of the major leagues until 1976, but in 1894 the company was on the verge of a different success story when basketball's Naismith asked Spalding to invent a special ball for the new indoor game.

By 1879, the league's leader in homers, Charles "Long Charley" Jones of the Boston Red Caps, still managed to slug only nine on the year. Pitchers remained the dominant stars, with John Montgomery Ward winning forty-seven games that year for the Providence Grays. One big reason for such dominance is that the pitching distance in those days was only forty-five feet.[9] It's a wonder anyone got a hit, let alone home runs, but it certainly helped that pitchers were throwing underhand. In 1883 they were allowed to throw side arm but still not overhand. By 1880, however, home runs were beginning to be noticed. On May 1, Mike "King" Kelly of the Chicago White Stockings slammed the first Opening Day homer. The following month, Boston's Charley Jones became the first major-league player to hit two home runs in the same game; in fact, he did so in the same inning. His was a notable feat, since the league leaders that year, neither of whom was Jones, hit only six in the whole season.

In the pre–antitrust exemption days, baseball competition was alive and well. An American Association was formed in 1881 to compete with the National League, and it immediately began a price war, charging only twenty-five cents to attend a game, or half the entrance fee for National League games.[10] The fans still did not see many home runs, though, with the Buffalo Bisons' Dan "Big Dan" Brouthers hitting only eight to lead the National League. But they saw plenty of overall hitting as Adrian "Cap" Anson batted .399 on the season for the Chicago White Stockings.

On May 1, 1883, an impressive crowd of more than twelve thousand spectators, including President Ulysses S. Grant, saw the New York Gothams (later called the Giants) beat the Boston Beaneaters, 7–5. That same year baseball saw a much different threshold event when, on August 10 (some sources say July 20), Chicago superstar Cap Anson refused to take the field against the Toledo Mudhens, because they had on their roster a black catcher, Moses Fleetwood "Fleet" Walker. "If you want me to play, you'll have to get that [Negro] off the field," Anson reportedly warned. Although the Anson challenge is widely quoted, it so happens that the teams played anyway. Some accounts say Anson relented, while others note that Walker was injured and couldn't play in the first place. The more detailed story seems to be that Walker was indeed injured, but the manager inserted him in center field anyway when he heard about the Anson edict. Anson reportedly relented when threatened with a forfeiture of both the game and the game receipts. Regardless, the incident prominently injected issues of race into major-league baseball. Meanwhile, by the end of the year, the home run count was creeping up, with league leader William "Buck" Ewing hitting ten for the National League's Gothams and Harry Stovey slugging fourteen for the Philadelphia Athletics.

In the spring of 1884, a healthy Fleet Walker took the field as the catcher for Toledo and apparently was the first black player to appear in a major-league game. Even his teammates were not wholly receptive, though. Pitcher

Tony Mullane would not follow his catcher's signs simply because he was black; however, Mullane openly called Walker the best catcher he'd ever had. Even with talented black players on the outs and pitchers still dominant, nonetheless, that season saw a surge in home runs.[11] Ned Williamson of the Chicago White Stockings would slam an impressive twenty-seven homers to lead the National League in 1884.

One goal the early home run leaders could not achieve was sustained power over many years. Even with 27 homers in one year, Williamson did not become the career leader in the pre-Ruth era. That honor belonged to Roger Connor, who managed 138 total home runs during a long career of belting long balls from 1880 to 1897. The next two decades, which preceded Ruth's appearance, are called the dead-ball era, but not entirely because of the ball. In fact, no meaningful technological changes "deadened" the ball during this time. From the inception of the American League in 1901 until the elimination of the spitball in 1920, scoring suffered and home runs were sparse. The era ended abruptly in 1920 when the spitball disappeared and the game's emphasis shifted from "small ball" strategies of bunts, sacrifices, and moving runners gradually around the bases to a more robust offense, including the "long ball," or home run. But the spitball was not banned overnight. Those pitchers who used it were grandfathered in, so the pitch remained in use until Burleigh Grimes retired in 1934. Yet the dead-ball era ended quickly. Baseball historians pegged its demise as 1920, the year Ruth was sold to the Yankees and slugged 54 home runs, a single-season record that shattered his own mark of 29 set only the previous year. With Ruth's performance, the lively ball era was born.

At six-foot-three and 220 pounds, the prior career home run king, Roger Connor, was a formidable slugger for any era. Largely unknown today, he was the undisputed home run king not only during his career but also for two decades thereafter—or until the lively ball era when slugger Babe Ruth came on the scene. Although he did slug seventeen homers during the 1887 season, Connor's overall home run career more approximated the style of Hank Aaron (1954–1976) than that of the prodigious Ruth. Connor was consistent and showed incredible longevity, accumulating a large number of home runs over an extended period. With his stunning power, he became the first big-league player to hit a grand slam—a two-out, bottom-of-the-ninth shot to come from three runs down in September 1881—and was the first player to clear the massive original Polo Grounds in New York, where he launched a mammoth shot over the right-field fence onto 112th Street. The latter feat was so spectacular that a number of blue-blooded fans reportedly took up an impromptu collection and raised enough to present a $500 gold watch to the ominous hitter.[12] In 1888, Connor became the sixth player to garner three homers in a single game. That monstrous feat, punctuating a spectacular home run career, led to his team being called the Giants.

Later that same year, a budding young writer, twenty-four-year-old Ernest L. Thayer, sold a baseball poem to the *San Francisco Examiner* for the notable sum of $5.00. As noted previously, Thayer's "Casey at the Bat" would become the most recognized and enduring work of baseball literature.[13]

Abner Doubleday, who was a Union commander at Fort Sumter at the advent of the Civil War and fought in four noted battles, including Gettysburg, passed away in 1893. On the field, baseball continued to progress. Prior to the year's regular season, baseball reacted to the prowess of the game's pitchers by increasing the pitching distance to sixty feet, although the actual length was erroneously recorded at sixty feet, six inches, where it remains today.[14] On April 21, 1898, Phillies's pitcher Bill Duggleby became the first player to hit a grand slam in his first major-league plate appearance.[15] No one has done it since. Bobby Bonds, father to the notorious Barry Bonds, did manage to slug a grand slam in his first game in 1968 but not his first trip to the plate.

At the turn of the century in 1900, the National League reorganized by buying out its weaker teams. At the same time a new competing league was being formed in Chicago called the new American League, which had no formal relationship to the old American Association that disbanded in 1891. Charles Comiskey moved his St. Paul, Minnesota, team to Chicago, where it became the American League White Sox. The new league started a bidding war for players, including one of the top stars of the day, the

Phillies' Nap Lajoie (pronounced La-ZHWAH), who bolted to the American League Athletics to avoid salary cap issues and to earn more dollars. That move led to a lawsuit, which the National League won. Then Lajoie went to another American League team, the Cleveland Broncos, and the Ohio courts proved more sympathetic and did not block the move. Playing during the era of Ty Cobb, Lajoie was one of the best second basemen in history, batting a stunning .426 in 1901—the highest season average for a position player in American League history—and leading the league in home runs with 14.[16] While playing in Cleveland, Nap became so dominant that in 1903 the team changed its name from the Blues to the Cleveland Naps. After Nap's departure, the team held a naming contest and eventually became the Indians.

As the post-1900 modern era emerged, home run totals settled back to modest historical norms. No hitter managed more than nine per season from 1876 through 1882. As late as 1917, Wally Pipp led the American League in single digits with nine homers, and in 1918 Clifford "Gavvy" Cravath led the National League with only eight. One factor was pitching, which improved almost overnight thanks to Elmer Stricklett. In 1905, Stricklett, a journeyman pitcher for Brooklyn, surprised the Giants with a wholly new elusive pitch, the spitball. The spitter may have originated by accident when a wet field moistened the ball one day, but Stricklett seems to have been the first to deploy the pitch in a major-league game.[17] When thrown correctly, the spitball is a wicked breaking pitch that changes direction dramatically because the slippery wet side creates less friction with the air, causing the dry side to drag and bend the flight of the ball. The home run leaders in both leagues that year consequently could not manage double-digit homers for the first time in the short history of the two competing leagues. Interestingly, the unpredictable spitter may have also had a much different type of impact on the game, for it was during 1905 that many catchers, including Cleveland's Jay Clarke, began wearing soccer shin guards under their uniforms. Until then, catchers' legs had been largely unprotected.

Meanwhile, the commercial success of baseball was showing itself in new ways. For instance, in 1905 Honus Wagner became the first player to endorse a bat and have his signature engraved on it when he inked a Louisville Slugger deal with J. F. Hillerich & Son. Then, in 1907, in what may have been the first commercial endorsement of its kind, baseball icon Ty Cobb landed a marketing deal of a different sort by endorsing Coca-Cola.[18] Cobb wound up with a sizable holding of Coca-Cola stock, which was said to be worth in the range of $12 million upon Cobb's death in 1961. Such deals may have done more to influence the game of baseball than originally thought, for in no small way did this new endorsement phenomenon lead to the importance of big-time plays, players, and home runs. As noted, Ralph Kiner knew where to find the Cadillacs. But Oakland slugger Reggie Jackson ("Fans don't boo nobodies") added geography and endorsements to the equation when he talked about New York while also evoking the ghost of Ruth: "If I played there, they'd name a candy bar after me." Then he did go to New York in 1977, and the Reggie Bar debuted in 1978.[19]

In 1908 a little song with a big heart titled "Take Me Out to the Ballgame" appeared and would become the virtual anthem of baseball. The following season in 1909, the Detroit Tigers' Ty Cobb was at the top of his game on the field. He led the American League in every major offensive category—batting (.377), slugging (.517), RBIs (107), hits (216), stolen bases (76)—including home runs, although he managed only nine round-trippers on the season. The next season, money and fortune would affect the game in new ways with Cobb and Lajoie locked in a tight race for the league's batting title. The Chalmers Motor Company promised a new car to the winner of the batting crown, adding fuel to the Cobb-Lajoie rivalry. Near the end of the season, Cobb had the lead and decided to sit out the final game while Lajoie opted to play a doubleheader against the St. Louis Browns.

The irascible Cobb was hardly a league favorite, so the Browns' third baseman played off the bag almost in short left when Lajoie came up to the plate. Lajoie did not notice at first, but he hit a triple anyway before getting the idea to bunt toward third every at-bat. In the two games Lajoie managed eight hits in nine at-bats and even reached base on the ninth try, which was deemed an error and not a hit. Lajoie thus appeared to win the crown and even received congratulatory notes from Cobb's own teammates. But officially Lajoie had not quite bested Cobb, who won the crown batting .3850687 to Lajoie's .3840947. Finding itself in the middle of a hot controversy, the Chalmers Company wisely opted to grant a car to both players.[20] So Cobb led the league in hitting officially at .385, while Lajoie garnered the most hits with 227. Neither of them led in home runs, however. That honor went to Jake Stahl of the Red Sox, who hit ten homers on the year.

With on-field exploits making headlines, baseball also was making an impact on America. That same year, 1910, President William Howard Taft began the tradition of presidents throwing the first ceremonial pitch. Meanwhile, another poem embedded itself in American pop culture when the *New York Evening Mail*'s Franklin Adams wrote "Baseball's Sad Lexicon," which played on the emergence of an enduring phrase about the Cubs' infield double-play combination—"[Joe] Tinker to [Johnny] Evers to [Frank] Chance." The following year, Shoeless Joe Jackson batted a sparkling .408, yet he still finished second to Ty Cobb's .420. Cobb missed the Triple Crown that year, falling one home run short, but he did win the new Chalmers Award devised for the league MVP. John Franklin "Home Run" Baker, whose name says it all, managed eleven homers on the season to take the American League lead, but he fell short of the record for the Cubs' Frank Schulte, who slammed twenty-one to lead the National League.

In 1912, the year the *Titanic* sank, the Cubs' Henry "Heinie" Zimmerman almost pulled a Ty Cobb by winning five of the six major offensive categories in the National League, including the top batting average at .372 and the league lead in home runs with fourteen. By 1913, Cobb, Shoeless Joe, and Home Run Baker all topped various American League categories. Cobb batted .390 with Detroit, Jackson garnered 197 hits for the Cleveland Naps, and Baker clubbed twelve homers with an impressive 117 RBIs for the Philadelphia Athletics. The major-league leader in home runs, however, was Gavvy Cravath of the Phillies, who slugged nineteen and had 128 RBIs for tops in the National League.

Off the field, American culture was still in the twilight of a repressed Victorian era that would break free during the Roaring Twenties. But on the field, major-league baseball was already breaking free as an irreverent game of mischief and deception and even came under the influence of gamblers. In these ways, baseball was a platform for a bursting sense of rebellion, similar to rock and roll five decades later. The greatest player of the era was Ty Cobb, who was so good, so cutting edge, and so unmistakably irreverent that he could have been a modern superstar.

In 1914 Cobb likened baseball to war and called batters the heavy artillery, an apt observation by the no-holds-barred center fielder who played the game with reckless, even dastardly abandon. It was a poignant comment, too, as 1914 saw the beginning of "the war to end all wars," World War I, although America would not enter that conflict until much later. Further, during 1914 a real economic war ignited on and off the baseball field—one that would change major-league baseball forever—when a third league, the Federal League, debuted on April 13. Formed to compete head-on with the National and American Leagues, it began by raiding players from both. On Opening Day, the new Federal League featured 172 former major-leaguers, including dozens of star players like Joe Tinker and dominant pitcher Mordecai "Three Finger" Brown.[21] A salary war soon followed, with the majors forced to pay more and more to keep their own stars, and National League owners did not overlook this punch in the pocketbook.

Major-league baseball, though, continued to flex its cultural and economic muscle, and as the game flourished, state-of-the-art stadiums were conceived and built, including Chicago's new Weeghman Park. This northside structure soon became a veritable baseball shrine, but it was not the original home of the Cubs. The competing Federal League's team, the Whales, occupied the stadium in 1914 and pressed the established Cubs (which were formed in 1876 but did not officially adopt the Cubs' moniker until 1907 after the team's nickname, coined in 1902, began to stick) and the other major leagues by competing on Chicago's turf. The National League fought back and attempted to freeze out the new Federal League in a war over star players, but the Federals countered with an antitrust lawsuit.

The U.S. antitrust laws had been in place since Congress passed the Sherman Antitrust Act of 1890, and federal trustbusters had already used their powers against the powerful John D. Rockefeller's Standard Oil. Chicago federal judge Kenesaw Landis, an antitrust expert, had once fined Standard Oil for violating the laws, so when the Federal League sued, it chose Chicago as its venue. Landis, a staunch baseball fan, arm-twisted a settlement, but the Baltimore Terrapins franchise would not join in, choosing to continue its fight against the National League. The legal battle went all the way to the U.S. Supreme Court and became the foundation for the curious baseball antitrust decision that has insulated baseball from antitrust laws since 1922.

Meanwhile, in 1914 another development, which went largely unnoticed at the time, would ultimately affect baseball even more than its antitrust status would. On April 22, an emerging pitcher debuted for the minor-league Baltimore Orioles, shutting out the Buffalo Bisons. But the real story began with the signing of that pitcher five weeks earlier. On February 14, 1913, Washington Senators' pitcher Joe Engel attended a baseball game that his alma mater, Mount St. Mary's College, played against St. Mary's Industrial School. He was impressed with the latter's nineteen-year-old pitcher named George H. Ruth and brought the kid to the attention of Jack Dunn, the owner of the Orioles. (The official Babe Ruth website says the brothers at St. Mary's had invited Dunn to come observe Ruth.[22]) Dunn worked Ruth out and offered the youngster $250 per month. Because Ruth was still a minor, Dunn had to become Ruth's legal guardian, too. Impressed by the kid's age and youthful appearance, the other players referred to him as Dunn's newest "babe."[23] The name stuck, and "Babe" Ruth soon transformed baseball in a way that no one has ever done for any other team sport.

The Orioles did not retain Ruth long. By July 9, 1914, the Orioles had sold the Babe to the Boston Red Sox in a three-player deal worth $8,000, and two days later Ruth debuted for Boston. A crowd of a little more than eleven thousand people saw Ruth strike out the first batter.[24] Although he was not involved in the final decision, Boston did go on to win the game.

In the meantime, the Federal League kept pushing. The Chicago team (which adopted the name "Whales" in 1915) enticed star pitcher Walter Johnson to take a $10,000 signing bonus and $20,000 per year on a three-year deal, forcing Senators' owner Clark Griffith to make Johnson a counteroffer of $12,500 per year and to reimburse the Whales for Johnson's signing bonus, which Johnson was allowed to keep. Significantly, Charles Comiskey reportedly loaned Griffith $10,000 to help pull off that coup. Although the Senators successfully retained Johnson, by 1915 legions of other traditional big-league stars bolted for the new league. On January 5, 1915, the Federal League officially filed its antitrust suit, with Chicago owners James Gilmore and Charles Weeghman leading the way. They partly wanted to bolster their legal grounds for the Chicago venue. On the field that year, the Phillies' Cravath was pushing the home run envelope, slamming twenty-four to lead the National League. With money and competition both on and off the field driving the game as never before, baseball was about to discover the marquee value of the home run.

After the Federal League's Baltimore franchise took the antitrust case to the Supreme Court, as part of the settlement, the Chicago Whales disbanded. Owner Charles Weeghman, together with an investor group that included William Wrigley, Jr., was allowed to purchase the Chicago Cubs from Cincinnati publisher Charles P. Taft, half brother to President Taft.

On July 21, 1915, Ruth, who was still primarily a pitcher, took a rip at history from the other side of the plate. Swinging from the heels, he connected on a pitch that sailed completely out of Sportsman's Park in St. Louis, cleared Grand Boulevard, and landed 470 feet from home plate. It was the longest home run ever to leave Sportsman's at the time and was a precursor to much bigger records for Ruth and baseball.

The 1916 season would offer a number of less dramatic yet key threshold moments that set the stage for the home run's ascension in a few short years. Weeghman moved the newly acquired Cubs to his new Weeghman Park at Clark and Addison, where the team played for the first time on April 20, 1916, before a crowd of twenty thousand people. The stadium would become Cubs Park, and then Wrigley Field in 1926 after Chicago industrialist William Wrigley purchased the team from Weeghman and the other investors. Wrigley Field was state of the art at the time, and it would be the site of much major-league history. Over time, its dimensions would prove friendly to long-ball hitters, and its lakefront breezes would play havoc with fly balls and home runs. On May 14, 1916, Rogers Hornsby belted his first home-field big-league home run for St. Louis; in June the star pitcher Ruth slammed a home run in three consecutive games; and in October, Boston won the World Series behind Ruth's pitching. The Babe still owns the record for winning the longest complete game in a Series, with a 2–1 victory over Brooklyn in fourteen innings.

On the field Wally Pipp led the American League in home runs by slapping twelve for the Yankees, while the Cubs' Fred "Cy" Williams and the Giants' Dave Robertson tied for the National League lead, also with twelve each. But perhaps the most important baseball moment occurred well after the season was over when, at year's end, a New York theatrical agent and producer—originally from Peoria, Illinois—bought the Red Sox for a reported $500,000. Four years later, Harry Frazee would not only change baseball history, but he also would change the game of baseball and even a notable slice of America itself.

Proving that he, too, could hit the long ball, in 1917 Ty Cobb took a rip at Ruth by slugging a grand slam at Sportsman's Park with a ball that traveled even farther than Ruth's record blast.[25] Neither Cobb nor Ruth led the league in homers that year, for the American League home run leader was again Wally Pipp, who had only nine on the season.

Boston owner Frazee surely made one of the all-time great baseball blunders when he sold Babe Ruth to the Yankees in 1920, but he had already made one of his better moves in 1918 by *not* selling Ruth when New York first came knocking. On May 6, 1918, Babe Ruth took the field as a position player for the first time, batting sixth, playing first base, and slamming an impressive home run against the Yankees. It was then that Yankees owner Col. Jacob Ruppert first approached Frazee about parting with Ruth. Frazee was not selling—yet.

By the end of the 1918 season, Ty Cobb was back on top, leading the American League in hitting at .382, but the slugging pitcher Ruth found himself on top in two non-pitching categories. For the first time, Ruth led the American League in home runs, tying the Athletics' Clarence "Tillie" Walker with eleven on the season. Yes, it was still a modest total, but Ruth also led the league's slugging percentage at .555 and, more important, acquired a taste for long-ball prowess, if not glamour.

Known in baseball annals as Frank "Home Run" Baker, the third baseman earned his long-ball nickname by winning two World Series games with home runs against the Giants in 1911. Baker was with the Philadelphia Athletics at the time. He led or tied the league in home runs four times and played in six different World Series from 1910 to 1922. His career total of ninety-six homers, logging forty-eight first for the Athletics and another forty-eight for the Yankees for six years, was impressive for his day, and his peak seasons came during the dead-ball era. Wielding a heavy fifty-two-ounce bat (Roger Maris would swing a thirty-three-ounce bat thirty-five years later), Baker was a recognized hitter. He was "one of the greatest hitters I ever saw," noted Red Sox manager Bill Carrigan.[26] Athletics manager Connie Mack echoed the praise: "[Frank] Baker is one of the most dangerous hitters in baseball today and is the type of cleanup batter all pitchers respect."[27] Tellingly, the only player that the irascible Ty Cobb actually admitted to spiking on the base paths was, indeed, Frank Baker.

When asked about George Herman Ruth, Baker's praise exceeded even his own accolades: "I hope he lives to hit one-hundred homers in a season. I wish him all the luck in the world. He has everybody else, including myself, hopelessly outclassed."[28]

Baseball before Ruth was ruled by dominant pitchers who could win thirty, forty, or more games a year, with a few genuine hitters—for example, Lajoie, Cobb, Pipp, and Baker—thrown in among them. After Ruth, many revered pitchers from Jay "Dizzy" Dean and Robert "Bob" Feller to Sanford "Sandy" Koufax and Roger Clemens would grace the game. Going on to rule the game, however, would be such marquee sluggers as Kiner,

Mays, Aaron, Mantle, Maris, Jackson, Kaline, Gehrig, and even the troubled likes of McGwire, Bonds, and Canseco.

More important, baseball had hitters before Ruth joined the game, but after Ruth appeared, they became sluggers. His prowess changed the game forever. It was a sports feat attempted by the likes of Wilt Chamberlain, Michael Jordan, Muhammad Ali, and others, but never had a sports threshold so significantly altered a game, a nation, or even history the way Ruth did. Certainly athletes played baseball *in* America before Ruth's era, but after Ruth, baseball *was* America.

RUTH:
THE QUANTUM LEAP

Even casual fans recognize Ruth's immortal number 714 as the total of his lifetime big-league home runs, but few are acquainted with his final shot, a blast for the ages. The grand finale of Ruth's career offers a symbolic image of his work at the plate, a transformation of baseball that not only moved the bar forever but also changed the nature of the bar itself.

On May 25, 1935, the "Bambino" lumbered to the batter's box at Forbes Field in Pittsburgh, one of the National League parks where Ruth found himself playing at the twilight of his career as a member of the Boston Braves—an ironic send-off given his Boston roots and storied sale to the Yankees in 1920.[1] According to the opposing pitcher Guy Bush, who had relieved starter Red Lucas that day, the forty-year-old Ruth was noticeably "fat and old."[2] Ruth still had smacked a two-run shot in the first inning, then followed with another two-run blast in the third. But those hits were simply his warm-up.

After adding a single in the fifth, Ruth came to the plate in the seventh inning. His very last round-tripper was the first to clear the right-field grandstand's roof, reportedly landing 600 feet from home plate. It was the longest home run ever hit at Forbes Field and made Ruth the first player to achieve three-homer games in both leagues.

Forbes Field was almost twenty-six years old at the time, and it would continue to host many of baseball's great moments until its demise in 1970. It featured an innovative three-tier grandstand and offered luxury suites, ramps, and elevators when it opened on June 30, 1909. The cavernous park's original dimensions were 360 feet to left field, 376 feet to right, and a daunting 462 feet to dead center.[3] It is unlikely that Ruth's final shot actually cleared a grandstand 600 feet away, since most historians recognize Mickey Mantle's alleged 565-foot home run at Griffith Stadium to be the longest tape measure homer; moreover, physicists believe that no baseball can be launched much more than 500 feet under human power with a wooden bat (and no wind). But that information, in itself, is a part of the Ruth legacy and lore.

Babe Ruth was undeniably a superstar, and he reportedly earned a collective $1 million in baseball compensation over his long career (one report suggests $1,076,474, and another computes the total at $910,696).[4] He received little additional endorsement income, however, because in those days sports endorsements were not yet a common or lucrative marketing tool. Ty Cobb had pioneered a few endorsements, but his millions came mostly from investing extremely well and taking early equity stakes in Coca-Cola (which he also endorsed) and United Motors, which later became part of General Motors. Moreover, the law did not recognize the unique property rights in one's own image and likeness, as it does today, so the players could not develop and own their images as a protectable brand. In those days a ball player's $1 million career was a stunning achievement, but it paled against the income of the top contemporary heavyweight boxing champions who were capable of earning that much for one fight. Yet even this dichotomy provided another opportunity for Ruth to change America, and the story does not begin in New York or even in the world of baseball.

On September 22, 1927, two heavyweight gladiators entered the championship ring at Chicago's Soldier Field to face off in what would become one of the most storied sporting events of all time. Jack Dempsey was a vicious fighter with a wicked punch who had lost his title to challenger Gene Tunney on September 23, 1926. Almost a year later to the day, both fighters were back in the ring before a massive Chicago crowd of more than 104,000 people. Already ballyhooed as one of several "fights of the century," this "long count" fight featured a historic boxing blunder that would endure as one of the sport's infamous moments when Tunney benefited from extra time to recover from Dempsey's knock-down punch (see also chapter 6). The live gate proceeds were $2.6 million, with Tunney raking in $1 million, or more than Ruth's entire career earnings, from an hour-long performance.[5]

During both 1930 and 1931, Ruth had earned his highest annual baseball salary, $80,000, from the Yankees. When asked why he earned more than the president of the United States in the midst of the Great Depression, he famously retorted, "I had a better year." By 1935, his final year, Ruth's salary remained at a relatively robust $35,000, but it paled against Tunney's $1 million "long count" payday or, for that matter, Dempsey's own take in Chicago of $450,000. (For an approximation of contemporary dollars, multiply each total by a factor of 12.)

In terms of fan interest, national pageantry, and stunning paydays that dwarfed those of any other sport, boxing was truly king well into the Roaring Twenties. While much of the sporting world had focused on the Dempsey-Tunney spectacle, however, that same day Babe Ruth quietly slammed a home run—his fifty-sixth—against the Tigers as New York eked out an 8–7 win. On September 30, 1927, only eight days after Tunney's big win, Babe Ruth set a milestone sports record with a long-ball shot in Yankee Stadium against the Senators' lefty Tom Zachary. Instead of an opposing outfielder, Joe Forner, a longtime Yankees fan seated in right field, caught Ruth's sixtieth home run.

A little more than a week later, on October 8, the Yankees completed a four-game sweep of the Pirates to take the World Series title. With that victory, Murderers' Row became forever embedded as a team for the ages in any sport. Also, America became a different place after Ruth's sixtieth home run because baseball's broad appeal immediately accelerated. Unlike boxing, fans recognized that baseball was a team sport (notwithstanding its one-on-one drama), was less brutal than boxing, and followed a regular schedule, taking place almost every day from spring through early fall. Key championship boxing matches were infrequent, although for decades they still commanded attention because of all the pageantry that accompanied such rare spectacles. But baseball became a permanent fixture of summer, and Ruth's home runs served as the driving catalyst by offering an image of power much as a knockout punch did. Indeed, sometimes a key home run is still called a knockout punch, especially when it puts the game away. Boxing's influence is not completely extinct, although America's interest in boxing has waned. Baseball surpassed boxing as America's sport beginning in 1927, a Ruth-driven change that the advent of radio in the 1920s and then television in the 1950s helped popularize. The complete transition did not happen overnight, because such fighters as Max Baer, James "Cinderella Man" Braddock, the "Brown Bomber" Joe Louis, and Rocky Marciano would go on to provide enough momentary bursts of glory to keep boxing relevant. By the time baseball with the likes of Willie Mays and Mickey Mantle was on television every day in the 1950s, the fate of boxing had been sealed. When Muhammad Ali exploded on the scene in the 1960s, heavyweight championship boxing had an important resurgence, but it proved to be more of a last gasp than a permanent comeback.

The 1927 "year of Ruth" is still seen as the pinnacle of all baseball seasons, one so entrenched in lore that the term "the '27 Yankees" continues as the gold standard of dominance and as a metaphor for the ultimate plateau of any team in any sport. But more than anything else, Ruth's last home run at the close of the season, the immortal sixtieth, drove Ruth, the Yankees, and baseball over the top, affecting America unlike any home run before or since.

The Babe's career in Yankee pinstripes began in legendary fashion when Boston sold him and suffered the resultant "curse of the Bambino." His professional career ended with a record-setting home run that capped the journey that America made with baseball and home runs from 1914 to 1935. Remarkably, in ten out of the twelve seasons immediately following his New York debut in 1920, Ruth individually would slam more home runs than the entire Red Sox team, demonstrating the power of a metamorphosis we now simply call Ruth and largely explaining the lingering ill will between the Red Sox and Yankees.

Ruth was a star from the beginning, but in the early days nearly all of his work was from the pitching mound. Yet even then the Babe thought about hitting, studied hitting, and used the sweet swing of Shoeless Joe Jackson for his model. "I may be a pitcher," he conceded to the famed New York sportswriter Grantland Rice in 1919, "but first off I'm a hitter."[6] By September 8, 1919, still wearing the Boston uniform, Babe Ruth accomplished a major feat and tied John "Buck" Freeman's twenty-year-old record from his power season of twenty-five home runs. But Ruth was hardly finished. On September 24 Ruth powered a ninth-inning shot that left the cavernous Polo Grounds altogether and, as the *New York Times* reported, to that point was the longest home run ever hit there.[7] It was home run number 28 that year for Ruth, and it may have been the most significant home run that season, or *any* season, up to that point. Ruth would slam one more long ball on September 27, but the penultimate shot had come *against* the New York Yankees at their home field. It was as if a cannon had exploded and blasted a missile over the wall, out of the Polo Grounds, and straight into America's destiny. It burned an immediate impression in the minds of the Yankees brass, for by the next season those same Polo Grounds became the home field where Ruth would play *all* of his home games in Yankee pinstripes.

Ruth's sixtieth home run stunned America, and Bobby Thomson's dramatic 1951 "shot heard round the world" found widespread recognition—thanks to radio and television—with most people widely regarding announcer Russ Hodges's exuberant reaction "The Giants win the pennant!" as the most famous home run call of all time. Ruth's 1919 blast, however, may have had the most cumulative impact on baseball, since it set in motion the first in all the Yankees' dominoes that would so transform baseball and then America. It is well documented that Broadway producer and Red Sox owner Harry Frazee needed cash, and the Yankees wanted Ruth. Everyone would be happy with Ruth moving to New York—except the jilted fans of Boston. From that platform, Ruth would transform baseball into a slugger's game of American power, reflecting the larger-than-life captains of industry who thought big and grew even bigger while hitting the ultimate home runs of business and success in America: John D. Rockefeller, Andrew Carnegie, Andrew Mellon, Thomas Edison, and then the New York Yankees. His impact on the Yankees was felt not only in 1920 but also over many subsequent decades, including the George Steinbrenner years of Yankee success on and off the field. But by the end of 1919 season, thanks to Frazee's cash flow problems and the Yankees' foresight, Ruth was about to become a symbol of the Roaring Twenties' Big Apple stage of New York City.

Meanwhile, as the 1919 season drew to a close, discussions arose between New York gambler Arnold Rothstein and the Chicago White Sox players who had clinched the American League pennant on September 24. On September 29, or two days after Ruth's then record-setting twenty-ninth homer, Rothstein began his own assault on baseball history when he agreed to fund payoffs to various Sox players to rig the 1919 World Series. Through Rothstein's intermediaries, Sox players Arnold "Chick" Gandil and Edward "Eddie" Cicotte found themselves with $10,000 payments to throw Series games. All in all, eight players eventually agreed to take $20,000 each for every White Sox loss.

Rothstein bet at least $370,000 on Cincinnati to win the Series, including an additional $100,000 when he learned that the "fix" had been successfully implemented.[8] Cicotte was the starting pitcher for Game 1 on October 1. He hit the first batter he faced. That was the prearranged signal—the "fix" was in. He made a bad throw in the fourth inning, botching a double play that led to the Reds' scoring five runs and taking the game 6–1. The rest is history, but less widely known is that White Sox owner Charles Comiskey had suspected tampering after that first game, and *The Sporting News* had heard rumors of a fix. Comiskey even told American League president Byron "Ban" Johnson about his suspicions, but Johnson at first dismissed the conspiracy theory as the product of sour grapes.

During the course of the Series, word spread that another gambler was barging in to bet on the Sox and offering more money for the Sox *not* to blow the Series. More money was then salted among Sox players Joe Jackson and three others, but Fred McMullin and George "Buck" Weaver did not receive any. The Sox lost the Series in six games, even though Cicotte had led the league with twenty-nine wins (with thirty complete games on the year), a 1.82 earned run average (ERA), and a winning percentage of .806 while leading the White Sox team to a pennant-winning season of thirty-six games over .500. After the Series, another $40,000 was distributed to various players under the terms of the clandestine deal, including $5,000 to little-used McMullin. Weaver still took no money, had a good Series, and consistently denied his role in any game-fixing scheme until his death. Although Weaver would spend the rest of his life trying to clear his name and it appears he did not participate in the fix, even after his death, Weaver is still banned from baseball.

In 1919 the Reds won the World Series, and Detroit's Ty Cobb again led the American League by hitting a sparkling .384, while Babe Ruth had stolen the spotlight with 114 RBIs and a record-setting twenty-nine homers, one of which had sailed a reputed 600 feet out of the Polo Grounds and into the annals of American lore. Ruth's home runs were not only frequent and came in bunches—he slammed a quantum-leap fifty-four jacks in 1920 during his first year with the Yankees—but his blasts were sometimes of staggering distance and often occurred at propitious moments.

In 1920 rumors of a livelier ball being in use swirled to little avail, for Ruth transformed the game into an eye-popping spectacle and brought baseball and America a new brand of long-ball entertainment. Meanwhile, the alleged lively ball had little effect on the other hitters. Ruth's fifty-four homers were almost *triple* the nineteen that second-place George Sisler of the Browns had and surpassed every other team's totals except for that of the Phillies, whose players hit a collective sixty-four in a small park. While no proof demonstrated that the ball was altered at this time, much evidence pointed to how the game itself was changing. Ruth's perceived "lively balls" inspired other hitters to adjust their approach, collectively causing baseball's home run transformation. For instance, Ruth not only swung for the fences but also began to turn on the ball as modern power hitters do. Many other batters soon followed his lead, influencing team philosophies about the use of the long ball.

During Ruth's inaugural New York season in 1920, the "Black Sox" World Series scandal blew wide open. Chicago authorities had begun the season investigating Cubs games. They sniffed a fix in the Cubs-Phillies contests in May and again in August when team president William L. Veeck received a number of anonymous telegrams, and possibly two phone calls, warning that a game was going to be rigged later that same day, August 31. After the Chicago press got wind of the fix and started to run stories, a grand jury was convened to begin an official inquiry. Suspicious Cook County judge Charles McDonald also steered the grand jury's attention to the 1919 World Series. When Giants' pitcher John "Rube" Benton testified that his teammate Harold "Hal" Chase had won $40,000 betting against the Sox in the Series, the grand jury shifted its focus exclusively to the White Sox. (Much betting on baseball, even by players, took place in the game's early days. No express baseball rule prohibited gambling until Kenesaw Landis implemented one in 1926, but rigging games was another story. Landis policed the leagues through his broad "best interests of baseball" powers.)

Four days after Benton's testimony, Eddie Cicotte cracked under oath, admitting the fix and implicating others. Eventually eight Sox players were indicted, and Landis banned all eight from baseball for life. As it happened, all the players were acquitted at trial, but the Chicago jury verdict was less than convincing, since the hometown jurors danced and celebrated with the players afterward. The ban remained and included Shoeless Joe, who had played well in the Series but had nonetheless taken part of the bribe money, and Buck Weaver, who did not accept any money but apparently had knowledge of the scheme.

On November 12, 1920, Chicago federal judge Kenesaw Landis was named the first independent commissioner of Major League Baseball, largely to counter the gambling scandal and to rebuild baseball's credibility by ruling the game with an iron hand. Landis, though, was not the first choice. The owners had originally approached William Howard Taft, the former president of the United States and a sitting Supreme Court justice, who was an ardent baseball fan. But Taft chose to remain on the bench, a position of influence that he still held when the Supreme Court issued its famous 1922 ruling that effectively exempted baseball from federal antitrust laws.

As baseball progressed in the 1921 season, Ruth continued his long-ball rampage, often with home runs clubbed in bunches. On May 7, 1921, in Washington against Walter Johnson and the Senators, Ruth slammed an estimated 520-foot shot over a tall center-field wall, the longest home run hit at Griffith Stadium to that point. Later that month Ruth launched a 535-footer beyond the center-field bleachers in St. Louis, the longest home run ever hit at Sportsman's Park. On July 18, he rocketed a purported 575-foot monster that some say went as far as 600 feet—or the length of almost two football fields—at Navin Field in Detroit. This blast may have been the longest home run not only in Detroit but also anywhere in the history of the major leagues. However, since actual tape measure analysis did not come into vogue until the days of Mickey Mantle, only the estimates of witnesses are left to assess the length and legend of Ruth's longest homers.

Even with his Navin Field shot, Ruth's summer barrage was simply getting started. Thirteen days later on July 31, 1921, Ruth launched a reputed 560-foot missile over the deep right-center double-deck roof at the Polo Grounds and bested his own 1919 blast, which had caught the Yankee ownership's attention when Ruth was still with Boston. Shortly thereafter, Ruth performed his long-ball magic at Comiskey Park in Chicago on August 17, sending one deep to center field, or 550 feet from home plate. By the end of 1921, Ruth had done the seemingly impossible by slamming 59 home runs, including five that traveled more than 500 feet, all with a lofty batting average of .376 to lead New York to its league title. Moreover, during July, Ruth had already bested the previous career home run mark of 138 held by Roger Connor, yet Ruth was by no means finished.[9]

Remarkably, if 1921 was not prodigious enough in its own right, writer Bill Jenkinson in 2006 suggested that Ruth had actually hit even more home runs that year. By analyzing the balls hit toward the 500-foot center field in the Polo Grounds and foul balls that newer rules would have deemed fair, and adjusting for other similar effects, Jenkinson calculated a reconstituted mark of a transcendent 104 total dingers.[10] Some argue that the Polo Grounds' odd shape helped Ruth as much as it hindered him, pointing out the unusually short left (279 feet) and right (258 feet) fields. Regardless, Ruth was still a home run machine, especially when compared to his overall competition.

For the next forty years, only Ruth himself would surpass his home run record of 1921, although two others came close—Jimmie Foxx with 58 National League shots in 1932 and Hank Greenberg's 58 American League homers in 1938. During the ten years immediately before Ruth's move to New York, the average major-league leading home run total each year (including both leagues) was 13.55. The ten seasons following Ruth's move to New York, including 1920, the leading home run average nearly tripled to 39.55. This jump was primarily owing to Ruth's own skill, since Ruth led the league eight times and averaged a formidable 50.875 during those same eight seasons.[11]

Clearly baseball had undergone a metamorphosis. After Ruth's home run barrages, the long ball dominated baseball offense in every decade from the Roaring Twenties to the New Millennium. The game would never be the same. Part of the reason for the change was Babe Ruth's performance, and as previously noted, another factor was radio.

Rudimentary baseball broadcasting had begun as early as the 1890s with game-time telegraph reports sent to bars, where patrons could follow big-league games in a crude version of the Internet sports tracking of today. Sometimes those reports would be displayed on outdoor "playographs," or large billboard devices that drew crowds of inner-city onlookers, especially during World Series play. None of those attempts influenced the game more indelibly than radio broadcasting would.

Conservative-leaning contemporary historian Paul Johnson pegs the birth of the modern world as we know it at exactly 12:38 hours GCT on May 29, 1919. At this precise moment astronomer Arthur Eddington successfully tested Albert Einstein's general theory of relativity, noting the gravitational bending of light around the sun during a South Atlantic solar eclipse.[12] Physics, and the multidimensional universe of nuclear physics, have worked to explain the essence of the universe as humans understand it. Eddington's observation occurred in the same year that Babe Ruth launched the longest home run, crushed his first grand slam, and broke all the prior seasons' home run marks in the baseball universe. The concurrent emergence of Ruth at the defining moment of the modern world may itself have been a coincidence, but other related developments were afoot that coalesced into the majesty of baseball as we know it.

Apparently 1919 was a seminal year as Einstein's theory in physics and Ruth's quantum leaps of baseball physics were unleashed almost concurrently. If they were not enough, the temperance movement in America finally prevailed. Prohibition was enacted by means of the Volstead Act in October 1919, ironically unleashing America's naughty, freewheeling personality that manifested itself in the speakeasy subculture that made the 1920s roar. Prohibition also led directly to the growth of organized crime, which was driven by lucrative underground breweries and gambling, and fostered such big-time gamblers as Arnold Rothstein, whose impact on baseball is still felt today. Fittingly, that year Babe Ruth also discovered the hard-ball value of swinging from the heels, and as a pitcher who was under less pressure to perform at the plate, Ruth was able to exploit that luxury.

Ruth had begun the 1916 season batting ninth as the starting-day pitcher for the Boston Red Sox. That season he became the ace of the Boston pitching staff with a record of 23-12 and an ERA of 1.75 that led the entire league. Ruth also led all the Boston pitchers and most of the position players in batting average at .272. In 1916 Ruth started 40 games as a pitcher and allowed no home runs but hit three himself, logging a unique season on the mound by slugging more homers than he yielded. Even though he was a good hitter, Ruth the pitcher could afford a few mistakes at the plate, so he experimented with his hitting. By 1917 he led the entire team in batting at .325 but hit only two home runs while leading the league in complete games (35) as a pitcher. While still primarily a pitcher, Ruth felt comfortable risking more strikeouts and adopted a go-for-broke swing. In 1918 the Sox used him more extensively as a position player, playing in 95 games while starting only 19 as a pitcher. He continued to experiment with more power at the plate, hitting eleven home runs, but led the league in strikeouts. By 1919, when he clubbed the record twenty-nine home runs, his pitching starts were down to fifteen, but he batted .322 in 130 games. By the time he arrived in New York, Ruth only pitched in 5 games for the Yankees; otherwise, he was exclusively an outfielder.

That Prohibition encompassed virtually all of Ruth's marquee New York career is fitting. Ruth was shipped to New York in 1920, where he made history for the better part of fifteen years until his final Yankees game on September 30, 1934, less than one year after Prohibition was repealed on December 5, 1933. Although the nation had been officially deprived of the spirits of alcohol, a swing-for-the-fences giant in the game of baseball had kept the people entertained. During Prohibition much of America's other forms of entertainment went underground, creating vast business opportunities not only for bootleggers but for gamblers as well. And what is better to gamble on than baseball? Horse races attracted their share of gambling interest, as well as big-time boxing, but those matches were too few and far between. Baseball games happened virtually every day.

But something else happened during the era of Ruth and Prohibition that would change communication, entertainment, and baseball. Perhaps it began on Christmas Eve of 1906, when the wireless operators on numerous ships stationed off the coast of New England shared a near religious experience when suddenly, amid the stark beep-beep-beeps penetrating the cold silence of the North Atlantic, came the sound of a violin playing "Silent Night."[13] Voices then appeared over the gentle tones of the violin and read from the Gospel of Luke. Heaven, it seemed, had arrived on earth.

Radio became widely commercialized during the Roaring Twenties at precisely the time of Ruth, home runs, and Murderers' Row, and it spread through America at a breathtaking pace. The original radio signals were crude and spotty until the development of a continuous wave transmitter, giving the signals enough audio transmission quality to make early talk radio feasible. This breakthrough led to the proliferation of radio communication, including the formation of RCA.

By 1920, the Westinghouse Company launched the first licensed radio station in America, 8XK in Pittsburgh, and soon relabeled it as KDKA. The first broadcasts were entertainment oriented and featured music and an announcer reading the newspaper aloud. Then radio discovered the value of breaking-news coverage with KDKA broadcasting the Warren Harding–James Cox presidential election returns on November 2, 1920.[14] One day in 1921 a young engineer named Harold Arlin was walking by the KDKA facility and was intrigued by the technical side of this radio innovation, so he went into the station and found an audition being held for the position of announcer. Arlin auditioned, too, and got the job.

On August 5, 1921, Harold Arlin brought a wooden plank into the stands at Pittsburgh's Forbes Field, placed it across the arms of his seat, set a telephone on it, and began to report on the game in progress between the Pirates and the Phillies.[15] Everything Arlin and KDKA were doing that day was essentially happening for the first time, including the whole concept of transmitting baseball games live via radio. In the early days the reporting may have been "live," but the broadcasts were often retransmissions, with the reporter calling in the game and an announcer at the station actually broadcasting the game over the airwaves. When teams traveled on the road, the reports arrived via Teletype, so the broadcaster also had to re-create the games' sounds and feel for the listening audience.

When radio began transmitting baseball games during 1921, Ruth had hit his fifty-nine home runs, and the Yankees were on their first-ever run for the pennant. Ruth's games did not become a part of broadcasting history, however, until the 1921 World Series. At first many owners and even the league felt that radio might ruin baseball by keeping fans at home instead of paying for tickets to see the games live. Their stance was shortsighted for two major reasons: first, baseball on the radio would generate more fan interest and actually help raise attendance at the parks, and second, no one had yet thought of the idea of collecting fees for broadcasting rights, sponsorships, and commercials, all of which would become lucrative beyond the owners' dreams. Until then, those same owners did not fear airing the World Series on the radio, correctly believing that no fans would miss those games—radio or no radio.

WJZ in New Jersey broadcast the first game of the 1921 World Series by disseminating reports of the games over the airwaves, and concurrently KDKA broadcast live via a direct link to play-by-play announcer Grantland Rice. The broadcast was a resounding success, but most owners continued to resist putting baseball on the radio for the regular season. Pittsburgh proved to be an exception, as did the emerging entrepreneur from Chicago William Wrigley. An astute marketer and promoter, Wrigley had built a chewing gum empire from his original soap company before purchasing the Chicago Cubs in 1915 from Charles P. Taft. Wrigley immediately grasped the idea of radio's potential for commercial application. Chicago's WGN Radio broadcast the Cubs' Opening Day live on April 14, 1925, from a makeshift broadcasting platform installed on the stadium's roof.

Wrigley would broadcast more and more home games on a semi-regular basis, then road games via the game re-creation technique, and eventually all home games continually. After 1925, the Cubs' home attendance dramatically increased by 114 percent (the five-year average, per game, starting in 1926 compared to the five-year average before 1925), even though the team did not dramatically improve in the standings (except for 1929, when they lost the World Series.). In fact, the Cubs were fourth in National League attendance in each of 1924 and 1925 but jumped to first for the next seven years.[16] As Wrigley had envisioned, radio was billboarding the games—bringing baseball to parlors, hospitals, filling stations, prisons, and fans everywhere—and generating a broader interest in the sport.

Typical of any emerging technology, the progression of baseball on the radio was not without its flaws. At first, radios were called radiophones and the announcers radiologists, a term that would gain more traction much later in the medical profession. The original broadcasters were mostly sportswriters who were good at writing but not necessarily at talking, and those who could speak often didn't. The "purist" announcers mistakenly believed that only the baseball action should be reported, so they left extraordinary amounts of dead air between swings and pitches. Baseball's slow pace only aggravated the announcers' painfully boring approach to sports broadcasting.

Eventually the deliberate pace of baseball ended up as one of the game's greatest assets, especially for radio. The announcers learned that dead air could be filled with conversation, stories, statistics, and friendly chatter, thrilling legions of listeners who grew attached to the broadcasters and the word pictures they painted. Baseball thus had the perfect pace for radio, where words were the only tools to describe the image and feel of the games in progress.

The novelty of radio and its power to transmit news and ideas swept the nation as consumers spent $60 million on radios in 1922, up to $430 million in 1925, and $843 million in 1929.[17] As noted, early radio broadcasts were crude and uninspired, often with announcers playing opera, reading newspapers articles, or recounting the police blotter entries. Programs as we know them today were not yet imagined, and scripted radio shows were not produced until the 1930s and 1940s. But baseball was different: it provided instant content, drama, and the familiar voice and conversation of a friendly announcer. Baseball became part of the family experience rather than remaining a distant game. The announcers' descriptions of baseball painted a virtual image of the game for the radio audiences while the exploits of their heroes unfolded on the field. Soon baseball would become integral to the image of America itself, incorporating the long-ball irreverence of a burgeoning nation.

"I watch a lot of baseball on radio," said former president Gerald R. Ford in 1978.[18] Indeed. Ruth, radio, and the Roaring Twenties had all converged to reinvent and spread the game of baseball across America precisely during a time of American expansion and confidence.[19] In 1922, an estimated 5 million people heard the World Series; by 1949 the Series' audience would grow to 26 million and then to 88 million listeners in 1968. Baseball had become America's pastime, and the home run would drive the game to new heights of drama and excitement. Even the home run itself was perfect for radio, taking up to four electrifying seconds to unfold after the resounding crack of big-league lumber. No wonder the home run call itself would take on a life of its own as announcers competed to bring its drama to living rooms, parlors, barbershops, farms, bars, filling stations, and neighborhoods across America.

It might be, it could be, it is a home run!
—HARRY CARAY[20]

☆ 5 ☆

THE MISSILES
OF MUDVILLE

Ruth established himself as an American icon against the backdrop of Duke Ellington, Al Jolson, and George Gershwin during an era of jazz, booze, gangsters, radio, and the emergence of baseball as America's game—the latter owing more to Ruth than to any other individual player. Because of his involvement, the image of Ruth represents an especially romantic slice of American lore; however, in life the Babe was competitive to a fault, a bit nasty (even though he had a soft spot for children), self-centered, and noticeably acerbic.

One of the most famous home runs in baseball history is Ruth's "called shot" at Chicago's Wrigley Field during the 1932 World Series, and its notoriety was largely a product of Ruth's personality. After a day of his relentless trash talking with the Cubs' bench during Game 3, history and video seem to suggest that the Babe pointed his bat toward the outfield, then ripped a mammoth blast an estimated 440 to 490 feet that landed well beyond Wrigley's deep center-field wall. The verbal jousting, the pointing of the bat, the length and drama of the home run, and its occurrence during the World Series all contributed to the lore of that home run regardless of whether it was really an intentionally called shot. With Ruth, the legend is imminently believable. Commenting on Wrigley Field, the quick-tempered Ruth topped

73

off the run by saying, "I'd play for half my salary if I could hit in this dump all the time."[1]

Whether Ruth really pointed to the outfield where his next hit would land, in the stands at deep center field, is a matter of debate. Several photos and films have survived, and all clearly show Ruth pointing the bat in some kind of gesture toward the outfield. Some witnesses say he was pointing to the pitcher Charlie Root, others to the Cubs' bench where catcalls and trash talk had targeted Ruth all day, and some of the images appear to confirm the legendary gesture during Ruth's fifth-inning plate appearance. Regardless, Root's next pitch, a curveball, took a 440-plus-foot ride into major-league lore.

That Ruth simply would have waved his bat to the pitcher or even to the Cubs' bench does not seem likely. The video evidence makes a case for the called shot's legend. As noted in the film *The Man Who Shot Liberty Valance*, perception is sometimes the better part of reality: "When the legend becomes fact, print the legend."[2]

But some think maybe the called shot was not legend in the first place. "Don't let anybody tell you differently. Babe definitely pointed," insisted the Cubs' field announcer Pat Pieper, who watched the whole sequence unfold.[3] Or maybe another witness may be more convincing: U.S. Supreme Court justice John Paul Stevens attended that game as a young boy with his father. He recalled, "My dad took me to see the World Series, and we were sitting behind third base, not too far back. . . . Ruth did point to the center-field scoreboard. And he did hit the ball out of the park after he pointed with his bat. So it really happened."

Perhaps the final word belongs to Ruth himself, who confirms most of the story and explains the rest:

Aw, everybody knows that game, the day I hit the homer off ole Charlie Root in Wrigley Field, the day October first, the third game of that thirty-two World Series. But right now I want to settle all arguments. I didn't exactly point to any spot, like the flagpole. Anyway, I didn't mean to, I just sorta waved at the whole fence, but that was foolish enough. All I wanted to do was give that thing a ride . . . outta the park . . . anywhere.[4]

When Ruth arrived in New York in 1920, America was undergoing major changes. That year, for the first time, more Americans were living in cities than on farms. With its "cathedral" parks planted in urban neighborhoods, baseball drew city-sized crowds. The following year, Albert Einstein won the Nobel Prize for physics. During that glorious year of 1927, when the Yankees welcomed Murderers' Row, not only did Charles Lindbergh make his historic transatlantic flight, but Al Jolson also starred in the first talking picture, Henry Ford sold his fifteen millionth Model T, and the home run emerged as the marquee image of baseball and America.

Although World War I ended in 1918, it was an uninspired baseball year, as each league batted a mediocre .254 during a war-shortened season. Batting averages crept up in 1920, with the National League hitting a combined .270 and the American League posting .283.[5] Home runs went up dramatically in 1920, though, with a 41 percent increase compared to 1919.[6] Ruth himself had much to do with the surge, since his own league-leading total of 54 in 1920 added 17.1 percent to the number of home runs hit in the rest of the American League that year (315) and was precisely 600 percent of Wally Pipp's league-leading 9 home runs in 1917. And as home runs multiplied, so did the fans' excitement and attendance.[7]

While the Yankees made Ruthian headlines throughout the 1920s, other teams also experienced a dramatic increase in their offense. Largely lost behind the fame of Murderers' Row, for instance, were the 1921 Detroit Tigers led by thirty-four-year-old player-manager Ty Cobb. That entire Tigers team batted a stunning .316, the best single-season team average in the history of the American League, but they still finished twenty-seven games behind the invincible Yankees that year.[8] The 1921 Tigers actually logged more base hits than the 1927 Yankees did (1,723 to 1,644), but the 1927 Murderers' Row team clubbed 158 home runs to only 58 for the 1921 Tigers. As a result, the Yankees won and achieved near immortality while the good-hitting Tigers slid into obscurity.[9]

Ruth would continue to excel through the 1920s, except for 1922, which turned into a short season for the Babe, who was suspended until May 20 for playing in off-season barnstorming games. Thus, in 1922 Ruth failed to lead the American League in homers, while in the National League, Rogers Hornsby not only slammed forty-two long balls of his own but also led the league in hitting (.401), slugging (.722), RBIs (152), and hits (250). Ironically, even though it was a relatively "off" season for Ruth, the Yankees broke ground in the Bronx for the new (now old) Yankee Stadium, where Murderers' Row would make its lasting mark.[10]

Before a massive inaugural crowd for Opening Day 1923, Ruth added to his legend by popping Yankee Stadium's first home run ever, a three-run shot in front of more than seventy-four thousand fans, a staggering baseball crowd for any era. With that blast, sportswriter Fred Lieb of New York's *Evening Telegram* christened the stadium "the house that Ruth built," and the legend of Ruth grew bigger than life.[11]

Babe Ruth was not merely a New York phenomenon; indeed, he captivated the nation. A syndicated feature called What Ruth Did Today began appearing in newspapers across the country. Interestingly, as the entire Ruth mystique built throughout a career that included hundreds of games not only in New York but also in Chicago, St. Louis, Detroit, and elsewhere, estimates suggest that fewer than 5 million different individuals actually saw Ruth play.[12] The combined attendance for all his games was a much bigger number, of course, but that total included repeat fans. Millions more read about the Babe in newspapers, watched him on newsreels, and heard many of his exploits on the radio.

Although radio broadcast hundreds of Yankees games, the lingering resistance to baseball broadcasting actually kept games off the radio in New York until 1939. Many owners, especially those in two-team cities, restricted radio broadcasts. In 1934 the owners of all three New York teams—the Yankees, Giants, and Dodgers—colluded to ban radio broadcasting and even prevented visiting teams from re-creating games for their listeners. Aside from being counterproductive, this action would likely have been deemed a violation of antitrust laws, which expressly prohibit a "contract, combination, or conspiracy" in restraint of trade; however, baseball's bizarre antitrust exemption from the 1922 Federal League decision insulated the game and the owners. This baseball blackout lasted until 1938 and encompassed the final years of Ruth's career and many years during Lou Gehrig's era.

Meanwhile, during Ruth's era, 2.5 million radios were in use in the United States by 1924. Rogers Hornsby tore up the National League, earning a .424 average and 227 total base hits, while Brooklyn's Jack Fournier led that league in homers with twenty-seven. But Ruth continued to dominate all other power hitters, slamming forty-six home runs on the season with a .378 batting average. Plagued with health issues and personality conflicts with the Yankees' manager, Miller Huggins during the following year, Ruth slipped a bit in 1925, playing in only ninety-eight games, while teammate Bob Meusel led the Yankees and the American League with thirty-three home runs.

Nonetheless, 1925 was a threshold year for radio, home runs, and a newcomer named Gehrig. Before the 1925 regular season, the minimum distance for a ball to qualify as a home run increased from 235 feet to 250 feet. The increase is not surprising, but the remarkably short distance required both before and immediately after 1925 stands out. That same year the major leagues adopted balls with a new cork center, Rogers Hornsby batted .403, and the Tigers' Harry Heilmann logged a .393 season average. On April 17, at the beginning of the season, Babe Ruth underwent surgery for a stomach abscess and missed every game through May, a stretch when the powerful Yankees could muster only a 15-25 record. On June 1, though, the Yankees' game changed when Ruth returned to the lineup, and youngster Lou Gehrig appeared as a pinch hitter, replacing baseball's odd man out, Wally Pipp. But it was not until the following day, June 2, 1925, that the real legend of Wally Pipp was born. After a pitch smacked Pipp in the head during warm-ups, the coach replaced him as a starter with the twenty-one-year-old Gehrig, who proceeded to club three hits on the day in an 8–5 victory over the world champion Washington Senators. Some accounts say Pipp simply had a headache to become baseball's historic odd man out. In truth, he was injured by the errant pitch, and Gehrig did replace him, but he did not slide into total obscurity. A Yankees regular since 1915, Pipp remained on the team's roster for the rest of 1925 and was sold outright to the Cincinnati Reds before the 1926 season. Pipp was not a stiff, however; he played 1,872 games during fifteen years in the big leagues and collected 1,941 hits for a lifetime .281 average. He even managed ninety home runs, not a bad feat considering the era. In fact, Pipp actually led the league in home runs in 1916 with twelve and again in 1917 with nine, although Ruth's fifty-four jacks in 1920 dwarfed Pipp's eleven. After suffering that pop on the head, though, Pipp was never the same. For that matter, neither was the baseball nation.[13] To this day, baseball observers often invoke the image of Pipp when a team starter is injured and a better bench player replaces him.

Meanwhile, radio received a double boost during 1925. On April 14, the Cubs began regular season broadcasting via WGN and WMAQ Radio in Chicago, a wildly popular move that both validated radio and increased attendance in the stadium. And in July 1925, WGN planted a microphone in far-away Dayton, Tennessee, a small town near Chattanooga. The station's management was following what it figured would be an interesting case.

On March 21 Tennessee enacted the Butler Act prohibiting the teaching of evolution in the public schools. By May, the American Civil Liberties Union actively sought a local teacher to test the case. Town leaders saw an opportunity for local fame and fortune and offered up the local biology teacher and football coach John Scopes, who agreed to be a guinea pig.

National orator, fundamentalist, and perennial presidential candidate William Jennings Bryan took up the cause for religion against evolution, and the case lured famed Chicago super-lawyer Clarence Darrow into the fray for the defense. With lines drawn for the legal battle of the century, WGN saw an opportunity. At a then stunning cost of $1,000 per day, WGN paid for dedicated phone lines to broadcast the court proceedings live.[14] Bryan and Darrow squared off before the international press, including the *Baltimore Sun*'s famous columnist, H. L. Mencken. In a forerunner to the O. J. Simpson murder trial seventy years later, the Scopes case became a media entertainment juggernaut when for the first time WGN broadcast a live courtroom battle. It gave credibility to radio as a mainstream medium capable of delivering spot news field reporting around the country and boosted its prospects for sports reporting, including baseball. At the time,

WGN had already broadcast the Indianapolis 500 race, college football, and the Cubs' Opening Day contest with the Pirates.

Radio carried the World Series every year starting in 1921, first without paying any rights fees. In 1934 Commissioner Landis had inked a four-year, $400,000 radio deal with Ford Motor Company that demonstrated the economic power of baseball broadcasting.[15] Advertising revenues exploded upward. By 1946 the Gillette Safety Razor Company had replaced Ford by paying $150,000 per year. In 1949, Commissioner Albert "Happy" Chandler consummated a seven-year World Series radio broadcast deal with Gillette and the Mutual Broadcasting System worth $4,370,000.[16]

In the meantime, a 1926 article proclaiming that baseball was in decline and was no longer "The Great American Game" appeared in *Time* magazine under the following headline: "Sport: Baseball Slipping." The piece was predicated upon a then recent survey of ten thousand athletic directors of elementary schools, high schools, colleges, and other organizations, in addition to interviews with sports editors, coaches, and sporting goods manufacturers. Among all the sports, baseball was ranked fourth in apparent popularity. Football ranked higher as a direct result of the stardom of Harold "Red" Grange, the "Galloping Ghost," whose superhuman efforts against the University of Michigan's powerhouse football team had made him famous overnight in 1924.[17]

Time's 1926 prediction of baseball's demise was premature and certainly reminiscent of the well-known Mark Twain line "The report of my death was an exaggeration." Although the following year would negate any such thoughts with the assistance of radio, Ruth, and all the Babe's men— Gehrig, Meusel, and the rest of Murderers' Row—1926 still had one more legend in the making, thanks also to Ruth, radio, and the New York press.

An eleven-year-old New York boy named Johnny Sylvester was reported to be severely ill on the eve of the World Series. The boy's family sent a telegram to the Yankees on behalf of their son, a big fan. The Yankees sent back an airmail package containing two balls—members of the Cardinals signed one, several Yankees players signed the other—plus a personal message from Ruth predicting a homer for Sylvester. The press had a feel-good news day, especially when Ruth *did* hit the round-tripper. The story gave the reporters a headline moment that suddenly anointed home runs as the cure for many ills, from losing to even death, so it would seem.

In Sylvester's case, the truth was trampled by the legend, leaving the real episode almost unrecognizable. Some reports had Sylvester dying, even predicting his death within thirty minutes. No one seems to know for sure what his malady was, with some saying blood poisoning and others recounting everything from spinal fusions to sinus infections. The most credible guess seems to be a forehead injury after a horseback riding accident at the family's country home. Hollywood later embellished the story even further in a film titled *The Babe Ruth Story*, which depicted Ruth at the kid's hospital bed promising to hit a home run for the dying youngster. Sylvester had not been in the hospital at all, however; he had been home in bed throughout the incident. Further, Ruth did not make the home run promise in person. But Ruth really did hit the homer. In fact, he smashed three altogether, and wonder of all wonders, the duly inspired Johnny Sylvester was cured.[18]

The backstory is even more interesting, if not incredulous. Sylvester was almost certainly not dying. After all, he was home in bed and not in the hospital, although during that era not every seriously ill patient went to the hospital. Also, apparently his parents or the doctor concluded that the World Series game would be too exciting, so Johnny was not allowed even to listen to the game on the radio. Little Johnny's parents didn't stay with the "dying" boy; they went to the game! Finally, at the outset of the following season, Ruth was told that Sylvester had fully recovered. Ruth, who did not recall the incident, reportedly replied, "Who the hell is Johnny Sylvester?" But it was too late. The legend of Johnny Sylvester and the inspirational healing powers of the almighty home run were already well known.

Then came 1927. Ruth slammed sixty homers, or four more than the Athletics, which hit more than any other American League team did that year. Lost in the excitement of Ruth's new record was that of Lou Gehrig, who crushed forty-seven home runs of his own in a spectacular achievement. Combined, the rest of the entire team hit a total of fifty-one home runs that season.

Eight years later, Ruth's sterling career came to its inevitable close with his four-hit, three-homer day at Forbes Field in Pittsburgh. Meanwhile, the other home run stars of the game made their own marks on history. The same year of Ruth's finale, Hank Greenberg had 110 RBIs—not for the season but at the All-Star break. And Greenberg challenged Ruth's record with a fifty-eight-homer season of his own in 1938, a year when baseball moved his team's final three games of the season in Cleveland to a bigger park with a bigger field purportedly to accommodate larger crowds. The new venue was Lakefront Stadium, which seated seventy-eight thousand fans and had an extremely deep center field of 467 feet. Some suggest the league made this move to a larger field really either to help preserve Ruth's record and image or to handicap Greenberg, who was Jewish. Neither idea is implausible given Ruth's star power and Commissioner Landis's reputed anti-Semitism.

Greenberg was one of the greats, as were Willie Mays, Mickey Mantle, Jimmie Foxx, Ralph Kiner, and other long-ball sluggers who took baseball to literal and figurative new heights. But Ruth was an epiphany. He proved baseball was not dead, as *Time* had pontificated. Instead, it was about to explode on an upward trend that would last until the World Series's cancellation in 1994, and then beyond, thanks again to the steroid era of Barry Bonds, Mark McGwire, Jose Canseco, and dozens of others.

Ruth not only slammed the long ball but also hit for average, finishing with a lifetime .342 mark. Overall, Ruth would lead the league in runs scored eight times, homes runs twelve times, RBIs six times, and walks no fewer than eleven times. Although 1927 remains his banner season, actually the 1920 season propelled the game in a new direction, a year that made 1927 possible and directly influenced such other long-ball years far in the future: 1956, 1961, and 1998. As noted in chapter 4, not only did Ruth go to New York and swing for the fences as the spitball was banned, but baseball also instituted another major change that transformed the approach to situational hitting, stolen bases, and base-running strategy. Prior to 1920, baseball teams used the same ball throughout the game, even retrieving it from the stands when possible, and replacing it only where mandated. This rule favored the pitchers, who could throw scuffed and battered balls; penalized hitting; and rewarded small-ball strategy. Using fresh, undoctored balls unlocked the potential of the long ball and helped the Babe change the sport forever.

The years preceding Ruth's home run barrages were called the dead-ball era for good reason. Following 1920, the lively ball era is easy to recognize by the numbers. In 1921 players scored 4,546 more runs than they did in 1918—11,928 versus 7,382—but they took 502 fewer stolen bases, or 1,487 instead of 1,989.[19] More important, the home run numbers suddenly went off the charts, with long-ball production up by nearly 300 percent from 235 league-wide home runs in 1918 to 937 in 1920.

Not only were home runs up dramatically, but their inherent excitement also caused league attendance to jump as well. In 1920 the Yankees drew 1,289,422 fans to the park, breaking the Giants' attendance mark of about 900,000 fans set in 1908, a whopping increase.[20] The Yankees, which had been founded in 1903 as the New York Highlanders, originally played at Hilltop Park but in 1913 joined the Giants at the Polo Grounds. Although the Giants had been playing there since 1911, upon Ruth's arrival, the Yankees began to outdraw the Giants. Breathtaking home runs were the biggest reason: the first sixteen that Ruth hit there all went over the roof or landed in the second deck. Only one other hitter, Joe Jackson, had cleared the roof at the Polo Grounds and only once in 1913 during the dead-ball era.

The Giants resented the Yankees' success in their ballpark and felt they could increase their own attendance with more scheduling flexibility, but they had little room to maneuver with a cotenant at the Polo Grounds. So the Giants began to push the Yankees out after only a few years, a timely exodus given Ruth's emerging star power. The Yankees made the most of it, constructing a new state-of-the-art Yankee Stadium on a ten-acre parcel across the Harlem River but still within eyesight of the Polo Grounds. Not merely a ballpark, the Yankees' new home offered three-tier seating for the first time and was among the first to be called a stadium. When the new stadium finally opened on April 18, 1923, it smashed the single-game attendance record with 74,200 fans, or close to double the old mark of 42,000 fans for a 1916 World Series game in Boston.

Ruth christened the new Yankee Stadium with a signature long-ball bomb. Bob Shawkey, the Yankees' winning pitcher that day, put the threshold moment into perspective: "Once the Babe homered, the fans cheered forever. . . . Babe owned the day. And that was just fine; he was born to be in the spotlight." Years later Ruth's wife, Claire, recounted that home run and the Babe's own take on it, saying, "He definitely talked about it more than any other home run he ever hit. . . ." She also felt that the moniker "house that Ruth built" would never have been inspired without that dramatic first-day homer.[21]

Which of Ruth's home runs was the greatest? Was it his longest shot, the record-setting bomb in Washington? Was it the called shot in Wrigley? What about the first homer at Yankee Stadium or his last at Forbes Field or the first record breaker in 1919 or the immortal sixtieth in 1927? Ruth's home runs not only won games but also brought in the fans. Further, America would never be the same after Ruth. As it happens, neither would Japan.

Ruth, Gehrig, Foxx, and others routinely took their big lumber on all-star tours of Japan, where American baseball proved extremely popular. American baseball players toured in 1908, 1913, 1920, 1922, and 1931. During the 1934 tour the Babe slugged thirteen home runs during eighteen exhibition games against local teams and became an icon in Japan. Massive crowds waved American flags as Ruth passed in parades.[22] It is no coincidence that the Great Tokyo team, the first Japanese professional club, was established at the end of 1934 and then took its own barnstorming tour to America in 1935. That same team still exists today, now called the Yomiuri Tokyo Giants. The Japanese ambassador to the United States directly attributed the surge in Japanese baseball to "the Babe Ruth effect."

Ruth became a legend in a country that takes its legends seriously. Ruth is still revered in Japan in the twenty-first century. In 2002 a statue of Babe Ruth was erected in the Yagiyama Zoological Park, the exact place where Ruth had slammed his first home run in that country on November 4,

1934. "Babe Ruth," said the Japanese ambassador in 2006, "is still considered the 'King' [in Japan]."[23] As of 1955, even after World War II, a bronze plaque at the Koshien Stadium in Osaka listed the most famous personalities in Japan of the previous forty years. All the names were Japanese except one: Babe Ruth.[24]

American baseball influenced Japan so profoundly that it even affected World War II. The catcher Morris "Moe" Berg took so many photos and films of Japan during the tours that they later proved useful to the U.S. War Department. And during the war, the Japanese shouted insults about Ruth to the Americans on the battlefield, believing that their derision of such an icon would be helpful to their cause. The U.S. government even considered sending Ruth to Guam to deliver a message personally to the Japanese people, a propaganda move that would have positioned Ruth as something of a "Tokyo Rose" in reverse.

After the war, a passionate group in New Jersey founded a baseball league for boys aged thirteen to fifteen under the curious banner of the Little Bigger League. In 1954, Ruth's widow gave the group permission to use the name the "Babe Ruth League," as it is still known today. One of the top amateur leagues in the world, the Babe Ruth League as of 2010 had fifty-six thousand teams fielding youngsters worldwide. Some players will go on to greater baseball success, as did former Babe Ruth Leaguers like Carl Yastrzemski, Rod Carew, George Brett, Nolan Ryan, and many more.

Babe Ruth was born in Baltimore in 1895 at a small row house near the original Baltimore Orioles' minor-league park. It was almost demolished at different times over the years but was salvaged for good in 1974 and became a museum supported by the nonprofit Babe Ruth Birthplace Foundation. In the 1980s the museum's mission expanded and became the official museum of the Baltimore Orioles and the former Baltimore Colts football team. Located not far from the Camden Yards ballpark, the museum attracts sixty thousand visitors a year.

Ruth and baseball came a long way from the early days of the sport. Back in 1845, the only allowable home runs were the inside-the-park variety, since the rules stated that a long ball hit over the fence would be considered a foul ball, not a home run. The home run was little more than a baseball afterthought until Ruth appeared. His impact was so great and so lasting that it transcends baseball. At the end of 2010, *The Sporting News* still listed Ruth as the greatest slugger in the game's history, putting him ahead of record holders Mark McGwire and Barry Bonds.[25] Of the top fifty sluggers, Ruth, the first, stamped the home run onto the baseball map and into the American lexicon.

Did Ruth change America? Do home runs affect American culture and not simply baseball? Consider this definition of the word "culture": "The system of shared beliefs, values, customs, behaviors, and artifacts that the members of society use to cope with their world and with one another, and that are transmitted from generation to generation through learning."[26]

Anthropologists, however, do not always agree about what culture actually is. Some recognize a classical cognitive culture, which, according to Clifford Geertz, is essentially "an historically transmitted pattern of meanings embodied in symbols, a system of inherited conceptions expressed in symbolic forms by means of which men communicate, perpetuate, and develop their knowledge about and attitudes toward life."[27]

The common theme in how we define culture appears to include shared beliefs, artifacts, and symbols that represent a means of coping with life and each other. The home run is one such symbol. It is a metaphor for triumph in America. Each home run on the field offers several seconds for the players and fans to savor a lofty feat of height, distance, and success. It affects how Americans think of themselves, express themselves, and see themselves and even how others see them. Yes, there are slam dunks, blitzes, and knockout punches, but nothing is savored quite like the home run spectacle. And nothing else in professional team sports quite symbolizes the American competitive culture of free enterprise, success, and failure as the home run does. After all, America is known as a place that swings for the fences and as a land of opportunity where most people have a chance at the home run in sports, business, and life. Winning is widely encouraged in America, as elsewhere, but winning big is the American dream. "If at first you don't succeed, try, try again" is a well-known mantra of success and failure. Even

Ruth evoked it and was known to say, "Every strike brings me closer to the next home run." In their hearts, most everyone wants a shot at the big prize, to win it all, and to hit the metaphorical home run.

To this day America invokes Ruth's greatness and still competes with him in mind. Indeed, when any of Ruth's records are challenged—for instance, when Hank Aaron finally bested the career homer mark in 1974, then when Barry Bonds broke it, and certainly when Roger Maris caught and passed the revered sixty-homer season plateau—it creates a front-page controversy.

Babe Ruth passed away on August 16, 1948, at the age of fifty-three, fewer than thirteen years after his final big-league home run. More than 200,000 people filed through Yankee Stadium, where Ruth's body lay for two days. They paid their respects and said good-bye to a man who, at the time, held the major-league home run record. Hundreds of thousands of additional fans lined the streets of New York for the Babe's funeral procession, and a flood of telegrams poured in from mourners around the world. In the end, Ruth asked that 10 percent of his estate be used "in the interests of the kids of America."[28] This bequest, perhaps, was the Babe's final home run.

THE HOME RUN THAT CHANGED AMERICA

Sixty, count 'em, sixty. Let some son-of-a-bitch top that.
—BABE RUTH, 1927[1]

As the Roaring Twenties came to define the free-spirited, burgeoning success of America, baseball provided its long-ball, swashbuckling swagger. Babe Ruth's explosive home runs were unlike anything anyone had seen before in baseball. A great deal more happened on September 30, 1927, however, than Ruth's slugging his final home run of a baseball campaign for the ages.

With one fell swing of big-league lumber, the epicenter of the baseball universe shifted from Chicago—the home of Commissioner Kenesaw Landis and Major League Baseball's corporate offices, as well as the city's perennial winners in the Cubs and White Sox—to New York City. That same blast also propelled Babe Ruth past Jack Dempsey as the leading sports icon in America and lifted baseball over boxing in national opinion. These moves would influence both the personality and perspective of twentieth-century America.

Babe Ruth's record-setting sixty long balls not only punctuated the great 1927 Murderers' Row season but also helped forge the Yankees' enduring mystique and still represent the most major-league home runs ever hit in a 154-game season—a standard that can never be broken in the current 162-game era. That record equaled the combined homers of the Phillies' Cy Williams and the Cubs' Hack Wilson, who shared the National League crown that year with thirty each. One decade earlier, the American League's leader had been Wally Pipp, who slapped only nine dingers the whole 1917 season.

Earlier, on September 22, 1927, fans had watched as Ruth strode to the plate and faced Detroit's Ken Holloway. In the waning moments of the ninth inning, Ruth smashed his fifty-sixth home run of the year, the second-most homers of any big-league season and three shy of Ruth's own mark of fifty-nine that he had set in 1921. Yet as noted earlier, more than 104,000 people swarmed into Chicago's Soldier Field that same day to witness what would become one of the most important sports matchups of the century, namely, the long-awaited heavyweight rematch between boxers Jack Dempsey and Gene Tunney.[2]

The Dempsey-Tunney fight was the biggest attraction in American sports, even larger than baseball was. To this day no major-league baseball game has attracted a crowd of more than 104,000 people in person, and champion Dempsey, in his heyday before losing to Tunney in 1926, was probably a greater figure than Ruth himself at that point. Prior to his magical 1927 season, Ruth had inked a new three-year deal for a salary of $70,000 per year, an extreme amount for the time but far less than the $1 million that champion Gene Tunney raked in for the Dempsey bout alone. (Tunney actually earned $990,000 that night and volunteered to contribute $10,000 of his own money so he could receive a check for an even $1 million.)

Arriving in Chicago on crowded trains from New York and elsewhere, the Dempsey-Tunney throng overflowed local hotels, and the city required a special police brigade of twenty-eight hundred officers and detectives to control the endless mobs. Six special trains were added onto the New York–Chicago schedule, the New York Central and Michigan Central lines braced to carry twenty-two thousand fight fans on the twenty-hour run from the Big Apple, and special trains ran from Cleveland, Detroit, Rochester,

Columbus, and Boston. By this time, the revered Dempsey had become the challenger, having lost to the likable Tunney a year before in Philadelphia, and the world anticipated a fierce comeback by the Manassa Mauler.

The Dempsey-Tunney rumble during Ruth's assault on home run history symbolized an unofficial clash between boxing and baseball as Ruth and the Yankees wrested public sentiment from a distant ring in Chicago to a fateful diamond in New York. Although one swing from Ruth would eventually tip the balance, boxing, like Dempsey himself, would not surrender easily. In the seventh round of their 1927 rematch, Dempsey cornered Tunney and pummeled the champion with a flurry of rights and lefts. A wicked combination of eight punches, half to the chin, floored Tunney. As Tunney struggled to find his legs, Dempsey hovered, ready to smash the fallen fighter as he rose. Yet this night was different. In accordance with a new rule, the referee ordered Dempsey to a neutral corner, but at first Dempsey failed to respond. Accounts differ, but it appears that four to seven seconds elapsed before Dempsey retreated from Tunney. After that delay, when the official counting finally began, Tunney took a full nine-count before rising. Collectively, the champ benefited from more than fourteen seconds to gather himself and then dropped Dempsey to the mat in the following round. Eventually the match went the full distance, with Tunney the boxer out-pointing Dempsey the fighter for a unanimous decision, and the "long count" became a permanent fixture in American sports lore. Boxing was still supreme—but not for long.

Ironically, the Dempsey camp had lobbied for the neutral corner rule. The match the year before had been uprooted from Chicago to Philadelphia to remove the fight from the shadow of gangster Al Capone, a Dempsey fan whose underworld influence in the Windy City made promoters nervous. Nonetheless, the rematch went back to Chicago, and conspiracy theorists suggested various possibilities of foul play, none of which has actually been proven.

But the unusual sequence of the Dempsey-Tunney long count could not be dismissed easily because of gambling. The whole nation was still reeling from the debacle that forever tainted the 1919 World Series, but according to the *New York Times*, as much as $10 million or more was bet in advance of the marquee boxing rematch, a startling sum for 1927.[3] At the time, major-league baseball was still dealing with post–Black Sox gambling issues and cleaning house through much of the 1920s. In November 1926, Ty Cobb suddenly had resigned as manager of the Detroit Tigers, and Tristram "Tris" Speaker announced his retirement as the Indians' manager less than four weeks later. These events were linked to letters that implicated both men in rigging a Tigers-Indians game back in 1919.

In January 1927, one of the ousted Black Sox players, Charles Risberg, implicated the 1917 Sox in a scheme to fix four games with the Tigers. Twenty-nine players responded to the commissioner's inquiry and admitted that the Detroit pitchers received the payment of $1,000 but "only as a reward" for taking a four-game series from Boston.[4] Landis did not suspend the players, but he did inject a new rule into the game banning such "gifts" to opposing players.

This case was not the only skullduggery to surface before the 1927 season. When a bookie from Cincinnati accused the great Rogers Hornsby of losing more than $90,000 on horse races and then stiffing him, Landis served up harsh words but no punishment. Previously, Landis also addressed the accusations about the 1919 Tigers-Indians game that had caused Cobb and Speaker to resign. The commissioner held a secret hearing, but the chief accuser against Cobb and Speaker failed to appear in person. Moreover, Cobb and Speaker both threatened to quit baseball rather than be punished for a hearing in which they could not face their accuser. This time the commissioner exonerated both players. Within days, Speaker signed a lucrative deal to manage the Senators, and Cobb signed with the Athletics, extending the careers—and legends—of both.[5]

On April 12, the Yankees opened the 1927 season at home before a staggering baseball crowd of 72,000.[6] The Twenties roared in full swing on and off the field. It was a burgeoning age evidenced, in part, by the proliferation of literature from such varied authors as Hermann Hesse, Marcel Proust, Franz Kafka, E. M. Forster, Thornton Wilder, Sinclair Lewis, Ernest

Hemingway, A. A. Milne, Upton Sinclair, Agatha Christie, Bertrand Russell, Edgar Rice Burroughs, and Virginia Woolf. All of them published books in 1927 alone.

But the year burst ahead not only for the written word but also for music. Louie Armstrong and Duke Ellington were performing jazz for an eager nation while the airwaves were filled with works by Irving Berlin, George Gershwin, Oscar Hammerstein and Jerome Kern, Richard Rodgers and Lorenz Hart, Noel Coward, and Hoagy Carmichael. Many Americans can still hum at least four popular songs of the day: "Ain't She Sweet" (Jack Yellen and Milton Ager), "Blue Skies" (Irving Berlin), "I'm Looking over a Four Leaf Clover" (Mort Dixon and Harry Woods), and "My Blue Heaven" (George Whiting and Walter Donaldson). Broadway served up *Showboat*, *The Desert Song,* and *Funny Face,* among many other shows, while the classics featured works by such enduring composers as Béla Bartók, Arnold Schoenberg, Dmitri Shostakovich, and Igor Stravinsky. The cinema was still ensconced in the silent era with grand offerings like Cecil B. DeMille's *King of Kings,* and some movies even featured baseball, such as *Casey at the Bat* with Wallace Beery and ZaSu Pitts. One film starred the real-life slugger Ruth, who played the semi-fictional character Babe Dugan in a forgettable feature titled *Babe Comes Home.*

By October, the Babe took his rightful place on the Big Apple's stage for the World Series in the midst of a worldwide surge in communications. Not only was radio still being commercialized, but also the first transatlantic phone call from New York to London took place that year. Bell Telephone may have one-upped both radio and telephones when it successfully transmitted an experimental visual image over the air, leading to the invention of television.

Charles Lindbergh also helped bring the world closer together in 1927. Undeniably a world hero after his transatlantic flight, "Lucky Lindy" returned to Washington, D.C., in June aboard the USS *Memphis,* with a convoy escort of warships and planes, and President Calvin Coolidge welcomed him personally. None other than Chicago mobster Capone had been among the first to push ahead of the crowd and shake Lindy's hand, illustrating Capone's status, even though the notorious gangster was only twenty-eight years old at the time. But in June 1927, no one was bigger than Lindbergh. New York welcomed him with a record ticker tape parade that drew four *million* onlookers, then he went on a ninety-two-city barnstorming tour of America.[7] The United States had become a nation that truly loves its heroes and had placed Lindbergh high on the national pedestal.

Meanwhile, on May 22, 1927, the day after Lindbergh's arrival in Paris, George Herman Ruth donned his number 3 jersey, stepped into the batter's box in Cleveland, and lofted his tenth home run of the year. The Babe had clubbed four homers in April, and he added twelve more in May, with the month's final shot coming at the expense of Philadelphia pitcher Howard Ehmke on May 31.

Yet Ruth's magic was slightly tarnished, for not only had the Yankees lost the 1926 World Series to Rogers Hornsby's Cardinals in seven games, but also Ruth had made the final out in the last game. Ruth had already homered in the close 3–2 contest, but in the ninth inning with two outs, the plodding Babe walked and then was gunned down trying to steal second with slugger Bob Meusel at the plate.[8] But did that final out inspire Ruth and help to ignite the Yankees next season!

Ruth had failed to deliver a home run in the Yankees' 1927 season opener, a historic contest in its own right, since no fewer than thirteen eventual Hall of Fame players took the field that day. The visiting Philadelphia Athletics featured manager Cornelius "Connie Mack" McGillicuddy and such notable players as Cobb, Jimmie Foxx, Robert "Lefty" Grove, and Al Simmons. Leading the Yankees were the two of the biggest names in baseball history, Ruth and Lou Gehrig, complemented by pitcher Waite Hoyt and their manager Miller Huggins.[9]

Ruth, in fact, went homerless in New York's first three games, but he broke through with a solo blast on April 15 at home against the Athletics. Then Ruth truly served notice in the month of May, slamming two home runs on May 1 against Jack Quinn and left-hander George "Rube" Walberg. He ended the month the same way, slugging two long balls in his fourth consecutive game and bringing his total to sixteen for the young season. But Ruth was hardly the only slugging machine on the prodigious Yankee team. Teammate Gehrig made his own statement swing on May 7 and became the first to blast a grand-slam ball into a new right-field pavilion installed at Chicago's Comiskey Park as New York blanked the Sox 8–0.

Teammates Earle Combs, Tony Lazzeri, and Meusel were also among the league's leaders in numerous offensive categories. Combs would finish sixth in the league in batting with a .356 average, while Meusel was second in stolen bases with twenty-four, and Lazzeri tied for third with twenty-two. Lazerri was also a factor in home runs with eighteen, third best in the entire league but still only third best on his own team behind Ruth's sixty and Gehrig's forty-seven.[10] Batting second behind Earle Combs, Lazerri was no stranger to home run power. The second baseman had clubbed sixty homers while in the Pacific Coast League, and in 1936 Lazerri would become the first major-leaguer to hit two grand slam home runs in the same game.

Demonstrating an unfathomable balance of pitching and power, the Yankees finished first, second, and third in the league not only in home runs but also in earned run averages. Pitcher Wilcy Moore at 2.28 led the field, followed by workhorse Hoyt (256.1 innings and twenty-two wins) with a 2.63 ERA and Urban Shocker checking in at 2.84.[11] But no one had a better year than the Ruth-Gehrig duo, who delivered a combined 107 round-trippers. Ruth drove in 164 runs that year, a remarkable total that bested the other league's leader by 33; yet the Babe could only finish second on his own team behind Gehrig's stunning 175 RBIs, which led all of baseball by a wide margin. Ruth and Gehrig also finished first and second in slugging percentages (.772 and .765, respectively) while Gehrig was league runner-up in hitting at .373.[12]

Over the ensuing decades, the Yankees would produce no fewer than four of the greatest slugging pairs in major-league history: Ruth and Gehrig, Gehrig and Joe DiMaggio, Mickey Mantle and Yogi Berra, and eventually Mantle and Roger Maris. Other magnificent duos have played on the Yankees—for example, Dave Winfield and Don Mattingly—and other teams featured great batters, such as Athletics stars Jimmie Foxx and Al

Simmons, who were great rivals to the Yankees' Ruth and Gehrig. And legions more followed, including the Tigers' one-two punches Hank Greenberg and Charlie Gehringer, the Braves' Hank Aaron and Eddie Mathews, the Giants' Willie Mays and Orlando Cepeda, the Orioles' Frank Robinson and John "Boog" Powell, the Pirates' Willie Stargell and Roberto Clemente, the Phillies' Mike Schmidt and Greg Luzinski, and a host of Dodgers paired up among Edwin "Duke" Snider, Gil Hodges, Roy Campanella, Carl Furillo, and Jackie Robinson.

But Ruth and Gehrig were the best of the best, slamming home runs, making history, creating legends, and winning with abandon. They took New York to 110 victories in 1927 and led the Murderers' Row Yankees to back-to-back World Series sweeps in 1927 and 1928. By 1931, the pair would again break their own records for combined runs scored (312) and runs batted in (347), marks that stand to this day. Ruth and Gehrig terrorized the league from 1925 through 1934, a full decade of long-ball mayhem.

The 1927 season is still one of the best years in baseball ever, though, mostly because of Ruth's record and the Murderers' Row mystique but also because it was Gehrig's breakout year. The Yankee first baseman, whom many suggest was the best first baseman in the history of the big leagues, batted fourth in the lineup behind Ruth and, importantly, ahead of veteran slugger Bob Meusel. Having Meusel for protection led to better pitches for the young Gehrig, and he was certainly up to the challenge. Even more significant to history was Ruth's batting ahead of Gehrig; the position ensured a diet of hittable pitches for the Babe and, as it happened, for posterity.

Although his home run assault continued with nine more in June, Ruth could not shake Gehrig until later in the year, setting the stage for one of the great home run races in major-league history. On July 4 in front of seventy-four thousand fans at Yankee Stadium, Ruth went five for seven in a holiday doubleheader against the Senators. Gehrig slammed two home run shots, leading New York to lopsided victories of 12–1 and 21–1 and pushing past the great Babe Ruth in the 1927 home run chase.

Five days later in Detroit, Ruth clubbed two more as the Yankees scored nineteen runs in a drubbing of the Tigers. The Babe reached the halfway point when he slammed number 30 against Cleveland on July 12, but then number 3 cooled off, going homerless for twelve days. On July 24 at Chicago's Comiskey Park, he hit number 31, a blast that gave Ruth at least one home run in every big-league park that year. Two days later, in a doubleheader against St. Louis, Ruth slammed two more homers in the first game—one in the first inning and another in the sixth—and both came at the expense of pitcher Milt Gaston. On July 28, Ruth crunched his last home run of the month, again in St. Louis, giving the Bambino thirty-four jacks as the oppressive heat of August loomed.[13]

As late as August 1, Gehrig still led the home run race, but then his pace slowed. Ruth clubbed his third homer of the month on August 16 in the fifth inning against Chicago. It measured 520 feet and was the first home run over the Comiskey roof when it sailed over the 75-foot right-field deck. Even so, Ruth still trailed Gehrig's thirty-eight jacks by one. The following day, though, the Babe smashed his own number 38 and followed with five more by the end of August, giving him forty-three on August 31.[14]

Ruth's first homer of September came on the second. September 6 show-cased a threshold game that foreshadowed a month of long-ball wonder. The Yankees faced the Red Sox in a doubleheader at Boston. In the first game, Ruth slammed two homers, with one clearing the center-field fence and becoming one of the longest home runs in Fenway Park's history. New York won the first game decidedly, 14–2, but Boston survived yet another Ruthian blast to take the second contest, 5–2. Ruth was not finished, though. He clubbed two more at Boston the next day, giving him five round-trippers in two days and a total of six that first week of September. Ruth smashed two home runs in one day twice more in September—one pair coming at Cleveland's expense on September 13 and another double homer in a game against Washington on September 29.[15]

Meanwhile, Ruth had reached the fifty-homer plateau on September 11 in the fourth inning of a game against St. Louis. The Yankees dominated the Browns that year, more so than all the other teams, winning a record twenty-one games against St. Louis in one season. Ruth hit number 51 on September 13 as the Yankees clinched the pennant with a pair of wins over

Cleveland. By September 18, Ruth's total of fifty-four jacks was crowding his own league record of fifty-nine. Gehrig was still making headlines, too, cracking the third grand slam of his bourgeoning career by July 4. He was en route to forty-seven home runs and a league-leading 175 RBIs on the season as the Yankees' great one-two combination pressed on.[16]

Then, on September 27, with the bases loaded, Ruth entered the batter's box to face the Athletics' pitching legend Lefty Grove, the prior season's league leader in both strikeouts and earned run average. The classic pitcher-slugger confrontation ultimately proved no contest. The Babe hammered his fifty-seventh home run of the year, and the grand slam game winner inched Ruth closer to the sixty-run threshold. On September 29, Ruth clubbed a home run in the first inning against the Senators. Then with the bases loaded in the fifth, he walloped yet another grand slam. With that blast, Ruth caught his own league mark of fifty-nine amid a deluge of September long balls that scored runs in bunches.

The last game of the year was October 1 against the Senators, but Ruth did not have to wait that long. Ten thousand fans appeared at Yankee Stadium on September 30 for the penultimate game of the year. The small size of the gate is interesting, for Yankee Stadium was capable of drawing crowds that reached seventy thousand or more, a number exceeded on Opening Day and again on July 4 that year. With Ruth closing on his 60th home run, a larger gathering would have seemed more likely, but that observation is made in the hindsight of long-ball mania and reviews of the crowds who witnessed Hank Aaron's 715th homer, Mark McGwire's 61st and 62nd, and Barry Bonds's 71st. Ruth started that trend. Only after he hit his vaunted record did America go home run crazy.

Ruth had first set his record of fifty-nine back in 1921 while still playing at the Polo Grounds. It took the Babe six years to challenge his own mark. Meanwhile, as noted earlier, in 1922 Ruth could not even lead the league in home runs after a season-opening suspension for illegal barnstorming shelved both him and Bob Meusel until May 20. In 1923 Ruth was back, leading the league with forty-one jacks and winning the MVP. In 1924 he led the league again with forty-six, but in 1925 teammate Meusel took center stage with his own league best at thirty-three. In 1926 Ruth clubbed forty-seven more to top the league in homers, slugging percentage (.737), and RBIs (146), and he set the stage for the magical 1927 season of Murderers' Row.

With one out in the eighth inning on September 30, 1927, George Herman Ruth lumbered to the plate, gripped the handle of his bat, and then took an epic swing, crushing a right-field blast off Washington pitcher Tom Zachary. The game-winning home run broke a 2–2 tie. The Yankees' bench pounded their bats in approval as Ruth rounded the bases and then saluted the fans. "Sixty, count 'em, sixty," Ruth crowed. "Let some son-of-a-bitch top that."

Zachary, who had thought the ball was foul in the first place, added his own commentary years later when asked about the historic moment. "If you really want to know the truth," he began irreverently, "I'd rather have thrown at his big fat head."[17]

Gehrig, with his .373 average, was one of five hitters over .300 in that starting lineup, including Ruth's lofty .356. The team bested every other major-league club by more than a hundred home runs, and the Yankees led the leagues with a remarkable team batting average of .307. Ruth had clubbed seventeen homers in September to pull away from Gehrig in the home run battle, but Gehrig still won the league MVP.[18] (In those days, a player could not win the MVP—then called the League Award—twice, so Ruth was already out of the running.) Ruth's total of sixty jacks was nearly an immortal feat for any era but especially so in the context of his times. Teams in the 1990s and beyond often slug more than two hundred home runs per year, but when Ruth set the record, he had single-handedly slammed more long balls than every other *team* in the league. Even Gehrig, with forty-seven, had out-slugged all but three other teams on his own. No wonder the entire lineup went down in history as Murderers' Row. The 1927 lineup wasn't the first Yankees team with that moniker, which was first used in 1919 to describe Frank "Home Run" Baker and Wally Pipp, but the 1927 pairing of Ruth and Gehrig virtually erased fans' memories of the original duo. The 1919 team also featured an outfielder with a future in football, George Halas, who helped found both the Chicago Bears and the NFL.[19] In the early 1920s the NFL was gaining popularity behind the star power of Red Grange, the NBA did not yet exist, and boxing was still a top draw.

On October 2, 1927, the *New York Times* ran a piece on the Babe that began, "What this big, good-natured, uproarious lad has done is little short of a miracle of sport."[20] The article then pointed to Ruth's magnificent 1927 comeback as the source of this reverence and even noted the great Dempsey by contrast. "What Dempsey couldn't do with his fists, Ruth has done with his bat. He came back."[21] The *Times* was alluding to the relatively mediocre season Ruth had had in 1925, appearing in only ninety-eight games, hitting twenty-five home runs, and having a mortal .290 batting average. Some thought his age was beginning to take a toll, too. Ruth had been twenty-six years old when he set his previous record at fifty-nine runs in 1921, and he was thirty-two when he hit number 60. "Put it in the book in letters of gold," the *Times* continued. "It will be a long time before any one [*sic*] else betters that home-run mark, and a still longer time before any aging athlete makes such a gallant and glorious charge over the come-back trail."[22]

Five times from 1921 to 1927 boxing gate receipts topped $1 million, and Jack Dempsey was featured in all of them. After 1927, boxing would not see such a frenzy until two generations later when Muhammad Ali captured the world's attention and led a heavyweight boxing resurgence that may have been boxing's last genuine gasp. By then it was too late, however; baseball had already been crowned the new king long before.

Baseball clichés began to supplant boxing terms in American slang. Although not jargon, the name "Baby Ruth" remains widely recognizable as that of a popular candy bar. The true origin of the name, however, remains controversial. The Curtiss Candy Company launched the Baby Ruth candy bar in 1920, the precise year of Babe Ruth's dramatic debut with the Yankees. By 1921, Ruth sued Curtiss Candy, alleging that the company illegally exploited his famous name for its own profit. Ruth lost, but the courts at that time were unfamiliar with the endorsement concept as it is known today. Subsequent historical accounts differ. Some suggest the candy was named either for Grover Cleveland's daughter Ruth—rather unlikely, since she had died seventeen years earlier—or for the granddaughter of the president of the Williamson Candy Company, where the recipe was reportedly born. The idea of naming a product after a competitor's grandchild is also a stretch. Maybe the Curtiss Candy Company did name the bar after a child named Ruth, but it would be a distinction without a legal difference, for using that child's name was almost certainly a pretext to exploit the more famous ballplayer's cachet. Would the Baby Ruth bar have become a nine-decade bestseller had it been named the "Abigail Bar" or the "Mildred Bar"?

Ironically, at least one boxing term—namely, the "one-two punch"—became mostly a baseball reference commonly used to describe the top two hitters in any lineup, such as Ruth and Gehrig, Mantle and Maris, and all the others. Sometimes other sports use the term to refer to their formidable duos, too—such as Earvin "Magic" Johnson and Kareem Abdul Jabbar, Michael Jordan and Scottie Pippen, and LeBron James and Dwayne Wade. This usage echoes the Ruth-Gehrig meaning of the term rather than hearkening its boxing origin.

The 1927 Yankees scored 6.3 runs a game and led the American League in runs, hits, triples, home runs, walks, batting average, on-base percentage, and slugging average. The team's .488 slugging percentage is still a major-league record.[23] The heart of Murderers' Row comprised five durable sluggers, four of whom—Ruth, Combs, Lazerri, and Gehrig—played in at least 151 of the 154 games on the schedule. (Gehrig played in every game, keeping his famous consecutive game streak intact.) Four of those hitters—Gehrig, Lazzeri, Meusel, and Ruth—each drove in more than a hundred runs, and four batters had slugging percentages greater than .500, including Ruth's .772 and Gehrig's .765.

Baseball was popular before 1927, of course, and the days of Cobb, Cy Young, Walter Johnson, Shoeless Joe Jackson, and many others are still legendary. But on September 30, 1927, America morphed into a long-ball society, and in many ways, then baseball truly *became* America, a game that was an integral part of everyday life and encapsulated the essence of America itself. The game mirrored our country's capitalist home run approach to baseball and business, and it soon took over our language, culture, and slices of our history. Ty Cobb and Nap Lajoie were magnificent hitters, but neither hit with unprecedented power. Not until the people witnessed Ruth's home runs did their excitement for the Yankees and major-league baseball grip America, then symbolize it. With its down-home announcers and home run spectacles, baseball helped transform many of our parents and grandparents, thus affecting who we all are as a nation. With Ruth's surge, the game overshadowed such other celebrated figures as Dempsey, Lindbergh, Charlie Chaplin, and even President Coolidge.

With its emerging superstars, baseball set the stage for athlete endorsements by bigger-than-life sports heroes at a time when the radio medium was taking hold, thus inventing sports broadcasting as we know it today. It is no coincidence that in the fall of 1927, the demand for radios increased dramatically. While Ruth was making his run at history in September, RCA introduced a new line of Radiolas. The most popular model, the Radiola 17, cost $157.50, could run on house current instead of batteries, and was simple to operate.[24] This new product fostered the proliferation of radio, and soon listeners heard more baseball—and home runs—on the radio.

Before 1927, boxing had been the unchallenged king of sports. During that fateful year, boxing lost its prize marquee Jack Dempsey while Ruth, Gehrig, and the '27 Yankees were dominating the baseball world as had no other sports team before them or since (although Mantle and Maris would provide a good imitation in 1961, and later NBA stars would make a good run at it). That shift to baseball altered the personality of an entire nation. We are no longer a society built in the image of Dempsey, Tunney, Joe Louis, or even Ali, although television helped Ali make a bid for lasting individual greatness that ultimately surpassed Ruth's worldwide recognition. We are now a society rooted in the spirit of Ruth, Gehrig, and a Murderers' Row team born in the dirt and grit of the house that Ruth built.

☆ 7 ☆

THE IMMACULATE DECEPTION

*[Gaylord Perry] should be in the Hall of Fame with a
tube of KY jelly attached to his plaque.*
—GENE MAUCH[1]

Baseball is an irreverent, larcenous team sport driven by dramatic one-on-one confrontations between powerful hitters and deceptive pitchers. While hitters recoil to swing for the fences, the pitchers rely mostly on deception to stop them. After all, they have to throw the pitch generally in or near the strike zone. All the pitcher can do is throw it faster or employ myriad tricks by changing speeds, altering the path of the pitch, and engaging in a series of mind games to keep the batter off balance.

When baseball banned the spitball and thus encouraged offense, especially home runs, the competitive balance shifted. Suddenly teams placed a bigger premium on the ability to throw tricky illegal pitches, namely, the spitter and its numerous permutations. The most infamous master of baseball larceny from the mound is Gaylord Perry, the first pitcher to win the Cy Young Award in both leagues.[2]

Stealing signs and using the hidden ball trick, corked bats, spitballs, brushback pitches, and even the legal but elusive knuckleball—all are ploys to gain a competitive edge. Such machinations are part of the charm and thus the lore of baseball.

Curveballs curve because the ball can be thrown from a variety of grips whereby the ball's spinning, raised seams create different forms of drag against the air. The laws of physics require the ball to change directions as the force vectors adjust to the resulting imbalance. Better pitchers can control the pitch for strikes and have various curve techniques so that each pitch is potentially different, forcing the batter not only to adjust to the ball's flight but also to guess its speed and its trajectory.

The spitball is effective for many reasons depending on what type of doctored spitter is thrown. In some cases, the wet side of the ball has less friction against the air, exacerbating the ball's inevitable break. Some pitchers, like Perry, will also load one side of the ball with grease—petroleum jelly, K-Y Jelly, Preparation H—making that side heavier and distorting the flight of the ball. Some will also adjust the drag on the ball by scuffing or nicking it, while others enhance the effect of a spitter by moistening their fingers to reduce the rotation of the ball as it leaves the hand, allowing for a speedier version of the knuckleball pitch. Perry was known around the leagues for his illegal proclivities, which gave him a mind game advantage over befuddled batters. Not only was Perry caught from time to time, but he once even endorsed a brand of petroleum jelly.

Edward "Whitey" Ford, the Yankees' great pitcher during the era of Yogi Berra and Mickey Mantle, reputedly cut the ball with his wedding ring and sometimes added a mixture of baby oil, turpentine, and resin.[3] If a pitcher applies a lubricant to his forefinger and middle finger, his overhand fastball will slide off his fingers with the effect of an amplified split-finger fastball and drop precipitously since there is less backspin.[4] The spitball, greaseball, and all their variations are illegal pitches because they create too much imbalance in the game; without a corresponding increase in the pitcher's talent or effort, these pitches quash the offense and most notably the marquee attraction of baseball, the almighty home run.[5]

The knuckleball, a legal pitch, has similar attributes and the same effect, but pitchers find it extremely difficult to master. They throw the ball with a grip that prevents the ball from spinning when released, and it is very hard to do, especially with enough velocity to keep hitters from watching, reacting, and pasting it into the stands anyway. Neither the pitcher nor the catcher, who has to use a special, noticeably larger mitt, knows where the ball will go, as wind drag on the ball's seams is unpredictable and uncontrollable. The batter is also clueless, which is the whole point of the pitch. Thus, baseball banned using moistened fingers; otherwise, pitchers could throw unpredictable balls with more speed that would be nearly unhittable.

A significant chapter in the annals of baseball cheating is directed to the balance and imbalance between the pitcher and the batter. Bat speed is essential to the equation, separating big-league batters from those in the minors. Greater bat speed allows the batter to "catch up" to deceptive pitches, essentially providing an additional split second to his swing. The hitter uses this micro difference first to see the spin of the ball as it is released, giving him a clue as to what is coming and the ability to calculate a better guess as to the ball's speed and trajectory.

The quickness of a batter's swing is increased by his having stronger hands and sheer talent and by using a lighter or shorter bat. Shorter bats don't cover as much territory, though, and they have less leverage and power behind them. Lighter bats have less mass to deliver enough force upon impact to be seriously effective. The hitter can compensate by building his strength either with training and practice or illegally with performance-enhancing drugs. Or the hitter can make a longer bat lighter in ways that increase the torque of the swing.

Enter the "corked" bat. Drill a cavity near the end of the bat, take out a chunk of wood, and replace it with a much lighter substance, and the illegal corked bat is born. Players have experimented with corked bats for decades. Slugger Sammy Sosa, the first player ever to hit sixty-six homers in a season, used a corked bat in a Cubs game against Tampa Bay on June 3, 2003. The bat splintered during the game, revealing the cork insert for all to see. Sosa denied using the bat intentionally, saying that he used the corked bat for batting practice and that he picked it up accidentally in the game against the Devil Rays. Although possible, his claim strains the bounds of credibility, especially considering that the aging Sosa was hitting .285 and had only six homers that season. He was striking out frequently, often because he chased bad pitches, especially wicked sliders. At the time, he also was coming off an injury and had had two hits in his prior fifteen plate appearances. This incident occurred at the beginning of the post-steroid era, so if Sosa had ever been on steroids, he probably was not taking them that 2003 season.

Sosa was suspended for his transgression, but does the cork really help a slugger enough to justify the risks? During the sixteen years prior to Sosa's suspension, four other big leaguers were caught and suspended for using corked bats: the Dodgers' Wilton Guerrero (1997), Chris Sabo of the Reds (1996), Albert Belle during a stint with the Indians (1994), and the Astros' Billy Hatcher (1987). Belle's story offers perhaps the most intrigue. When he was caught, the umpires confiscated the bat as usual, but someone later broke into the White Sox's clubhouse and stole the evidence, giving the whole episode a "bat-gate" mystique.[6]

Robert K. Adair, perhaps the foremost expert on the physics of baseball, is not convinced that cork was effective in the first place. In his book *The Physics of Baseball*, Adair debunks the value of cork.[7] Yes, the drilled hole does reduce a typical ash bat's weight by about 1.5 ounces, but the cork, rubber, or other filler adds another half ounce. Further, in the process the bat loses its ability to transfer energy to the ball—the filler's elastic energy, even of rubber, is not enough to propel the ball—thus making the corked bat possibly less effective as a hitting tool. Adair suggests a better approach to batters: choke up on the bat handle, use a shorter or slightly lighter bat in the first place, or sand the barrel of the bat down from 2.5 inches to 2.4 inches in circumference.[8]

The lighter a bat gets, the easier it is to swing, assuming it still has enough weight to get the job done. For example, a bat used for whiffle ball is much lighter, but it won't hit a regulation baseball far. In general, the lighter bats increase the ability to make contact, but they lose an element of power. In 1962, the year after Roger Maris's record-breaking season of sixty-one homers, Maris experimented and practiced with five different bats weighing from thirty-three to forty-seven ounces. Each bat was a replica of what notorious home run hitters previously had used, including the heavy forty-seven-ounce model that Babe Ruth used in 1927.[9] The results confirmed the relationship between mass and distance: the heavier the bat was, the farther the ball traveled. Added weight detracts from bat speed, quickness, and hitting for average, so the heavy bats do come with a price.

Perhaps sensing the delicate balance between speed and effectiveness, and cheating and not cheating, the great Yankees third baseman Graig Nettles found himself swinging a doctored bat in the fall of 1974. Nettles played in the majors for twenty-two years, including a long run with the New York Yankees from 1973 to 1983 when the Yankees won four pennants. Known for his Hall of Fame–caliber defense at third, Nettles was a mediocre hitter with a career .248 average, but he did have surprising power, slugging 390 total home runs, including a career-best 37, in 1977. On September 7, 1974, Nettles took a solid rip at the plate, shattered his bat, and abruptly sprayed no fewer than six Super Balls across the infield, nearly becoming the first hitter to ground out to all bases at one time. Even with a career fielding percentage of .961 at the "hot corner" of third base, 390 career homers, and 1,314 RBIs in 2,700 big-league games, Nettles is also remembered for the Super Ball incident.[10] Largely forgotten is the outstanding, outlying month of April in that troublesome 1974 season when he slugged 11 home runs. One can only wonder whether there was a correlation between those homers and a tampered stick.

Unlike Albert Belle's mystery bat, Sosa's corked bat did not disappear. Chicago collector and president of Harry Caray's Restaurant Group, Grant DePorter, bought it at auction for $14,404, held it for nearly eight years, and in February 2011 was suddenly inspired to study the infamous bat further by using available CAT-scan technology. The test revealed a marvel of larcenous engineering, sports columnist Rick Telander of the *Chicago Sun-Times* noted in February 2011: "The cork in the bat begins an inch and a half below the beveled top, and it continues down the barrel for almost a foot. A circle the size of a 50-cent piece was drilled straight down, though slightly off center, until the barrel narrowed too much to continue farther."

Ground cork was jammed throughout the cavity and glued in place with some sort of paste. Moreover, the top of the bat had been ingeniously screwed together, the whole bat was painted black and varnished, and Sosa's number 21 was painted over the top in silver marker, thus disguising the rigged bat even more.[11] As a result, Sosa's bat was lighter without sacrificing length. Although he theoretically could have made contact more often, his effort did not appear to have worked very well. In any event, Sosa's bat-gate scheme was deficient in that it lacked sufficient mass to increase the likelihood of home runs.

Baseball has tolerated cheating since the game's inception. More than a century ago, when only one umpire worked the games, John McGraw of the Baltimore Orioles would hold on to the belt of opposing runners tagging at third on sacrifice flies. Ridiculous as that now sounds, players still use similar tactics in football and, in particular, basketball, where clandestine shirt tugging is a virtual art. With more umpires and limited singular action, the belt trick is impossible to use in major-league baseball today, but the game has found other ways to tip the competitive balance, such as trapping balls in the outfield, stealing signs, growing the grass long in the infield, and deploying variations of the spitball and the occasional corked bat, the effect of the latter being somewhat dubious. Various superstitions, such as fidgeting with the batting gloves in the batter's box, crossing oneself, wearing the same dirty socks or worse, and even invoking curses, are endemic to the game of baseball as well. Other sports sometimes exhibit similar superstitions about socks, underwear, pregame rituals, and so on, but neither the NBA nor the NFL has curses, at least of the proactive variety. There is something of a "Madden curse," named for the former coach and commentator John Madden. Some have pointed to a drop-off in the performance of players who are featured on the cover of the popular Madden video football games as a curse of sorts, similar to the adage about those who appear on the cover of *Sports Illustrated*. Strategic curses and hexes are largely left to the singular game of baseball.

Cheating provides color, excitement, and personality to an otherwise cerebral, sometimes banal game where on-field action is limited to intermittent bursts sandwiched between intervals of downtime. Simply put, since base-ball has time to cheat, it often does. But cheating also leads to scandals, especially when larceny exceeds the bounds of allowable gamesmanship. A charging outfielder pretending to catch a trapped ball by exuberantly show-ing it off in the glove and the catcher "framing a pitch" by subtly gliding his glove closer to the strike zone to induce a called strike are examples of widely tolerated ploys within the norms of baseball. Much more dubious are head-hunting brushback pitches, sliding into base with high spikes, and secretly using steroids—all deemed unacceptable in the context of the modern game—although spitballs and other mischievous tricks do still appear from time to time.

Overt rigging of the games has always been eschewed for any legitimate sport, for such conspiracies eliminate competition and destroy the contest altogether. Such manipulation was exposed in what some regard as the greatest sports scandal of all time, the rigged 1919 World Series and subse-quent lifetime ban of eight Chicago White Sox players. Sports gambling is only a step removed from sports manipulation, and when that line is crossed, the sport ceases to exist as a genuine contest.

Perhaps even more scandalous, however, is the steroid pandemic of the 1990s and early 2000s when many baseball records were tarnished and the integrity of the game was reduced to rubble. Remarkably, even as the truth came out, major-league baseball took a head-in-the-sand, see-no-evil stance and still recognized players' statistical records, although the fans seem less willing to embrace these new bloated marks. A vaguely defined but decid-edly real distinction exists between acceptable manipulation and intolerable cheating, although those limits may vary among fans, players, and umpires. Game rigging by gamblers is at the top of the proscribed list of transgres-sions, a point that star player and manager of the Reds Pete Rose knows well. In 1989 he was banned from the game for life as a result of his baseball gambling, even though no overt game fixing on his part was ever discovered. Steroid-induced home runs are not legal, either, although they have been largely tolerated in the record books. The accused players' distorted records are allowed to stand, even as the Hall of Fame voters shun these players.

But the annals of baseball lore seem to have a special place for doctored pitches. Not only is Gaylord Perry in the Baseball Hall of Fame, but his records also stand untarnished. Further, he is celebrated, if not revered, for his transgressions. Over the course of his career, Perry won 314 games, collected 3,534 strikeouts, and of his 690 career starts, pitched a staggering 303 complete games. (A complete game in the new millennium is a notable accomplishment.)[12]

Gaylord Perry actually pitched until age forty-five, but he was not caught throwing an illegal doctored pitch until his twenty-first season in big-league ball. Batters long knew Perry's larcenous reputation and invariably lost the fragile mind game of hitting against him, for Perry's unproven but widely regarded reputation kept batters off balance regardless of whether he actually threw his junked-up pitches during the course of any given game.

Illegal pitches are effective because only a small difference can lead to a big change in the status quo. Studies have shown that a typical big-league curveball breaks when it is about halfway to the plate and deviates only about 3.5 inches from a straight line. But the effect creates a perceived deflection of up to 14 inches by the time it reaches the plate, a distinction that is made more dramatic from the batter's perspective.[13] A bird's-eye view from the side angle of the curveball's trajectory shows a gradual deviation off-line, but of course the batters sees all pitches head-on as they leave the pitcher's hand and experience an illusion of a wicked break. Why? When the eye picks up the pitch, the brain interprets its likely arrival point at the plate as though it will graze the inside corner while it actually hits the outside corner, giving the illusion of a 14-inch break right at the plate.

The knuckleball is a different beast. The physics behind it are not the same, since a really good one does not spin at all. The knuckler takes about 600 milliseconds to reach the plate and is slower than a curveball and a fastball (550 milliseconds and 400 milliseconds, respectively). Its flight begins to change around 150 milliseconds after the release, floating about eleven inches off a straight line and reaching its maximum deviation when the pitch is less than 200 milliseconds from the plate. At that point the knuckleball becomes a mindless, out-of-control fluttering missile. It might wander back to the middle of the strike zone, rise over the catcher's head, drop into the dirt, or sail behind the batter. Since the blink of an eye takes about 150 milliseconds, the final stages of the pitch are difficult to follow. Moreover, following its first 300 milliseconds is largely irrelevant as the first half of the ball's trajectory has little to do with the second half.[14]

So how do these pitches relate to cheating? The unpredictable greaseball can be thrown like a curveball and at the speed of a curveball, or it can be gunned as a fastball. If the imbalance of the ball is exacerbated, all the normal lines of trajectory are disrupted, not only wreaking havoc on the batter's sight lines, timing, and concentration but also placing a higher premium on his bat speed to make up for the confusion. This mayhem partly explains why the spitball was banned at the dawn of the home run age in 1920, why steroids became a popular antidote for wicked fastballs and sliders in the 1990s, and how Gaylord Perry could pitch so effectively for so many years.

The steroid monsters might never find their way to Cooperstown, but Perry, who eventually admitted using greaseballs and other creative, substance-aided pitches, was inducted into the Hall of Fame anyway (although it took three tries). And as with hardball politics and robber-baron business, that attempt to gain an edge is reflected in both baseball and America.

After all, playing hardball is how John D. Rockefeller built the mammoth Standard Oil from a consortium of oil drillers and distributors, partly inspiring and then evading federal antitrust laws. ("Competition is a sin," he once said.) And it is how the 1951 Giants caught the Dodgers and launched a tainted home run into major-league destiny. Although he has historically denied cheating on his most famous homer, batter Bobby Thomson has sometimes hedged the idea of his stealing that home run, since the Giants caught the Dodgers in the 1951 pennant race with the help of an elaborate system for stealing signs. Coach Herman Franks used a telescope to read the catcher's signs and then sent a signal about the pitch to the bullpen. From there, someone would immediately relay it to the batter. The process was a wonder of timing and ingenuity as well as larceny. As for Thomson, he admits to the sign-stealing season, even during the pennant-winning game, but still denies that his walk-off blast was stolen.[15]

Such shenanigans are hardly unique to baseball or America. Some believe trickery is how John F. Kennedy won Chicago in 1960 by a huge margin, then all of Illinois by only 8,858 votes, and finally the nation, with the help of Illinois' 27 electoral votes. At the time, Richard J. Daley, the powerful Democratic mayor, tightly ruled Chicago, and his city had a history of engaging in questionable voting tactics, especially ballot stuffing and the purported appearance of dead people at the polls. Although less dramatic, hardball shenanigans are likewise a part of big-league lore, including how Gaylord Perry won 314 games for eight different big-league clubs from 1962 to 1983 with rigged pitches. Even the Yankees' great Whitey Ford had a creative repertoire of junk-aided machinations to doctor the ball, including mud clumps around the mound to load the ball, his wedding ring to nick pitches, or the help of catcher Elston Howard who sometimes cut the ball with his belt buckle.

Pitchers, batters, managers, and coaches have all been guilty of such misdeeds. Even the groundskeepers entered the act. The notoriously creative Gene Bossard family, which maintained the field at Chicago's Comiskey Park with larcenous ingenuity, soaked the outfield to aid the Sox's sinkerball pitchers so thoroughly that the outfield was sometimes referred to as Bossard's Swamp. They even kept the first and third baselines slightly elevated to help keep speedster Jacob "Nellie" Fox's bunts in fair territory.[16] In 1981 the Seattle Mariners' manager, Maury Wills, once had the Kingdome batter's box enlarged by a foot toward the pitcher. This alteration gave his hitters a chance to catch the wicked breaking balls of the Athletics' Rick Langford a little early, a point that the A's irascible manager, Billy Martin, strenuously made.[17]

The culture of baseball skullduggery is long, deep, and endemically American. It reflects the country's unbridled capitalism, perseverance, corner cutting, and sometimes illegal quest for victory, beginning with America's defiant Declaration of Independence through the days of Rockefeller, Al Capone, hardball presidential elections, and baseball's recent steroid era. As noted previously, in 1910 the maligned Tiger Ty Cobb was in the hunt for one of his twelve batting titles and had an eight-hit edge over rival Nap Lajoie of Cleveland. The whole league hated Cobb, who had a nasty temper, would slide with spikes up if necessary, and once even bludgeoned a disabled fan in the stands.[18] So during a season finale doubleheader with Cleveland, the Browns' manager attempted to shift the batting title to Lajoie by instructing his third baseman to play off the base. Lajoie bunted to the hole in the defense at third and had seven hits. Cobb won the title, besting Lajoie .3850687 to .3840947.[19] Years later a review of the records showed Cobb had been awarded one hit too many during the season, and Lajoie should have won outright. Commissioner Bowie Kuhn refused to change the record books, opting to preserve legend over fact—albeit a Browns-aided dubious "fact."

Baseball, in the end, begs an oxymoronic question of morality: is there such a thing as "cheating fair"? Every time an NBA player flops on the court to coax a foul call or an NFL lineman holds an onrushing defender, the players are cheating, whether they are caught or not. But these tactics are within the normal expectations of the game since they happen often and during the normal course of every contest. Baseball is replete with such tolerated infractions, giving the game an edgy personality with a boyish charm. Golf is more for Tom Sawyer–like players who are charming but play within the rules; football is for bullies; and baseball features players who have a Huck Finn sense of mischief. In the game of baseball, skullduggery is expected and somewhat tolerated. After all, boys will be boys.

But such matters beg the dilemma that inevitably follows: does the end justify the means? Spitballs, greaseballs, corked bats, stolen signs, and mushy outfields tread dangerously close to much greater transgressions, such as racial segregation. And fifty years after Jackie Robinson's debut, baseball again tested the bounds of morality with a different approach to manipulating history. In 1998, amid the euphoria of home run power reminiscent of the long-ball seasons of Mantle-Maris and Ruth-Gehrig, the great steroid era was in full swing. The rest of America simply didn't know it yet.

THE GAME OF
INFAMY

In June 1944 during the darkest hours of World War II, the great Yankees' center fielder Joe DiMaggio stepped to the plate before an anxious crowd of thirty thousand fans.[1] "Joltin' Joe" peered at the opposing pitcher, pulled back his bat, and ripped a 453-foot monster home run that not only left the stadium but also sailed into baseball posterity like no other ball off DiMaggio's bat. This tape measure blast occurred not at Yankee Stadium or Fenway or Comiskey; instead, it happened at Honolulu Stadium beyond the shallows of Pearl Harbor, where DiMaggio's Seventh Army baseball team exhilarated the capacity crowd. He dropped his bat and circled the bases only eight hundred meters from the sunken hull of the USS *Arizona* and its 1,102 souls entombed beneath the Pacific. Given the circumstances and surroundings, it may have been the Yankee Clipper's most poignant home run.

Earlier, when the baseball season began during the spring of 1941, the German Army had controlled Poland already for the better part of two years and had occupied Paris for nearly a year. It was an extraordinary time in world history. During that fateful season before the attack on Pearl Harbor, baseball offered a number of big-league milestones, some moving, some lasting, and many entwined with a world at war.

With America's entry into World War II, baseball, which had already become an indelible part of America, took an even greater place in history. Baseball had captivated America for many decades, particularly after the introduction of Babe Ruth and Lou Gehrig, Murderers' Row, and the home run, but during World War II, baseball *became* America in a much different way. As the United States entered the war, the military draft raised two million servicemen in an extraordinary expansion of the armed forces and national defense. Not surprisingly, the major leagues offered up many able-bodied young men, the first of whom was the Phillies' pitcher Hugh Mulcahy, inducted into the armed forces on March 8, 1941, almost nine months before Pearl Harbor. A much bigger star, Detroit's Hank Greenberg, was drafted in May 1941, going from league MVP in 1940 to a soldier in the U.S. Army making $21 a month. On May 6, he slammed two home runs against the Yankees and then left baseball to enlist before his draft notice even made it to the mailbox.

Parenthetically, at the beginning of the season the Dodgers had debuted a new batting helmet that two Johns Hopkins surgeons devised after the rash of baseball "bean wars" the prior year. It was a good idea but did not really catch on for many more seasons. The Pirates began using helmets in 1952, but Major League Baseball did not mandate batting helmets until 1971. Meanwhile, the war years were still the "good old days" of chewing tobacco, throwing spitballs and brushback pitches, kicking dirt on the umpire, blasting home runs without a steroid liftoff, and enjoying the feel of a cool breeze through the batter's cap.

In May 1941, when Greenberg went off to war, the great thirty-game winner Dizzy Dean retired. On the other side of the plate, the Yankees' Joe DiMaggio, who had not yet joined the war effort, already had begun hitting safely for several games in a row. Thus he started his famous hitting streak, which some now regard as the most unassailable record in baseball, if not in all team sports. By May 27, the streak was up to twelve games thanks to a four-hit game in Washington.[2] Six days later, however, another Yankee ended his own streak when the great Lou Gehrig finally succumbed to ALS. Astonishingly, Gehrig died on the sixteenth anniversary of the day he had first broken into the Yankees' starting lineup in 1925. His longtime teammate Babe Ruth attended the funeral along with countless dignitaries and other baseball royalty.

Three days after Gehrig's funeral, DiMaggio's streak had reached an impressive twenty-two games. One day later, the Yankee Clipper added two more games, playing a doubleheader sweep over the Browns, and unloaded four hits on the day, including three home runs. DiMaggio's assault on history made for an extraordinary summer in the last baseball season when America was still mostly unmarred by the scourge of World War II. His consecutive-game hitting streak reached fifty-six in the middle of the summer of 1941, and on July 17, it was finally over. During his record run, DiMaggio had garnered ninety-one hits, including fifteen home runs, and batted a lofty .408. Remarkably, Joe immediately started a new streak the next day, going sixteen in a row. Thus, he actually had hit safely in seventy-two out of seventy-three games, a string that is even more implausible and impressive statistically.[3]

By season's end, a twenty-year-old youngster in St. Louis began an enduring long-ball career when he slammed his first home run on September 23. Stanley Frank Musial would not retire from the game for twenty-two more years, a span that saw 3,630 hits, including 475 home runs.[4]

That same 1941 season was winding down on September 28 when young slugger Ted Williams, a pure hitter with a picture-perfect swing, found himself batting .39955, or statistically .400 when rounded from the fifth decimal. His manager Joe Cronin had offered Williams the option of sitting out a scheduled doubleheader to preserve his virtual .400 average, but the twenty-three-year-old would have none of it. After all, the real unrounded number still began with a three, so he took the risk and proceeded to play against the Athletics. That day the legend of Ted Williams began. He collected seven total hits, including a home run; lifted his average to a stellar .4057, rounded in the record books to .406; and was the last major-leaguer to achieve the mystical .400 threshold. No one had done it in the majors since 1930, and no one has done it since. Even with all those hits over all those games, Joe hit .357 on the season, falling far short of Williams's average. Joe did lead the league in RBIs with 125, though, and his streak was duly rewarded when he won the American League MVP.

From DiMaggio's hits to Gehrig's death to Williams's .406 average, 1941 was already a distinct year for baseball milestones, but the magic was not over yet. The season would end in style with a Yankees-Dodgers subway World Series. Two months after a Yankees victory, a Japanese armada launched an attack against the United States. On December 7, 350 planes flew in the raid in two separate waves, the first leaving at 6 a.m. and the second group fifteen minutes later. Each wave reached Peal Harbor less than two hours after launch. Together they sank or damaged twenty-one ships and killed 2,335 American servicemen, and President Franklin Roosevelt declared December 7 a historic "day in infamy."[5]

Two days after the bombs fell, the game's youthful hero Bob Feller became a hero of a different sort when he rushed to enlist, becoming the first major-leaguer to do so. Feller, who pitched for the Cleveland Indians during his entire big-league career, was only twenty-three years old, yet in the previous three seasons he had already won seventy-six American League games and led the league in both wins and strikeouts each time. Even with those accomplishments and many more over his prolific career on the mound, in 2010 Feller continued to regard his military service as his greatest achievement. The war deeply affected baseball by taking more and more stars from the game—some forever—but baseball would soon have its own profound effect on the war. Sometimes the game's relationship to the war effort was direct. For instance, before the Chicago Cubs could install their new lights at Wrigley Field for the 1942 season, the military conscripted the light standards for use at the Great Lakes Naval Air Station on the shores of Lake Michigan and north of Chicago.

More significant, though, was Roosevelt's presidential edict that major-league baseball should continue during the war years. On January 15, 1942, Roosevelt sent to Commissioner Kenesaw Landis a one-page letter, now remembered as baseball's "green light letter," wherein the president proclaimed that keeping baseball going for its morale and entertainment value would be in the best interests of the country. This decision, more than any other single event in an era besieged by war and radical change, was the tipping point for baseball becoming integral to America. On the precipice of America's greatest crisis of the twentieth century, the president deemed that the country needed the diversion, the continuity, and the symbolism of baseball.

Ultimately Roosevelt was careful to leave the final decision to Landis, who then opted to play ball—albeit without black ballplayers, even though it would have been the perfect time to integrate the major leagues. The Negro leagues also had lost many players to the armed forces, and the remaining players from both leagues might have better reinforced the major-league ranks. Instead, Kenesaw Landis issued a statement—a bold-faced lie—that Negroes had never been banned from baseball during his tenure, notwithstanding that no black ballplayer had ever appeared in a big-league uniform while Landis was commissioner. Missing their own chance at history, the Chicago White Sox had taken a close look at both Jackie Robinson and Nate Moreland in March 1942 but refused to sign either one. Kenesaw Landis, after all, was still commissioner. When Branch Rickey finally signed Jackie Robinson to a minor-league stint in Montreal in October 1945, Landis had been dead for only eleven months.

Meanwhile, major-league owners met in February 1942, a month follow-ing Landis's decision to keep playing ball during wartime, and approved two All-Star Games. One was scheduled to occur in Cleveland between current big leaguers and the armed forces, which, by game day, would have inducted several major-league players. This game would feature the traditional All-Star Game's winning team, which that year happened to be the American League, against the service all-stars, and the proceeds would go to the Army-Navy Relief Fund. That contest attracted more than sixty-two thousand fans and raised $120,000, including an allocation for baseball equipment and gear for the armed forces' baseball teams. The American League won the game 5–0, and many fans at home listened to the game's Mutual Radio broadcast fea-turing announcers Bob Elson, Waite Hoyt, and Jack Graney.[6]

The owners at that time also approved more night games, although that decision soon ran aground, especially on the East Coast, where the War

Department thought that the added lights could be helpful to Nazi submarines lurking near the Atlantic shore. Under orders, the Giants and Dodgers thus canceled their remaining night games. One tradition that did gain traction, directly because of the war, was the playing or singing of the National Anthem at the start of the game. Previously, teams had done so for marquee games like Opening Day. The wave of solidarity triggered by World War II brought that patriotic tradition to every game, and it has become a custom for all major sporting events.

On May 22, 1942, Boston slugger Ted Williams was sworn into the navy, although he did not have to report for duty until after the baseball season—and quite a season it was. Williams won the American League's Triple Crown, batting .356 with thirty-six home runs and 137 RBIs. Remarkably, he again failed to win the MVP. Having lost out to DiMaggio and the streak in 1941, this time he lost to the Yankees' Joe Gordon. A second baseman, Gordon had a nice year, hitting .322 with eighteen homers, but it was hardly a Triple Crown season on the heels of a .406 year.

Although Williams would once again see military service during the Korean War and became a genuine war hero, he did not actually see combat during World War II. Moreover, he seemed reluctant to enter the armed forces in 1942, and at that time the fans saw the behavior as almost traitorous. The late Ted Williams is now largely revered, of course, and is duly remembered for his long wartime service to the country, but many confuse his Korean War heroics with his less significant contribution to World War II. But Williams's World War II effort, or lack thereof, was not entirely his own fault.

The draft board had initially classified Williams as 3-A, which amounted to a deferment because his mother was totally dependent on him for financial support. Once America officially entered the war, the board changed his status to 1-A, or draft eligible. Williams, however, appealed this new classification and won, stating that he would nonetheless enlist once he had fully funded a trust for his mother. The outraged public viewed Williams as a draft evader, an unwelcome label during World War II. The public outcry was so intense that Williams finally felt pressured to enlist in the navy.

Once in the armed forces, Williams dived in head first and opted to train as an aviator. Naval doctors discovered that Williams actually had superior 20/10 vision, which likely had contributed to his extraordinary hitting ability.[7] Once in the service, Williams was an outstanding student and even set training records for naval gunnery. He was in Hawaii awaiting his war assignment when World War II came to a close.

With many real baseball stars in the armed forces, Hollywood got into the act and partially filled the void by churning out movies about baseball and its heroes, such as the acclaimed *The Pride of the Yankees* starring Gary Cooper as Lou Gehrig. Sometimes, though, the real stars themselves returned to the game. Babe Ruth (age forty-seven) and Walter Johnson (age fifty-six) appeared before sixty-nine thousand fans jammed into Yankee Stadium and helped raise $80,000 for the Army-Navy Relief Fund. Between games during a twin bill, Johnson actually pitched to Ruth, who obliged the fans and history by slamming one into the right-field stands.

In 1943, the war modified baseball's spring training when teams were ordered to play closer to home and reduce their travel. On the big screen, the war was the topic of many Hollywood films, not the least of which was *Casablanca*. Released nationwide in January 1943, it is still acknowledged as one of the all-time great films. Before the 1943 season, Bill Veeck attempted to buy the Phillies, but the other owners blackballed his bid, and the team was sold to William Cox instead. This sale was particularly controversial, for Veeck maintained that he had told Kenesaw Landis of his intention to add black players to the Philadelphia roster, a move that would have made perfect sense, since the war had severely depleted the ranks of available players. Veeck was suggesting that Landis was a racist and was behind the restrictive efforts. Some historians, however, doubt whether Veeck had actually told Landis of his plans to hire black ballplayers.[8] Meanwhile, that same year there were race riots in Harlem and Detroit. In Detroit the rioting tore the city apart, eventually helping set the stage for societal changes on and off the baseball field.

Two days after the Phillies' sale, Phil Wrigley and Branch Rickey announced the formation of the All-American Girls Softball League with four midwestern teams. Meanwhile, the St. Louis Cardinals began advertising for players to fill the decimated ranks of their minor-league teams and the big-league club, but baseball continued to deny legions of qualified blacks the chance to play major-league ball or even to perform in the minor leagues.

On July 28, Ruth was back yet again. This time he helped raise $30,000 for the Red Cross by managing a squad of Yankee old-timers against a service team of recent major-leaguers, including Ted Williams, whose team won the game 11-5.[9] Remarkably, no big-league player had been killed in the war throughout 1942 and 1943, but their luck ran out on April 20, 1944, when Elmer John Gedeon's plane was shot down over France. Gedeon had appeared in only a handful of Senators games before the war, but he died a hero.

Only two major-league games were scheduled for June 6, 1944, but both were postponed by the D-Day invasion. An Allied armada of five thousand vessels carried more than 100,000 troops, together with heavy support equipment, to the shores of Normandy, France. On the first day 100,000 Allied soldiers successfully made it to shore, but more than 9,000 were killed or wounded that day on the blood-soaked beaches.[10] Among those who successfully landed at Normandy was the great Yankees catcher Yogi Berra. Altogether 15 million Americans served during the war, with about 500 from the ranks of big-league baseball and another 4,000 from minor-league teams.

No American had a greater direct impact on World War II than Gen. Dwight Eisenhower, who led the Normandy invasion, and it turns out that baseball had a huge impact on Eisenhower. After Ike became president of the United States in 1953, he wistfully admitted his regret that he had never made it as a big-league ballplayer. He recounted how he and a friend used to go fishing as boys back in Kansas and shared their dreams of greater things. His friend wanted to be president, while Ike wanted to be a major-league baseball player like Honus Wagner, who led the National League in batting eight times while playing for Pittsburgh. "Neither of us got our wish," Eisenhower lamented.[11]

By 1944, star pitcher Dizzy Dean was back in baseball, calling games for the often-hapless St. Louis Browns. Dean was an engaging, prolific talker, a natural for baseball broadcasting with his resonant voice, his down-home southern accent, and his many colorful stories about the game and its players. It would take an act of the War Department to silence him, and it did when it banned the reporting of any weather conditions over the air-waves to prevent the enemy from learning too much information about the homeland. One day, when the Browns experienced a long rain delay, Dean could say nothing about the weather. Finally he suggested that fans "look out the window" if they wanted to know the reason for the game's delay.[12]

On November 25, 1944, Commissioner Landis performed one of his more noteworthy acts for baseball and posterity by dying in a Chicago hospital. Although Landis repeatedly denied keeping black ballplayers out of the game, he had maintained the leagues' strict segregation during his tenure as commissioner. Landis was big on fiction: it was also during his tenure that baseball was legally deemed not a business in interstate commerce. His successor, Happy Chandler, acknowledged Landis's role in perpetuating the all-white major leagues, and Branch Rickey tested the new regime by signing Jackie Robinson without meeting any league resistance. Bill Veeck, who had not been allowed to acquire the Phillies and stock the team with Negro ballplayers, was by this time the owner of the Cleveland Indians. Veeck soon followed Rickey's lead and this time was allowed to sign and keep blacks on the Indians' roster, including the first black player in the American League, Larry Doby.

Before the beginning of the 1945 baseball season, the heirs of Col. Jacob Ruppert sold the Yankees team to a consortium of Larry MacPhail, Dan Topping, and construction magnate Delbert "Del" Webb. Ruppert had owned the Yankees from December 31, 1914, until the day of his death, January 13, 1939, for a twenty-five-year reign. Ruppert had guided the Yankees to unprecedented greatness, including one of the most influential personnel moves of any sport when he stole Babe Ruth from the Red Sox at the end of 1919.

When the Yankees' sale finally went through in 1945, the war had so depleted the ranks of the major leagues that teenagers and the disabled filled the final roster spots. Cincinnati's fifteen-year-old pitcher Joe Nuxhall had an auspicious debut on June 10, 1944, losing to the Cardinals 18–0. One-armed hitter Pete Gray fared better, however. On May 20, 1945, Gray had an all-star day for the St. Louis Browns with four hits in a doubleheader sweep of the Yankees. Gray played in seventy-seven big-league games in 1945, garnering fifty-one hits for a remarkable .218 season average.[13]

During the spring of 1945, vaudeville comedians Bud Abbott and Lou Costello took their classic "Who's on First?" routine of baseball double-talk to the big screen in a film titled *The Naughty Nineties* and left an enduring baseball contribution to American culture. Although Abbott and Costello had debuted the bit in 1936 and subsequently performed it on radio, the movie version ensured widespread exposure. The routine's uniquely American play on words at the time offered a small escape from the relentless war headlines of the day.

On two separate but equally momentous days during August 1945, American planes released atomic bombs on the Japanese mainland. The Germans had already surrendered on May 7, 1945; by August 14, when Japan acquiesced to the Americans' terms of surrender, the war was finally over. More than 70 million soldiers had been mobilized worldwide during the massive global conflict that took the lives of more than 17 million combatants and an estimated 35 million civilians, including European Jews; Russians, many of whom starved during the 900-day siege at Leningrad; Chinese; and legions of other innocent casualties of war.[14]

As America pulled itself together and dusted off the ravages of war, baseball symbolically returned to its pre-1941 form. Only ten days after the Japanese surrendered, Bob Feller returned from the navy to pitch for Cleveland. A crowd of more than forty-six thousand fans saw him strike out twelve batters in a victory over Detroit.[15] En route to the World Series in 1945, the Tigers were boosted by the return of Hank Greenberg, who belted an emphatic grand slam on September 30 against the Browns. With legions of healthy major-leaguers returning from the war, the days of the disenfranchised replacement players were limited, including the Browns' one-armed Pete Gray, who played his final game that day against Greenberg's Tigers. The thirty-year-old rookie's big-league career began and ended that season. The major leagues set an attendance record in 1945, as the game's star players came home. Hank Greenberg played in only seventy-eight games for Detroit that year, but he powered thirteen home runs and drove in sixty to help the Tigers win eighty-eight games and the American League pennant.

Whether contributing to the war effort or taking on such threshold topics as racism, labor-management disputes, antitrust, drug abuse, steroids, religion, or runaway capitalism, baseball has been at the forefront of nearly every significant American issue for more than a century. The backstory of Hank Greenberg, one of the most prolific home run hitters in all of baseball, offers a compelling example. Tall and lanky, Greenberg was physically built the same way as Ted Williams, plus he could hit for power as Williams did. But Greenberg was also the son of Jewish Romanian immigrants, rendering him decidedly different among the ranks of big leaguers, especially in those days. Nonetheless, when he was still a teenager, the Yankees, Senators, and Detroit Tigers all came calling and offered playing contracts to the promising first baseman. The Giants gave him a look, too, but in an unflattering reflection of the Giants' scouting efforts, they decided the kid had too little major-league potential. Because Greenberg could see that the Senators and Yankees already featured star first basemen, the youngster opted for Detroit.

At first young Hank stayed in school at New York University to please his father, but he left after a year and spent two years being groomed in the minor leagues. It took a year for Greenberg to blossom. After a decent but not memorable rookie season in 1933, Greenberg's batting exploded. During Greenberg's next seven seasons before the war, he would slam at least forty homers three times, lead the league in home runs three times, achieve all-star status four times, and bat over .300 with more than 100 RBIs every season (excepting an injury-shortened 1936).

In his second year Greenberg led the Tigers to the World Series, which they lost to the Cardinals. Then he did it again in 1935, and the Tigers beat the Cubs to win the title, but largely without Greenberg, who broke his wrist in Game 2. But his performance in 1935, with a league-leading thirty-six homers and a stunning 170 RBIs, had already made it clear that Greenberg was an offensive machine. In 1937 he bested his own RBI mark with 183 and almost caught the all-time RBI leader Gehrig, who had 184 in 1931.

The American League waited thirty-four years before Roger Maris surpassed Babe Ruth's milestone sixty-homer season in 1961, yet Hank Greenberg almost did it in 1938 when he garnered fifty-eight home runs with five games to go in the season. With no offense to Maris, Greenberg did so in only 150 games.[16] Greenberg's assault on long-ball history in 1938 seemed almost inevitable, but it was not to be. The reason could have been fate, Karma, fatigue, good pitching, bad luck, or even anti-Semitism.

Hank Greenberg was not the first Jewish player in baseball, but he was the first Jewish superstar. The first Jewish players in the majors debuted before 1900: Lipman "Lip" Pike (1876), Jay Pike (1877), Jake Goodman (1878), Ike Samuels (1895), Leo Fishel (1899). Several others, such as pitchers Bill Cristall (1901) and Harry Kane (1902), played in the early 1900s. By the time Greenberg debuted on September 14, 1930, thirty-six Jewish ballplayers had played at the major-league level (counting Erskine Mayer, whose father was Jewish).[17]

Among the first was Moe Berg, a catcher who debuted on June 27, 1923, and later made a significant contribution to World War II. Now largely forgotten, Berg was a highly intelligent, eccentric individual who spied for the U.S. government in the 1930s and 1940s. Berg graduated with high honors from Princeton in 1923 and was proficient in many foreign languages: Latin, Greek, French, Spanish, Italian, German, and even Sanskrit. He also graduated Columbia Law School and was good enough to play in the major leagues from 1923 to 1939. He was a journeyman big-leaguer overall, but Berg did have his strengths—a crafty intelligence and a cannon arm. In 1929 he played in 107 games for the White Sox, and batted .287 with forty-seven RBIs. Although he spent much of his career as a second- or third-string catcher, Sox pitchers Ted Lyons and Tommy Thomas preferred Berg as their catcher. Later, playing in Washington, Berg set an American League record, catching in 117 consecutive games from 1931 to 1934 without making an error.[18]

Berg took home movies of Tokyo in the 1930s during a barnstorming exhibition tour with a host of major-league stars, including Babe Ruth and Lou Gehrig, and turned the film over to the U.S. government. In 1942, the U.S. Army Air Forces used his films to plot the famous Jimmy Doolittle raid on Tokyo in retaliation for the attack on Pearl Harbor. Later Berg served as a goodwill ambassador to South America; worked as a nuclear spy in Europe; won the Medal of Freedom, which he characteristically refused; and dazzled the nation with his wit and intelligence on a radio quiz show called *Information, Please*. After that appearance, Commissioner Landis was inspired to write directly to Berg: "You did more for the image of baseball in half an hour than I have since I became commissioner." His spy work revealed Germany's progress in nuclear bomb research and influenced the Manhattan Project. After his death in 1972, his sister, Ethel Berg, claimed the Medal of Freedom on his behalf, and it is now featured in the Baseball Hall of Fame. His friends included Joe DiMaggio, Jimmy Breslin, Casey Stengel, Nelson Rockefeller, sportswriter Jerome Holtzman, Nobel Prize winner William Fowler (physics), Will Rogers, the Marx Brothers, and dozens of society women whose company he enjoyed.[19]

Moe Berg was mostly an average ballplayer, with a lifetime .243 average and six total home runs, but he enjoyed baseball and played for five major-league clubs over a span of seventeen years. Moreover, his impact on World War II was as much or greater than any other big-league player had. Not only did his home movies contribute to the Doolittle raid in the Pacific, but while in Europe Berg also worked on secret codes, translated documents, reported on missile projects and German bacteriological warfare capabilities, and arranged for Italian aeronautical engineer Antonio Ferri to escape to the United States in 1944. He even merited the attention of President Roosevelt, who said, "I see Berg is still catching well."[20]

Moe Berg had never fit in with the blue-blooded elite when he was an undergrad at Princeton, and while Berg and all the early Jews in baseball experienced various forms of anti-Semitism, no one experienced the problems Hank Greenberg faced. Only two Jewish players, superstars of the highest caliber, are in the Baseball Hall of Fame—Greenberg and the

Dodgers' great pitcher of the 1950s and 1960s, Sandy Koufax. (It would be three Jewish players, counting Lou Boudreau, who was reared a Catholic but had a Jewish mother.) But as an early superstar in the 1930s, Greenberg was a lightning rod for anti-Semitic trashing.

Already with an admirable batting average and obvious long-ball prowess, Greenberg drew still more attention to himself in 1934 during Rosh Hashanah and Yom Kippur. Greenberg himself was not particularly devout, but because his father insisted that he respect the high holy days, Greenberg did not play against the Yankees during Rosh Hashanah. The Yankees won that day, although Detroit won the pennant anyway. Greenberg, however, would remember that day when he walked into temple instead of the batter's box. He received a standing ovation, and the experience moved and humbled him.

The year 1934 saw tumultuous times in American and world history, including in the annals of baseball. The nation of Israel was still only a dream while Adolf Hitler and the Nazi machine prepared for war against the world and particularly targeted Jews and people of color, among others. It would be two more years before world-class sprinter Jesse Owens would embarrass Hitler at the 1936 Berlin Olympics, but American blacks and Jews at home were still struggling for acceptance. During a 1935 World Series game against Chicago, for instance, the Cubs' bench vocally trashed Greenberg as a "Christ killer" and "Jew bastard" and rode the slugger so viciously that the umpire gave a warning to the offending players. Longtime commissioner Landis was also horrified—he fined the umpire for interfering.[21] George "Birdie" Tebbetts, Greenberg's teammate over the years, later called Greenberg the most abused man in baseball aside from Jackie Robinson. His observation is particularly poignant since Robinson himself would sometimes refer to Greenberg as his own idol for much the same reason.

As Greenberg grew in stature at home, Hitler's power began to grip the world. As the Nazi regime gained visibility and influence, Greenberg recoiled. "I came to feel that if I, as a Jew, hit a home run, I was hitting one against Hitler," he later reflected.[22] In no small way baseball did fight the Nazis, both symbolically with home runs and literally by supplying legions of major-league heroes like Greenberg for military service. The Tigers' star was actually discharged from the service on December 5, 1941, but turned around to volunteer again when Pearl Harbor was bombed two days later. As fate would have it, Greenberg was then shipped to the Pacific and not war-torn Europe, but he was prepared to answer the call of duty regardless.

World War II had arrived on the eve of baseball's true golden age and on the heels of Ruth, Gehrig, and Murderers' Row, and people still had fresh memories of past baseball heroes: Cobb, Nap Lajoie, Wagner, Cy Young, and Walter Johnson. Baseball had so permeated America that it was inevitable the servicemen would take baseball into the war theater. The War Department concluded that as many as 75 percent of all American fighting forces played or watched baseball during the war, although some of what passed as baseball was closer to underhand softball.[23] Only circumstances of space and equipment defined the difference, so considering the constrictions of war, this distinction was immaterial. The soldiers played whatever form of baseball they could come in army bases, in supply lines, or on the front.

During a 1944 invasion of Tulagi in the Pacific theater, a spontaneous baseball game broke out amid a contingent of surrounded Marines. Battle-worn and weary soldiers found a suitable dead branch to swing, scraped together some bases, and proceeded to play, scoring runs and even arguing with impromptu umpires—all without a ball! No matter, the game must go on even in the midst of war-induced chaos.

"Without baseball, we would sink back to the dark ages," concluded one sergeant named Louis Eanes, whose plea for the support of wartime baseball was printed by *The Sporting News*.[24] Pvt. Wayne Ashworth added to that sentiment, saying, "Discontinue baseball and you remove something from our morale—something only baseball can fill."[25] Ashworth was referring not to the morale of folks at home but to that of the soldiers at the front. Even if they could not see a single big-league game, they could follow the scores, argue baseball, and hold onto the homespun glue that was baseball, and that gave stability and meaning to the fight, even in the foxholes of Europe and the Pacific.

But Private Ashworth was not entirely correct. Baseball *could* be brought to the troops, even baseball with a major-league flavor. Although the servicemen loved seeing the traveling shows from home featuring movie stars, entertainers, and pinups like actress Betty Grable, the army brass found that the soldiers responded more to the big names of baseball such as Stan Musial and Fred "Dixie" Walker.

During these times of war, instead of Commissioner Landis, many viewed the midwestern commander near Chicago, Capt. Robert Emmet, as the top man in baseball. As commander of the Great Lakes Naval Training Station, Captain Emmet oversaw 35 percent of all new navy recruits nationwide as they were funneled through the facility. Emmet was a baseball man who drew crowds of up to ten thousand sailors to watch baseball games featuring some of the greatest military teams ever to play the ball.[26] Not only did Emmet cherry-pick the best ballplayers among the hundreds of thousands of recruited seamen, he also had access to scores of actual major-leaguers in uniform, like Bob Feller and Johnny Mize. Competitive to a fault, Captain Emmet even began to recruit big-league players as ringers for his teams, almost the way today's college football and basketball coaches cull the ranks of America's high schools. Emmet scanned the major leagues for players who were likely to be drafted, contacted them, and persuaded them to enlist in the navy so they would get shipped through the Great Lakes training facility.

As a result, Great Lakes teams were among the best in the armed forces. Emmet's 1942 team featured eleven major-league players and compiled a record of 63-14. Led by Johnny Mize, the 1943 squad went 52-10-1, while the 1944 team entirely featured major-league players and posted a record of 48-2 against other service teams.

Baseball in the armed forces became so big that there was a great demand for equipment. Stateside big-league teams donated millions of dollars' worth of equipment that was shipped to servicemen around the world during the war. One of those servicemen was the great Joe DiMaggio, who found himself in the U.S. Army Air Forces—but getting there was not easy. In 1942, the season following his unparalleled hitting streak, fans booed DiMaggio because he had not yet joined the war effort. So in February 1943, he finally succumbed. Eventually playing in the Hawaiian service league in 1944, DiMaggio lit up the armed forces, hitting a .401 average over the course of ninety games, including his symbolic shot at the Honolulu stadium.

Most of America's 15 million fighting men and women were hardly as famous as Joe or Hank or the other 500 big leaguers, but each was a hero of sorts. For example, Elmer Gedeon, who was the son of major-leaguer Joe Gedeon, had enjoyed a five-game stint with the Senators in 1939, but with three total hits he never achieved stardom—until Nazi artillery destroyed his plane during a pre-Normandy bombing run. From 1935 to 1939, Elmer had been a football and baseball man at Michigan, where he also excelled in track as a two-time Big Ten champion in both the 120-yard and 70-yard high hurdles. After he was drafted, he trained as a pilot and became a captain in a European theater bomb group. Gedeon piloted a B-26 Marauder during a raid against a German buzz-bomb facility on April 20, 1944, which happened to be Hitler's birthday. Antiaircraft fire struck Gedeon's B-26, and it went down in flames over Saint-Pol, France. His body now lies at the Arlington National Cemetery.[27]

While men played baseball at American battle groups everywhere, the game also surfaced in some of the most unlikely venues, prisoner of war (POW) camps. Altogether about 130,000 American servicemen were captured during the course of World War II.[28] While playing baseball was impossible at the horrific death camps, it did spring up with remarkable regularity at most other POW camps. In the better German-run camps, for instance, dozens of teams played in organized leagues throughout the summer months. While those teams featured mostly Americans, they also included many Canadians, British, Australians, New Zealanders, some Japanese, and even a few Germans. Sometimes lacking equipment and often facing space and other limitations that mandated underhand pitching, the men played baseball, one way or another.

Back in the states, the YMCA collected ping-pong balls and paddles, baseballs, gloves, bats, and other sporting goods. It then shipped the equipment to the International Red Cross, which, for the most part, had access to the prisoners of war. One YMCA letter from 1945 suggests that the organization distributed more than 1.7 million pieces in this manner.[29] The stabler, longer-term stalags fielded many teams and saw the usual baseball arguments and complaints about umpiring, recruiting ringers for various teams, paying off better players with cigarettes and chocolates, gambling, and even the rigging of games.

Some POW camps even held the occasional "home and away" games, when teams would travel from one compound to an adjacent compound At Stalag Luft I in Germany, prisoners were allowed outside the gates to follow their teams to a neighboring stockade, but the practice came to a halt after men escaped from Stalag Luft III, made famous in the 1963 Hollywood film *The Great Escape*. The Germans worried that these games and the crowds of onlookers could offer diversions for mass escape attempts, but they did not stop the games. Rather, the Germans constructed additional fences to augment the main camp fences and allowed the baseball games to continue. Stalag Luft III housed as many as ten thousand prisoners at its peak, and apparently as many as two thousand of them were ballplayers who participated in the various organized baseball games, which included up to five games per day during the summer months. German concerns about escape were justified, for tunneling activity often occurred during the distraction offered by major games.[30]

Austria's Stalag 17B was even larger, holding up to thirty thousand prisoners, mostly from the United States, Russia, France, and Italy. The Americans eventually took over five of the camp's twelve compounds and formed baseball teams with names like the Wildcats, Bomber Aces, and Luftgangsters. Stalag IIIB in Furstenberg, Germany, actually produced an eventual major-league ballplayer, Newton "Mickey" Grasso.[31] After playing with various lesser clubs, Grasso finally caught on with an International League team in the minors, then worked his way up to a spot as a batting practice and bullpen catcher with Joe Cronin's Red Sox. With a taste of the majors and the hope of a real shot at "the show," Mickey was drafted into the U.S. Army. During the winter of early 1943, Grasso was among six thousand Allied prisoners captured by Gen. Erwin Rommel's Afrika Korps. He spent two years as a prisoner, mostly at Stalag IIIB, located about sixty miles southeast of Berlin. Before long Grasso was instrumental in developing baseball teams and leagues in the POW camp, and the sophisticated organization included minor and major leagues, American and National divisions, and even a World Series. After the war, Mickey gave professional baseball another shot and became a journeyman big-league catcher. He debuted with the New York Giants on September 18, 1946, eventually appearing in a World Series game in 1954 as a late-inning replacement for the Indians, a team that featured pitchers Bob Lemon, Early Wynn, and Bob Feller.

Also appearing in the stalag baseball leagues was a promising player named Augustine "Augie" Donatelli, who would make a big-league name for himself as one of the most high-profile, respected umpires in major-league history. Donatelli had been a B-17 tail gunner with seventeen bombing missions under his belt before being shot down over Berlin in March 1944. He umpired games at Stalag Luft VI soon thereafter and played shortstop for a POW team that made it to the Luft IV World Series during the summer of 1944.[32]

Meanwhile, many teams played baseball at POW camps in the Pacific as well and sometimes in the steamy jungles against their Japanese captors, who loved the game. POWs even played baseball along the River Kwai in Burma, where members of the famed Lost Battalion were held captive at the Kilo jungle camps. Escape was impossible, and 133 of the 500 Americans held captive at Kilo did not make it out alive. The prisoners were assigned to work on the so-called Death Railway and constructed the railroad that was depicted in the 1957 film *Bridge on the River Kwai*, although as it happens, the bridge story itself was fictional. In one of these Kilo camps the Japanese guards challenged the American prisoners to a baseball game to celebrate the emperor's birthday in 1944.[33]

After the war ended in 1945, Hank Greenberg would find himself back home and playing for Detroit in the World Series. His Tigers beat the Cubs. Less than two weeks later, the Dodgers' Branch Rickey forever altered the American and baseball landscapes by signing Jackie Robinson and sending him on October 23, 1945, to the Montreal minor-league team with the Dodgers' organization.

With one Jackie Roosevelt Robinson, baseball was about to shift its focus from overseas to a much different front-page conflict at home. While Moe Berg directly contributed to the Doolittle raid on Tokyo, and Greenberg blasted both home runs and real guns against the Nazis and their death camps, Jackie Robinson had been preparing to take on American baseball and the world in a different way. And with a middle name like Roosevelt, how much more American did Jackie have to be?

The 1945 World Series was the first peacetime fall classic since 1939. It featured slugger Hank Greenberg, who slammed a key three-run homer in Game 2, slapped three doubles in Game 5, and contributed a surprise sacrifice bunt in a crucial Game 7. That particular Series would become famous for two other reasons, both involving the Tigers' opponent, the Chicago Cubs: it would be their last World Series appearance in the twentieth century (and beyond), and it would be the source of one of baseball's more interesting mystical events, resulting in the infamous "Curse of the Billy Goat," which has allegedly kept the Cubs out of World Series play ever since.

Greek immigrant Billy Sianis owned Chicago's famed Billy Goat Tavern, a watering hole for dozens of renowned journalists that featured a goat mascot. He had purchased two tickets to Game 4 of the Tigers-Cubs Series, one for himself and one for his mascot goat. Billy himself, a valid ticketholder, was allowed to attend with owner Phil Wrigley's personal permission, but stadium personnel instructed Billy to leave the goat outside. Sianis telegrammed Wrigley to ask why, and Wrigley curtly replied, "Because the goat stinks."[34] Legend has it that Sianis then proclaimed his lasting curse, "The Cubs will never win a World Series so long as the goat is not allowed in Wrigley Field." Cursed or not, the Cubs lost that Game 4, lost the Series, and haven't been back since.

As noted earlier, football, basketball, and most other team sports do not have notable curses, but baseball is different. It is replete with curses, superstitions, and mysticism and not only in America. In Japan, for instance, one team suffers from the "Colonel Sanders curse," after an incident suggesting that baseball was more the cause than the effect. When the Hanshin

Tigers won their league championship in 1985, a disturbed crowd stole and then threw a statue of Colonel Sanders from a Kentucky Fried Chicken shop into the river. The Tigers have not won again.

Meanwhile, the Billy Goat Curse's influence did not stop at the gates of the World Series. Largely owing to the staying power of the irreverent curse and the Sianis family's flare for marketing, the Billy Goat experience was immortalized still further in 1978 when *Saturday Night Live* and its stars performed a sketch based on the tavern. Don Novello (also known on camera as Father Guido Sarducci) actually wrote the bit when he was employed as an advertising copywriter in Chicago. The bits featured Chicagoans John Belushi and Bill Murray, who is also a devout Cubs fan, and fellow cast members Dan Aykroyd and Laraine Newman. Murray and Novello would stop by the Billy Goat for years afterward, reminiscing about the "cheezborger, cheezborger, cheeps, no fries" skits.

Situated on lower Michigan Avenue between the buildings housing competitors the *Chicago Tribune* and the *Sun-Times* (the *Sun-Times* later moved down the river to accommodate the new Trump Tower), the Billy Goat made its mark on American literature and journalism as a favorite hangout of Chicago's great names in the print and electronic media. David Brooks, from the *New York Times,* wrote:

> Twenty-five years ago when I was in Chicago beginning my career, I used to go to the Billy Goat Tavern to drink like a reporter. The Billy Goat—half relic, half tourist trap—was under Michigan Avenue between The Tribune and The Sun-Times. It had laminated articles, half-forgotten bylines, and pictures of dead reporters tacked all over the walls. I could sit and imagine I was breathing the same air that had been inhaled by George Ade, Nelson Algren, Ben Hecht, Theodore Dreiser, Eugene Field and Mike Royko.[35]

Billy Goat patrons would certainly have included them all and probably also included Saul Bellow and James Farrell, both of whom were contemporaries of the Billy Goat and one of its most famous fixtures, political columnist Royko. Along the way, many local celebrities and numerous national figures stopped in for a burger or beer at the Billy Goat.

Ben Hecht, a Chicago reporter who went to New York and then Hollywood, wrote a number of top screenplays, including *The Front Page* and Alfred Hitchcock's *Notorious*. Hecht died in 1964, the same year the Billy Goat moved to Michigan Avenue from the West Side where it had stood on Madison Street near today's United Center since 1934. Reporters from the *Sun-Times* and *Chicago Tribune* frequented the Billy Goat, trading barbs and war stories over beers and burgers for decades and no doubt influencing the news, journalism, and even politics of Chicago. Baseball icon Bill Veeck was a mainstay, as were legions of sports reporters, including Tim Weigel, Bill Jauss, Bill Gleason, Ben Bentley, ESPN's Lester Munson, and many others.

"The Goat's" national influence is undisputed. Not only has it been home to prize-winning journalists, sports icons, and *Saturday Night Live* regulars, but it also has been visited by the likes of Jimmy Breslin, President George H. W. Bush, President George W. Bush, President Bill Clinton, Secretary of State Hillary Clinton, Vice President Al Gore, Jon Stewart, Harrison Ford, John Cusack, Jewel, Frank Sinatra, and dozens more. But with all that exposure, the Billy Goat's true legend is inextricably tied to baseball, without which there would be no mystique and no mystical influence on baseball, literature, journalism, and America itself.[36]

Both baseball and the nation had endured and been affected by the global holocaust of World War II. Occurring soon after the close of the war, the Billy Goat Curse's influence on baseball and the tavern's subsequent brushes with literature and pop culture are anecdotal but not atypical. More typical, ballplayers cross themselves or wear the same underwear or socks over and over or go through a litany of egocentric exercises on the mound or in the batter's box, where many a hitter has driven pitchers and fans to distraction. All in the name of superstition and mysticism, they engage in these compulsive routines to tip the balance of the fragile craft we call baseball. (The film *Bull Durham* mocks such shenanigans when the fictional pitcher Nuke LaLoosh starts wearing Annie Savoy's garter during games, inspiring the Crash Davis quip, "The rose goes in the front, big guy.")

Meanwhile, with Jackie Robinson already signed to a Dodgers contract in 1945, major-league baseball and its traditions were about to change America forever.

MANIPULATING
HISTORY

*Baseball has done more to move America in the right
direction than all the professional patriots with
their billions of cheap words.*
—MONTE IRVIN[1]

Who hit the greatest home run in the history of baseball? It could have been
Bobby Thomson's pennant winner in 1951, Mickey Mantle's tape measure
blast at Griffith Stadium, or maybe Babe Ruth's 1919 stunner that left the
Polo Grounds altogether and caught the attention of the Yankees' Jacob
Ruppert. But if we define "home run" the way it is commonly understood
in the vernacular of contemporary American language—achieving a lofty
goal or milestone, especially in dramatic fashion—the greatest baseball home
run may have been embodied in a person, Jackie Roosevelt Robinson. What
other player did more to change not only baseball but also America itself?

Abraham Lincoln may have inked the Emancipation Proclamation on
January 1, 1863, but society did not change its approach to race overnight.
America and baseball have been part of an extended sociological continuum for more than a century, a symbiotic match that is partly accidental yet
in many ways deliberate. Branch Rickey integrated the major leagues by

bringing Negro league star Robinson to the Dodgers in 1947. And while Robinson is widely celebrated for diversifying baseball, his courage in stepping up to the plate helped show Americans the possibility of achieving not only an integrated game but also an integrated nation.

Monford "Monte" Irvin was one of the first black ballplayers to follow Jackie Robinson to the big leagues, where he batted .293 over a span of eight seasons. Irvin had begun his career with the Negro leagues' Newark Eagles and eventually hit .458 for the New York Giants in the 1951 World Series.[2] On August 6, 1973, Irvin was inducted to the Hall of Fame in a class that included one of history's greatest pitchers, Warren Spahn, as well as one of the all-time great position players, Roberto Clemente.

It took more than twelve years after Robinson debuted for the Dodgers, but by July 21, 1959, when Boston inked Elijah "Pumpsie" Green, every major-league team had signed at least one black ballplayer. In 1974, exactly twenty-five years later, fully 27 percent of all baseball players were African American. Baseball would be forever changed on and off the field, and black players are still rewriting its record books, notably regarding two premier marks the game has to offer—the single season and career home run standards. One of America's remarkable ironies, however, is that by Opening Day of 2007, the number of African American players had dropped precipitously, all the way down to 8.2 percent. One profound difference between the 1940s and the 2000s is that before Robinson's era, the paucity of blacks was entirely involuntary. Still, the rapid decline of African Americans in the game, voluntary or not, is an enigma.

The major leagues will long be remembered for the blatant segregation that began in the nineteenth century during the time of White Stockings star Cap Anson's unofficial but openly stated "no Negros" rule, an exclusionary practice that extended to the post–World War II era of Robinson and even beyond. Baseball's refusal to embrace or even acknowledge the black ballplayer was a disgrace, one that reflected the racist character of American culture itself.

When the Dodgers signed Jackie Robinson, baseball took America by the tail and began to yank the whole nation in a new direction. That epiphany was more than symbolic, and the timing could not have been better. It affected the entire country and helped set the stage for the civil rights movement during the 1960s. Civil rights and baseball made significant headlines beginning in 1947 and during the 1950s with Jackie Robinson, Willie Mays, and other emerging African American stars. At the same time, in 1950, two key cases about equality in education—*Sweatt v. Painter* and *McLaurin v. Oklahoma Board of Regents of Higher Education*—reached the U.S. Supreme Court, and Thurgood Marshall, then with the National Association for the Advancement of Colored People's Legal Defense and Education Fund, represented both plaintiffs. The landmark *Brown v. Board of Education,* also a Thurgood Marshall case, was appealed to the Supreme Court on October 1, 1951, and decided in May 1954.[3] The biggest, most frequent front-page headlines of the day, however, featured Robinson, Mays, and their contemporary African American ballplayers. Maybe the fact that *Brown* was decided soon after Robinson's emergence was a mere accident of history, but that prospect seems unlikely, since it is inconceivable that the Supreme Court would not have noticed or in any way been influenced by the Robinson-led revolution.

Even though baseball had been staunchly segregated before 1947, it nonetheless managed to integrate and to make a remarkable contribution to American culture seven full years before the Supreme Court did the same for American public schools with the *Brown v. Board* case in 1954. Although the game's connections to *Brown* are indirect, baseball has a history of unique precedent in American law. No sport has had a more enduring connection to jurisprudence than baseball, a unique and often quirky bond that extends for at least two generations before Robinson and through today.

Nap Lajoie, a Hall of Fame second baseman who still holds the American League season batting record at .426, was one of baseball's early superstars. In 1902, the Supreme Court of Pennsylvania upheld an injunction that prevented Lajoie from bolting the National League to join the upstart band of competitors called the American League. Undaunted, Lajoie left for Cleveland anyway, where an Ohio court let him play, thus enhancing the new American League's credibility, changing baseball history, and creating the model for modern sports free agency.

A few years later, the 1919 Black Sox gambling scandal broke and, among other consequences, led to the appointment of an independent baseball commissioner, Kenesaw Landis, whose mandate was to rid baseball of the gambling scourge. Widely known for its impact on baseball and Landis's notorious suspensions that followed, the Black Sox episode also led to a court case that ended with a federal jury in Chicago rendering a hometown verdict and fully acquitting all the players. Although the trial had less historical impact than the suspensions did, baseball would soon flex its precedent-setting muscle. In 1922 the Supreme Court issued the most influential legal ruling in baseball history by finding that major-league baseball is not a business in interstate commerce, effectively insulating the game from federal antitrust laws. Thus began the misnamed "baseball antitrust exemption," which remains one of the most recognized rulings not only in baseball but also in all of American jurisprudence.

On July 9, 1958, Casey Stengel and Mickey Mantle appeared before a Senate committee investigating baseball's unique antitrust exemption. Stengel did not disappoint as he spewed waves of "Stengelese" baseball double-talk that was sometimes hard to follow but nonetheless simplistic in its premise and always entertaining. Stengel's lengthy but colorful soliloquy to the Senate produced some of the most remarkable testimony ever given to Congress, but it was one-upped moments later when Sen. Estes Kefauver asked Mantle if he anything to add. Mantle's reply—now widely misquoted as, "I agree with him"—was memorable for its brevity: "My views are just about the same as Casey's."[4]

In 1972, the Supreme Court reaffirmed its implausible stand on the baseball antitrust law with a written opinion authored by Justice Harry Blackmun, who was inspired to add a list of his eighty-eight favorite major-league players in the text of the ruling. A bizarre insertion in its own right, that list almost humiliated the court further, for his original roster failed to name a single black ballplayer. It was an especially egregious oversight, since the player who brought the case at hand was Curt Flood, a noted black outfielder for the St. Louis Cardinals who had been traded, unjustly he felt, to the Phillies. Flood had even raised the race issue and publicly denounced the reserve clause as a thowback to the days of slavery. According to published reports, meanwhile, Justice Thurgood Marshall, who as noted earlier had previously represented plaintiffs in several landmark civil rights cases, reportedly noticed Blackmun's omission, whereupon Blackmun amended it to include Jackie Robinson, Leroy "Satchel" Paige, and Roy Campanella.

Further, Justice Blackman pressed on. While dismissing Flood the ballplayer, if not the man, Blackman indulged himself by penning more than seven hundred astonishing words of baseball editorializing, plus still more in footnotes. He made observations on baseball's romance and early history, going all the way back to the mid-1800s: "It is a century and a quarter since the New York Nine defeated the Knickerbockers 23 to 1 on Hoboken's Elysian Fields June 19, 1846. . . ."[5]

Blackmun, though, was not the only judge to embellish a court ruling with his love of baseball. In 1975 the *University of Pennsylvania Law Review* published "The Common Law Origins of the Infield Fly Rule," an article that tracks the similarities between baseball evolution and legal precedent.[6] It has become one of the most commonly cited law review articles among modern judicial opinions. Although the 1922 antitrust exemption may have been the court decision with the greatest direct impact on baseball, sports, and ultimately America itself, the infield fly article better symbolizes the symbiotic relationship between baseball and the nation by spotlighting the similar evolution of both baseball law and American law.

Baseball's infield fly rule originated sometime in the 1890s—the precise year is subject to debate—during an era of particularly dirty play. Its purpose, then and now, is to prevent a fielder from purposefully dropping an infield pop-up to convert a single out into a double play. The rule evolved from this special need, much in the way the American common law develops as a matter of course; hence, the author of the infield fly article, William Stevens, explored "whether the same types of forces that shaped the development of the common law also generated the Infield Fly Rule." Stevens's piece inspired much more reaction than he anticipated. Subsequent articles appeared on the wisdom of its contents, with some paying tribute and others draped in sarcasm about law and law journal editors.[7]

American common law is a fluid function of necessity, a Darwinian evolution of logic and principle that developed into law as the judiciary recognized the common practices and expectations of the people. Dodger Branch Rickey aptly described the progression of the common law in his lasting observation about hardball fortuity that validates the bond between baseball and America: "Luck is the residue of design." Capitalism, politics, and law are each defined by a "make your own breaks" continuum of cause and effect that is driven by needs and solutions. So is baseball. And so, most probably, was *Brown v. Board of Education*, a post-Robinson ruling that partially caused and concurrently reflected an American cultural shift that began to tolerate racial protests while becoming more open to moves toward integration and equality.

Baseball symbolizes the moxie that drove immigrants to Plymouth Rock and Ellis Island. Baseball has always been about taking chances, with players guessing at a fastball, throwing to home over the cut-off man, or recklessly diving head first into third base in a cloud of dust. Law, life, and baseball are defined much the same way—trying, dusting off, licking wounds, and diving in again—for sooner or later "luck" will inevitably smile upon those who persevere. But what may be deemed luck in hindsight was initially called planning by those who dared to try new things, thus revealing the true formula for what we call luck: planning plus effort.

Such was precisely the dynamic that led to the publication of Stevens's infield fly article, which then gained considerable traction as judges noticed its provocative logic. Its author had attempted many times to have his own *Penn Law Review* publish it. Finally, after graduation, he talked a new regime into running the piece, but only as an aside to another article and without his byline. It may have been sheer luck that Fifth Circuit judge John R. Brown noticed the article, but the judge dug further to give the author proper credit in the court's written opinion in *Kessler v. Pennsylvania National Mutual Insurance Co.*, a ruling handed down in 1976, the year after the aside was published.[8] The judge in *Kessler,* a lawsuit over an automobile and tractor trailer collision, apparently found that the lure of baseball was too much to resist. Thus, the opinion opened with a bit of baseball sarcasm: "A multi-party, multi-claim, multi-court Donnybrook in which all have at one time or another lashed out against each for all or any part they could get, this Tinker-to-Evers-to-Chance ended when our suitors were put out by an infield fly."[9]

So not only did the *Kessler* opinion "set precedent for the *Aside* article as precedent," but it also corroborated Branch Rickey's thesis about luck as a function of design. Had Stevens not persevered, Judge Brown could not have discovered the article, let alone embraced it in the text of his ruling.

Stevens's infield fly piece went on to become one of the most widely recognized and quoted law review articles of all time. When Stevens passed away in 2008, the *New York Times* ran an insightful tribute that summarized the influence of Stevens and his essay article on American law, and therefore baseball itself, including this excerpt:

> Published as a semi-parodic "aside" in June 1975, "The Common Law Origins of the Infield Fly Rule" quickly achieved legal fame, in part because nothing like it had ever appeared in a major law review, in part because of its concise, elegant reasoning. It continues to be cited by courts and legal commentators. It is taught in law schools. It is credited with giving birth to the law and baseball movement, a thriving branch of legal studies devoted to the law and its social context. It made lawyers think about the law in a different way.[10]

Taking Rickey's point a step further, law is always the residue of experience, and in some cases it is also the residue of truth. No sport impacts American language as baseball has, and no baseball figure has influenced that vernacular as Stengel did. Although oddly confusing at times, the beauty of Stengelese is its simple devotion to truth, as in, "You gotta have a catcher or you'll have a lot of passed balls."[11]

Sooner or later all baseball discussion gets around to luck, if not luck's cousin in the law of unintended consequences. Baseball maintains such a fragile balance among success, failure, and luck that superstition became a part of the game almost from its inception. Its players still have the quirkiest habits and most annoying fidgets in all of sport. Some batters readjust their gloves after every pitch, others cross themselves in a religious devotion to God and hardball, and some wag their bats to complete distraction while many others spit, shuffle around the mound, or compulsively step in and out of the batter's box. Baseball players, moreover, are widely noted for refusing to change socks during a hitting streak, for oiling or boning their bats, for kissing a necklace or other charm, or even for patting a hunchback batboy and mascot as the pennant-winning White Sox did in 1919.

Many players seriously thought Eddie Bennett, the hunchback mascot for the Sox, had a meaningful role in the team's success. The White Sox won the pennant in 1919, but when the World Series' gambling scandal broke, their batboy lost his charm and was dumped. Bennett went back home to New York and spent a short time with the Dodgers in his native Flatbush neighborhood, and the Dodgers won the pennant in 1920. The Yankees then grabbed Bennett for their own magical spell and proceeded to win six pennants and three World Series titles from 1921 to 1932. History would argue that Ruth and Gehrig had more to do with that streak than Bennett did, but the Yankees still took Bennett, who developed a personal friendship with Ruth, to hedge their bet.

Branch Rickey, as noted earlier, was not a proponent of magic, spells, or hunchbacks. His own take on luck as "the residue of design" relied more on effort and planning than kismet. Stengel's own succinct take on luck echoes that of Rickey: "You make your own luck." If anyone believed in making his own breaks, it was Bill Veeck, one of the premier showmen of the game. He had little money as baseball moguls go, but he still managed to own three big-league clubs at various times: the Browns, the Indians, and the White Sox. But his most famous contribution to the luck-as-residue-of-design theory was undoubtedly Eddie Gaedel, Veeck's dwarf batter who walked on four pitches during one fateful plate appearance on August 19, 1951. Gaedel is listed at a mere three feet and seven inches tall, which meant his strike zone from the knees to the chest was extremely small. Some estimate that when he crouched, the strike zone was only a few inches, presenting an almost impossible target for pitchers. With Gaedel in the batter's box, had Veeck gone too far in making his own breaks for those hapless St. Louis Browns? Would a team of little people disrupt the game and evoke a "dwarf batter" rule for the same reason the infield fly was needed? Diminutive batters or not, baseball is *largely* a game of deception and trickery, so what about curveballs, spitballs, greaseballs, and boned or even corked bats? Some of those machinations are legal, some barely legal, and some prohibited altogether, but they all share the common purpose of achieving an edge by manipulating luck.

In truth, was "getting an edge" a complicit motive behind the baseball's antitrust exemption in 1922? Did the game manipulate that result, and if so, did baseball go too far? Did the courts? Veeck's take on the Supreme Court antitrust ruling, conveyed during the 1972 Flood case, aptly states the issue: "When the Supreme Court says baseball isn't run like a business, everybody jumps up and down with joy. When I say the same thing, everybody throws pointy objects at me."[12]

Veeck's observation may sound whimsical, but in a meaningful way, such paradoxes are precisely the point about baseball. The game has a no-holds-barred approach to winning—and to history. The much-ballyhooed Robinson experiment, for example, did not occur in a vacuum. Jack Johnson won the heavyweight title in 1908, asserting the credibility of the black athlete. Johnson gained great notoriety as the champion at a time when boxing was king. He was often a front-page story in the mainstream press, and his fame was a source of much pride in the African American community. Johnson's wealth allowed him to have a car, girlfriends, and even some legal troubles when the white establishment found it hard to accept his accomplishments and notoriety. His high-profile reign became divisive, even to the point of inspiring that still famous search for the "great white hope." Johnson became one of the first people prosecuted under the federal Mann Act, which was passed in 1910 to proscribe the transportation of minors across state lines for sexual purposes. Presiding was Judge Kenesaw Landis, who later became commissioner of baseball and was known, among other things, for keeping baseball segregated. The Johnson prosecution is now widely regarded as having been a racist legal maneuver. Then came Jesse Owens, the world's fastest man, who proved his prowess at the 1936 Berlin Olympics and took four gold medals, showing up Hitler's disgruntled "Master Race." Owens's popularity benefitted from the passage of time after Johnson's headline days, and it helped that Jesse had taken on the Nazis, who in time would become widely hated. A hero on and off the track, Owens was an inspiration to millions, including Jackie Robinson. And in the ring again, the likable Joe "Brown Bomber" Louis held the heavyweight boxing crown from 1937 until his retirement in 1949, a span longer than any other heavyweight champion enjoyed before or since.

When Owens and Louis made history, they also made Rickey's job easier. For one, he was spared the effort of proving the worth of black athletes in general. But Rickey and the Dodgers still took a big chance when they selected Robinson as the first player to be responsible for showing that a black man could both *become* a big-league baseball player and be *accepted* as one. Robinson was not the only player the Dodgers had considered. Rickey had worked out two other black ballplayers as early as April 1945, but he rejected the other candidates when they did not demonstrate the requisite skills.

Signing Robinson was one thing, but could he succeed? Could he handle the pressure of playing the game and carrying a torch for racial justice? Those questions were answered as the fateful 1947 season unfolded. Robinson's visibility and success gave hope and renewed pride to millions of black Americans. When Robinson debuted at Ebbets Field, more than half the fans in attendance were black.

The 1947 campaign proved a tough year for Jackie, though. Everywhere the team played, Robinson had to break new ground, shake old stereotypes, and display great poise during a season of relentless verbal abuse. Robinson was "the loneliest man I have ever seen in sports," observed New York columnist Jimmy Cannon.[13] When that first year was all over, Jackie had managed a .297 season at the plate, led the league in stolen bases, and was named National League Rookie of the Year. His dignity and work ethic ensured his rightful place in the national spotlight, where he caught the attention of many—no doubt including the Supreme Court justices and certainly at least one president, Dwight Eisenhower, who was a staunch baseball fan.

Over the ensuing years, Bill Veeck brought Larry Doby to Cleveland, followed by an aging Satchel Paige and many other black ballplayers. Soon the floodgates opened, and black players flourished. Even that success, however, did not mean racism was dead; indeed, it still exists today. But Robinson, Doby, and the other African American ballplayers together bravely contributed to a process that is still ongoing.

During the seven years leading to the 1954 *Brown v. Board of Education* landmark ruling, black ballplayers continued to make headlines. Don Newcombe was named Rookie of the Year, Campanella was National League MVP three times, Mays exploded as the 1951 Rookie of the Year, Saturnino "Minnie" Minoso led the American League in stolen bases, and Doby topped the American League in home runs. Of course, Jackie Robinson, who had started it all, continued to star for the Dodgers.

In 1948, only one year after the Robinson breakthrough, President Eisenhower issued an order formally desegregating the U.S. armed forces that was probably not a mere coincidence. Forces of racial change were at work in America, but none was more dramatic than Robinson's headline news. Certainly many African Americans had fought during World War II, but Eisenhower took the necessary step of clearing up the official military records on segregation at an opportune time. As a devoted baseball fan who sometimes lamented his own failure to become a big-league ballplayer, Eisenhower would have observed, and could have been influenced by, Jackie's successes both on and off the field.

President Eisenhower was from Kansas; Robinson was discovered playing Negro league ball for the Kansas City Monarchs, where he hit .387 in 1945; and an eight-year-old girl who was forced to travel several miles to school in Topeka, Kansas, rather than attend a neighborhood school only blocks away, solely on the basis of her skin color, helped trigger the *Brown v. Board* case. All these connections to Kansas may have been coincidental, but given the Karma of baseball, one could forgive posterity for finding a deeper connection.

Whether by fate, spells, or simply progressive thinking, the confluence of Robinson's milestone year followed by Eisenhower's order for military desegregation and the *Brown v. Board* breakthrough in 1954 together ushered in a watershed breakthrough for the equal acceptance of black citizens. Black players were front-page news every year from Robinson to *Brown*. The stories showed America their home runs, class, and character, pulling the country closer when racial strife off the field would yank it in the opposite direction of hate, fear, and disgrace.

When writing the opinion for *Brown*, the court had little choice but to notice Robinson and those who had followed. Although the written opinion was extensive, the essence of the *Brown* ruling was profoundly simple, as evidenced by one succinct, powerful sentence: "The separate but equal doctrine of *Plessy v. Ferguson* has no place in the field of public education."[14] But the driving force behind that ruling is subtler, as Chief Justice Earl Warren hinted in the text of the findings back in 1954. "Today . . . many Negroes have achieved outstanding success in the arts and sciences as well as in the business and professional world," observed Warren, who then built the crux of the decision upon that premise.[15]

The court did not specifically mention baseball because it was making a case for education and not sports. Yet by 1954, *nowhere* was the success of the black man more visibly demonstrated than on the ball diamond, or in the ring with Joe Louis, and certainly more so than in business. Indeed, the court could not help but think of the success blacks were achieving in sports and particularly in baseball, since by then Robinson's achievements were almost daily news. Moreover, Robinson had already been an accomplished student-athlete at the University of California–Los Angeles (UCLA), where he became the university's only athlete ever to letter in four sports: football, basketball, baseball, and track and field. With his success in college, Robinson's example extended to education, making it easier for many in a predominantly white America to accept that black students should be afforded the same opportunity as white children everywhere, especially in the public schools. Indeed, the Supreme Court noted, "We cannot turn the clock back to . . . 1896 when *Plessy v. Ferguson* was written. We must consider public education in the light of its full development and its present place in American life throughout the Nation."[16]

In 1955, only a year after *Brown*, Rosa Parks refused to yield her seat to the white patrons of a Montgomery, Alabama, bus. Eleven years earlier, Robinson himself had been arrested for not moving to the back of a bus while serving in the U.S. Army. Baseball, meanwhile, had set the national standard for "separate but equal" by relegating black ballplayers to the Negro leagues. Then Jackie and the other black pioneers of major-league ball, including the great Willie Mays, earned some of the biggest baseball headlines of the early 1950s. Given the Supreme Court's long relationship with baseball, when the court noted in its 1954 decision that blacks had "achieved outstanding success" in a multitude of endeavors, it must have partly meant the national example that was unfolding on both the baseball diamond and in the news.

When the Supreme Court had upheld the "separate but equal doctrine" with *Plessy v. Ferguson* in 1896, it echoed the established precedent for the rest of America, including big-league ball. Although now largely a footnote to history, the first African American major-leaguer was not technically Jackie Robinson. As noted in chapter 3, that distinction likely belongs to Moses Fleetwood Walker, an outstanding catcher who debuted on May 1, 1884, but was soon released because, among other things, white pitchers were reluctant to work with a black catcher or follow his pitching signs. That reaction was hardly surprising, since only the year before, the White Stockings' Cap Anson had rudely demanded that Walker get "off the field."

Then in 1949, more than fifty years after Anson's antics, the state of Kansas enacted General Statute 72-1724, which permitted Kansas cities with populations greater than fifteen thousand to maintain separate but equal school facilities for Negro and white students. The state passed the law during the height of Jackie Roosevelt Robinson's national fame. As with the *Plessy* court's following society's attitude about integration, which was punctuated by Anson's proclamation, the *Brown* court took judicial notice of Branch Rickey's counterargument that enabled Jackie Robinson to pioneer his own statements on the field.

Baseball's personality is uniquely American. The game emulates the rough-and-tumble approach to business and life when it features irregular fields of play, embraces the trickery of curveballs and spitballs, and takes great chances in full view of world opinion. The game is sometimes its own worst enemy, however, as when it fostered overt segregation and then had the audacity to lie about it. Kenesaw Landis, baseball's most powerful commissioner and apparently its lead racist for more than two decades until his death in 1944, consistently and brazenly denied the obvious segregation of baseball. As seen previously, Landis repeatedly insisted that black players were not banned from major-league ball, and two years before his death, he boldly proclaimed, "There is no rule, formal or informal, or any understanding—unwritten, subterranean, or sub-anything—against the hiring of Negro players by the teams of organized baseball."[17] Undaunted by his own incredulity, the commissioner punctuated his incongruous position with one final untruth: "Negroes are not barred from organized baseball . . . and never have been in the 21 years I have served."[18]

On March 18, 1942, five full years before his official debut, Jackie Robinson tried out for the big-league Chicago White Sox. The Sox made no offer and missed a golden chance for team immortality, though signing Robinson would certainly have provoked the wrath, and likely rejection, of the commissioner. Months after Landis's death in 1944, Robinson auditioned for the Red Sox, but the team likewise made no offer. With Landis out of the way, Branch Rickey and others were free to consider the possibility of hiring black ballplayers. He had already scouted two Negro players—Terris McDuffie and Dave "Showboat" Thomas—but signed neither and kept looking. On August 13, 1945, Rickey, Walter O'Malley, and John L. Smith bought controlling interest in the Dodgers. Meanwhile, Dodger scout Clyde Sukeforth observed Robinson playing for the Kansas City Monarchs of the Negro leagues, and on August 28, two weeks after buying into the Dodgers, Rickey found himself offering Robinson the chance of a lifetime. They signed a minor-league deal on October 23,

1945. The death of baseball segregation began a year after the death of Landis himself.

Robinson may have suddenly appeared in the big leagues, but he had not entirely emerged from nowhere. The first four-letter athlete in UCLA's history, as a junior Jackie averaged a stunning twelve yards per carry on the football field, and in basketball he led the Pacific Coast Conference in scoring for two straight years.[19] Unfortunately, discrimination was no stranger to Robinson even at college; he was left off the all-conference first, second, and third teams in basketball. Emulating Jesse Owens in track, Robinson also won the National Collegiate Athletic Association long jump in 1940 and was an Olympics favorite until World War II caused the cancellation of the games that year. Robinson was also a star swimmer and tennis player besides playing more than a little baseball.

At age twenty-eight, Jackie's maturity was a factor in his big-league success, for along with his string of honors, including the National League Rookie of the Year in 1947 and the MVP in 1949, he endured great hostility. After Robinson, the doors of baseball opportunity opened for Mays, Hank Aaron, Clemente, and the rest. Baseball continues to further integrate and today has become an international sport that embraces not only whites and blacks but also Hispanic, Asian, Venezuelan, Dominican, Puerto Rican, Cuban, and Jewish ballplayers. The game now reflects the melting pot image of America by showcasing minorities and honoring the great Robinson experiment with its continuing example of racial and ethnic equality. The players recognize their debt to Robinson. Willie Mays himself may have said it best: "Every time I look at my pocketbook, I see Jackie Robinson."[20] More recently, Robinson's number 42 was retired from all of Major League Baseball on April 15, 1997, helping to preserve Jackie's lasting legacy.

Players did hit many great home runs before Jackie Robinson did, and many more have done so since. But the literal and figurative complexion of those home runs changed on April 18, 1947, when Robinson, in a Dodgers uniform, became the first black player in the modern major-league era to smack a home run.

Robinson was not an overpowering home run hitter, but he had great speed and was particularly adept at stealing bases. He led the league with twenty-nine stolen bases in his rookie year and stole thirty-seven in 1949, not only leading the league but also logging the highest total in nineteen years. In 1954, the very year of the *Brown v. Board* decision, Jackie Robinson become the first National League player in twenty-six years to steal his way around all the bases.[21]

The relationship among Robinson, *Brown v. Board*, and the progression of equality both on and off the field may now seem obvious. No one connected the dots of history better, however, than California congressman Adam B. Schiff did in his February 2004 congressional address commemorating the fiftieth anniversary of the *Brown* decision: "On April 15, 1947, Jackie Robinson would take the field to play for the Brooklyn Dodgers—a pioneer as the first African American to play major-league baseball. Not only did Robinson open the door to pro sports for other African American athletes, but his remarkable accomplishment also would help chip away at prejudices in the minds of Americans and jumpstart the process of dismantling existing barriers throughout our society."[22]

Robinson had truly "knocked one out of the park." Sixty years after his debut, on August 7, 2007, Barry Bonds—an African American with an outstanding baseball pedigree thanks to his major-league father, Bobby Bonds, and his godfather, Willie Mays—stepped to the plate and launched lifetime home run ball number 756 over the wall and into a firestorm of history. But without Robinson, Bonds's achievement would not have been possible.

The last time the career home run mark had been eclipsed was on April 8, 1974, when Henry Aaron slugged number 715 to left-center field in Atlanta before an anxious crowd of 53,775. As noted earlier, that year fully 27 percent of all major-leaguers were African American, but their participation declined steadily. In 1995 they were reduced to 19 percent of all major-leaguers, then 10.8 percent in 2003, and the 2007 low of 8.2 percent.[23] As recently as June 1958, two big-league teams—the Tigers and the Red Sox—did not have any black ballplayers, and by the start of 2007, the majors had come full circle, as Atlanta and Houston were lacking African American players.

The speed, grace, and romantic lure of basketball and football have played a major part in this decline. African American players are in the majority in both sports, and they dominate professional basketball. Fewer little leagues and other organized baseball programs operate in the inner cities, but there are limitless basketball hoops, especially in the post–Michael Jordan era.

According to census figures in 2010, African Americans comprise about 12.6 percent of the U.S. population,[24] yet around 65 percent of NFL players and up to about 75–80 percent of NBA players are black.[25] The NBA is changing and experiencing an influx of white European, Russian, and Chinese players. Soon, it may become as international a game as baseball is today.

Still, population statistics can be misleading. In the 1930s boxing was largely a "white" sport, and Jewish players reigned in basketball. Nat Holman, the star of the original New York Celtics, was Jewish, and Jewish players dominated college teams such as the St. John's teams of the 1920s. Even the founder of the Harlem Globetrotters, Abe Saperstein, was a Jewish kid from Chicago who played basketball at the University of Illinois. The early history of basketball reflects a threefold phenomenon: basketball was always suited for inner-city play and for those players from the inner city who decades ago were often Jewish, especially in and around New York City. At the time, blacks were excluded from many walks of life, including pro and major college sports. Finally, not many blacks attended college in those days; therefore, they were certainly not found in large numbers on college basketball teams except for at the all-black colleges. North Carolina College's innovative coach, John McLendon, was emphasizing fast-break basketball as early as 1944.

Today African Americans are not being pushed from baseball because of a lack of ability or talent. Instead, some are opting to play other sports while others are being partially culled by a baseball draft and minor-league system that embraces foreign players. A wealth of international baseball talent comes from Japan, which took an interest in the game in the 1930s, and from Korea, as well as Latin America.

Of all the sports Jackie Robinson played at UCLA, baseball is generally regarded as his weakest. With Robinson's speed, strength, and demonstrated leaping ability, had he come through the athletic ranks today, he might have opted for football over baseball, especially given the promise he showed on the college gridiron as a running back and punt returner. But in Robinson's college days, young black Americans looked up to top track athletes like Jesse Owens, boxing champions like Joe Louis, and the likes of James "Cool Papa" Bell, Satchel Paige, and Josh Gibson in the Negro leagues.

Today's NBA and NFL offer glamour and money and attract many black superstars like LeBron James and Kobe Bryant. Major-league baseball can provide similar rewards, but could baseball itself be partly to blame for the declining participation of black ballplayers? Jackie Robinson never lived to see a black manager in the major leagues, and at the start of 2007 only two African Americans were at the helm in baseball. In 1974 when Aaron bested Ruth's all-time home run mark, then commissioner Bowie Kuhn was noticeably absent. When Major League Baseball proclaimed April 15, 2007, as Jackie Robinson Day and had one player from each team wear Jackie's league-wide retired number 42, many still accused baseball of racism over white America's cool response to Bonds, who had a surly personality and faced persistent accusations of steroid use. Then, when Bonds was about to break Aaron's mark, Commissioner Bud Selig struggled with whether to attend the game. He did not want to condone Bonds's reputed use of steroids, yet his absence would look all too reminiscent of Kuhn's apparent 1974 boycott of Aaron. Selig, in fact, missed Bonds's breaking the record with home run number 756 in San Francisco on August 7, 2007; however, the commissioner had been in San Diego for the record-tying number 755 days before.

With its embrace of many foreign players, meanwhile, major-league baseball is becoming a genuine rainbow league. But it cannot afford to lose its most poignant color component of that rainbow, the one whose acceptance the courageous Jackie Robinson pioneered. The man remains a genuine hero to many.

When asked about his own sports hero, Robinson could have said Jesse Owens, Joe Louis, or maybe Satchel Paige; instead, he named Hank Greenberg, the mild-mannered Detroit slugger who had endured seasons of anti-Semitism during the 1930s and 1940s. Greenberg's final year in the majors, 1947, was Robinson's first. That year Greenberg played for Pittsburgh in the National League, and he met Robinson for the first time when they collided at first base in a game on May 17, 1947. Among Robinson's numerous attributes of ability, courage, and character, apparently he was color blind, too. That lack of prejudice places him a different class altogether. He joins such men as Martin Luther King, Jr.; big-league icon Branch Rickey; and that colorful baseball champion of the downtrodden, William Veeck, Jr., who once called baseball "an island of surety in a changing world."[26]

★ **10** ★

THE MISSILES
OF CAMELOT

I've found that you don't need to wear a necktie if you can hit.
—TED WILLIAMS[1]

Two missiles ushered in the 1960s. One launched astronaut Alan Shepard as the first American in space on May 5, 1961, and another clanked into the right-field stands at Yankee Stadium on October 1, 1961. Both came after great national anticipation, both made headlines, and both left indelible marks on American history.

The baseballs that the Yankee M&M boys Roger Maris and Mickey Mantle launched in bunches in 1961 represented a new era of headlines and home runs, but they also defined a resurgence of American swagger. The United States was about to test the limits of change with a new form of rock music, a misplaced brand of war, and a dramatic expression of free speech and social protest that harkened back to the American Revolution with its grassroots intensity. The 1950s milestones of Jackie Robinson and *Brown v. Board* were also revolutionary, but the intensity of the civil unrest and populist rage in the 1960s was unlike anything the country had experienced since the Civil War. Among the first to shake the foundations was a sullen kid with a big swing, Roger Maris.

The 1961 season arrived as the new, charismatic president, John F. Kennedy (JFK), settled into the White House. JFK had vowed to win the space race by landing a man on the moon and bringing him home before the end of the decade, all ahead of the Russians—a goal inspired by the daunting success of Russia's Sputnik satellite in 1957. The 1950s had been a successful postwar decade, but they also had been a relatively complacent transitional period after the war-torn years preceding them. Then the colorful, tumultuous, and anarchistic 1960s arrived, bringing the Beatles; Woodstock; Vietnam; the assassinations of JFK, Martin Luther King, Jr., and Robert "Bobby" Kennedy; and a new form of edgy social comedy from Lenny Bruce, George Carlin, and Richard Pryor. Our sentimental national metaphor, the New York Yankees, would also undergo a temporary but symbolic fall from grace. While the Russians may have motivated Americans by successfully launching the Sputnik satellite, an impressive and unnerving feat, Roger Maris grated America's soul by tarnishing three baseball icons all in one swing: Babe Ruth, Mantle, and the mystical sixty-homer season.

Baseball in the 1950s was still the all-American game and sported such household names as Willie Mays, Larry Doby, Duke Snider, Stan Musial, and Don Newcombe. Fans saw plenty of home runs as a personable young Hank Aaron gained traction, while the irascible veteran Ted Williams made his marks, some as a soldier in Korea and the rest on the baseball field. Almost on cue, the pre-1960s baseball era was punctuated by the final home run from none other than Williams himself, one of the greatest of the old-school sluggers. On September 28, 1960, Ted Williams slammed home run number 521, then walked off the field and into posterity. It was a powerful moment for Williams, baseball, and America. He was not the only major-leaguer to club a homer in his final at-bat—seventeen players had done it before him—and two years later, almost to the day, Don Gile did it again for Williams's team, the Boston Red Sox.[2] Gile's effort, though, was anything but historic, for it was only the third home run of his entire career. Of all the players on the list (forty-five men at the end of the 2012 season), Ted Williams was by far the most prolific, high profile, and relevant. He blasted through the revered 500-homer plateau at a time when the 500 club was special and elusive. Williams's achievement was all the more remarkable, since he had also fought in two wars that shortened his baseball career by almost five full seasons.

Most of those final at-bat homers came from a variety of unknowns, but genuine stars launched several. Albert Belle homered in his last plate appearance on October 1, 2000, retiring with the second-most career long balls in the final at-bat club, but his 381 dingers were well behind Williams's total. Of the players on the list of final at-bat homers, thirteen men hit their *first and only* career home run in that last appearance, thus giving them two places of distinction. Other hitters of distinction on the final at-bat homer list include the great Mickey Cochrane (119 career home runs), for whom Mickey Mantle was named; the steady Yankee-turned-announcer Tony Kubek (57); Joe Rudi (179); Ray Lankford (238); and Todd Zeile (253).[3]

But given his irascible personality, the venerable history of the Red Sox, and the sheer magnitude of his hitting prowess, Williams's shot was both dramatic and poignant, adding still further to his legend and anointing him as one of the most memorable hitters in baseball history. His aura stirred great debate for decades while fans argued whether the aging Williams or Joe DiMaggio was "the greatest *living* career hitter." Both had big egos, too; each regarded himself as the greatest. History would probably side with Williams, but it is hard to overlook DiMaggio's famous fifty-six-game hitting streak, the record that baseball pundits believe might never be broken. Then again, Williams, having batted .406, was the last batter to break the .400 barrier. Hence, the debate continues even though the game and America lost both players years ago.

One feat Williams did not accomplish was hitting a homer in his *first* big-league appearance. Through the 2012 season 113 players had done so, although most of their names have been lost to the dusty annals of baseball trivia. One of the more familiar names, however, was not a hitter at all but pitcher Hoyt Wilhelm, an eventual Hall of Famer whose effort earned him a dual distinction since that first home run was also his last. Wilhelm played twenty-one years without launching another. Twenty-eight players (through

2012) actually homered on the first *pitch* they ever faced in the majors. But of the 113 who had homered in their first appearances, only two managed the exclusive distinction of slamming one in their second trip to the plate as well—Keith McDonald (July 4, 2000) and Bob Nieman (September 14, 1951).[4]

One member of the first at-bat homer club, pitcher Dave Eiland, had given up a home run to the first batter he ever faced in 1988. He became the only player to do both when he hit a home run in his first plate appearance in 1992. A total of sixty-five pitchers managed to give up homers to the first batter they ever faced, including a handful of recognizable names like Bert Blyleven, Jeff Suppan, Ken Holtzman, Dickie Noles, and the Cardinals' power pitcher and Hall of Famer Bob Gibson.[5] Fastballer Gibson yielded a number of homers over the years, but most opposing hitters failed to get enough wood on the ball to matter.

Ted Williams left the game as a legendary power hitter, but he also had compiled a .344 lifetime average and tied for fifth all time among those with at least 5,000 career at-bats. Moreover, Williams was only .002 away from third place on the lifetime list, plus he had the most home runs of anyone in the top seven and second most in the top thirty behind only Babe Ruth (714). Barry Bonds, the lifetime home run leader with 762 (saddled with an implied asterisk due to the steroid era), did not even make the list of top hundred career batting averages with his mark of .298. Coincidentally, on the career average list, Bonds's name is tied with another great player who failed to make the top hundred in hitting but who was arguably better than both Bonds and Williams and who made a landmark impact on the game, if not on America itself: Mickey Mantle.[6]

Playing during the same era as Ted Williams, Mantle hit more home runs (536) than Williams, yet Williams's lifetime average was much higher than either Mantle or Bonds achieved. Moreover, while Bonds had a higher on-base average plus slugging percentage (OPS) ranking than Mantle's (fourth place versus twelfth), the second-place Williams was better than both of them and behind only Ruth. Although all batters still pale next to Ty Cobb's top lifetime batting average of .366, Cobb only hit 117 career homers during a dead-ball era that virtually shunned the long ball. Further, Mantle's 536 total is still well behind Bonds's and is only sixteenth on the all-time homer list (before the 2012 season).[7]

Ranking only sixteenth on the career home run list and not ranking at all among the top 100 career batting averages, was Mickey Mantle really so special? His charisma, his impish behavior, the boy-like gleam in his eye, and his twelve different World Series appearances are a big part of Mantle's magic, but a closer look at number 7's statistics reveals even more. Mickey Mantle was a switch hitter who mastered both sides of the plate and drove opposing pitchers and managers to distraction. Among major-league baseball's switch hitters, Mantle remains the statistical leader in four major categories (or five if counting strikeouts). His OPS was highest at .977, his on-base percentage the best at .421, he had the most walks with 1,733 (seventh on the overall list of all batters), and, of course, Mantle led the switch hitter group with a stunning 536 regular season home runs.[8]

But most of all, a majority of Mantle's seasons did not end in September. He played in sixty-five World Series games, a staggering number of nearly a half season (especially when the regular seasons ended at the 154-game mark). During those championship games Mantle established ten World Series records. Among them he came to bat 230 times, had eighteen home runs, forty RBIs, forty-two runs scored, and walked forty-three times for 123 total bases.[9] Mickey Mantle was an all-star in sixteen of his eighteen seasons and was MVP three times during a career that included seven World Series titles—the latter being a meaningful total given Mantle's own historic 7 uniform, a number virtually identified with Mickey in the same way number 23 signifies Michael Jordan to basketball fans.[10] (Few but the most devoted fans today can peg the uniform numbers of Babe Ruth or DiMaggio or Mays or Barry Bonds, but many still connect number 7 with Mantle, especially in New York.) Even Mantle's batting average is understated by his career hitting at .298. Ultimately he was a victim of his own tenacity, coming to bat 875 times during his final two years, his seventeenth and eighteenth seasons, when he brought his overall average down significantly by hitting .245 and .237, respectively.[11]

"The best prospect I've ever seen," said Branch Rickey of Mantle in 1951. Mantle's own manager, Casey Stengel, strengthened that sentiment: "That kid can hit balls over buildings."[12] Mantle ranks fifth best among the all-time great center fielders and still owns one of the best baseball seasons any player has ever logged, the only season perhaps that truly rivals Babe Ruth's magical 1927 campaign.[13] In baseball annals four seasons are defined simply by the years themselves without further explanation: 1927, 1947, 1961, and Mantle's singular 1956. Mantle was only twenty-four years old at the time, but his 1956 season was a year to end all baseball years. Not only did he win the elusive Triple Crown that season by hitting .353, slamming fifty-two homers, and knocking in 130 runs, but he also led the league by scoring 132 runs. Moreover, he compiled a league best .705 slugging average, becoming only the ninth player to top the .700 mark in all of baseball history.[14]

Mantle was seventeen years old when the Yankees first signed the promising slugger in 1949. When he joined the big club in 1951, Mantle showed a unique propensity for power and speed, as well as grace. The fair-haired country kid from Oklahoma was touted as the next great Yankee outfielder, destined to replace the aging Joe DiMaggio. Mantle did not disappoint and indeed showed promise during that first season with 341 at-bats, thirteen homers, and a respectable sixty-five RBIs, but his blazing outfield speed, ironically, would soon become his Achilles' heel.

Mickey Mantle could cover a wide swath in the outfield while tracking down fly balls and cutting off liners to the gap, but his talent would contribute to one of his greatest weakness, a bad right knee that would hamper his speed and interfere with his home run power. As noted previously, in his first year in the majors, Mantle played in the 1951 World Series against the Giants. While intercepting a drive from the great Willie Mays, Mantle abruptly pulled up to avoid crashing into DiMaggio and tore up his right knee.[15] Mantle would never be quite the same. He may have ended his 1951 season on a stretcher, but the hobbled Mantle who showed up for seventeen more seasons was still faster than most players and certainly better than almost anyone who ever donned a big-league jersey.

The next year Mantle was back and DiMaggio was gone, so Mickey took over in center field. He batted a star-caliber .311, hit twenty-three homers, and drove in eighty-seven runs, while his speed helped him to score ninety-four runs that year. His numbers were good enough to earn an all-star berth, the first of his fourteen straight all-star seasons. But Mantle continued to improve for several seasons during his prime years, scoring a league-best 129 runs in 1954 and leading the league in home runs with thirty-seven in 1955. Then came 1956, the first of Mantle's three MVP seasons. The second was back-to-back in 1957 when he hit a stunning .365 and propelled the Yankees into the World Series for the sixth time in his first seven Yankee seasons. Yet when Mantle's numbers eased a bit in 1958 and 1959, the New York fans proved fickle and even booed Mick, especially when the foundering team was headed for third place during the 1959 campaign.[16] Mantle was still an all-star in 1959 when he logged 541 plate appearances and 31 home runs, but he only batted in 75 runs while hitting a nice but decidedly mortal .285.

With a third-place finish, the Yankees began looking for more offense. They found it in Kansas City, trading away five players for another promising young slugger, Roger Maris. It is difficult to imagine a more fateful move for the Yankees than their acquisition of Maris—save for taking advantage of Boston's 1920 gaffe and buying Ruth—especially since this one was motivated partly by Mantle's sub-superstar year, one that paled in comparison only to the highest bars that he himself had already set.

The New York fans wanted to love their overachieving boy wonder in Mantle, but they had already fallen victim to a more potent aphrodisiac called winning. Roger Maris's first years in New York may have been a wake-up call to the formidable Mickey Mantle. Maris pressed him to the power alleys of performance, almost catching the Mick's forty homers for the team lead with his own thirty-nine. Mantle led the whole league again with 119 runs scored, but his .275 average had slipped even further. The newcomer Maris then did the unthinkable by winning the MVP award. A precursor to greatness, Maris's trenchant 1960 campaign showed that his 1961 season was no random fluke.

The Big Apple sat at the dead center of the world stage in 1961. Home runs rained down at Yankee Stadium and anywhere else the Yankees played. Mantle not only found himself back in the good graces of New York fans but also again became their darling as he slammed tape-measure home runs with a boyish charm and big-league smile. The Mick was back and so was New York; but even though Maris was a big part of the team's newfound winning formula, Roger soon became the odd man out.

Many have written about Maris's distant personality, for he is remembered as a quiet and sullen character, but more than his demeanor added to his travails. Mickey Mantle had already paid his dues, having brought New York back to the world of winning before he lost his edge as well as the Series. So when he climbed all the way back in 1960 and 1961, he was treated as the prodigal son. The city, even the entire country, felt free to embrace Mantle again, so America's bonds to the Mick grew immediately stronger and even more emotional than before. Unfortunately for Maris, he entered the New York baseball world at precisely the wrong time, although in fairness, he was a big part of the reason that the Yankees and Mantle were winning in the first place.

By overachieving, winning, failing, then winning again, Mantle had become more human, therefore rendering him someone with whom regular baseball fans could identify. To a large degree Maris's poor relationship with the fans was his own fault, having acted distant and cold, but the timing of Mantle's legacy-in-the-making was out of Maris's control. In 1961 Maris hit an immortal sixty-one homers against Mantle's remarkable fifty-four and drove in more runners with 141 RBIs (including his own sixty-one runs) to 128 for Mantle. The Mick stole twelve bases to none for Maris, and Mantle led the league in slugging percentage at .687. Although he struck out more times than Maris did (112 against 67), his .317 batting average was much higher than Maris's .269. All those home runs and the Ruth legacy they surpassed, however, impressed the MVP voters who, for the second straight year, gave the top honor to Roger Maris. Today the OPS stat gets more attention than it did in 1961, and Mantle's on-base plus slugging was a lofty 1.135 to .993 for Maris. The nod in another contemporary number, wins above replacement (WAR), also goes to Mantle. Leading the American League in that department with 10.2, Mantle loomed over Norm Cash, in second place with 8.9, and Maris, who was tied for fifth in the league at 6.7.

Mantle walked 126 times in 1961, and that statistic helped him to an on-base percentage of .448, or the fourth highest of his career. Maris walked only 94 times, partly because pitchers were careful not to walk him with Mantle following in the batting order for most of the season.[17] As a matter of fact, of Maris's 94 bases on balls, not one of them was intentional, even though Maris was a power hitter, suggesting that opposing managers preferred to take their chances with Maris's swing rather than putting him on base ahead of Mantle.

Maris's home runs notwithstanding, Mantle still proved to be the darling of the media. He gave a good interview and could work the press better than most baseball players. He was at the top of his game with the added story line of his injuries, courage, and perseverance. Mantle, therefore, received good ink while, in the end, the press and the public dismissed Maris. They felt he had robbed baseball. Not only did he break its most revered record, which was held by its most storied player, Ruth, but he also had beaten Mickey Mantle, the sentimental favorite, to the punch.

The 1961 season was like none other since the monster 1927 season of Murderers' Row. The year 1961 had captured America, a time when even non-baseball fans began to follow the Yankees. Mantle, Maris, Ruth, and the home run race made headlines everywhere.[18] The excitement of that season's campaign was quite similar to the 1998 home run season of Mark McGwire and Sammy Sosa but with two major differences: Maris and Mantle played on the New York stage and for the same team, usually batting next to each other in the order. The Sosa-McGwire race may have been reminiscent of the Mantle-Maris contest, but 1961 match more closely resembled that of another historic Yankee duo, Babe Ruth and Lou Gehrig.

By the time 1963 had arrived, the great and charismatic Mickey Mantle was on the downside of his illustrious career, a slide helped along when Mantle collided with an outfield fence in Baltimore, tore the cartilage in his left knee, and broke his left foot. Mantle missed about 60 percent of that season. For most of his career Mantle played hurt to some degree, a serious impediment to a player known for speed and hustle. Many players recounted days where they could not believe how the hurting Mick had gutted out his games and demonstrated a determination that earned him their respect. "He is the only baseball player I know," observed teammate Clete Boyer, "who is a bigger hero to his teammates than he is to the fans." In the case of Mantle, who was popular to a fault, that observation said a great deal. The level of respect he enjoyed extended beyond his own team and even to the rival Red Sox. Noted Sox favorite Carl Yastrzemski, "If that guy were healthy, he'd hit 80 home runs." Imagine Mickey Mantle playing a few years later with the benefit of better surgery techniques, anti-inflammatory medications, painkillers, or steroids—not for artificial power but for healing. Maybe he would have lived up to the musings of Nellie Fox: "On two legs, Mickey Mantle would have been the greatest ballplayer who ever lived." As it was, he had earned his spot in the team picture, front and center.[19]

Despite all that admiration, the Mick was hardly perfect. He respected the game and its players, often running the bases with his head down to avoid showing up opposing pitchers, but he drank heavily, chased women, and abused his already damaged body. He thought he would die young, as his father had, so he lived with reckless abandon. Mantle's explanation has the ring of an excuse rather than of a noble concession to fate, but his belief may well have contributed to his fearless success on the field.

Mickey Mantle did die young at age sixty-six on August 13, 1995, after serious bouts with alcoholism and liver cancer. In the end, though, Mantle died with a profound sense of perspective if not honor. He finally realized that he was truly a role model and pointed to his example of how not to live one's life. "Don't be like me," he warned others in a candid concession to reality, essentially a "home run" warning in its own right. Poignantly, until the 2012 season, Mickey Mantle's twelve walk-off home runs remained tied for the career lead with four other players: Jimmie Foxx, Stan Musial, Frank Robinson, and Babe Ruth.[20] The record held up until slugger Jim Thome clubbed his thirteenth, a pinch-hit walk-off home run for the Phillies, on June 23, 2012.

Even in death, Mantle made history. His former teammate Bobby Richardson gave a eulogy that inspired those who heard it and is still highly regarded among followers of the game. While the address was not the greatest good-bye in baseball history—that honor goes to Gehrig's "luckiest man" speech—it may have been the best send-off, a dubious although eminently appropriate distinction for the Mick and for Bobby Richardson. "If you know Mickey," Richardson said, "he was always laughing." He knew Mantle laughed in spite of, and perhaps because of, his insecurities about death.

Mickey Mantle was the stuff of legends. The Griffith Stadium home run shot in 1953 traveled somewhere between 510 and 565 feet, depending on how much legends are allowed to trump fact. Either way, it is still regarded as the longest official blast in major-league history. Remarkably, Mantle is largely credited with the longest unofficial shot, too, with that alleged 656-footer he launched during an exhibition game at the University of Southern California. For longtime Yankee fans, his most memorable homer may have been the ball he crushed on May 22, 1963, during his shortened season from colliding with that wall in Baltimore. Although the ball "only" traveled to the 370-foot mark, it had been on a much farther track since it was still 115 feet high when it struck the right-field facade at Yankee Stadium.[21] Many witnesses insist that the ball was still rising, stirring estimates of a 600-foot homer had it not hit the stadium rooftop's latticework.

Babe Ruth hit a monster shot in his rookie season with Boston that clunked onto the sidewalk about 470 feet from home plate, but Mantle's Griffith Park homer is thought to have started baseball's modern tape measure approach to determining memorable long-distance home runs. Although distances of 500- and 600-foot home runs are fodder for baseball debate, they are largely more mythical than factual. As noted earlier, in 1982, IBM implemented a system of computing the distance of long balls by calculating where they would land if unobstructed. Until 1995, it only credited the Tigers' Cecil Fielder with a home run of more than 500 feet, when he hit a 502-footer that sailed over the left-field bleachers at Milwaukee's County Stadium. One reliable measurement occurred when

"King Kong" Dave Kingman crushed one that left Chicago's Wrigley Field and slammed against the third house past Waveland Avenue, a wind-aided but still impressive measurable distance of 530 feet.[22]

Owing to a lack of technology and a genuine interest, teams did not regularly keep measurements of home runs in the old days and not even for Maris and Mantle in 1961. In 1998, when two of the game's most prodigious long-ball hitters squared off, Sosa and McGwire together were credited with six home runs that were deemed to have traveled at least 500 feet. Five belonged to McGwire, with the longest pegged at 545 feet, and Sosa's went 500 feet.[23] Even with modern IBM estimates and the rise of McGwire and other power sluggers, Mantle may have slammed the longest extrapolated blast as well. That 1963 facade shot has been recalculated to a ridiculous 734 feet after factoring in the wind and accounts about the ball still rising when it struck the overhang.[24]

Legend is a part of baseball, and tall home run tales are the basis of much baseball lore. Having played with a legend on a championship team and becoming a dominant winner in his own right, Mickey Mantle is among the greatest of all ballplayers. His association with legends, ironically, may have been the ultimate downfall of Mantle's teammate, the unwitting Roger Maris. Not only did Maris best the image of Ruth in 1961, but he also tarnished the image of the popular Mickey Mantle, who failed to catch Maris in the home run race to destiny. Maris, it seems, had to both overcome the ghost of Ruth and compete with two Mantles—the actual Mickey, with his actual records, and the myth of what Mantle could have been if, as Yastrzemski commented, he had been healthy. Even so, Mantle and Maris showed little personal rivalry, with the media hyping most of it and the fans perpetuating it. Mantle even pulled for Maris to beat Ruth's record when, near the magic season's end, it had become clear that the injured Mantle could not.

In the final analysis, Roger Maris's sixty-one home runs did change baseball; however, Mickey Mantle accomplished far more, for he charismatically reflected America and its perceptions of success. He was the consummate all-American boy—handsome, witty, charming, talented—and ranks among the most outstanding ballplayers in the history of America's game. With a uniform number 7 that needs no further explanation, a long-ball reputation as the father of the tape-measure home run, and a holder of ten World Series career records, Mantle was the face of baseball *and* America. His boyish face appeared on sports and other magazine covers, folks wrote songs about him, and he was a box office draw on the road.

Throughout the Mick's retirement and for still more years after his death, baseball continued to look for the next Mickey Mantle—a charismatic slugger with speed, power, and infectious smile. Many players, like the outgoing Sammy Sosa or the respected Ken Griffey Jr., captured America's attention for brief moments, but baseball has not discovered another Mickey Mantle. Neither has America.

In 2003, the Chicago White Sox drafted Brian Anderson, a good-looking young outfielder with speed, power, and blond hair. Some noticed his similarities with Mantle, especially during his first big-league game in Chicago. He arrived with a $1.6 million signing bonus in 2003 and good promise, hitting two home runs for the big-league club near the end of the 2005 season.[25] Then the Sox won the 2005 World Series. Fans and even a few pundits began to wonder whether Brian Anderson could be as promising as the Mick was. Eventually Anderson's hitting proved inconsistent and lacked power, and he hit only eight home runs in 405 plate appearances in 2006. With his speed and strong arm, Anderson became little more than a defensive outfielder in 2007 and 2008. Soon thereafter, the White Sox gave up on him altogether, and he bounced from team to team. Brian had the looks, the speed, and a big arm in the outfield, but the similarities ended there. So close and yet so far. (During spring training in 2010, Anderson began the long process of converting himself into a pitcher by working his way through the Kansas City Royals farm system on the mound.)

But failing to capture the magic and success of the Mick was hardly Brian's fault; the aura of Mickey Mantle toppled far greater stars who fell equally as hard. Ask the late Roger Maris.

It was all I lived for, to play baseball.
—MICKEY MANTLE[26]

Frank "Home Run" Baker's batting grip (1912). *Photo courtesy Library of Congress, Prints and Photographs Division*

The cavernous Polo Grounds during the 1912 World Series. The Yankees would begin playing home games there in 1913 and share the park with the Giants through 1922. The only player ever to slam a home run ball completely over the roof and out of the park was Babe Ruth. The Polo Grounds were the site of Bobby Thomson's 1951 pennant-winning walk-off blast and Willie Mays's "the catch" in Game 1 of the 1954 World Series. *Photo courtesy Library of Congress, Prints and Photographs Division*

Wrigley Field, built in 1914 by the owner of the Chicago Whales, is the second-oldest existing major-league park after Boston's Fenway (1912). It was the site of many significant home runs by Ernie Banks, Sammy Sosa, Mark McGwire, and others, but the most famous of all was Babe Ruth's "called shot" homer during the 1932 World Series, an audacious blast that is still debated among fans, witnesses, and historians. Did Ruth really predict and point to where the ball would land before slugging it into the seats? *Photo courtesy the National Baseball Hall of Fame Library (Cooperstown, NY)*

An overhead view of the massive Griffith Stadium in Washington, D.C., where Mickey Mantle's legendary 565-foot shot left the stadium altogether, inventing the tape measure home run and contributing to the American lexicon. *Photo courtesy the National Baseball Hall of Fame Library (Cooperstown, NY)*

The home run has long been a staple of American culture beyond baseball, evidenced by this vintage sheet music cover. *Photo courtesy the National Baseball Hall of Fame Library (Cooperstown, NY)*

Playground baseball in America during 1918 when Ty Cobb was a star, Babe Ruth was still pitching for the Red Sox, and the season home run record stood at twenty-seven. *Photo courtesy Library of Congress, Prints and Photographs Division*

Serving hot dogs to fans at Brooklyn's Ebbets Field on October 6 before Game 2 of the 1920 World Series between Brooklyn and the Indians. Brooklyn won the game 3–0, but Cleveland would take the series. *Photo courtesy Library of Congress, Prints and Photographs Division*

Peerless Babe Ruth is seen making a new record with his third home run in one day during a double header between the Yankees and Senators, in 1920. *Photo courtesy Library of Congress, Prints and Photographs Division*

Babe Ruth shown slugging his immortal home run number 60 on September 30, 1927, the long ball that would haunt baseball and America for the better part of a century. Ruth's own take on it: "Let's see some son-of-a-bitch match that." *Photo courtesy the National Baseball Hall of Fame Library (Cooperstown, NY)*

President Franklin Roosevelt about to throw the Opening Day pitch in Washington, D.C., 1934. Roosevelt was a devoted fan of baseball, and his "green light letter" on January 15, 1942, paved the way for major-league ball to continue during World War II, thereby influencing wartime America at home. *Photo courtesy the Franklin D. Roosevelt Library*

Babe Ruth, *left*, with Yankees owner Jacob Ruppert in 1934. Ruppert purchased Ruth from the Red Sox in December 1919, altering the course of major-league history and American culture. *Photo courtesy the National Baseball Hall of Fame Library (Cooperstown, NY)*

A deep center field and a shorter right-field line are depicted in this 1936 view of Yankee Stadium. Opened in 1923, the stadium's short right field mimicked that of the Polo Grounds, where Ruth originally honed his home run prowess, and was probably constructed intentionally to exploit Ruth's left-handed power. *Photo courtesy National Archives and Records Administration*

Ronald Reagan announcing Chicago Cubs games for radio station WHO, Des Moines, Iowa, between 1934 and 1937. While traveling with the Cubs on an exhibition tour to California in 1937, Reagan stopped at Warner Brothers studios for a screen test that soon led to his acting career. *Photo courtesy the Ronald Reagan Library*

Lou Gehrig batting against Cleveland in 1938 during his record streak of 2,130 consecutive games played. In 1938 he had 689 plate appearances, but only 33 more in 1939 until ALS halted his career. His "luckiest man" address on July 4, 1939, is still regarded as one the great American speeches of the twentieth century. *Photo courtesy the National Baseball Hall of Fame Library (Cooperstown, NY)*

THE WHITE HOUSE
WASHINGTON

January 15, 1942.

My dear Judge:-

Thank you for yours of January fourteenth. As
you will, of course, realize the final decision about the
baseball season must rest with you and the baseball Club
owners -- so what I am going to say is solely a personal
and not an official point of view.

I honestly feel that it would be best for the
country to keep baseball going. There will be fewer people
unemployed and everybody will work longer hours and harder
than ever before.

And that means that they ought to have a
chance for recreation and for taking their minds off
their work even more than before.

Baseball provides a recreation which does
not last over two hours and a half, and
which can be got for very little cost. And, incidentally,
I hope that night games can be extended because it gives
an opportunity to the day shift to see a game occasionally.

As to the players themselves, I know you agree
with me that individual players who are of active military
or naval age should go, without question, into the services.
Even if the actual quality of the teams is lowered by the
greater use of older players, this will not dampen the
popularity of the sport. Of course, if any individual
has some particular aptitude in a trade or profession,
he ought to serve the Government. That, however, is a
matter which I know you can handle with complete justice.

Here is another way of looking at it -- if
300 teams use 5,000 or 6,000 players, these players are
a definite recreational asset to at least 20,000,000
of their fellow citizens -- and that in my judgment is
thoroughly worthwhile.

With every best wish,

Very sincerely yours,

Franklin D. Roosevelt

Hon. Kenesaw M. Landis,
333 North Michigan Avenue,
Chicago,
Illinois.

An image of Roosevelt's signed green light letter, which the *Chicago Sun* called the most significant contribution to baseball in our time. The original is located at the Franklin D. Roosevelt Library in Hyde Park, New York. *Photo courtesy the National Baseball Hall of Fame Library (Cooperstown, NY)*

Jackie Robinson at the Dodgers' clubhouse still wearing his minor-league Montreal jersey. Branch Rickey had signed Robinson to the Dodgers' Montreal Royals farm team in 1945, two years before Jackie's major-league debut and nine years before the Supreme Court desegregated American schools. The court likely noticed Robinson's success for the Dodgers, and the favorable media reports may have partially influenced its landmark *Brown v. Board of Education* decision. *Photo courtesy the National Baseball Hall of Fame Library (Cooperstown, NY)*

Bobby Thomson cracked possibly the most famous home run in major-league history when his "shot heard round the world" captured the 1951 pennant for the Giants. Although later thought to have been aided by stolen signs, the allegations did not taint his feat, perhaps partly due to baseball's larcenous legacy of stolen signs, spitballs, hidden balls, and corked bats. *Photo courtesy the National Baseball Hall of Fame Library (Cooperstown, NY)*

Monte Irvin greeting Willie Mays after Mays's twenty-ninth home run of the 1954 season. Many regard Mays as history's best all-round major-league player. The opposing catcher is Roy Campanella. All three African Americans had followed Jackie Robinson to the majors, but in 1954 four teams still had no black ballplayers: the Yankees, Phillies, Tigers, and Red Sox. *Photo courtesy the National Baseball Hall of Fame Library (Cooperstown, NY)*

Baseball commissioner Ford Frick (1951–1965) at his desk. He tainted Roger Maris's record of sixty-one home runs by suggesting it should be qualified for coming in a 162-game season, even though no other season or career records—not even the bloated steroid marks of the 1990s—have been so designated. Frick's comments would continue to be treated as the infamous Roger Maris asterisk, even though an actual asterisk never really existed. *Photo courtesy the National Baseball Hall of Fame Library (Cooperstown, NY)*

Casey Stengel managed the New York Yankees from 1949 to 1960 and is the only person to manage five World Series–winning teams in a row (1949–1953). Stengel later managed the original New York Mets, where his "Can't anybody here play this game?" outburst became immortalized in baseball and American lore. *Photo courtesy the National Baseball Hall of Fame Library (Cooperstown, NY)*

Ted Williams, shown batting in 1958, may have been baseball's greatest overall hitter. The last man to bat .400 with .406 in 1941, Williams's lifetime .344 average remains tied for seventh best all time—and none of the others played after 1937. He clubbed 521 career home runs in spite of missing almost five full seasons while serving in the armed forces. Williams's "career walk-off" home run when he left the game in the eighth inning on September 28, 1960, at age forty-two, only added to the slugger's legacy. *Photo courtesy the National Baseball Hall of Fame Library (Cooperstown, NY)*

Mickey Mantle striding home after hitting a September homer in 1959 at the peak of his career. Some of Mantle's home runs traveled so far that he is credited with inventing the "tape measure home run," now a staple of American lore and slang. *Photo courtesy the National Baseball Hall of Fame Library (Cooperstown, NY)*

Maris's left-handed power swing broke Babe Ruth's single-season mark of sixty home runs, the Holy Grail of baseball records. Maris was largely shunned for besting both the icon Ruth and popular teammate Mickey Mantle in 1961, and his home run record, set during a 162-game season, has been tainted with a fictional yet symbolic asterisk. *Photo courtesy the Arthur Rickerby Collection, the National Baseball Hall of Fame Library (Cooperstown, NY)*

Although Roger Maris was never inducted to the Baseball Hall of Fame, his 1961 jersey and the bat and ball from his historic sixty-first home run can be found there. *Photo courtesy the National Baseball Hall of Fame Library (Cooperstown, NY)*

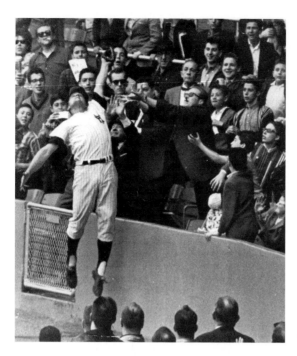

Roger Maris was a solid athlete who not only slugged 275 major-league homers but also prevented a few. Shown here, he's robbing an opposing home run on May 7, 1962, with an impressive vertical leap. *Photo courtesy the National Baseball Hall of Fame Library (Cooperstown, NY)*

Two home run hitters with differing styles. The Senators' mammoth Frank Howard towers over the flashy Reggie Jackson on July 23, 1969. *Reprinted with permission of the DC Public Library, Star Collection,* ©Washington Post

Hank Aaron slamming career home run number 715 in 1974, eclipsing Babe Ruth's immortal lifetime record of 714 home runs. Even though Jackie Robinson had desegregated the major leagues in 1947, Aaron's achievement would not receive full recognition and acceptance for another twenty-five years. *Photo courtesy the National Baseball Hall of Fame Library (Cooperstown, NY)*

Dodger Kirk Gibson's game-winning home run to take Game 1 of the 1988 World Series against Oakland's ace reliever Dennis Eckersley. The injured Gibson did not start the game, and while pinch-hitting in the bottom of the ninth inning with two outs, he needed either a walk or a home run, since he could not run the bases. His ensuing walk-off blast may have been the most improbable home run in World Series history. *Photo courtesy the National Baseball Hall of Fame Library (Cooperstown, NY)*

Barry Bonds in 1993 before the looming steroid era would transform dozens of players into home run machines. The fifty-homer season had been achieved only eighteen times from the beginning of the major leagues through 1993 and twenty-three times since 1993. The top six home run seasons of all time occurred from 1998 through 2001. Barry Bonds would hit the most ever with seventy-three in 2001. *Photo courtesy the National Baseball Hall of Fame Library (Cooperstown, NY)*

Slugger Mark McGwire as a member of the Oakland Athletics in 1997, one year before the great home run chase against Sammy Sosa. McGwire would be the first to break the Roger Maris home run record and achieve seventy home runs in 1998, although Sosa would be the first to achieve home run number 66 that same year. Both Sosa and McGwire would later be linked to performance-enhancing substances. *Photo courtesy the National Baseball Hall of Fame Library (Cooperstown, NY)*

Sammy Sosa seen crushing a ball circa 2001, his season of sixty-four homers and a league-leading 160 RBIs. Sosa lost the home run crown to Barry Bonds that year, but he is the only major-leaguer who has achieved a sixty-homer season three times. *Photo courtesy the National Baseball Hall of Fame Library (Cooperstown, NY)*

THE RISE AND FALL
OF ROGER MARIS

It's like obituaries, when you die they finally give you good reviews.
—ROGER MARIS[1]

Time magazine's Man of the Year for 1961 was John F. Kennedy, the engaging world leader who took on the Cold War, resurrected the space program with a New Frontier vitality, and brought the romance of Camelot to Washington.[2] His youth, passion, and wit complemented his frat boy charm and prankish casualness. Kennedy's charisma and intellect helped him shrug off the Cuban Bay of Pigs debacle that April, making him perhaps the original "Teflon" president two decades before Ronald Reagan, the president for whom that moniker was ultimately coined.

Kennedy and Mickey Mantle were different in many ways, but their striking similarities and their impact on the early 1960s are inescapable. Both were pranksters, both were products of the American dream—politics and baseball—and both were icons. They had captivating smiles, a twinkle in the eye, and effusive personalities. They also had bum legs and a bit of a limp. Moreover, each man received rave reviews in life and great accolades at death. Not so for their contemporary Roger Maris, who had sunken eyes and a distant, sometimes combative persona and anticipated receiving "better reviews" in death. Remarkably, all three died rather young: Kennedy at age forty-six; Maris at fifty-one, after losing a bout with cancer; and Mickey, who also fell to cancer, at age sixty-three. Of the three, Maris's topping of the American icon Babe Ruth ultimately earned him more scorn than praise. In the end, although Maris's reputation has fared better in death, especially in the post-steroid era, his legacy resembles the sullen Richard Nixon's more than it does that of Kennedy or even Mantle. Though certainly not as dramatic, the public viewed Maris's success over both Mantle and Ruth as though Nixon had dethroned Kennedy.

Nixon, of course, was defeated by his charismatic counterpart, Kennedy, while Maris betrayed the romantic expectations of history by eclipsing Ruth, Ruth's revered home run record, and the affable Mickey Mantle all at once. Further, Maris's demeanor continued to overshadow his success on the field. "You ask Maris a question," observed Casey Stengel, "and he stares at you for a week before he answers."[3] Even Maris seemed resigned to his place in baseball history. "I was born surly," he acknowledged after the close of the 1961 season, "and I'm going to stay that way."[4]

Maris was born Roger Eugene Maras in Minnesota in 1934 and changed his last name in 1955. He grew up in Fargo, North Dakota, where he excelled in football, basketball, and track. His high school did not have a baseball team, but Maris became a star player for the local American Legion team. An all-state running back, Maris turned down a football scholarship to Oklahoma, accepting an offer from the Cleveland Indians instead. In 1958 Cleveland traded Maris to Kansas City, where he showed promise as a hitter, but he was traded again less than two years later to the New York Yankees. When he stepped to the plate for the first time as a Yankee in 1960, Maris was a seasoned pro at twenty-five years old. He did not disappoint. He slammed two home runs to go with a single and a double. The Yankees won the pennant that year, then would notch four more in a row. Maris himself, though, was destined for even more.[5]

While poet Robert Frost had expressly declared Kennedy to be a "man of destiny," a label that fit the young president well,[6] Kennedy's life was brutally cut short. Unlike Kennedy or Mantle, though, Maris did not seem much like a man of destiny at the time. Maris would actually derail baseball's chosen one, Mickey Mantle, achieving success at precisely the wrong time and the wrong place in history, a fate that cast him as more of a villain than an icon.

To many ordinary Americans in 1960–1961, society may have seemed to be acting similar to an adolescent than the angry young adult it would become later in the decade. Yes, the Cold War loomed, but it did not seem to produce imminent danger, except for Kennedy's Bay of Pigs misstep with its nuclear implications. It was still a time when Chubby Checker was on the pop charts and movies such as *The Parent Trap* flickered in theaters coast to coast. In 1961 a gallon of gas cost 27 cents and the average new house cost only $12,500.[7]

When astronaut Alan Shepard ushered in a new space age on May 5, 1961, Roger Maris had clubbed two home runs en route to what would become one of the greatest baseball seasons ever. Maris went on to hit eleven home runs in the month of May, plus fifty more as the season continued. Not only did Maris slug sixty-one, but Mantle also added fifty-four in a neck-and-neck race that lasted until the final month, when Maris finally pulled ahead. Overall, the Yankees set a team record for home runs with at least another twenty each from Moose Skowron, Elston Howard, Yogi Berra, and Johnny Blanchard.

Lost in the national hysteria was the entire Detroit Tigers' team, a juggernaut that won 101 games and still finished a distant second to the Yankees' 109 wins. The Tigers even featured their own home run duo of Norm Cash, who slammed forty-one while leading the league in hitting at .361, and Rocky Colavito, who launched forty-five homers and drove in an impressive 140 runs. Outside of Detroit and the staunchest baseball fans, the Tigers' 1961 season is largely lost to posterity. Meanwhile, on the west coast, Willie Mays had become the ninth major-league and the first African American ballplayer to slam four homers in one game,[8] but this year would be remembered for the great home run chase in New York. The energized drama, featuring suspense, great personalities, and history, captured national headlines.

As discussed previously, baseball is a sport of curses, such as the Red Sox's Curse of the Bambino, the Cubs' Billy Goat Curse, and many others as well. One event not normally associated with hexes was the Maris-Mantle duel, but it may have been cursed as much as any of the others. It was not subject to a magical curse but to hexes in the form of trash-talking dares, the type that players often use to rankle their rivals. It began with Ruth himself, who dared anyone to equal his 1927 record: "Let's see some son-of-a-bitch match that."[9] The awe-inspiring number of Ruth's homers and his brash persona anointed the Babe's record as something of a holy grail. Any hopeful record breaker was thus preordained as a "son-of-a-bitch" (SOB), and Maris was the perfect SOB foil. Hall of Famer Rogers Hornsby piled on, adding his own insult during the midst of the record 1961 run: "Maris has no right to break Ruth's record."[10] His comment possibly invoked the new 162-game season argument, since the American League schedule was stretched in 1961 to create a season that was eight games longer than the 154 contests during Ruth's day. Making matters worse, the National League still had a 154-game schedule in 1961, for it did not expand until 1962. On July 17, 1961, Commissioner Ford Frick publicly called for a qualification of the new homer mark because of the new 162-game season and virtually cursed the record before it happened. It was a shortsighted, ignorant proclamation. After all, many baseball records set after 1960—team records, pitching wins in a season, career and season home runs, hits, walks, errors—also benefitted from those eight additional games each season. Any player's mark could profit from one 162-game schedule or a whole career of them.

The Frick remark is widely remembered as an asterisk, but an express asterisk was never in the official record books. Frick had never even used that term in his comments; instead, he had said that if the players took more than 154 games to break Ruth's record, "there would have to be some distinctive mark in the record books." New York sportswriter Dick Young actually suggested the asterisk.[11] As it happened, until 1991 Maris's home run record was in fact listed separately in the record books. It was a ridiculous distinction since, again, no other records received this qualifier, including Pete Rose's all-time hits mark that broke Ty Cobb's record in 1985.

During a career of twenty years, for example, those eight extra games would add up to 160 contests, or a full season's worth. Remarkably, on the one hand, Rose is not a recognized player in good standing, yet his record stands. On the other hand, Maris is not banned from baseball, but his record is considered tainted. Moreover, neither Rose nor Maris is in the Hall of Fame, although both broke the seemingly invincible records of two distinctly different baseball icons.

Much has been written and debated about the Baseball Hall of Fame and its various inductees, admissions criteria, and voting standards. For Maris and other qualified veterans to be elected, they first have to meet the objective criteria of ten major-league seasons and other qualifying standards. Then 75 percent of the reconstituted Veterans Committee, comprised of ninety voters, must elect them. The official criteria the committee must use is succinct: "Voting will continue to be based upon the individual's record, ability, integrity, sportsmanship, character and contribution to the game of Baseball."[12]

Traditionally, the committee also looks into the player's overall "body of work" regardless of the significance of particular contributions. The "integrity, sportsmanship, character" qualifications have always been problematic given the irascible collection of knaves and racists that have already been admitted to the hall, and it will continue to be relevant and controversial over the coming years as the committee considers the steroid-era players. Many players from the 1990s, such as Mark McGwire and Barry Bonds, are tainted, but other cases involve minimal steroid use, as with Alex Rodriguez, or highly suspected use, as in the case of Sammy Sosa. The steroid debate is one thing—certainly the committee has grounds to invoke the sportsmanship conditions with many steroid-era players—but the Roger Maris issue continues to be troubling, especially since Maris was never linked to steroids or other character issues. Fittingly, however, his final two home runs of 1961, the ones that tied and broke Ruth's record, now have renewed relevance as the Hall of Fame discussion in the post-steroid era gains traction.

The chiefly cited reason for barring Roger Maris from Cooperstown is usually a vague reference to his entire body of work, as though the 1961 season was not enough to merit entry and as if the rest of his career was a dud. Had Maris done little else beyond breaking Ruth's mark, such a milestone should itself be worthy of consideration as a meaningful "contribution to the game of baseball." But, in fact, Roger did achieve much more during his baseball career. He appeared in no fewer than seven different World Series (over a span of nine seasons), including two that occurred after he left the Yankees to play with the St. Louis Cardinals. Although his World Series marks were less than stellar overall, Maris did have his postseason moments. For instance, he powered the Cardinals to a seven-game victory over the storied Red Sox in 1967 by hitting .385 with ten hits and seven runs batted in.[13] He also won the American League MVP not once but twice, both times over the reigning darling of baseball, Mickey Mantle—and the first such title was bestowed in 1960 before his record-setting season.

The Maris home run record remains particularly relevant today because, ironically, it may still be the one truly legitimate season home run mark. His record certainly is the only one on the books that is not tainted by the steroid era that occurred from the mid-1990s to the early 2000s. (Apparently the era extended a little beyond that period, considering Manny Ramirez and his sudden 2011 retirement plus Ryan Braun's close call with a positive drug test and fifty-game suspension that was successfully appealed in 2012. Ramirez had received a hundred-game suspension for failing a drug test, then retired. Afterward, the suspension was reduced to fifty games, and he attempted a comeback with Oakland.) Yet Major League Baseball still seems to focus on Maris, qualifying his record as somehow illegitimate, and the tarnish relentlessly keeps the Yankees slugger from Cooperstown. Meanwhile, the other home run records from Sosa, McGwire, and Bonds remain intact, even though none of those players have a meaningful chance for Hall of Fame legitimacy in the near future, if ever.

Prior to the 2011 season, baseball's Hall of Fame included 295 players, managers, players from the Negro leagues, and a few others, such as Commissioner Kenesaw Landis. Without belaboring the many names now lost to posterity, a random sampling of less recognized, and therefore somewhat invisible, Hall of Famers includes David Bancroft, Elmer Flick, John "Pop"

Lloyd, Walter "Rabbit" Maranville, and Zach Wheat.[14] All were undoubtedly deserving of induction in their day; however, many other inductees fell short on the sportsmanship standard. As noted earlier, Hall of Fame great Ty Cobb was known for dirty play on the field and had a close brush with gambling allegations. Roger Maris will never slide into obscurity, though. He not only remains an indelible part of big-league baseball history but also is a memorable part of American culture. The Maris-Mantle home run chase touched virtually the entire baby boomer generation in some manner, yet its members still ignore Maris. Apparently shunning Roger Maris has gone on so long that it has become its own baseball tradition. And baseball prizes its traditions.

Articles, dedicated websites, and numerous grassroots campaigns have called for Maris's induction into the Hall of Fame. Recounting all the arguments would be an exercise in restating the obvious, but one salient comparison stands out: in 1960, Maris's first MVP year, the Pirates' Bill "Maz" Mazeroski cemented his career with one crowning home run that won the World Series in the ninth inning of Game 7 over the Yankees. It was a feat worthy of accolades and continuing distinction. But was that home run enough to earn Bill Mazeroski a place in the Hall of Fame, especially while Roger Maris is denied entry? Yes, the Mazeroski home run was one of the best clutch hits in recent times, and a genuine seventh-game walk-off homer is a storybook hit if ever there was one. For changing the 1960 World Series maybe the home run itself should be in the Hall of Fame, but it did not change baseball and only left a negligible impact on America.

Mazeroski did best Maris in total number of games played and played more years in the league (seventeen versus twelve). He barely edged Maris in total RBIs, with 853 compared to 850 for Maris, although Mazeroski needed five more years to achieve those 3 additional RBIs. Both players hit exactly .260 for their entire careers, but Maris clubbed 275 home runs to 138 career round-trippers for Mazeroski, or nearly double the number. Maris played in seven World Series in nine years, while Maz went twice, appearing in only one game in the 1971 version. Maris was league MVP twice.[15] Mazeroski was never MVP, although once he finished eighth and another time at twenty-third in the voting. In comparing home run seasons, Mazeroski's best was nineteen in 1958,while Maris's was the home run season of the century during which he slugged twenty homers in one thirty-day stretch in May and June.[16] Mazeroski's best RBI year was 82 in 1966, but Maris knocked in 112 in 1960, another 141 in 1961, and 100 in 1962 for three straight years of 100 or more runs batted in.[17] Mazeroski gained admittance to the Hall of Fame because he was a fine athlete and a credit to baseball. By the same token, then, Maris's case is compelling. Maris had a better year in 1961, a better overall career, and more World Series appearances, and he broke the holiest of all baseball records. Except for his personality and his awkward brush with icons, asterisks, and history, Roger Maris likely would have been admitted to Cooperstown long before Mazeroski was in 2001.

As it happens, the ball that sailed over the outfield fence for homer number 61, the bat that Maris used to hit it, and his Yankees home jersey are all enshrined in Cooperstown. The man who wore the uniform, swung the bat, and hit the ball over the fence, however, is not there.

When Maris slammed his historic shot over the wall at Yankee Stadium, which somewhat fittingly came against the storied Red Sox, Roger Maris and the Bostonian John F. Kennedy crossed paths more than metaphorically. Kennedy sent the accomplished slugger a telegram just before the 1961 World Series began: "My heartiest congratulations to you on hitting your 61st home run. The American people will always admire a man who overcomes great pressure to achieve an outstanding goal."[18]

Roger Maris had begun the 1961 season on top of the world. With a hefty raise in pay from $18,000 in 1960 to $32,000 the following year, the reigning MVP drove to spring training in a new 1960 Buick.[19] By the end of May, a breath of spring was in the air, accompanied by a scent of history in the making. As of May 30, 1961, Roger Maris already had clubbed eleven home runs and Mickey Mantle had launched thirteen. On that same day in 1927, Babe Ruth had belted fourteen, and the first hints of an impending brush with baseball fate were beginning to emerge. A curious suggestion of adversity also was in the air, an almost mystical omen about the Maris record.

Pitcher Bob Turley, Maris, and teammate Bob Cerv were at a midwestern coffee shop when a youngster asked for their autographs. They all signed a piece of paper, but Maris mischievously signed his as Babe Ruth. It struck Roger as funny, but the boy's parents were less than amused. The next day the newspapers chided Maris for being a jerk, although according to Turley it was only a joke. But the controversy refused to go away. "It was something Roger had to deal with all year," Turley reflected years later.[20]

The 1961 home run chase transfixed America. Even the word "chase" gives energy to the events themselves as fans and nonfans followed the action. As the lofty Ruth milestone became vulnerable, Ford Frick's edict of having to hit the homers by the 154th game loomed, but 1961 was the first year of the longer American League season. Frick, it turns out, was a staunch fan of Ruth's, and he had developed a close personal relationship with him. Frick had covered Ruth as a sportswriter in New York; became Ruth's bridge partner, golfing companion, and ghostwriter; and was protective of Ruth's legacy. If either Mantle or Maris could match or break the record within 154 games, the new record would not require special treatment. It remains unclear, though, what would have happened were it broken more than once in the final eight games. Difficult as it may have been, Maris nearly obliged. As of the season's 154th game, Roger Maris had actually clubbed fifty-nine, but he could not manage any more that day.[21] It took him all eight remaining games to hit two more, but he finally hit the record breaker on the last day of the season.

On October 1, 1961, the season's sixty-first home run left the bat of Roger Maris and sailed over the right-field wall and into destiny, clanking into box 163D at Yankee Stadium, section 33. It also proved to be the winning run in a 1–0 victory over the Red Sox, the first time Maris had won a 1–0 game with a home run. The homer not only won the game and obviously broke the baseball record for the ages, but it also gave Maris the league title in RBIs with 141 and runs scored at 132. Poignantly, although Roger drove in sixty-one of his own runs, many of his other runs came at the behest of Mickey Mantle, who, for most of the season, batted behind Maris in the order.

Mantle was present for the record-setting homer only in spirit. He had to watch Maris's fateful home run from his hospital bed, where he was being treated for complications from a flu shot (it had struck and infected a bone) that sidelined him on September 11, stalling his own home run total at fifty-six. With nineteen days left in the season at that point, Mantle may have been able to catch both Ruth and Maris, but he could not overcome the infection. At the time of his illness the two sluggers had been neck and neck, for Maris had slammed number 56 on September 9 against the Indians' James "Mudcat" Grant. Mantle took Maris's record-setting blast well, though. "I watched it closely on television," he said, "and I got goose bumps all over my body."[22] Mantle saw Roger go to the plate two more times that day, but the sixty-first homer was all he could muster, striking out in the sixth inning and popping out to the second baseman in the eighth.

Roger Maris held that season home run record for thirty-seven years, or three years longer than the Babe himself had owned it. But for the steroid era, Maris might still be the record holder. Hank Greenberg, who nearly caught Ruth decades earlier when he slammed fifty-eight homers in 1938, was vocally critical about the injustices that Maris had suffered. "I thought the thing that really hurt the season and hurt Roger was Frick's ruling about the 154 games," Greenberg observed. "That was just damn stupid. What was the difference? Conditions always change in baseball—day ball to night ball, new towns, new teams, new parks. They don't make rulings every time something like that changes."[23]

Indeed. "They" did not even qualify Barry Bonds's career record, which also happened during the era of 162-game seasons and apparently was partly propelled by the use of steroids. As widely reported in March 2011, Bonds' own attorney formally admitted Bonds used steroids during his opening statement to the jury in the criminal trial over Bonds's allegedly lying to a grand jury regarding drug use in baseball. But the lawyer further asserted that his client had only accidentally used a steroid cream. So Bonds "accidentally" took steroids and hit 73 home runs en route to a career record 762 long balls, even though no one before the tainted 1998 season had ever hit past 61. Hank Aaron, the prior career record holder at 755 homers, never once hit as many as 50 in a season. In April 2011, a federal jury found Bonds guilty of obstruction of justice for lying to investigators, but the jury was deadlocked on three other related counts. By 2012, Bonds was arguing his own case to be inducted into the Hall of Fame.

A broader question derived from the Maris-McGwire-Bonds aberration and related injustices is, is America becoming too complacent about unfairness? No, America has not given up on fairness altogether and sometimes allows the overuse of fairness to drive too many political agendas, but occasionally America can be immune to institutional inertia. Simply because the steroid records are still tolerated or because Roger Maris has always been shunned or because at one time African Americans were denied the right to play major-league ball or because myriad other baseball injustices were once accepted, such transgressions should not be embraced into perpetuity. Consider the absurd "baseball is not a business in interstate commerce" rationale behind the game's antitrust exemption, for instance. Simply because it has been in place since 1922 hardly means that the ruling is right. To the contrary, such front-page subterfuge creates a backdrop of futility that undermines the essence of what America is or at least what it is supposed to be. Americans feel used sometimes and have a fatalistic impression that seems justified when such obvious ploys are allowed to persist. Most knowledgeable fans understand that baseball is as much an interstate business as the NFL is, that black baseball players were unfairly banned from the game far too long, that Bonds's records are suspect, and that the excuses behind the Roger Maris exile are another trumped-up foil to spin history the way baseball sees it. No wonder Americans feel the "deck is stacked." To feel that the Supreme Court and baseball can manipulate the desired result, even when the truth seems obvious, is disquieting. But even so, baseball can still do its part to make amends logically and fairly.

If baseball desires to maintain its fragile status as America's game, it should rectify such chicanery, not perpetuate it. Even the discomfort with black players lingered well beyond Jackie Robinson's threshold season of 1947. The Yankees waited eight more years before they featured a black ballplayer, and the Red Sox were not integrated until 1959. After Robinson, it took twenty-eight years for a team to hire a black manager, Frank Robinson in 1975; thirty years for the game to embrace a black general manager, Atlanta's Bill Lucas in 1977; and all the way until 2006 for the Negro leagues' players to be recognized and for Cooperstown finally to admit seventeen players and executives.

Baseball did the right thing by inducting the Negro leagues' players to the hall. It was a great step in recognizing, then abrogating the past. The steroid era and other aberrations need to be handled the same way if baseball is going to regain the public's trust. Qualifying all the records that emerged during the steroid era will be impossible because determining which ones are tainted, which players were guilty, and what impact performance-enhancing drugs actually had will be impossible. But one approach can partially cleanse the record books and—as with the induction of the Negro players—can at once acknowledge and partly rectify problem: resurrect the asterisk. Give both Roger Maris and Hank Aaron an asterisk that serves to recognize their respective season and career home run marks by designating them as "the last home run record holders in the pre-steroid era." This designation would recognize the steroid problem without accusing any single individual and would duly qualify the initial records without disturbing the other obviously bloated home run records that will tarnish the game for decades. For that matter, Ruth could use an asterisk, too, as the home run record holder for a 154-game season. This way everyone deserving—Ruth, Maris, Aaron, and even Bonds—remains in the record books legitimately.

But does such a qualification really matter? Is baseball that important? Are not the nation's compelling issues of war, economics, the environment, jobs, and bouts with recessions or worse more important? Sports do not trump war and democracy, but matters of baseball integrity are not merely a sporting issue. Roger Maris's and Hank Aaron's records should not be saved simply for the players' sakes or even for baseball's sake. They should be resurrected, acknowledged, and honored to uphold a much larger principle, namely, truth. In the wake of a national financial meltdown in 2008, the arrest of Ponzi scheme artist and former stock market chairman Bernie

Madoff that same year, a contested presidential vote in 2000, and the concurrent steroid era that diluted the entire history of baseball records, Americans are skeptical of our institutions everywhere from Washington to Wall Street to even Cooperstown. Baseball has the power and the responsibility, however, to rectify part of that feeling of futility by embracing the truth. The game—and America—will be all the better for baseball's effort.

Otherwise, baseball will be left with a progressively heightened dilemma. Can the Baseball Hall of Fame continue to ignore the steroid-era players, even those not linked to performance-enhancing drugs? In January of 2013, not one player was enshrined in the Hall from a potential class of thirty-seven names, including Sammy Sosa, Mark McGwire, Barry Bonds, Roger Clemens, Curt Schilling, Craig Biggio, and Mike Piazza.[24] Remarkably, that same month, Lance Armstrong, the embattled cycling icon, finally came clean, admitting to a plethora of drugs, doping, and cheating—and he will pay a heavy price. Meanwhile, will no players from the 1998–2001 era be recognized by the Baseball Hall of Fame, even though their records stand, and even though several were probably not on steroids? And will Roger Maris still be shunned, even though he was a credit to the game and was never juiced?

STEALING HISTORY

With a long legacy of spitballs, corked bats, stealing signs, and manipulating the infield grass or foul lines, not to mention the traditional spitting and a litany of other impish behavior, baseball has long been a mischievous game on the field of play. But by banning players of color from the game for so long, then by manipulating who is in the Hall of Fame (the hall's voters act separately from Major League Baseball, but the latter deemed Rose ineligible), and even by qualifying records as in Maris's case or allowing other tainted marks, such as Bonds's home run records, to be sustained, baseball skullduggery is hardly confined to the playing field itself. One surprising place where baseball appears to carry a disproportionate level of influence is in the U.S. government, including the Oval Office and the Supreme Court.

What happens on the field not only influences American culture in varying degrees, but it also helps define the very essence of America. As already noted, one specific example of the game's continuing impact is the now infamous "called-shot" World Series of 1932 between the Chicago Cubs and New York Yankees. Wrigley Field was still a relatively new ballpark at the time, having been built as Weeghman Park for the Federal League's Chicago Whales in 1914, but even in the early days before the famous outfield ivy was installed in 1937, it was no stranger to baseball legends.

With New York leading in the 1932 Series two games to none, the Yankees faced an especially hostile Chicago crowd. The surprising level of antagonism led to epithets tossed across the field from the players, the benches, and the belligerent fans. Many young boys and men may have attended the game with their fathers that day, but only one grew up to become a Supreme Court justice. John Paul Stevens would go on to a stellar career, a mainstay on the court for an extraordinarily long term of nearly thirty-five years until his retirement in 2010.[1] He supported women's rights, demonstrated by his voting record on abortion and a woman's right to choose, as well as affirmative action for the hiring of women. He upheld the Miranda warning, said Congress could regulate guns in schools, and favored the obligation of the Boy Scouts to accept gay scoutmasters. Justice Stevens was widely regarded as a left-leaning moderate, although certainly more conservative than Justice William O. Douglas, whom he replaced.

When the late Charles H. Percy, a liberal Republican, recommended Stevens to the Seventh Circuit Court of Appeals (located in Chicago) in 1970, Richard Nixon nominated him. Five years later, President Gerald Ford nominated Stevens for the Supreme Court, and Stevens was confirmed nineteen days later by a Senate vote of 98–0.[2] Stevens was not a one-dimensional ideologue. Within a year he found himself agreeing with the majority to end a nationwide moratorium on the death penalty, and he dissented in a ruling that found the burning of the American flag is protected free speech. Still, on many major points and issues, he fostered a liberal view. Almost thirty years later, Stevens wrote the opinion that allowed terrorists detained at Guantanamo Bay the right to challenge their incarceration in U.S. federal courts.

Baseball was in Justice Stevens's blood and may have influenced his role in the 1951 congressional report on organized baseball that, among other things, endorsed the need for a reserve clause tying players to their teams. An antitrust expert stemming from his early days as associate counsel to Congress's Monopoly Power Subcommittee of the Judiciary Committee, Stevens ended his career on the high court with a blockbuster opinion against the NFL. In its threshold *American Needle* case in 2010, the court rejected the NFL's central argument that its entire league of teams is really one entity and not a collection of separate units. Had the NFL won that decision, it may have derailed the entire union decertification and antitrust lawsuit as a tactic against the NFL lockout in 2011.[3]

The history of baseball's relationship with the Supreme Court is so intertwined that it became a part of the court's psyche for a hundred years. Some of baseball's greatest influence on the court came from William Howard Taft, who in 1910 started the tradition of presidents throwing the ceremonial first pitch of the baseball season when he tossed the Opening Day ball on April 14.[4] After his presidency Taft was appointed to the court and served as chief justice when in 1922 the court's ruling in *Federal Base Ball Club of Baltimore, Inc., v. National League of Professional Base Ball Club*s established baseball's antitrust exemption.[5] Taft was a rabid baseball fan who had been a power-hitting second baseman during his high school days in Cincinnati, then excelled as a member of the baseball team at Yale University. As noted previously, his half brother, Charles Phelps Taft, was an owner of the Chicago Cubs from 1914 to 1916 when the rival Federal League sprang up and sued the National League in that same *Federal Base Ball* case. This connection was a bit incestuous, especially given the court's ruling that big-league baseball was not a business engaged in interstate commerce.

Other presidents have had links to and influenced by the game of baseball, connecting the game to White House traditions. On June 6, 1882, President Benjamin Harrison was the first sitting president actually to attend a big-league game. Before that, Presidents Andrew Johnson (1865), Ulysses Grant (1869), and Chester Arthur (1883) had invited organized teams to the White House. The rotund Taft was the first president to attend a major-league game outside of Washington when he saw the Pirates play in 1909 and allegedly started the tradition of the seventh-inning stretch when he stood to stretch his own legs—although a number of sources suggest that story may be more legend than fact. About three weeks later, Taft became the first sitting president to attend *two* big-league games on the same day, which he did while in St. Louis.[6]

On October 9, 1915, Woodrow Wilson became the first president to attend a World Series game, and in 1924 Calvin Coolidge became the first president to throw the opening pitch of the World Series. In later years, FDR was the first to attend an All-Star Game, Harry Truman was the first to attend a night game, Richard Nixon was the first to throw the Opening Day pitch at a site other than Washington (Anaheim), and Ronald Reagan became the first to watch a game while actually sitting in the dugout.[7] Moreover, Reagan is widely known for announcing Cubs games from an Iowa radio station in the 1930s, and in 1988 he was at it again, broadcasting play-by-play for an inning and a half during a major-league game. Later Bill Clinton became the first to throw the opening pitch from the mound (and make it to the catcher), then he and Vice President Al Gore became the first executive team to attend a game together when they attended Cal Ripken's record 2,131st consecutive game. More recently, President Barack Obama, a White Sox fan, spent some time in the broadcast booth and has tossed his share of ceremonial pitches. But perhaps George W. Bush had them all beat, for he actually was a co-owner of the Texas Rangers before making it to the Oval Office.

Even more presidents were big-league fans, such as Dwight Eisenhower, who lamented his inability to play major-league ball. Some had a widely recognized affinity for the game, as did Nixon, who also had an indirect influence on the sport, having appointed four of the five justices on the 1972 court that ruled against outfielder Curt Flood and failed to overturn the *Federal Base Ball* antitrust exemption. But the president who may have influenced the game most was Taft, who appointed six justices to the Supreme Court—the most by any president except George Washington—and who became chief justice in 1921, right before the court rendered its most influential baseball decision.[8]

By the time Taft took his seat on the bench, the court was already packed with baseball fans. In 1912, when news broke that the justices were following the World Series' scores and allegedly being distracted during sessions, there arose a vocal public outcry. The *New York Times* even published a harsh letter to the editor on October 21 that exposed the court's close interest in World Series games.[9]

On May 29, 1922, the Supreme Court rendered one of its most famous decisions, which became one of its most widely misunderstood rulings when it effectively exempted Major League Baseball from the federal antitrust laws in the *Federal Base Ball* case. With many Supreme Court opinions running twenty, fifty, or more pages, the *Federal Base Ball* opinion stands out not only for its far-reaching conclusions but also for its remarkable brevity. The entire ruling was confined to fewer than two full pages. The decision is also noteworthy because it may have been manipulated, and therefore virtually stolen, by the baseball powers of the day.

What really happened? First, the court did not expressly exempt baseball from the antitrust laws; rather, it said the laws do not apply to big-league baseball because it is not a business engaged in interstate commerce. The ruling is often misquoted to suggest that the court believed "baseball is not a business," but that interpretation is misleading. Instead, the court held that the business of baseball was not a part of "interstate commerce," per the operative words in the sentence.

Even in 1922, big-league baseball was a multimillion-dollar enterprise whereby professional ball players traveled from state to state on trains and played in mammoth stadiums seating thousands of people for large sums of money. Starting in 1921, some games, notably the World Series, were also broadcast over the radio. So what was the Supreme Court's thinking?

Possibly the court genuinely believed baseball was not a business at all or that playing baseball was more of a pastime than a form of commerce, let alone interstate commerce. After all, the Sherman Antitrust Act of 1890, which created the antitrust laws, was still a relatively new concept that the judiciary had not yet fully explored. Or maybe the justices simply felt that the antitrust laws were not intended to be applied to games at all, even profitable ones. But if the court really did feel that way, the question then becomes why?

Perhaps the court wanted to insulate baseball from the reach of the federal antitrust laws, since it did precisely that with its ruling. A plausible explanation is that the Supreme Court was concerned about what the antitrust laws could do to baseball rather than how baseball might be running afoul of the antitrust laws. The game was already a sacred national institution, as evidenced not only by baseball's effect on the whole country when Babe Ruth was redefining sports history but also by the court's sentimental and noticeable attachment to the game during the 1912 World Series. And it helped that by 1921 Taft, one of the great fans in the history of baseball, was at the helm as chief justice.

Yet, being a devoted follower of the game is one thing, but neutralizing the entire statutory scheme of antitrust regulation for the sake of a lucrative sports juggernaut is another. In matters of law, nothing happens in vacuum, so taking the *Federal Base Ball* case in the context of the times suggests that the court was more than simply waxing sentimental. The Sherman Act outlawed any "contract, combination, or conspiracy" in restraint of trade, and if that conspiracy was interstate in nature, the federal laws would certainly apply.[10] The law was enacted because of the vast power and fortunes that the country's biggest industrial powers at the time had amassed after the Civil War.

Postwar America had experienced an explosion of industrial growth that was fueled by a number of contributing factors, including Reconstruction in the South and the rapid development of railroads that connected the industrial Northern states and linked them to the West. Competition was so fierce and the costs to expand manufacturing so great that some enterprises turned to price fixing to bolster their profits and cash flow. In 1863 John D. Rockefeller established a refinery and built it into the world's largest oil refining enterprise by 1868. In 1870 Rockefeller began buying up the competition and rolling the companies into one controlled group that would later become Standard Oil. In 1882, Rockefeller created Standard Oil of New Jersey as a means to control his complex trust empire, a series of companies that included Standard of Ohio, Standard of Indiana, Standard of Iowa, and others for Illinois, Minnesota, Kansas, Missouri, Nebraska, Louisiana, and New York. The New Jersey company controlled overseas operations and, for accounting purposes, directed the whole trust conglomerate. The trust consortium would also control such other recognizable brands as Esso, Amoco, Socony, Mobil, Chevron, Socal, Sohio, and more, making it one of the most complex, wide-ranging industrial giants in history.[11]

The business model of controlling industries and prices proved profitable, although it was not beneficial to the public and hardly worthy of American traditions of competition. Meanwhile, similar consortiums of trusts began to spring up in other industries, such as whiskey, sugar, meat packing, and tobacco. A similar accumulation of steel businesses became United States Steel in 1901. Meanwhile, all these trusts had caught the attention of Ohio senator John Sherman, who, in 1890, had succeeded in his quest to combat the monopoly giants with the passage of a sweeping antitrust act bearing his name.

In 1907, a Chicago federal judge had fined Rockefeller's Standard Oil empire a then staggering sum of $29,240,000, the maximum blow it could deliver for 1,462 restraint of trade violations. The *New York Times* called it "the most important case against a trust in the history of the United States."[12] And who was the judge behind such a far-reaching antitrust case? None other than the baseball's future powerful commissioner—the one who kept African Americans out of the game, the one who clamped down on the 1919 Black Sox gambling fiasco, and the one who ruled the game with an iron fist—Kenesaw Mountain Landis.

On May 15, 1911, the Supreme Court ruled that the Standard Oil trust should be broken apart. This red-letter day not only affected American businesses but also served as an epiphany for baseball.

In 1914 the Sherman Act was followed by the federal Clayton Antitrust Act, both of which paved the way for labor unions by statutorily exempting them from the reach of antitrust laws and laying specific ground rules for government scrutiny of certain large corporate mergers.[13] A Justice Department eager to wield its Sherman Act sword examined most major industrial empires. Even Major League Baseball caught the attention of Washington—and why not? A powerful league of team owners bound together and acted as a consortium to promote the business of baseball and to exert complete control over the chief source of their entertainment product, the players. The major-league agreement binding the owners and teams together, and specifically the reserve clause that bound the players to those owners, was on its face a "contract, combination, or conspiracy" in restraint of trade and a textbook antitrust violation.

Thus, baseball was already exposed to the trustbusters' scrutiny when another threshold event took place that changed the legal and business playing field of baseball dramatically and further exposed the league to antitrust liability. In 1919, the Chicago White Sox threw the World Series and took money from the notorious New York gambler Arnold Rothstein. This gambling conspiracy, which was not only a fraud on the opposing Cincinnati Reds but also on the public, gave baseball a spectacular black eye. The game reeled from this embarrassment, and the owners retaliated. This scandal was the catalyst that led to the call for an independent commissioner, someone who could take an ax to the offending players, clean up the game and its public image, and control the owners when necessary. This commissioner would really become an all-powerful baseball czar.

The owners first turned to William Howard Taft, one of the game's most powerful fans, who was also known for his antitrust expertise, but he was enjoying even greater powers on the Supreme Court and turned down the position. The owners turned to the next most powerful candidate they could find, Kenesaw Mountain Landis, the Chicago federal judge and antitrust expert who had already nailed Standard Oil and who was an unabashed Cubs, White Sox, and overall baseball fan. Landis skillfully used the White Sox gambling scandal to garner and wield great power over every aspect of the game. Taking office in January 1921 shortly after the World Series fix had been exposed, Landis took swift and decisive action and banned eight members of the White Sox team for life, denying several of those who are otherwise qualified for a place in the Hall of Fame.

The game was being cleansed in the public eye, but the effort was a two-edged sword: as Landis took more centralized control over baseball and its entertainment power became much stronger, the commissioner exposed Major League Baseball to even more antitrust scrutiny if not liability. When the Supreme Court in 1922 ruled that baseball is not a business engaged in interstate commerce and exempted it from the Sherman Act's reach, circumstances strongly suggest that the infamous antitrust exemption was likely no accident of fate.

The confluence of events point to one logical conclusion: baseball in general, and Landis in particular, manipulated the Supreme Court either directly by talking to the right people in the federal judiciary or indirectly by making a carefully orchestrated public case that could not have been lost on Chief Justice Taft. The case that dramatically changed the game of baseball for nearly a century was the *Federal Base Ball* decision of 1922 between the National League and the Baltimore franchise of the competing Federal League. The Federal League believed that the National League was conspiring to quash competition and to hoard players by preventing them from signing with the new league in 1915. Essentially the Federal League argued that Major League Baseball was another illicit trust that should be broken apart as Standard Oil had been in 1911. The original trial judge on the initial *Federal Base Ball* case was the same Kenesaw Landis who was commissioner when the 1922 ruling came down. Sometimes this Landis connection is glossed over, with some students of baseball history implicitly accepting such ties as coincidence and legal scholars not always appreciating the baseball significance along with the legal importance of what otherwise would be quite a remarkable, and decidedly unlikely, happenstance. But, in truth, Landis's involvement was no coincidence. The Federal Baseball League filed a case in Landis's jurisdiction in large part because of his dual passions for baseball and antitrust, and the court likely assigned it to him because of his recognized antitrust reputation. Further, baseball just as likely tapped Landis as commissioner because of his baseball affinity and antitrust acumen.

During the course of litigation, Landis repeatedly tried to press a settlement. His effort eventually resolved the controversy, except the Baltimore team chose to pursue its own antitrust claims as far as it could. The case led directly to the eventual *Federal Base Ball* ruling that effectively exempted baseball from antitrust regulations in 1922. Free agency for the players was at stake, as well as the existence of baseball as we know it—that is, a consortium of teams acting together to serve their own best interests. When Landis became commissioner, he did not give up his judgeship right away and opted to do both jobs, thus serving on the federal bench while overseeing baseball from the league's offices in Chicago. He did not vacate his judicial post until March 1, 1922. (The Federal Baseball League had filed the case in Federal District Court in Chicago in 1915. Landis arm-twisted a settlement, but when the Baltimore franchise refused to go along, its case was eventually argued before the Supreme Court on April 19, 1922, or six weeks after Landis officially resigned.) Some regarded Landis's dual role as judge and commissioner as a conflict of interest. In fact, in February 1921 Ohio congressman Benjamin Welty moved to impeach Landis for his alleged baseball conflicts, but no evidence proved any actual bias and the impeachment failed.[14]

Meanwhile, consider Taft. As a devoted baseball fan and antitrust expert whose half-brother at the time owned the Chicago Cubs, a chief rival to the Federal League's Chicago Whales, Taft had the motive and opportunity to play hardball with baseball's antitrust status—but did he? Another approach is to ask a related question: did the Supreme Court really believe what it was ruling? Justice Oliver Wendell Holmes penned the court's unanimous opinion in the case, so what was the court in general, and Holmes in particular, ruling in similar cases at that time?

First, consider on its face the absurdity of the antitrust ruling that baseball is not a business in interstate commerce. In an analogous series of cases between 1900 and 1910 concerning the constitutional authority of Congress to regulate commerce among the states in general, and to impose regulations upon the railroads in particular, the Supreme Court already had ruled that even empty railroad cars sitting stationary in a rail yard were instruments of interstate commerce. Yet the Taft court's decision held that baseball, by loading those cars with big-league ball players and hauling them from state to state to play in monster stadiums for millions of dollars in gate revenue, was *not* engaging in interstate commerce. Moreover, another decision handed down within a year after *Federal Base Ball* suggested that traveling vaudeville shows could be deemed engaged in interstate commerce. So ballplayers on moving trains were not considered engaging in interstate commerce, but jugglers and comedians were.

The vaudeville case of *Hart v. B. F. Keith Vaudeville Exchange* was decided in 1923.[15] It specifically tested the *Federal Base Ball* premise with the

Vaudeville Exchange attempting to rely upon a similar exemption. The court wriggled out of the quandary, though, by finding that the baseball teams' travel was incidental to the business of baseball in a way to preserve its "non-interstate" quality, while the Vaudeville performers had to haul scenery and equipment that was instrumental to the interstate nature of their commercial enterprise. If that finding sounds like double-talk, it is, especially since the same justice, Holmes, wrote both opinions:

> It is alleged that a part of the defendants' business is making contracts that call on performers to travel between the states and from abroad and in connection therewith require the transportation of large quantities of scenery, costumes, and animals. Some or many of these contracts are for the transportation of vaudeville acts, including performers, scenery, music, costumes and whatever constitutes the act, so that it is said that there is a constant stream of this so-called commerce from state to state.[16]

Apparently the court believes there is a distinction not only between hauling the baseball players and the vaudeville scenery but also between transporting scenery and baseball equipment.

Landis proceeded to rule baseball with his rigid will, inspiring some to call him "the only successful dictator in United States history," a label applied well before people used it in the Watergate scandal of the 1970s.[17] In 1975 in the aftermath of Watergate, baseball fan John Paul Stevens became a justice of the Supreme Court.

As noted earlier, three decades after *Federal Base Ball*, Stevens also became entwined with baseball, antitrust, and the *Federal Base Ball* precedent. Associate Counsel Stevens helped guide the 1951 congressional hearings on baseball antitrust matters, during which Casey Stengel unloaded his humorous double-talking diatribe on the game only to have Mickey Mantle then testify by "agreeing with him." Those hearings would provide a watershed moment for American sports. As Harry Fetter wrote in a retrospective on the career of Justice Stevens in 2010:

The 1951 hearings proved to be a turning point in the history of American sports. They had a more enduring impact than the much better remembered piece of that year's baseball history: Bobby Thomson's "shot heard round the world" that won the 1951 National League pennant playoff for the New York Giants. Never before had the business of a major league sport become the lead story on the nation's sports pages, spilling over, indeed, onto the front page. The business of sports had become, and ever after would be, the public's business as well.[18]

Baseball had never been publicly challenged in this manner, and Stevens did much of the questioning about baseball's business practices. Sports had become big business, and baseball had found itself in Congress's sights. The 1951 baseball antitrust hearings set a precedent for challenging the business of sports even as baseball made history with Thomson's unforgettable pennant-winning home run.

Stevens was not on the court when Curt Flood challenged the antitrust exemption and lost the 5–3 ruling in 1972. But given the romantic homage to the game contained in that opinion, one can wonder what impact Stevens, the liberal moderate and devoted fan, might have had on that decision. As it was, the court took a traditional and therefore protectionist stance where baseball was concerned. Justice Blackmun's opinion allowed the *Federal Base Ball* antitrust exemption to stand, even though the court conceded that the 1921 decision was wrong.[19] So why was the antitrust exemption not reversed? The court used the argument that it had been law so long that only Congress should change it. Congress never took the bait. Fortunately, the court did not take that position when it overturned the "separate but equal" race doctrines of *Plessey v. Ferguson* when it decided *Brown v. Board of Education* in 1954.[20]

The *Flood* opinion, which sets a dangerous precedent that goes far beyond sport, suggests three truths about baseball and America. First, baseball is so entwined with America that even bad baseball precedent has become sacred. Almost like the legend of Bobby Thomson's homer or the game's own aversion to instant replay, the Supreme Court cannot accept fact over legend or tradition when it continues to deny the game's role in interstate commerce. Second, it exemplifies how judges lose their good sense when dealing with sports cases in general and with baseball in particular. Third, the precedent that *Flood* established is the law of the land, and while technically it applies only to baseball, the decision also stands more broadly as a beacon of injustice and suggests that Washington is willing to ignore the law when it pleases, thus undermining public confidence. Maybe the court and Congress feel they are being cute with the baseball tradition of bad law, but the real message to the public is more hurtful and more dangerous: all justice is vulnerable to "the vengeful god of baseball."

That *Flood* stands as a monument to delusion or manipulation is bad enough, but Justice Blackmun's ramblings about the "New York Nine" and his list of eighty-eight favorite ballplayers trivialized the opinion itself. Lester Munson, a Chicago lawyer and noted ESPN sportswriter and legal analyst, wrote the following for *Sports Illustrated*:

> In drafting his 1972 opinion upholding Major League Baseball's antiquated reserve clause in the Curt Flood case, Justice Blackmun obviously consulted sources beyond the law library. A lifelong baseball fan who kept a copy of *The Baseball Encyclopedia* in his chambers, Blackmun relied on that work, as well as Lawrence Ritter's *The Glory of Their Times*, to produce what was a much a windy history of the national pastime as it was a legal decision.[21]

The *Flood* ruling as a whole and Blackmun's opinion in particular were slaps in the face of jurisprudence and logic. The ruling essentially agreed with Curtis Flood on the antitrust issue, but when it took the blatant position that only Congress should change the absurd exemption, that cop-out undermined public confidence not simply for baseball rulings but also in the law and the courts overall.

Judges generally have demonstrated an above-average affinity for including baseball references in their opinions and often where non-sports cases are concerned. This interest should hardly be surprising given the game's influence on American culture and language, but it also highlights how much the game has become a part of America itself. Perhaps this phenomenon is best demonstrated by the 1975 "aside" piece in the *University of Pennsylvania Law Review* titled "The Common Law Origins of the Infield Fly Rule." As discussed in chapter 9, the article pointed out that the common law has evolved much as the rules of baseball have.

According to law professors Robert Jarvis and Phyllis Coleman, the infield fly piece became one of the most frequently cited law review articles among all written legal opinions in America—a remarkable homage to the importance of baseball in American history, logic, and law. Initially published without a byline, its author became immediately famous anyway when the October 1975 issue of the *ABA Journal* did a piece on the clever "aside" and named the real author, young Penn law student William S. Stevens, who had lobbied hard to have the article published in the first place. Unfortunately, the Philadelphia lawyer and teacher died in 2008 of a sudden heart attack at age sixty without publishing more extensively on baseball. But he had always appreciated the opportunity to make his contribution to legal jurisprudence with a sense of humor: "My ego is simultaneously flattered and bruised by the notion that something I cranked out more than 25 years ago would prove to be the highlight of my professional and academic careers."[22]

Somewhat ironically, during the same year that Stevens's infield fly piece appeared, two far-reaching events occurred that would change baseball forever. First, after their incredulous loss in the *Flood* case, the baseball players finally gave up their pursuit of antitrust relief. Under the leadership of their union chief, Marvin Miller, the players turned to an alternate scheme of federal laws, the labor statutes. They strengthened their union and in 1975 served up two test cases to challenge the reserve clause from a different direction, or arbitration. Pitchers Andy Messersmith (Dodgers) and Dave McNally (Orioles) were selected as test cases to challenge the meaning and extent of the reserve clause that had permanently denied the players free agency for so long. Neither re-signed with their teams, and both took the reserve clause to arbitration. In 1976 the decision came down: the reserve clause, as written, meant that teams could force players with expiring contracts to stay with their teams only one time for one additional season, and afterward, they could be free agents. Further, the owners themselves were to blame for the decision, since they had drafted the clause. But baseball argued that a one-time-only renewal of a player's contract would automatically renew the one-time renewal clause into perpetuity. Their egregious argument was potentially a winner except for one detail: the owners also had inserted into the clause an ability to cut a player's salary by 25 percent each time that renewal happened. The two clauses together meant that a team could keep a player forever while concurrently reducing his salary until it reached virtually zero. The arbitrator ruled that this clause was not logical or fair or even lawful.

So off the field, 1975 was a landmark year when the players won free agency, while on the field the 1975 World Series between the Cincinnati Reds and the Boston Red Sox changed how baseball is broadcast and viewed—all because of one of the most famous home runs in Series history. The fall classic between the Red Sox and the "Big Red Machine" was one of the most dramatic and exciting contests in recent decades. It featured a cavalcade of stars, including Carlton Fisk for Boston and Pete Rose for the Reds. The powerful Reds led the Series three games to two, so Game 6 was a must-win for Boston. The score was tied 6-6 in the twelfth inning when Fisk stepped to the plate. Pat Darcy delivered his second pitch to Fisk, who responded with a deep drive down the left-field line. Since a home run would break the tie and win the game, the following four suspenseful seconds became one of the most dramatic intervals in World Series history as Fisk, focused on the ball, excitedly waved his arms to "will" the ball to stay fair. Whether fate was influenced as much by Fisk's sorcery as by his swing is a matter for baseball legend, but either way the ball stayed fair, barely, and ended the game as a stunning walk-off home run.

The game was already a classic contest before the Fisk homer. At one point when Rose entered the batter's box, he told Fisk, who was catching, that it was the greatest game he had ever seen. The network television lens lodged in the left-field wall, or the Green Monster, caught the entire orchestration of Fisk's home run swing. Beforehand, standard broadcast procedures followed the ball in flight, but this time the cameraman stayed focused on Fisk. The camera broadcast to the viewers Fisk's arms magically pushing the ball fair as he jumped up and down with anticipation.

Baseball television broadcasting changed at that precise moment as television networks realized the drama came from the players and not the small, round object sailing into the dark. Although television still shows the paths of home run balls, the broadcasts now make a point also of showing the players and the managers and their reactions. Although the cameraman later said rats in the left-field wall had distracted him and that the shot had been a coincidental accident, it seems more plausible that he, too, had been caught up in the moment.

Such long-ball milestones as Fisk's homer and Ruth's records evoke a great deal of baseball romance. Home runs make a huge difference in the game—both in the score and in the action. That drama not only affects the soul but also leaves a lasting influence on all that baseball touches, including presidents, the Supreme Court, and the laws of the land.

★ **13** ★

THE DEAD BALL
MALAISE

Before Andy Messersmith's legal action defeated baseball's seemingly impregnable reserve clause, the game had evolved in the image of the American dream: good young men playing a wholesome game. Or at least that was how it seemed on the surface.

Prior to 1976, the owners were in complete control. No player could leave his team for another club—even the superstars could not so much as threaten the leverage of free agency to achieve a better deal—and the players lost every counteroffensive they could muster. The players could not even convince the courts that big-league ball was a business in interstate commerce. But to the fans, the players, and the teams had become one and the same: Mantle and the Yankees were synonymous, Ernie Banks was Mr. Cub, Stan Musial was a St. Louis icon, and Willie Mays personified the Giants. Baby boomers can still recite large portions of the classic lineups from teams like Willie Stargell's Pirates or Lou Brock's Cardinals. The press also largely refrained from covering the private, especially embarrassing, moments of the players' off-field lives. But at what cost? Free agency suddenly removed much of that magic, but it also propelled the business of baseball to a more competitive model. Former pitcher Jim Bouton's bestselling tell-all book *Ball Four* had also lifted the cap of baseball silence for a glimpse at the game's grittier, more human, and often funnier moments.

Once Marvin Miller and the players' union finally cracked the reserve clause through arbitration, free agency was available, and the balance of power shifted in the players' direction for the first time. But did the owners learn from their defeat, fight back, and retake the economic ground they had lost? In truth, the ruling in Messersmith's favor was a narrow one, and even the arbitrator warned that it should not be taken too broadly.[1] The owners could have fought to change the language to something more justifiable, such as removing the salary reduction part from the perpetual renewals of the player's contract. They might have lost, but at least they would have retaken some of the diluted contractual territory and likely would have regained some momentum. They did not. The lords of the game had grown complacent, and the owners reacted in a flat-footed manner, almost in denial that their absolute power had been successfully challenged.

On the field, baseball was experiencing a home run malaise, a timely case of lethargy coinciding with the lackluster Jimmy Carter administration and a new economic phenomenon called stagflation. A frustrated Carter eventually blamed America itself, scolding the entire nation for wallowing in our own "national malaise." Carter would not recover, getting bounced for Ronald Reagan—union leader, movie cowboy, and baseball man. The reasons for Reagan's national political ascension were many, including lofty interest rates at home that reached a prime rate level of 21.5 percent per annum and the national embarrassment stemming from the Iran hostage crisis overseas. One contributing factor to his success, therefore, was the country's looking to feel better by harkening to better times. Roger Maris's great home run chase of 1961 was one diversion that remained fresh in the memory of most voters, and Ronald Reagan offered a sentimental link to the great American days of cowboys, baseball, and home run power.

When Roger Maris slammed homer number 61 into the Yankee Stadium's seats, the home run was king of baseball. But as the 1960s evolved, boredom took over on the field and in the stands. Major-league pitching had caught up to the long ball. Slugger Maris had been the American

League MVP in both 1961 and in 1960, but by 1968, the MVPs in both leagues were not hitters at all but pitchers—Bob Gibson and Denny McLain. Pitching dominated big-league games, and many baseball purists were thrilled as the pop of the catcher's mitt slowly replaced the crack of the mighty bat. Baseball, in effect, was devolving into its own malaise, at least on offense, and in its own way foretelling the Carter-era lethargy that would grip the rest of America by the end of the 1970s.

By 1968, the top batting average in all the American League was the paltry .301 that Carl Yastrzemski of the Red Sox mustered, the lowest league-leading average in the history of the big leagues. In the same year the Tigers' McLain achieved the unthinkable from the mound and logged thirty-one wins. Sam McDowell of the Indians struck batters out 283 times while teammate Luis Tiant posted an invincible league-leading 1.60 earned run average.[2]

In 1960 all top ten hitters batted greater than .300, from Ken Boyer's .304 for St. Louis to Dick Groat's .325 for Pittsburgh. In 1968 Pete Rose, a one-man hitting anomaly, did manage an impressive .335 in the National League; yet only six hitters in all of baseball broke .300 that year, including Yaz, who barely made it to the top of the American League. Slugging averages, which take into consideration both batting averages and power numbers, fell dramatically. The leader in 1960 was Frank Robinson for Cincinnati at .595. Maris was second with .581, Aaron third at .566, Boyer fourth (.562), Mantle fifth (.558), Mays sixth (.555), and Banks seventh with a .554 slugging percentage. By 1968 the leader for both leagues was Washington's Frank Howard, who slugged .552, which was lower than Banks's seventh-place total in 1960. Although Frank Howard, a mammoth of a man, did manage forty-four home runs in 1968, no one else made it to forty. Four of the top ten batters failed to reach even thirty homers. In 1960 three players—Banks, Mantle, and Aaron—had achieved forty or more homers, and all the game's top ten sluggers hit at least thirty-one.[3] Moreover, the following season, 1961, was one of the great home run years of all time: Maris clubbed sixty-one, Mantle hit fifty-four, and six more sluggers banged out forty or more.

The most dramatic difference in hitting between the early 1960s and the late 1960s is found in those slugging percentages. While 1960's numbers were impressive, 1961's percentages were overpowering. No fewer than seven players slugged more than .600, with the top four including Maris (.620), Jim Gentile from Baltimore (.646), Detroit's Norm Cash (.662), and Mantle's .687 topping them all. Cash added a .361 batting average to lead the majors, while all the top ten hitters logged .322 or better. Perhaps most impressive of all, in 1961 Mickey Mantle led both leagues in wins above replacement batting among all players with 11.9 versus second place Cash at 10.0.[4] By 1968 the wins-above-replacement batting leader for all players was not even a hitter; instead, the top player was St. Louis's fireball pitcher Gibson, who blew the league away with a 12.2 wins-above-replacement, compared to Yastrzemski in second place with 10.1. Third place was another pitcher, Tom Seaver, as was the fifth placeholder, the Cubs' Ferguson Jenkins.[5] All three pitchers did happen to be good hitters—an ability that was crucial to the batting WAR statistics—and Gibson and Jenkins were even capable power hitters. In 1961 no pitchers were in the top ten.

With pitchers fanning, batters whiffing, and fans yawning, baseball rediscovered its manipulative roots. After the 1968 malaise and before the 1969 season, baseball lowered the official height of the pitcher's mound from fifteen inches to ten inches. At fifteen inches—and with some mounds at "Mt. Everest levels" of twenty-five inches, as Stan Musial believed—the pitchers had an advantage of motion dynamics.[6] From a higher mound the pitchers had more room to work with to throw sinkers and sliders, and from the batters' vantage the balls came in hard at a subtle angle, making the pitches difficult to hit. For several years, pitchers had been gunning down batters with greater efficiency, so the league felt it had to respond.

The results were spectacular for the 1969 season, even during spring training. *Sports Illustrated* observed, "When you walk into any training camp it looks as if a mountain has been turned into a molehill."[7] A stunning fifty-four runs were scored in the first three spring training games in Arizona, and the Mets stepped up to the plate as though every pitch was telegraphed, pounding out twenty-two hits in one game. In 1968, Bob

Gibson had pitched a remarkable thirteen shutouts. Starting with 1969 he would log only eighteen more over the next seven years combined. Although Gibson still led the majors in batting wins over replacement among all players in 1969 with 11.7, slugging was back in style. Rose batted .348 while Roberto Clemente logged a .345 average, and all the top ten hitters managed .309 or better. Three players had slugging percentages greater than .600, with Willie McCovey leading the way at .656. And home runs were on the climb, with Harmon Killebrew clubbing forty-nine for Minnesota while Washington's Howard hit forty-eight and Oakland's Reggie Jackson banged out forty-seven. Moreover, in 1968 only three major-leaguers had managed at least 100 runs batted in, but one year later Killebrew's 140 led the league. Every one of the top ten knocked in 110 or more, besting Ken Harrelson's 1968 plateau of 109.[8]

The contrast between 1968 and 1969 shows that hitting had made a comeback, and clearly the pitching mound was the cause. By 1969, the first year of the lower mound, the two top home run leaders—Killebrew and Howard—slugged a total of 97 long balls, a noticeable jump from a paltry 80 for the top two spots (Howard and McCovey) the year before. Still, the magic was not all back, especially where the marquee home run was concerned. In 1974, Mike Schmidt banged out only 36 homers to lead the National League, while Dick Allen topped the American League with a mere 32 home runs. The two league leaders combined had slugged just 68 home runs, which represented the lowest total since 1946 when Hank Greenberg (44) and Ralph Kiner (23) hit for 67 on the season. By contrast, in 1961 Maris and the National League's leader, Orlando Cepeda, had managed 107 between them. Teammates Maris and Mantle fared even better, combining for 115, a mark that may stand for some time, especially now that the steroid era is over.[9]

After 1969, although batting was on the rise, the home run numbers steadily declined. In 1970 the combined leaders hit 89 homers, and in subsequent years the totals were 81, 77, 76, and 68, respectively. Fittingly, even as home runs declined in number, they retained their magic. In 1971, the cocky slugger Reggie Jackson crushed a home run during the All-Star Game in Detroit that stunned a national television audience. Playing at Tiger Stadium, Jackson unleashed the longest home run ever slammed in an All-Star Game and one of the longest in baseball history. Pirates pitcher Dock Ellis delivered a slider that Jackson powered hard to right center with such force that the ball struck an electrical transformer perched over the stadium roof about 100 feet above the field. On television the ball appeared to still be rising when it slammed into the transformer.[10] Had it drawn sparks, the image would have been a real-life version of Robert Redford's climactic light standard shot at the end of *The Natural*. Taking into consideration that evening's weather conditions and wind speeds, the time the ball took to complete its journey and fall back into the stadium, and other relevant factors, physicists for the Hit Tracker Online website calculated the ball would likely have traveled a legitimate 532 feet had the ball not struck the looming transformer.[11] Thus it would have been one of the longest home runs ever hit, anywhere, anytime. As it was, the stunned crowd drew audible breaths. Clearly, indeed, magic still occurred in such monster blasts; unfortunately, baseball was producing fewer and fewer of them during its real games.

A few years later a slight rebound in 1975 bumped the league leaders' combined homers to seventy-four, just one more than Barry Bonds would hit by himself in 2001. The total slipped to seventy in 1976, with Yankee Graig Nettles topping the American League with only thirty-two. Thanks to headline sluggers such as Jim Rice, George Foster, King Kong Kingman, Gorman Thomas, Ben Oglivie, and Reggie Jackson, home runs increased from 1977 to 1980, when the combined leaders banged out ninety-one, eighty-six, ninety-three, and eighty-nine. Then a brutal labor dispute shortened the 1981 season, in which the combined leaders managed a mere fifty-three homers. Even after the labor action, the game failed to return to the short-lived resurgence in homers it had glimpsed earlier. The totals did not break eighty again until the underrated Andre Dawson for the Cubs and, perhaps prophetically, an emerging Mark McGwire, who was then with Oakland, each launched forty-nine during the 1987 season.[12]

Then history repeated itself. Another labor action in 1994 had already disrupted the game when baseball canceled the 1994 World Series. Fans were outraged, and many abandoned the game altogether. Baseball sleep-walked through a four-year purgatory as betrayed fans were still unsure about their interest in the game. But in 1998, a long-ball spectacle jolted the game from its lingering doldrums with a home run show for the ages, a return to home run power that drew even casual fans back to baseball. Baby boomers were reminded of the glory days of Maris and Mantle, while younger fans reveled in the home runs sailing into record books and trouncing the old-timers' accomplishments.

The record for most home runs by teammates in the same year is still the 115 bombs that Maris and Mantle launched in 1961. Fortunately, the steroid era did not manage to erase that one record, which remains a testament to the special wonder of that Maris-Mantle duo. Even so, the pandemic of artificial power in the 1990s and 2000s rewrote and thus tarnished most home run records. Not only did Barry Bonds trash the home run marks of Ruth and Maris, but in 2001 he also blew through the elevated steroid-era standards that Sammy Sosa (66) and McGwire (70) had set in 1998. The 2001 Giants' tandem of Barry Bonds (73) and Rich Aurilia (37) combined for 110 teammate home runs. They merited second place in the all-time list and surpassed such time-honored duos as Babe Ruth (60) and Lou Gehrig (47) from the 1927 Yankees, Hack Wilson (56) and Charles "Gabby" Hartnett (37) from the 1930 Cubs, and the 1932 A's mark of Jimmie Foxx (58) and Al Simmons (35).[13]

Many years before the appearance of performance-enhancing drugs, Ruth and Gehrig had combined for enough home runs to make the duo list three of the top seven times, including taking second place behind Maris and Mantle in 1961. The only other duo in recent decades to appear on the list, after Maris and Mantle but before the steroid era, was Mays (fifty-two) and McCovey (thirty-nine), who had a total of ninety-one homers in 1965. Overall, various pairs of teammates have hit a combined ninety homers on twenty-six different occasions, nineteen of which came in 1996–2006, or the decade of performance-enhancing drugs in baseball.

The more recent 2006 Phillies' tandem of Ryan Howard (fifty-eight homers) and Chase Utley (thirty-two) seems to have escaped the steroid tarnish, since both began in the majors just after the steroid era and neither has been specifically linked to banned PEDs. (Players still do stumble, however, as suggested by the highly publicized alleged test failure of star Ryan Braun in 2011. Braun's resultant suspension was later overturned due to his successful argument about the test sample chain of custody;[14] whether he was fully exonerated could still be debated by fans and the public at large.)

Most of the top power hitters during the steroid era have been linked to drugs in some way. Several such sluggers, though, have not been linked, including Ken Griffey Jr. and Jim Thome. And Ron Gant, for example, who jacked twenty-six in 1998, rounded out the much loftier totals of bigger stars like Mark McGwire (seventy), and made the list of power duos apparently without the aid of performance enhancers. Gant was known for his chiseled physique but was not necessarily linked to steroids.[15]

Astonishingly, the 2001 Giants have not one but two pairs who made the top home run duo list concurrently—Bonds and Aurilia and Bonds again with Jeff Kent (twenty-two). The 1998 Cardinals of Mark McGwire served up not two but three pairs all at the same time: McGwire (seventy) and Ray Lankford (thirty-one), McGwire and Gant (twenty-six), and McGwire and Brian Jordan (twenty-five).[16] While not all players on the list are known steroid users, many are strongly suspected, and the league has questioned several about performance enhancers. Bonds, McGwire, Rafael Palmeiro, Alex Rodriguez, David Ortiz, and Manny Ramirez have all been linked to these drugs in some manner.

Baseball may never prove the precise boundaries of the steroid era or be able to assess fully the actual impact of the drugs themselves. Statistics suggest the affected time frame as running as long as perhaps 1996 through 2007. Looking at the combined home runs of the top player in each league, a noticeable jump occurs from 1994, with 83 from Griffey and Matt Williams, to 1997 with 105 from Griffey and Larry Walker. In between, three consecutive seasons saw three curiously large jumps—from 1994 to 1995, 7 more homers; 1995 to 1996, 9 more; and 1996 to 1997, 6 more—or up from 99 to 105. The tandem numbers from power hitters in the same league also remained high, peaking at 126 in 1998 (McGwire at 70 and Griffey at 56). Looking at the top two National Leaguer leaders—Sosa with 66 and McGwire with 70—their total of 136 clearly dwarfs Mantle and Maris's pre-steroid mark of 115, making them look almost like amateurs. Then, as suddenly as they had risen in the first place, the tandem totals began to decline. In 2007, they dropped to 104 and again to 85 in 2008 with drug testing firmly in place.[17]

Did the owners or the league offices actually plan the sweeping turn to performance-enhancing drugs? Probably not. No evidence of overt conspiracy or any such premeditation has surfaced. Further, it would seem a stretch to conclude the owners possessed either the foresight to infuse the league with steroids or the power to instigate a conspiracy of any such magnitude, especially since it would obviously necessitate player involvement. But the leagues could have taken passive advantage of the situation as it evolved or perhaps could have even manipulated it. The motive was already there—a need to address the post-1994 fan base malaise and related fallout—and the opportunity would have presented itself once players began using the drugs. At that point, all that baseball simply had to do was look the other way and let the pandemic spread. The situation is not so simple, since the players' union appears to have ignored it as well. Meanwhile, history does not lie: the baseball lords have perennially demonstrated a propensity to tweak and even manipulate the game of baseball to serve their own needs. So, historically speaking, allowing the steroid home run barrage to continue would hardly have been out of character.

Anytime baseball needed a boost of offense over the eons, the owners supplied it. The spitball was banned when Ruth went to the Big Apple, and suddenly home runs were in vogue. When the dead-ball era became the lively "rabbit ball" era, entire team batting averages soared to .300. Then when pitchers such as Gibson, Koufax, McLain, and others began to dominate, baseball lowered the pitching mound, and batting averages and home runs went up on cue. Years before, when antitrust laws became a threat to the game's business practices, then by hook, crook, or miracles the Supreme Court ruled that baseball is not a business in interstate commerce. But then came Messersmith and McNally, who spawned a free-agency ruling that blindsided the owners. When players soon began to shop for better deals, payrolls escalated as the players moved from team to team, making use of leverage they had not previously enjoyed.

Not all owners reacted the same way. Exacerbating this movement and salary escalation was a new breed of shoot-from-the-hip owners who were much less steeped in baseball tradition than they were governed by business savvy. One of this emerging breed was the Atlanta Braves' Ted Turner, an irascible, front-page innovator who reinvented television with the superstation concept and then changed the entire world of news dissemination with an initially ridiculed, all-news cable television station with the straightforward moniker Cable News Network. But before Turner launched this worldwide brand, he first turned his talents to baseball and baseball broadcasting.

Turner had purchased an Atlanta television station that relied on cheap programming in the form of old TV reruns when he jumped into professional sports by acquiring the Atlanta Braves baseball team. His reasoning was simple: baseball was good television content. A six-month season has 162 baseball games, and all the drama virtually produces itself. Baseball games don't need any scripts, writers, rehearsals, or much original production or direction. In its own way, sports programming was in the vanguard of the big-time reality shows, and Turner was among the first to recognize its full potential.

Turner was also the first to see the value of cable programming outside the normal geographic viewing area and thus used the Braves to convert his station into a national cable power. A natural huckster, Turner knew that promotion would drive programming and that winning would help drive the station's promotional efforts. Turner, a young and brash new owner and a dynamic innovator, was hardly confined by the tradition, let alone the fraternal stodginess, of Major League Baseball. Once pitcher Andy Messersmith had been sprung to free agency in 1976, Turner not only signed the star pitcher away from the Dodgers, which made news in its own right, but also gave him the number 17 and a new moniker for the back of his jersey, "Channel." As a result, the center-field camera covering the pitcher would show "Channel 17" on Messersmith's back in a salute to Turner's television station. Soon Channel 17 would be much more, as he expanded his vast entertainment empire into the Turner Broadcasting System,

Turner Network Television, the Cartoon Network, the MGM film library, the Atlanta Braves, and much more. Turner also bought the Atlanta Hawks NBA franchise for more sports programming. Its eighty-two regular season games almost all occurred during baseball's off-season.

Turner did not shake baseball traditions all by himself, though. Charles "Charlie" Finley was another unconventional owner who danced to his own drummer. Finley was a self-made Chicago businessman who purchased the Oakland Athletics. Labeled "Baseball's Barnum" by *Time* magazine in 1975, Finley and his antics made Turner seem almost conservative by comparison. With a team starved for attendance and cash, Finley implemented a number of promotions. He held greased pig races before games, offered half-price tickets to bald men, and featured a live mule mascot called Charlie O.[18]

Finley's innovations began to affect baseball in more significant ways. As early as 1963 he had already petitioned the league to allow bright multicolored uniforms, and the colors of green, white, and gold became associated with his early Athletics teams. The rest of baseball took note, and many teams adopted brighter uniforms over the years. He also brought flashy white shoes into play, experimented with orange balls, and even invented the concept of ball girls to retrieve foul grounders. Finley also helped push the idea of the designated hitter for the American League, which in turn influenced the home run records by extending the careers of aging sluggers whose position play may have slipped.

Finley's offbeat pranks ranged from silly to entertaining to innovative. At one point he paid players $300 to grow obnoxious mustaches, harkening back to the old days of baseball. He invented the idea of ball girls, and he even hired Miss USA to be a bat girl.[19] Finley's stunts were largely tolerated until they crossed the line, offending league sensibilities in general and Commissioner Bowie Kuhn in particular. When Finley took the helm of the Athletics in late 1960, the team was the worst in the American League, had finished thirty-nine games behind the Yankees, and had compiled losing records for seven straight years. Moreover, even when he moved the team to Oakland in 1968, Finley found that the ballpark was substandard, the fans were apathetic, and attendance was sparse. Miraculously, one thing the

A's had done right during their prior years in Kansas City was develop a credible farm system. They traded a number of players, including a young slugger named Roger Maris, but they kept many, too, some promising. By the late 1960s the team had enough emerging big-league talent to push the Athletics over .500 for only the fifth time since the Depression. Two of the early stars were a standout pitcher, Jim Hunter, and a brash, flashy home run hitter, Reggie Jackson.

Unable to resist his circus-style impulses, Finley took his new talent and repackaged it for the public, even assigning catchy nicknames to his players. He gave "Catfish" to Hunter and "Blue Moon" to pitcher Johnny Odom. Jackson, though, earned his name the old-fashioned way on the field when his post-season home runs gave him the "Mr. October" label. Armed with crazy names, big facial hair, big arms, white shoes, and thunderous home runs by players like Jackson, the Athletics began to win big. Not only did they win their division five times in a row, but also from 1972 to 1974 the A's were almost unbeatable, winning three straight World Series titles.

Then came free agency in 1976. With all of Finley's star-studded talent, salary demands were inevitable and too much to counter. Seeing that his players could simply move on, Finley seized upon an opportunity. He traded some players the usual way and then got the idea to "trade" others simply for cash, essentially selling his players to other high bidders around the league. Right before the major-league trading deadline on June 15, 1976, Finley sold the rights to three of his star players. Pitcher Vida Blue went to the Yankees for $1.5 million in cash (a deal sweetened when Blue signed a three-year contract extension just before the sale), while Joe Rudi and Rollie Fingers were shipped to Boston in a package deal for $2 million. Such price tags are meaningful even today, but in 1976 they were such lofty sums that league commissioner Kuhn intervened. Two days after the trade deadline, Kuhn threw together a quick hearing and then disallowed all three transactions on the grounds that such sales were "inconsistent with the best interests of baseball." Kuhn was concerned about where such actions might lead in the future, but he may also have been motivated by revenge and the possibility of finally being able to best the impish pest Finley where it counted the most, namely, Finley's pocketbook.

Charlie Finley had now been robbed of $3.5 million, and he was irate. One week later, Finley sued Kuhn in federal court, accusing the commissioner of arbitrary and unreasonable conduct. The case was heard in Chicago, then found its way to the Seventh Circuit Court of Appeals in Chicago.[20] The clash of personalities was inevitable, and the court battle inspired bouts of public warfare.

On the one hand, Kuhn was something of a nerd, a stiff, or as some called him, a stuffed shirt. He was six-foot-five but had been a lousy athlete. As a high school senior, Kuhn was approached by the basketball coach who could not help but notice his size. The coach knew more than a little about basketball, too, for he happened to be Arnold "Red" Auerbach, who one day would coach the Boston Celtics en route to a Hall of Fame career. But even Auerbach could not make a basketball player out of Kuhn and gave up trying.[21] Kuhn then went to Princeton and graduated law school at the University of Virginia. Afterward he joined the silk-stocking law firm Willkie Farr & Gallagher, which happened to represent the National League. Kuhn found himself immersed in major-league work for nearly two decades, became a baseball insider, and eventually was offered the job as commissioner.

On the other hand, Finley was brash, confident, and unpredictable—that is, anything but a stuffed shirt. Finley was an outcast and proud of it. As early as 1973, during the A's World Series dynasty, Kuhn had tried to discipline Finley, who announced that the commissioner could "shove it up his big fat ass." By 1976, Kuhn was returning the favor. When Kuhn vetoed Finley's fire sale, Finley publicly called him "the village idiot," then thought better of it and announced an apology to "village idiots everywhere."

Unfortunately for Charles O. Finley, the courts in those days were reluctant to interfere with the inner workings of private organizations like Major League Baseball. Charlie lost his case in 1978 and licked his wounds, then sold the team in 1980 to the Walter Haas family, the owners of Levi Strauss & Company. Charlie made out in the end, collecting $12.7 million for the team that he had paid $2 million for a controlling interest in, in 1960.

Meanwhile on the east coast, Roger Maris was winning his first MVP in the same year that Finley bought the Athletics, 1960. But even the mighty Yankees lost the 1960 World Series in seven games on the strength of Bill Mazeroski's walk-off homer. As the great Ted Williams would later confess, at this point the reeling Yankees offered him a lucrative deal to join the team mostly to pinch-hit. Williams declined. It did not matter, for beginning in 1961 the M&M boys would bring drama, power, and winning to the Bronx. But soon a pair of pitchers would be making headlines of a different sort from the mound.

After the Maris-Mantle slugging duel in 1961, the pitchers began to make their stand. Just as Mantle and Maris had been long-ball teammates, Sandy Koufax and Don Drysdale—two of the best pitchers in baseball—were also on the same team during the early 1960s. They were such a magnificent one-two punch that after the 1965 season, when the two of them combined for a 49-20 record for the Dodgers and won the World Series, Koufax and Drysdale tried jointly to negotiate a lucrative contract for themselves. The Dodgers' owners were caught off-guard, and Drysdale and Koufax staged their own mini-strike, holding out for thirty-two days. They wanted to share an unprecedented $1.05 million deal over three years. At the time, Mays was baseball's highest-paid player at $125,000 per year, but Koufax, with a record 382 strikeouts, and Drysdale, with twenty complete games, made an impressive case. They eventually settled for a more down-to-earth increase, giving Koufax $125,000 and Dysdale $110,000 (many reports differ by $5,000 for each player).[22] Koufax never earned more, for his last year was 1966, and although Drysdale played through 1969, his salary actually went down to $100,000 for two years before reaching $115,000 in his final season.

Meanwhile, from 1963 to 1966, Koufax and Drysdale pitched the Dodgers to National League first-place finishes three times, and the Dodgers won the World Series in 1963 and 1965. Drysdale could hit, too. In 1965 he batted .300 and slugged .508, totals lofty enough to justify his occasional use as a pinch hitter when he was not pitching.[23] Koufax didn't hit much, but neither did his opponents. He was with the Dodgers from 1955 through 1966, and in the 1960s he led the league in strikeouts four times and earned run average five times and was ultimately named an all-star six times. In World Series play Koufax compiled a stellar ERA of 0.95, or less than one earned run per game.

Because these pitchers were so valuable to the Dodgers and because the idea of a joint holdout was daunting and dangerous to the owners in general, baseball negotiated a provision in the next collective bargaining agreement to ban such joint negotiating outside the context of the customary collective bargaining activity. That provision was agreed to both ways, meaning the owners could not jointly act on the other side, either. This agreement might sound benign enough, but it later came into play during the great baseball collusion case that arose out of Commissioner Peter Ueberroth's attempt to control players' salaries during the 1980s.

Ueberroth had caught the owners' attention when he led the successful 1984 Los Angeles Olympics by securing major corporate sponsorships. He took the baseball helm on October 1, 1984, but insisted on greater authority to issue fines and negotiated a hefty salary that was almost double what his predecessor, Bowie Kuhn, had received. Ueberroth's first major effort was to mediate a dispute with the umpires, and by the following summer he managed to resolve a players' strike that lasted only a day. His tenure already seemed successful when he also managed to negotiate a $1.2 billion network television deal with CBS. He reinstated two of the game's greatest stars in Willie Mays and Mickey Mantle, both of whom Kuhn had been suspended for taking PR jobs with Las Vegas casinos. Ueberroth also fined a number of players for cocaine use and investigated the Pete Rose gambling scandals.[24]

Ueberroth was smart, aggressive, and brash. He told the owners they were foolish for signing multiyear player deals and for losing money by chasing pennants. Ueberroth instigated a clandestine owners' meeting whereby they agreed to suppress player salaries during the mid- to late 1980s. Union chief Marvin Miller later exposed the scheme and filed a labor action that would become known as the great baseball collusion case. One might suspect the owners felt insulated by their antitrust exemption; after all, their collusion was an obvious "contract, combination, or conspiracy" in restraint of trade.

During the winter months prior to the 1988 season, the owners had established an information bank to share detailed data about salary offers they made to each and every player, giving them inside information about the reality of the free-agent market. Only three players switched teams during that off-season, and their salaries were suppressed because the owners knew what offers were on the table before they left. The clubs either forgot or ignored an important point that had arisen out of the Koufax-Drysdale joint holdout two decades before. While a new clause in the collective bargaining agreement prohibited players from dual negotiating, the players' association had gained reciprocal language that prevented owners from bargaining in concert. Even though baseball was protected by its antitrust exemption, the owners had essentially given back much of that protection in the collective bargaining agreement. Ueberroth, when he engineered the owners' collusion scheme, therefore violated both the antitrust laws and the labor agreement with the union, specifically Article 18 barring such joint owner actions.[25]

A settlement ensued whereby an arbitrator would reallocate aggrieved players' claims for additional compensation from a pool to which owners contributed $280 million. In 1991, about eight hundred players filed claims that exceeded $1 billion in total. Several awards exceeded $1 million per player, including sluggers Carlton Fisk ($1.2 million) and Andre Dawson ($1.1 million).[26] Moreover, a number of other players received a second chance at free agency and increased compensation. The collusion case was embarrassing and costly to the owners; however, since it was a labor claim and not an antitrust action, the clubs were not penalized by treble damages. This point was not lost on the union, which later inserted the treble damage provision into the collective bargaining terms. (The antitrust laws provide that winners are awarded three times their actual damages as a punitive measure to discourage violations.)

Although the collusion case was resolved, the bad blood between the owners and the players may have contributed to the most contentious labor action to date, the 1994 work stoppage that canceled the World Series and soured the fans. Some blamed the owners, others blamed the perceived greed of the players, but a major segment of fans held it against baseball, regardless.

In 1978, a television audience that averaged 44,278,950 viewers had been drawn to the World Series, a classic big-market contest between the Yankees and the Dodgers. Each team featured a number of star players, including Reggie Jackson, Roy White, Graig Nettles, Ron Guidry for the Yankees and David "Davey" Lopes, John "Dusty" Baker, Ron Cey, Thomas "Tommy" John, and Don Sutton for the Dodgers. The games scored a lofty Nielsen rating of 32.8, which was much greater than the anemic 19.4 from the 1970 Series. With ratings that hovered in the 30 range from 1977 to 1981, baseball seemed to be on the right track. But the Nielsen ratings began to slide, dropping to 27.9 in 1982, then 23.3 the following year. By 1989 they logged a horrible 16.4 and were still only 17.3 in 1993. After the 1994 labor dispute, the Series' ratings and baseball's television draw never rebounded. It never again hit 20, instead taking another dive in the mid-2000s as the steroid-powered home runs stopped. By 2008 the ratings could not even manage double digits, coming in at 8.4 with just 13,635,000 viewers, although in 2009 the share did creep back up to 11.7.[27]

Baseball had enjoyed its moments throughout the 1980s, a decade that featured such prodigious sluggers as Schmidt, Dawson, and McGwire. Two of the most famous home runs in history occurred during the 1980s, one during the regular season and the other in the World Series, both providing outstanding drama for the television camera. On July 24, 1983, the Royals' George Brett slammed a ninth-inning homer off the Yankees' irascible closer Richard "Goose" Gossage to take the lead 5–4. Then Yankee manager Billy Martin complained to umpire Tim McClelland, who concluded Brett's bat had too much pine tar under the rules, threw the bat out of the game, and disallowed the home run. Brett's bug-eyed, explosive gallop from the dugout remains one of the iconic televised moments in the annals of baseball. The home run was later reinstated and the ninth inning concluded almost a month later on August 18, with the Royals winning "again."[28]

As entertaining as the Brett dinger and subsequent reaction may have been, Dodger Kirk Gibson's ninth-inning blast in Game 1 of the 1988 World Series against the Yankees endures as one of the most dramatic in Series history. That day Gibson's legs were so bad that he could not even take the field for warm-ups, let alone play. With the Dodgers trailing 4–3 in the bottom of the ninth inning, pinch hitter Mike Davis coaxed a walk from the formidable reliever Dennis Eckersley. Manager Tommy Lasorda surprised most of the players, the media, and millions of viewers when he called upon the injured Gibson to pinch-hit. Although he was the National League MVP that year, Gibson was severely hobbled by both a bad knee and an injured hamstring. Lasorda's call was particularly gutsy—or nearly insane—because Gibson could not have legged out a hit. The only possibilities were a walk, a hit batter, a passed ball, a balk, a home run, or nothing, with the latter being the most likely. At first he nearly took a walk as Eckersley ran the pitch count to 3-2. But then Gibson cracked the next pitch. Launching the ball deep into the right-field stands for a walk-off home run, Gibson did his best to circle the bases. It not only was the first time a trailing World Series team had won by a walk-off blast in the ninth but also would be Gibson's only plate appearance during the entire Series.[29] His truly unbelievable performance was forever memorialized by broadcaster Jack Buck, who saw it live and was audibly dumbfounded: "I don't believe what I just saw. I don't *believe* what I just saw!"

Then came 1994, when baseball would not have any World Series drama on the diamond but plenty of controversy off the field. At the end of the twentieth century a poll of baseball writers listed the most thick-headed baseball events of the century. The top ten included Brett's pine tar incident, the Roger Maris asterisk episode, the Red Sox selling Ruth to the Yankees, the White Sox taking a pass on Jackie Robinson, the 1919 Black Sox scandal, and near the top, the 1994 player strike and World Series cancellation. The baseball work stoppages drove a stake into America's gut, and even presidents were moved enough to speak out. "I would simply appeal to both sides to get the matter resolved so the American people can hear the cry, 'Play Ball,' again," said George H. W. Bush.[30] Regarding the 1994 labor dispute, Bill Clinton was publicly frustrated, "Clearly they are not capable of settling this strike without an umpire."[31]

The World Series' debacle of 1994 was the classic last straw, and it was much more than a common strike. After all, it involved baseball, the all-American game. President Bush summed up its importance in the American psyche: "The Fall Classic has become a metaphor for America's love with baseball. For a few golden days every October each of us becomes a self-anointed expert. The Fall Classic evokes a continuum of memories. We mark chapters in our lives by the World Series we recall.[32]

But soon the American metaphor would undergo its most radical metamorphosis. In 1995 Albert Belle hit the fifty-homer plateau, the first to do so in five years and only the fourth to hit fifty since 1965 when Willie Mays banged out fifty-two. The following year Brady Anderson clubbed fifty, more than doubling his best previous output, while Mark McGwire slammed fifty-two that same season even though he had played in only 130 games. In 1997 America was treated to its best home run chase since the 1961 Maris-Mantle duel when McGwire and Ken Griffey Jr., were neck and neck, with McGwire finally besting Griffey fifty-eight to fifty-six.

McGwire had been traded to the Cardinals in 1997 during the season and lost some of his long-ball rhythm; otherwise, he may have lodged a successful assault on Maris's single-season mark. But 1998 would be different. McGwire slammed home runs in each of his first four games, serving notice that this season would be special. Then Sammy Sosa erupted, breaking the big-league homer record for June with twenty round-trippers. With that, the greatest home run race of the past half century was on. Baseball would never be the same. America would not quite be the same, either, for the lingering fallout of 1998 would continue to tarnish the image of baseball and even notions of justice and fair play. The Hall of Fame's steroid debate will linger for decades, and each year will fuel new rounds of arguments over the impact of cheating in baseball and its effects on America.

☆ **14** ☆

SOSA-McGWIRE: THE SUMMER THAT ROARED

I threw a ninety-seven mile per hour pitch to [Mark]
McGwire, and it went out at a hundred and ten!
—POWER PITCHER RANDY JOHNSON[1]

Indeed, so went the entire 1998 season of long balls, nostalgia, and sheer wonder. That season culminated in a near mystical crescendo of two iconic American attributes—baseball and muscle.

On March 31, 1998, the imposing six-foot-five, 250-pound Mark McGwire stepped to the plate in the fifth inning against Los Angeles Dodgers pitcher Ramon Martinez in the St. Louis Cardinals' season opener. Martinez was a veteran pitcher who would start fourteen more games for the Dodgers in 1998 en route to a 7-3 record, but the Dodgers would not have a winning pitcher on this day. With three on and two out, McGwire recoiled, then launched a Martinez delivery 364 feet for the game winner. McGwire's first home run of the year started the season with a bang: a grand slam blast for the only runs St. Louis needed in a 6–0 shutout victory.[2]

No one knew what was in store for baseball, the almighty home run, or even America that day, but the fourth game into the season gave us a clue. When McGwire connected on a 419-foot shot against Don Wengert on

April 4, he had homered in each of his first four games. Ten days passed before he launched another, but pitcher Jeff Suppan paid the price. McGwire smashed not one but three long balls on April 14, the first two off Suppan, including one that sailed 424 feet. But then pitcher Barry Manuel yielded a super tape measure shot that was calculated at 462 feet. The season was fifteen days old, and Mark McGwire had already smashed seven home runs, three of them clearing 400 feet.[3]

On May 8, when McGwire slammed a 358-footer into the stands for the four hundredth home run of his already illustrious career, he did so in his 4,726th at-bat, making him the fastest major-leaguer in history to reach the four hundred plateau. But McGwire was simply warming up. His next home run, a 3-run mammoth blast that measured 527 feet, came four days later in the fifth inning against Milwaukee's Paul Wagner. Another four days later, McGwire crushed a Livan Hernandez pitch to the tune of 545 feet. That spectacular shot was the longest of McGwire's 1998 season and in fact surpassed the longest blast of the entire year by any player on any big-league club. McGwire's fourth-inning solo shot contributed to the Cardinals' 5–4 win over the Florida Marlins.[4]

On May 19 McGwire slammed three more, all of them traveling more than 400 feet, with one measuring 471 feet. Whether in bunches or one at a time, Mark McGwire hit home runs so often that by the end of May, he had cranked out twenty-seven and already had a very good season for most players. Thus he had a clear edge in his quest for the 1998 home run crown. Was there anyone in the majors who could catch McGwire, anyone at all who could match the slugger's unstoppable momentum?

Remarkably, McGwire would not be the first to reach sixty-six home runs that year. By the end of May, the Cubs' Sammy Sosa had clubbed a respectable thirteen home runs off National League pitching, but he was still well behind Mark McGwire's total. Then came June.

Sosa was originally listed at six feet tall and 165 pounds, consistent with his leaner, speedier days on the Rangers and White Sox plus his early days when he joined the Cubs in 1992. In 1990, the sleek Sosa had cracked ten triples for the Chicago White Sox during a season when he added twenty-six doubles for an overall slugging percentage of .404. By 1998, though, Sosa had morphed into a different hitter, one who appeared to be a more muscular slugging machine and who weighed more than 200 pounds, perhaps a great deal more. Despite a .308 season average, Sosa hit exactly zero triples that year, but he would garner the second-highest slugging percentage of his career at .647.[5]

April was a respectable month for Sosa, who banged out six homers in twenty-four days. In May he produced seven more, including multi-homer games on May 25 and on May 27. Suddenly, Sammy Sosa had crunched five home runs in six days, all of them soaring 400-plus feet, including a mammoth 460-foot shot on May 27 against Philadelphia's Darrin Winston.[6]

Who was this guy? "Playing in the afternoon with the sun shining, it's like playing in heaven," Sammy once proclaimed, endorsing the lopsided number of day games played at Wrigley Field even after the lights were finally installed in 1988.[7] It was built in 1914 at Clark and Addison as Weeghman Stadium to house the Federal League's Chicago Whales. Although the new northside ballpark had a seating capacity of 14,000, small by modern standards, the playing field extended 356 feet to right and a hefty 440 feet to center. Only the left-field line, at 310 feet, was inviting to hitters.[8] Chicago catcher Art Wilson hit the stadium's first home run on April 23, 1914. After the Federal League collapsed in 1915 and its antitrust lawsuit against the National League came apart at the seams seven years later, stadium owner Charles Weeghman bought the Cubs from the Taft family and moved the team to the north side to play at what would be renamed Wrigley Field in 1926. Wrigley's most storied home run is still Babe Ruth's 1932 called shot, but its other grand baseball moments include Ernie Banks' 500th homer on May 12, 1970; Pete Rose's 4,191st career hit, which tied Ty Cobb's record for the most in major-league history; and pitcher Kerry Wood's remarkable twenty strikeouts on May 6, 1998, when he fanned every single Houston batter, pinch hitter Bill Spiers included.[9] Wood victimized some of them three times, including the three hitters at the heart of the order: Jeff Bagwell, Jack Howell, and Moisés Alou. Five years later, playing as a Cub himself at Wrigley, Alou became a permanent part of the Cubs' lore when fan Steve Bartman grabbed a barely foul fly ball from Alou's reach—an incredible moment that preceded (some say, caused) a Cubs collapse only five outs short of reaching the World Series. Thanks to instant replay, YouTube, and the sheer impact of the moment, the Bartman debacle may still be the most famous Wrigley image of the new millennium.

According to Major League Baseball's official website (www.mlb.com), the most memorable home run at Wrigley was the "Homer in the Gloamin'" blast. Legendary Cubs catcher Gabby Hartnett, on September 28, 1938, slammed a one-shot pennant winner that the Entertainment and Sports Programming Network (ESPN) ranked as the forty-seventh all-time greatest home run in big-league history. The Hartnett homer was a walk-off shot that came as darkness rapidly descended upon Wrigley. Hartnett was also the team manager at the time, making it perhaps the most significant home run clubbed by any active baseball manager. Adding to the mystique, the umpires had been set to call the game for darkness after Hartnett's plate appearance, a move that would have negated the whole game as a tie to be replayed the next day.[10]

Sammy Sosa, then, may have been the perfect complement to Wrigley and its penchant for day games. Born on November 12, 1968, in the Dominican Republic, he learned the game of baseball in a sunny, warm, and humid environment, the perfect prelude to Chicago summers. His first big-league appearance was for the Texas Rangers when he was still twenty years old. In 1993, his second season with the Cubs, Sosa showed a proclivity toward home runs when he launched thirty-three in 159 games. Sosa thereafter became a reliable power hitter, slamming twenty-five long balls in 1994, thirty-six in 1995, and forty more in 1996. In 1997 he played in all 162 games and powered thirty-six homers and 119 RBIs, although he batted a mediocre .251 on the season.[11]

When the National League–leading Cubs collapsed famously in 1969 as they lost out to the surging Miracle Mets, the grueling day games began to overtake the Billy Goat Curse as the popularly accepted cause of the Cubs' perpetual futility, but Sosa embraced the sunshine as a slice of heaven. Then came 1998, the greatest home run season in Cubs history and one of the greatest in the history of baseball. Sosa's effort surpassed both Ruth's and Roger Maris's records with room to spare. With Mark McGwire already making noise for the St. Louis Cardinals—the fiercest Cubs rivals—Sosa was poised for his own surge. On June 1, 1998, Sosa drove a Ryan Dempster pitch 430 feet, then powered an Oscar Henriquez offering 410 feet. These first two home runs in June were his eighth in a row to measure at least 400 feet. The Sosa bombs would come in bunches from then on, with one homer each day against different pitchers on June 5, 6, 7, and 8. In one game on June 15, Milwaukee's Cal Eldred personally surrendered three more homers to Sosa, and on June 19 Carlton Loewer gave up two in a game for the Phillies. The following day, Philadelphia's pitching served up yet two more Sosa homers, with the second shot traveling a mammoth 500 feet and becoming Sosa's longest tape measure blast of his 1998 home run barrage.[12] Sosa's 500-foot shot came at Wrigley Field in a game that also featured pitcher Kerry Wood, who struck out eleven Phillies' batters to complement Sosa's two home runs. Poignantly, Wood that day hit his own solo homer, his first big-league round-tripper. By June 20, Sosa had slugged twenty homers in his last twenty-one games. That month alone he had already garnered sixteen home runs, setting a record for the month. With ten days to go, he had a chance at the major-league record for any calendar month, which stood at eighteen.

Sammy Sosa's sixteenth home run in June was a rocket off Philadelphia reliever Toby Borland. The ball sailed over Wrigley's left-field wall, exited the park, and eventually thumped onto a rooftop across Waveland Avenue. That roof was thought to be 440 feet from home plate, but had the ball not landed there, its speed and trajectory suggest it was a legitimate 500-footer, one of the few genuine 500-foot homers belted in big-league history. Matt Beech, who had yielded Sosa's first homer that day plus the Kerry Wood blast admitted, "I stunk."[13] The next day Beech was old news. The new victim was Philadelphia hurler Tyler Green, who gave up a 380-footer for Sosa's fifth home run in three days against the Phillies' pitching.

On June 30, 1998, Sosa slammed his twentieth home run of the month, a solid 364-foot drive against Arizona's Alan Embree. Twenty homers in one calendar month was an historic milestone. Ruth himself had never managed such a feat, nor had the heavy hitters Maris, Mickey Mantle, Willie Mays, Ted Williams, Hank Aaron, or even McGwire. Rudy York, who had banged out eighteen for Detroit, set the American League's mark for most home runs in any calendar month in 1937. Ruth and Barry Bonds hold the record for left-handers, each with seventeen. Ruth's came in September 1927 for the magical Murderers' Row Yankees; Bonds compiled his in May 2001. Mantle is on the all-time list, too, for hitting the most runs in a month for an American League switch hitter, bagging sixteen in May 1956, his Triple Crown year.[14]

At the end of the 2012 season, the National League's record for a switch hitter was still Ken Caminiti's fourteen. Before his death, Caminiti later admitted to steroid use and warned the world about the steroid pandemic in major-league baseball. Bonds would one day admit to steroids as well, although he maintained his use was accidental—a position rewarded in 2011 with a conviction for obstruction of justice. McGwire would also admit to a brush with steroids (or at least a "steroid-like" substance). Sosa never admitted to steroid use, although he put on muscle mass and hit homers in record numbers during the heart of the steroid era. According to stories in the *New York Times* and elsewhere in 2009, Sosa tested positive for steroids in 2003, linking even the charismatic Cub to the juice.[15] He was not directly connected to steroids for 1998, although the circumstantial evidence suggests otherwise. None of the other names on the monthly leader list played in the steroid era: Rudy York, Mickey Mantle, Babe Ruth.

Meanwhile, as Sosa was rewriting the record books in June, Mark McGwire had a unique month as well, slamming an array of homers that were impressive for their tape measure length. McGwire clubbed ten homers of his own, or only half of Sosa's record number, but a remarkable nine of them flew more than 400 feet. His second of the month was a 356-footer hit off Jason Bere, but all the others went 409–472 feet, with several in the 430-foot to 460-foot range. Then McGwire did the amazing: in July *every* homer he launched soared more than 400 feet. Three measured 405–415 feet, but four went 452 feet or farther, including his first one of the month, a 485-foot blast hit off Billy Wagner on July 11. The long ball McGwire stroked off Brian Bohanon six days later was a moon shot at 511 feet. During the 1998 campaign, in fact, McGwire would lift five jacks listed at 509 feet or better, including his longest on May 16 at a superhuman 545 feet.[16]

McGwire's eight homers in July, while a nice number, were not enough to stretch his lead over Sosa, who actually narrowed the gap by hitting nine. In the first ten days of July, however, Sosa and McGwire had combined for one solitary 432-foot home run, which Sosa hit on July 9. The All-Star Game, traditionally played in the first week of July, likely contributed to the drought. Sosa was resting a bad shoulder and missed the game altogether, so he was slow to get his timing back during the layoff. McGwire played in the game—not to mention also participating in the increasingly popular home run derby—and may have fatigued himself by doing so instead of resting.

The 1998 All-Star Game was one of the most entertaining of recent decades. Played at the hitter-friendly Coors Field in Denver, the game featured twenty-one total runs, thirty-one hits, and five stolen bases in a 13–8 slugfest won by the American League. The combined runs set an all-star record while the combined hits tied the all-time mark. The American League scored at least once in each inning, coming from behind twice. In the fifth inning the National League was down 5–3 when Barry Bonds muscled a 451-foot shot to score three runs. Neither McGwire nor Ken Griffey Jr., managed to homer in the game, but Ivan Rodriguez and Roberto Alomar each went three for four at the plate, with Alomar taking the game MVP honors.[17]

Before the game, McGwire competed in the 1998 home run derby, the popular pageant that pits sluggers against each other as a sideshow to the All-Star Game itself. Griffey won the contest with nineteen jacks over the course of three rounds, with Jim Thome coming in second with seventeen. McGwire managed only four homers, all in the first round, for a disappointing eighth place. He would redeem himself in 1999, however, with a stunning first-round total of thirteen homers. He did not officially win the

1999 contest, either, for he apparently wore himself out in that one prolific round, but most do remember that McGwire's performance was nothing short of electrifying. He found a lethal rhythm and not only banged out thirteen during the first round but also launched some of the most impressive moon shots in recent memory, with several flying toward the top of the light standards before they disappeared into the darkness. At the 2000 derby, Luis Gonzalez recounted McGwire's tape measure night: "I remember in 1999 sitting there watching Mark McGwire hit balls five-hundred ninety (590) feet. I just hope mine go three-hundred thirty (330) feet and go over the wall. . . ."[18]

In the meantime, with the 1998 All-Star break behind him and his shoulder rested, Sosa rebounded with a vengeance in August, slamming thirteen long balls that month. McGwire managed a respectable ten of his own, but Sosa still cut the lead again, this time by three, and outslugged McGwire for the third month in a row. Sosa finished the month strong with three homers in four days from August 28 to August 31. McGwire closed the month with only two in the final six days of August, but those statement shots measured longer than 500 feet each. McGwire rode the momentum into September, slamming four tape measure blasts of at least 450 feet in the first two days.[19] But Sosa refused to wilt. From September 11 to September 13, he clubbed four of his own with the latter two both measuring 480 feet at Wrigley Field.[20]

By this time the duo's assault on the record books was inescapable. After hitting two homers on September 2, 1998, Mark McGwire was at history's doorstep with fifty-nine home runs in the most prolific power season since Roger Maris's in 1961. But as of September 2, Sosa remained on McGwire's heels with fifty-six homers of his own. Then Sosa hit number 57 on September 4 and number 58 on the fifth. McGwire was up to the challenge, though, clubbing his sixtieth that same day, matching the immortal Ruth, and becoming only the third big-league player to reach that magical plateau.[21]

Yet Sosa would not go away, nailing his own sixtieth the next week. The full-fledged home run race between Sosa and McGwire included two other components—the shadow of Ruth and the legacy of Maris. Once McGwire and Sosa had reached Ruth's coveted sixty, they were locked only with the specter of Roger Maris in a battle for long-ball history. Then, on September 7, McGwire knocked a 430-footer off Mike Morgan to reach number 61, tying him for first place all-time and only one homer short of posterity.[22]

Chicago and St. Louis were crazy with excitement. By this time the Sosa-McGwire charge was no longer confined to the Midwest; indeed, it had become a national headline story reminiscent of the magical summer of 1961. The home run mystique was back, baseball was king again, and America felt great.

On September 8, one day after he had tied Maris's record, McGwire slapped a Steve Trachsel pitch 341 feet for home run number 62. Long-ball greatness belonged to McGwire and McGwire alone—save for Sammy Sosa still nipping at McGwire's heels.[23] Five days later Sosa smashed numbers 61 and 62 on the same day; then he pushed his own personal mark and the Cubs' team record to sixty-three runs on September 16. He was only a single day behind the blistering pace of McGwire, who had reached sixty-three runs the day before, September 15.[24]

Then McGwire belted number 64 on September 18. Sosa remained quiet for a week, but on September 23 he cranked two more against Milwaukee. With that game, Sosa stood at sixty-five home runs on the season. He had finally caught McGwire, the imposing slugger who had enjoyed such a fast start and then found himself tied with the affable power hitter from Chicago as the end of the 1998 season was quickly approaching.[25]

When the sun rose on September 25, both Sosa and McGwire had garnered sixty-five home runs, and their 130 combined long balls far surpassed the Maris-Mantle total of 115. But neither slugger was finished. The *New York Times* predicted a battle could go down to the "last swing."[26]

The great 1998 home run chase was so intense that the pennant races themselves were almost lost amid the tumult. As the season wound down, the Cardinals finally succumbed. While St. Louis had a winning season with 83 victories, enough ultimately to finish the year at four games over .500, the Cubs were in the hunt for a wild card ticket to the playoffs until the end. Eventually the Cubs secured the fourth playoff slot in the National League with a 90-win season, beating out the Mets, who finished 88-74, while the Atlanta Braves secured the top spot with 106 victories. With all the home run hysteria in the National League, the media paid little relative attention to the emerging American League story, where the Yankees were destroying their competition with a spectacular 114-48 mark, a full sixty-six games over .500 with a formidable 62-19 record at home.[27] Perhaps in the playoffs it would be another story, but the regular season belonged to Sosa, McGwire, and the almighty home run and not to the mighty Yankees.

After 138 games, Sosa and McGwire had been tied with fifty-five home runs each. They were tied again at sixty-two, then sixty-three, and once again at sixty-five. The usual front-runner McGwire could easily break into the lead, but Sammy Sosa had other intentions. As the final weekend of the season began, the *New York Times* called the home run slugfest "Baseball's version of hand-to-hand combat."[28] The Cubs were on the road in Houston when Sosa stepped to the plate and faced Jose Lima, a six-foot-two right-hander who was having a breakout year and who would finish at 16-8 on the season. Sosa proceeded to torch Lima for a 462-foot monster that propelled him to sixty-six, or one ahead of McGwire. Sosa became the first man to reach that milestone in big-league history.[29]

Although Sosa had set the major-league record for home runs, with his bat landing in the Hall of Fame as a result, McGwire had a swift answer. Sosa would hold the big-league record by himself for all of forty-five minutes, for McGwire, playing at home against Montreal, cranked a Shayne Bennett pitch 375 feet for his own sixty-sixth home run of the season.[30] Remarkably, earlier in the year Sosa and McGwire had faced each other in a Cubs-Cardinals contest while tied at forty-seven home runs each. In the fifth inning, Sosa slapped a 368-footer to take the lead at forty-eight, but in the eighth inning, McGwire clubbed a Matt Karchner offering 398 feet to tie Sosa. In the tenth inning, Sosa belted a 408-foot shot to regain the lead with forty-nine homers. Even then, Sosa had held the lead for only fifty-seven minutes. So twice that summer, Sosa had surged ahead only to lose the lead to McGwire less than an hour later.

That September, however, McGwire was about to go on a tear. He finished the season by slamming two on September 26, with both balls traveling more than 400 feet. Sosa was still in the hunt until McGwire sealed the contest the next day, the last game of the season, with yet two more home runs.[31] Sosa failed to hit even one more. The season, at long last, finally belonged to McGwire. The Cubs, though, survived to make the playoffs, while the Cardinals did not. Meanwhile, McGwire had written a new slice of baseball history and American lore. His final shot reinvented the meaning of home run prowess: on the last day in the final game of 1998, a veritable season in the sky, Mark McGwire had slammed his immortal seventieth home run, besting Ruth, Maris, and Sosa by a wide margin.

McGwire had hit five home runs on the final weekend of the season, authoritatively closing the door on a magical year. McGwire had slugged 180 home runs over the course of three years, but his last one of 1998 was special. Cardinals manager Tony La Russa said it was stranger than fiction, and even President Clinton weighed in, calling from his motorcade to congratulate McGwire. At first McGwire said he was speechless, but then he conceded, "I am in awe of myself right now."[32]

The San Diego Padres made the World Series after winning ninety-eight regular season games and emerging from the National League playoffs, but the powerful Yankees took the Series with a four-game sweep. But thanks to McGwire and Sosa, the World Series was not the top story in baseball.

The great home run chase of 1998 stands out among many national and world stories from pop culture to politics. The music world featured the Backstreet Boys, 'N Sync, and the Spice Girls, although the latter actually broke up in 1998. The scorched earth upheaval in Kosovo boiled over with the Yugoslav army and Serbian police clashing with the separatist Kosovo Liberation Army in Europe. King Hussein of Jordan and President Bill Clinton closed a peace agreement between Palestinian leader Yasir Arafat and Israeli prime minister Benjamin Netanyahu.

The most provocative story of the year may have been President Clinton's escapade with White House intern Monica Lewinsky. Independent counsel Kenneth Starr investigated the president's alleged abuses and released the Starr Report. The investigation proved interesting, not only because the whole Lewinsky affair led to Clinton's impeachment hearings based on charges of perjury and obstruction of justice, but also because Starr's conclusions about veracity sound remarkably similar to the transgressions alleged against Barry Bonds in his perjury trial over a decade later, a perhaps unfortunate commonality between baseball and the presidency.

Many of the year's headline stories, including Kosovo, the Netanyahu-Arafat accord, *Titanic* becoming the all-time box office leader, and the Clinton-Lewinsky debacle, are memorable but not readily linked to 1998 in people's minds. Yet many do remember the summer of 1998 for the great Sosa-McGwire home run chase. Their home runs may have transcended the other events partly because the home runs' stories took place over the course of many weeks, with new chapters written almost daily. They offered feel-good headlines from city to city across America during a baseball season that was reminiscent of Ruth and Gehrig, Mantle and Maris, and Roger Kahn's "boys of summer." The long-ball summer of 1998 and the steroid-induced home run barrage that followed remain a matter of public debate that often appears in the headlines, sometimes in the chambers of Congress, and even in the courtroom, from Bonds's conviction for obstruction of justice in 2011 to Roger Clemens's perjury case acquittal in 2012.

While baseball permeates American sentiment, as noted previously, home runs have become the symbolic essence of American brawn, capitalism, success, and national identity as expressed in our language and literature and in our cultural history. It has been this way since the days of Babe Ruth.

Although McGwire was the first to surpass Maris and achieve the seventy-homer plateau, Sosa would soon set a record for consistency, becoming the first and only player to smash at least sixty homers in three different seasons. None of the other big sluggers—Mantle, Hank Greenberg, Aaron, Mays, Williams, Jimmie Foxx, or Lou Gehrig—had managed that number even once. Indeed, in seventy-one years, only three different icons had managed to hit the sixty mark: Ruth, Maris, and McGwire. But Sosa not only powered sixty-six homers in 1998, but he also followed that campaign with

sixty-three more in 1999 and sixty-four in 2001. More amazing, Sosa's spectacular totals did not manage to lead the major leagues in the year they
were hit. McGwire outslugged Sosa in 1998 with seventy homers and again
in 1999 with sixty-five, and Bonds won the 2001 crown with a record seventy-three homers.[33]

Through the close of the 2012 season, the sixty-homer threshold had
been surpassed nine times in big-league history, and Sosa had three of those
seasons on his own. The fifty-home run mark had been reached forty-two
times through 2012, twenty-five of them since 1990. Somewhat lost during the race in 1998 scuffle were the Mariners' Ken Griffey Jr., who hit
fifty-six, and the Padres' Greg Vaughn, who also had a monster season with
fifty homers. Even Albert Belle contributed forty-nine homers in 1998, easily marking that single season as the most prolific collection of individual
home run campaigns in history.[34]

The string of record-breaking home run crescendos ground to a halt on
the West Coast in the shadows of the Golden Gate Bridge after Barry Bonds
pushed the all-time mark to seventy-three in 2001. But it had all started in
New York long, long ago—first at the Polo Grounds, then at the Yankee
Stadium—where Ruth hit his immortal sixty and Lou Gehrig hit forty-
seven more in the Murderers' Row year of 1927, Gehrig had another forty-
nine homers in both 1934 and 1936, Mickey Mantle hit fifty-two in 1956
and fifty-four in 1961, and Roger Maris hit his sixty-one in '61. Eventually
home runs would find their way back to New York with Reggie Jackson
and other notables, such as Alex Rodriguez, who had fifty-seven in 2002
and fifty-four in 2007.[35]

It was as though a long-ball epidemic had spread from east to west, as the
records stretched from the initial fifty-nine homers at the Statue of Liberty
to sixty in Chicago and seventy in St Louis and on to San Francisco, where
it finally settled at seventy-three jacks in 2001. First imagined in Stanley
Kubrick's futuristic film *2001: A Space Odyssey* in 1969, the year 2001 was
then immortalized by the chilling tragedy of September 11, America's new
day of infamy. Barry Bonds's and Sammy Sosa's home runs that year would
offer an escape from the aftermath of 9/11, but Bonds did not grip America

in quite the same way Ruth, Maris, Mantle, Sosa, and McGwire had done. The magic was gone, partly because Bonds was not particularly personable and because the tragedy of 9/11 was too overwhelming.

Baseball did play a role in healing America after 9/11, however, that was more than symbolic. And it would happen at Shea Stadium in—where else—New York.

☆ **15** ☆

NEW YORK, NEW YORK

On September 21, 2001, the Mets' catcher Mike Piazza stepped up to the plate at Shea Stadium and ripped a home run into the teeth of destiny. The Mets-Braves matchup was the first game after the 9/11 tragedy. Baseball was back. America was back.

The philosophical question of whether to play ball during wartime is itself a statement about baseball's place in America. In the 1940s, many believed that devoting substantial resources and energy to a pastime while Americans were fighting abroad and the citizens at home were subjected to rationing was sacrilegious. Owners may have wanted to keep baseball going for financial motives, but the war presented an inescapable dilemma. Shutting baseball down altogether would be extremely costly for the team owners, but pressing on in the face of a national emergency might seem insensitive, if not irreverent. When Commissioner Kenesaw Landis wrote to President Franklin Roosevelt and inquired about the propriety of continuing to play major-league ball, Roosevelt's green light letter of January 15, 1942, said, in part, "I honestly feel that it would be best for the country to keep baseball going."[1]

History would vindicate the decision to play ball, but one major newspaper, the *Chicago Sun* (a predecessor to the contemporary *Chicago Sun-Times*), was an early supporter, referring to the green light letter as "the most notable contribution to baseball in our time."[2] Decades later, the precedent that Landis set by playing ball during World War II, and Roosevelt's reasons for doing so, supported the league's resumption of play in the aftermath of 9/11. Roosevelt's had argued that major-league baseball is a "recreational asset" whereby the efforts of up to 6,000 ballplayers would be invested in the entertainment of "20,000,000 of their fellow citizens." His main point about the value of baseball to America was as true in 2001 as it was in 1942. From the political and practical perspectives, Roosevelt would have known the value of keeping Americans entertained, focused, and bonded. Roosevelt was also a staunch fan of the game and devoured the sports pages of six different newspapers. He threw the Opening Day pitch no fewer than nine times during his presidency, a record that seems safe given the current term limits on the chief executive.[3]

It is interesting to note that the Hollywood film industry received no such letter or permission from the Oval Office, even though Hollywood continued to employ thousands of people to create a much-needed, entertaining diversion for millions of Americans. Hollywood had already hit a significant prewar stride with a sudden string of extraordinary films in 1939 and 1940. Now remembered as perhaps the best year of Hollywood's golden age, the single year 1939 saw the release of ten of the industry's most remarkable films, including such classics as *Stagecoach; Wuthering Heights; Goodbye, Mr. Chips; Mr. Smith Goes to Washington*; the iconic *The Wizard of Oz;* the epic *Gone With the Wind*; and Charles Laughton's emotional portrayal in *The Hunchback of Notre Dame.*

World War II made its distinctive mark on Hollywood. Even before America entered the war, Charlie Chaplin released *The Great Dictator* in 1940, an anti-fascist lampooning of Hitler and the Nazi regime. The war became the overriding theme of many Hollywood offerings. The successful string of Tarzan movies continued throughout the 1940s. At least one of them pitted the famous Ape Man against the despised Nazis, who did, indeed, have a presence in Africa, although mostly in the northern regions of Morocco and Egypt.

Some World War II films were documentaries about the war or pro-
moted the war effort. Such top directors as John Ford, Frank Capra,
William Wyler, and John Huston made a number of them. Scores of dramatic films about the war were patriotic hits among audiences: *Wake Island*
(1942), *Guadalcanal Diary* (1943), *The Story of G.I. Joe* (1945), and *They
Were Expendable* (1945).[4] But one fictional film that debuted during the war
may have been the most significant of all of Hollywood's war-inspired
efforts, *Casablanca* (1942), the timeless Humphrey Bogart–Ingrid Bergman
love story set amid the French resistance efforts in Morocco.[5] Many credible sources still list it among the top five or ten films of all time.

Baseball also contributed to the Hollywood entertainment magic. In his
prologue to the *The Pride of the Yankees* (1942), Damon Runyon described
the biopic of Lou Gehrig as being about "a gentle young man who, in the full
flower of his great fame, was a lesson in simplicity and modesty to the youth
of America."[6] The film solidified the bond between baseball and America,
and it was well received at a time when America needed heroes at home as well
as overseas. Still highly regarded, it is often cited as one of the top ten sports
movies of all time. Remarkably, *The Pride of the Yankees* was nominated for
eleven Academy Awards in 1943, earning more than 1943's *Casablanca* (eight),
an impressive showing even though *Pride* ultimately won only one Oscar.

Another diversion with a distinctly American slant is comedy. When
Universal Pictures released *The Naughty Nineties* on July 6, 1945, World
War II still raged, and the "Who's on First?" comedy routine had already
become a beloved expression of the American experience. But for the first
time, most Americans were able to see Bud Abbott and Lou Costello's
genius in the film rather than simply hear it on radio. In a December 31,
1999, retrospective, *Time* magazine named "Who's on First?" the best comedy routine of the century, edging out performances by Monty Python and
Will Rogers. "It's absurdism mixed with the easy pleasure of confusion,"
explained *Time*, "and Bud Abbott plays the perfect cool logician to Lou
Costello's frustrated inquisitor in the Beckettian farce."[7]

Also in 1999, a consortium of experts was asked to choose and rank the
top speeches of all time. Lou Gehrig, one of the original Yankee superstars

and the subject of his Hollywood biography *The Pride of the Yankees*, was listed at number 73 for his "luckiest man" address on July 4, 1939.[8] The durable Iron Horse of baseball not only played a record 2,130 consecutive games during his seventeen seasons in the major leagues but also was a prolific power hitter who smashed 493 career home runs, including 47 homers and a stunning 175 RBIs for the Yankees with the 1927 Murderers' Row. He won the Triple Crown in 1934, slugging 49 home runs to complement his .363 batting average and 165 RBIs. When he finally retired in 1939 because of the deadly disease ALS, Gehrig had compiled a lifetime batting average of .340, still the fifteenth highest of all time. Of all the home run hitters, Gehrig was the most efficient at driving in runs. Of his career homers, 166 were two-run jacks while 73 more were three-run shots and 23 were grand slams. Among players with more than 300 home runs, Gehrig still holds the record for most runs driven in per homer (as of 2011).[9] His twenty-three grand slams for the same team set a major-league record that still stands; no one else could ever manage more. (On June 12, 2012, Alex Rodriguez also hit his twenty-third career grand slam but not all for the Yankees.)

Even with all his prowess on the field, Lou Gehrig was more than a long-ball hitter; he was the quintessential American. He was born in New York City to modest German immigrant parents and was the only one of their four children who survived. He attended Columbia University in 1921 on an athletic scholarship to play football but found himself in trouble for honing his baseball skills in a professional summer league—all on the advice of Yankees manager John McGraw. In 1923 he left school, accepted a $1,500 bonus to play for the Yankees, and started off at Hartford, where he hit .304. That effort caught the eye of the big club. The Yankees called him up in September, and Gehrig garnered twenty-six plate appearances. He did not disappoint, batting .423 in that short span, yet he was unassuming and modest to a fault. When asked about playing in Babe Ruth's shadow, Gehrig replied that it was indeed a big shadow, but he added that a shadow that wide provides a lot of room to spread your own wings and be yourself.

Lou Gehrig played his last official game on April 30, 1939, ending his streak of 2,130 consecutive games. He announced his retirement on June 21 and made it official on July 4, 1939, Lou Gehrig Appreciation Day, at Yankee Stadium. The ceremony took place between the games of a doubleheader with the Washington Senators. Among a host of Yankee teammates, such as Waite Hoyt, Bob Meusel, and Ruth, stood Gehrig's former Bronx teammate Wally Pipp, an excellent player with a long career who is now largely remembered as a footnote to Gehrig. The Yankees gave Gehrig an inscribed silver trophy, while even the hated rival Giants, who attended the ceremony as guests, contributed a commemorative plaque. A crowd of almost 61,808 fans waited for Gehrig to speak.

No complete recorded rendition of Gehrig's actual address exists. Portions of it survive from newsreels. Many who seem to remember it may actually be recalling Gary Cooper, who played Gehrig in *The Pride of the Yankees*. Cooper resembled Lou Gehrig and had a quiet, gentle confidence that was reminiscent of Gehrig's modest personality. Although he seems to look older in photos, the great Yankees' first baseman was only thirty-seven years old when ALS, now commonly known as Lou Gehrig's disease, finally claimed his life.

As noted earlier, Gehrig's speech is universally regarded as one of the great sports addresses of all time and among the best American speeches of the twentieth century. One attempt to rank all the great American speeches sparked a debate over its placement. Few disagree with its listing behind the great orations of Martin Luther King, President Franklin Roosevelt, President John Kennedy, Stokely Carmichael, and Clarence Darrow, but ranking Gehrig's effort behind offerings from Vice President Spiro Agnew, Barbara Bush, and Justice Clarence Thomas's foil, Anita Hill, seems misplaced.[10]

Lou Gehrig's heartfelt speech was all of 277 words. Delivered live, he spoke off the cuff before the throng of Yankee fans who were also celebrating Independence Day. In 1938 Gehrig played the entire season, slammed 29 homers, drove in 114 runs, and had an on-base percentage of .410. The next year he played in only eight games with a solitary RBI. For Gehrig, the American dream had come to an abrupt halt.[11]

Lou Gehrig Appreciation Day was a quintessential American moment, one that combined appreciation, resolve, sentiment, and baseball. By taking place on the baseball diamond, the speech combined what was best about the American character—that is, Gehrig's grace and humility, his courage, and his feats—with the great game of baseball. Only two years later, the man himself was gone. Ruth and Gehrig had been the greatest power tandem the game had ever seen, and they still are. Mantle and Maris were outstanding, but nothing in baseball can match the hitting prowess, the fierce competitiveness, and the historic significance of Ruth and Gehrig together in the Yankees' lineup.

This instance was not the first time that baseball and America shared poignant slices of history. Nor would it be the last. Baseball, for instance, has a particular link to the national anthem. The lyrics to "The Star-Spangled Banner" come from a poem Francis Scott Key wrote after he witnessed the impressive bombardment of Baltimore's Fort McHenry during the War of 1812. Set to music, it was first played before a baseball game on May 15, 1862, but was included only as part of a band concert. Although a congressional resolution did not make the song the national anthem until March 3, 1931, a military band played it during the seventh-inning stretch during the first game of the Cubs–Red Sox World Series on September 5, 1918. Notably, serviceman Fred Thomas, on leave from the U.S. Navy at the time, stood at attention. His patriotic act was particularly poignant since World War I still raged, the armistice not coming until later in the fall on November 11. In turn, Thomas's effort helped establish a new tradition of playing "The Star-Spangled Banner" at every World Series game and season opener from then on. Teams also had it played for each game when they happened to have a band available. Not until World War II, more than twenty years later, was the national anthem played regularly at major-league games, a tradition inspired by the war and aided by the availability of reliable public address systems.[12]

Yet, baseball's most significant connection to World War II was found on the battlefield. More than forty-five hundred professional players from the ranks of the majors, minor leagues, and Negro leagues served in the armed forced during World War II. Among those men who served, thirty-four would have Hall of Fame baseball careers, even though virtually all would lose a material portion of their big-league time to the war effort. Some of the most recognizable Hall of Famers to participate in World War II include Luke Appling, whose service interrupted his career with the Chicago White Sox from 1930 to 1950; Yogi Berra; Mickey Cochrane; Joe DiMaggio; Bob Feller; Hank Greenberg; Ralph Kiner; Bob Lemon; Johnny Mize; Stan Musial; Harold "Pee Wee" Reese; Robin Roberts; Duke Snider; Hoyt Wilhelm; and Early Wynn. Another was Phil Rizzuto, the undersized American League MVP in 1950 who also called the Yankees' games as a broadcaster for forty years until 1996.[13]

Also among the Hall of Famers was Ted Williams, who lost almost five full seasons while serving in World War II and Korea. During his latter tour, he became a war hero by flying thirty-nine combat missions as a U.S. Marine fighter and taking enemy fire on three different occasions. Many still regard Williams, who remains the last major-leaguer to bat more than .400 (.406 for the Red Sox in 1941), as baseball's best overall hitter. He won baseball's Triple Crown twice, plus he had a third "virtual" Triple Crown season, barely losing out in the batting average category by less than 0.001 percent for a statistical tie. As noted previously, Williams also had a valuable attribute for a big-league hitter and a Marine Corps aviator: ophthalmologists in the armed forces reported that his extraordinary eyesight "was a one-in-100,000 proposition."[14]

Williams had more than superior eyesight, pure athletic coordination, and power. He was a fierce, unwavering competitor who was compared to Gen. George Patton for his "no retreat, no compromise" approach to everything. It led not only to his historic .406 season but also to Williams's refusing to settle for a virtual .400 season (.39955).

During the war years Ted Williams impressed his commander John Glenn, the future astronaut and senator, when the slugger crash-landed a plane that was missing its landing gear, then calmly walked away as the aircraft smoldered. Hitting .406 must have seemed like child's play by comparison.

Williams's final day in baseball was no different than others in his entire career. He played surly, superlative, and more than a bit eccentric. On

September 28, 1960, the forty-two-year-old stepped to the plate at Fenway Park in the eighth inning against the Orioles. He crunched a 1-1 pitch into the stands for his 521st career home run, circled the bases, and disappeared into the dugout and posterity. He never emerged again as an active player, not even to take a bow or to play the field in the top of the ninth inning. With three games left, he simply retired. When asked how he felt about launching his final home run, Williams' response was typical: "I felt nothing."[15] If Williams could have hit 40 homers per year during the five years he was out of the game, he would have finished his career with 721 homers and overtaken the Babe's record. Williams made no fuss, however; he simply walked away a winner.

Before his 1947 major-league breakthrough, groundbreaking Hall of Famer Jackie Robinson also served during World War II. Robinson had been in Honolulu to play semipro football and was on a ship sailing back to the mainland when the Japanese attacked Pearl Harbor on December 7, 1941. Robinson was inducted on April 3, 1942; entered officer's training; and was commissioned a second lieutenant on January 28, 1943. Thereafter, however, he was subjected to so much racial discrimination during training at Fort Riley, Kansas, that he was transferred to Fort Hood, Texas. The military in those days was highly segregated, so the discrimination did not change. When a military bus driver ordered Robinson to the back of a bus, the soldier stood his ground. He was court-martialed for his stand against discrimination, so he was unable to leave for the European theater with his unit. Later Robinson was exonerated at trial and ultimately received an honorable discharge.[16] The racial incident that sabotaged Robinson's service left the U.S. Army looking much worse than Robinson did.

Jackie was hardly the only black ballplayer to serve in the armed forces during World War II. Legions of African American players were inducted or otherwise joined, including Larry Doby, who served in the navy during 1944–1945, and Monte Irvin, who was in the army in 1943–1946. Herb Bracken, a pitcher for the Cleveland Buckeyes, was 13-1 against the competitive Great Lakes Naval Station teams before shipping out to Hawaii. Elmer Carter of the Kansas City Monarchs served in North Africa and Normandy and was later wounded at the Battle of the Bulge, and Marlin Carter, from the Memphis Red Sox, was in the Pacific and saw Hiroshima and Nagasaki before returning home. Leon Day, with the Newark Eagles, landed at Utah Beach with the 818th Amphibian Battalion on D-Day. He survived the landing and served in the army until 1945. Henry "Hank" Thompson went from the Kansas City Monarchs to the Battle of the Bulge.[17] The complete list is extensive, including Chicagoans Henry "Hank" Presswood and Johnny Washington, both of whom served and survived their stints in the army. Presswood is a sweet, soft-spoken man living in Chicago. Washington, a talented storyteller, was shot and injured his knee in combat, but he still managed to play baseball when he returned. Tragically, none of these men served in an integrated branch of the armed forces, for President Truman's Executive Order 9981, officially desegregating the military, was not issued until July 26, 1948.[18]

While attending a Columbia University graduation, NBCSports.com contributor Filip Bondy once heard Noam Chomsky proclaim, "There are no heroes in sports."[19] Chomsky was wrong. There are examples too numerous to mention, not the least of whom are the heroes of actual battle like Ted Williams and Leon Day. Muhammad Ali helped stem the tide of the Vietnam War by challenging and defeating federal authorities in court. NFL player Pat Tillman in 2002 walked away from a lucrative playing contract and joined the U.S. Army to fight the Iraq War, ultimately paying for that decision with his life. Lou Gehrig gave one of the great American speeches on what should have been the low point of his life. Further, Jackie Robinson served in the military *and* was a genuine hero on the playing field, game after game.

Baseball's standing as America's game has been continually reinforced by the breadth of baseball's impact on America, from Roosevelt's green light letter to the tradition of playing "The Star-Spangled Banner" to presidents throwing the first pitch to players becoming war heroes to breaking segregation with integration and more. But nowhere was baseball more indelibly part of America than it was on September 21, 2001.

The fabric and foundation of America had been shaken ten days earlier, a day so tragic that it is remembered solely by its date. After the attacks on New York City and the Pentagon and the plane crash in Shanksville, Pennsylvania, America came almost to a halt, its skies empty after all air traffic had been grounded. Stunned workers went home, the news and sights of the tragedy played endlessly around the globe, and major-league baseball was canceled while the NFL delayed the second week of its season, making up the games in January. Within days after 9/11, when the twin towers were obliterated, taking with them 2,752 souls, players from the New York Mets and the NFL's New York Giants visited Ground Zero to support grieving families and rescue workers.

Major-league ball was on hold for ten days as America wept, then regrouped. On September 21, in the first ballgame played in New York after baseball's hiatus, the Mets met rival Atlanta Braves at Shea Stadium. With LaGuardia Airport across the way, multiple planes overhead were an eerie reminder of the hijacked jetliners. People did not know if another plane would be hijacked and feared another attack might occur anywhere, but undeterred fans filled Shea Stadium.

More than excitement was in the air that night. Everyone felt a surge of hope, a sense of unity, and an outpouring of pride. Then the New York Police Department Band took to the field. When it played "The Star-Spangled Banner" as Marc Anthony sang, all the players stood on the baselines as they do for the World Series. After the anthem, the players shook hands with each other and touched Americans' hearts. With the Mets wearing hats from the New York City Police and Fire Departments, all the players shook hands with the firemen and police officers on hand as well.[20] The first responders then left the field to the sound of "Amazing Grace."

Televised nationally, the game was an emotional catharsis. If baseball could go on, so would the world. The seventh-inning stretch arrived and singer Liza Minnelli stepped forward. Her rousing performance of "New York, New York" elicited tears, pride, joy, and sorrow all at once. As she belted out the words, with an escort of police and firefighters who danced behind her, fans in the stands waved hundreds of flags and signs that read "Always Remember," "Thank you NYPD," "I ♥ New York," and others.

As America watched on television, the Mets' Mike Piazza stepped to the plate in the eighth inning and cracked a two-run shot into the stands, sealing a 3–2 win over the Atlanta Braves.[21] It was a symbolic, improbable moment as the ball sailed over the outfield wall. It was as if baseball had given America permission to play once again and to laugh, rejoice, and return to its competitive, irreverent roots.

All the Mets players donated their paychecks for that game to a fund for relief workers and their families, or about $500,000 in total.[22] Five years later Piazza was still moved by the huge losses on 9/11 and reflected, "In death, those people taught us so much about living."[23]

It may have been only four seconds of glory, but Piazza's home run in 2001 helped heal a shell-shocked nation. His homer helped recall the Ruthian days of America's glory and all the Babe's men who would emerge from the great slugger's shadow.

A decade later, on September 11, 2011, Major League Baseball stumbled when it refused to allow the Mets players to wear New York Police and Fire Department caps on the tragedy's tenth anniversary, even as baseball itself was commemorating that fateful day. "Rules are rules," the game said, but this request came from Shea, where Liza, the police, and the firefighters had brought baseball and America back from the depths of horror. And it came from all of New York, a place where legions of fans had lost friends and family on 9/11. The swift and vocal national backlash excoriated the baseball brass.

Yet the nearly universal negative reaction did not suggest that baseball had diminished in importance; instead, it demonstrated the opposite: baseball continued to be important to the American experience. Baseball is still inseparable from great national meaning.

THE SCARLET NUMBER

While September 2001 was leaving its mark on the American landscape, Barry Bonds was at the peak of his career with a dual assault on posterity.

Although the 9/11 attack on America may have been directed at the World Trade Center and other specific targets, its deeper meaning leaves lingering questions about the nature of terrorism in the new millennium. While the escalation of the war terrorism rightfully overshadowed Barry Bonds's quest for the home run record, the backstory of his bid for greatness nonetheless begs more questions of Bonds, baseball, and history.

Bonds says his use of steroids was accidental. For taking that position, Bonds was, in part, rewarded with a conviction for obstruction of justice. Bonds was reportedly upset, nearly depressed, over the thunderous shots that Mark McGwire and Sammy Sosa had hit during what appeared to be a magical 1998 home run season. At the time, Bonds was perhaps the best all-around player in the major leagues. With Willie Mays as his godfather, an Olympic sprinter as his aunt, big-league star Bobby Bonds as his father, and the great Reggie Jackson as his distant cousin, Barry was a pedigree performer in every respect: the consummate five-tool ballplayer with speed and defense, he could run, throw, and hit for power and average. But in 1998 Barry Bonds was not even a footnote to that season's historic campaign.

A first-round pick of the Pittsburgh Pirates in 1985, Barry Bonds was listed at six-foot-one and 185 pounds, a svelte athlete who could run and dazzle fans in the mold of Roberto Clemente, who had also played for the Pirates.[1] By 2001 his body had swollen measurably, perhaps to 220 pounds or more, and eventually he could hardly run at all. But he could still swing for the fences.

In 1987, his second year in the majors, Bonds had nine triples with thirty-four doubles and ninety-nine runs scored, all reflecting his considerable speed and baseball talent. During his first six years, Bonds had respectable home run years slugging between sixteen and thirty-three per season while generally batting in the mid- to upper .200s (even .301 in 1990). Moreover, from 1989 through 1992, Bonds continued to make good use of his speed by averaging 41.5 stolen bases per season. But 1992, his seventh season, was a threshold year as Bonds led the league in runs with 109 and walks at 127, while posting a .311 batting average and thirty-four home runs, his career high to that point.[2] This breakout year for Bonds established him as a genuine star and earned him the National League's MVP honors. It was also his last campaign in Pittsburgh, a small-market team that could no longer afford to keep him.

In 1993, Bonds had another outstanding season, this time for the San Francisco Giants, where his father had played two decades before. He led the league in home runs with forty-six, RBIs at 123, and a slugging percentage of .677. He also had 126 more walks, a spectacular number, and a sparkling batting average of .336. Bonds also won his third MVP award. He continued as a solid player through 1997, leading the league in walks four times in a row and finishing high in the MVP voting each year.[3]

Then came 1998, an individual season that normally would have been lauded as a fabulous year for any ballplayer when Bonds hit forty-four doubles, seven triples, and thirty-seven home runs. He also had 122 RBIs, 130 walks, and a .303 average, all of which earned him an eighth-place finish in the MVP voting.[4] But his effort was barely a footnote in the record books in a year when Mark McGwire became the first to surpass both Babe Ruth's and Roger Maris's records with sixty-two homers and then Sammy Sosa became the first player to reach sixty-six home runs. By season's end, McGwire's seventy home runs appeared to be an unbreakable record for the ages.

As noted previously, Mark McGwire had also become a mountainous slugger who stood six-foot-five and weighed 250 pounds or more. (He had been listed at 215 pounds as a rookie.) In 1998 he not only slammed a home run every 7.27 at-bats but also launched them high and far, with ten measuring 501 feet or more that season, including his longest at 545 feet.[5] By comparison, Mickey Mantle allegedly had six tape measure homers that exceeded 600 feet, going beyond the 565-footer at Griffith Stadium that ranks as his longest official blast. To be fair, the measuring techniques in the 1950s and 1960s were less sophisticated, and a Yankee front-office employee actually stepped off Mantle's 1953 Griffith homer. Still, some of those homers are preserved on film or videotape, including the Yankee Stadium facade shot, so they can be analyzed more scientifically. Whether McGwire could smash tape measure home run balls as well as Mantle did is a matter of debate, but certainly McGwire's 1998 season was at the time the most prolific long-ball season in the annals of the game.

McGwire and Bonds had each broken into the majors in 1986. Bonds took time to develop his power, but from the beginning McGwire was no stranger to home runs, slamming 49 to lead the league in 1987, his first full season. Like Bonds, he made pitchers nervous, had a good eye at the plate, and thus led the league in walks with 110 in 1990. Except for shortened seasons in 1993 and 1994 largely owing to a foot injury, McGwire played nearly full seasons from 1987 through 1999 and averaged 45.5 home runs per year.

Except for those forty-nine homers in his first entire season, McGwire was consistent but did not have a true breakout year through 1995. Then in 1996 he led the league in homers with fifty-two, walked a personal best 116 times, and led the league in both on-base percentage and slugging average. He even batted .312, the first time McGwire exceeded .300 in any of his full seasons to that point. Unlike Bonds, however, speed was clearly not in McGwire's arsenal. Although McGwire did manage four triples in 1987 and one more in 1988, he did not hit another—his last career triple—until

1999. Besides those six triples, he also compiled an anemic twelve total stolen bases during his sixteen major-league seasons.[6]

In 1997, McGwire was traded mid-year from Oakland to the St. Louis Cardinals, where he played his final fifty-one games of the year. Then came 1998, his first full season in St. Louis, and it proved to be much more than a breakout year. McGwire led the league with a stunning 162 bases on balls, a .752 slugging percentage, and a milestone seventy home runs that reinvented baseball history and buried the historic marks of Ruth and Maris. Remarkably, though, McGwire did not win the MVP in 1998. Instead, he finished second in the voting for the best showing of his career.[7]

In 1998 the most valuable player was the camera-friendly and personable Sammy Sosa. Originally listed as a slight six-footer at only 165 pounds, Sosa broke into the majors with the Texas Rangers on June 16, 1989. After only twenty games in Texas he was traded to the Chicago White Sox, where he spent the rest of the 1991 season. In 1990 Sosa was a speedy right fielder who slapped ten triples to go with fifteen homers and a modest .233 batting average. He also managed to strike out 150 times, an unusually high number for a non-power hitter. In 1991 his RBIs (just 33), home runs (ten), triples (one), and batting average (.203, the lowest of his career) all fell off at once.[8] The Sox gave up on Sosa and traded him and pitcher Ken Patterson to the Cubs in exchange for the aging star George Bell right before the 1992 season.

At first the White Sox appeared to have the better end of the deal. In 1992 Bell clubbed twenty-five homers for the south siders, adding a more than respectable 112 RBIs, although his batting average (.255) and on-base percentage (.294) were suspect. He also led the league by grounding into double plays twenty-nine times that year. Sosa, meanwhile, batted .260 for the Cubs but hit only eight home runs and had 25 RBIs in sixty-seven games, a less-than-stellar performance.[9]

The following season, 1993, was a different story. Sosa played in 159 games with thirty-three home runs, 93 RBIs, ninety-two runs scored, and a career high in stolen bases at thirty-six.[10] Meanwhile, 1993 was Bell's final year in the majors. He managed only thirteen homers, 64 RBIs, and a weak .217 average. Bell was finished, but Sosa was only getting warmed up.[11]

Ensconced on one of America's sentimental teams, the Cubs, Sosa would soon take center stage at the venerable Wrigley Field thanks to his engaging on-camera personality plus his very big swing. But it did not happen at first. During his first seven seasons in the majors, Sosa averaged 18.6 home runs per year and never hit as many as 40 during that stretch. But in 1996, his eighth season, Sosa slammed 40 homers with a .564 slugging percentage—both numbers his highest to date—even though he only played in 124 games that year. In 1997, Sosa's progress stalled. He played in all 162 games with 694 plate appearances, matching his career best at that point with 119 RBIs, but even with 153 more plate appearances, he hit 4 fewer home runs than he had the previous year. Not only that, he had a league-leading 174 strikeouts.[12] Sosa was morphing into a different player, one with an all-out slugging mentality, but the transition would not be complete until 1998, Sosa's magnum opus.

It all came together in 1998. The Cubs fielded a team good enough for ninety wins and a playoff appearance under manager Jim Riggleman, while McGwire's Cardinals finished with eighty-three wins and third place in the division. This difference may have been the primary reason that Sosa snagged the MVP honors that year over McGwire and his seventy home runs. In 1998 Sosa had 722 plate appearances, the best of his entire career, and sixty-six home runs; moreover, he led the league with 134 runs scored, 158 RBIs, and, not surprising, 171 strikeouts. Somewhat tellingly, it was also the first full season of his career that Sosa did not hit any triples at all, perhaps partly owing to bad luck and partly to his apparent weight gain and heavily muscled frame.[13] By then, the once fleet-footed 165-pounder appeared to pack more than 200 pounds.

McGwire would only have one more sixty-plus season, but Sosa had two more, slamming sixty-three long balls in 1999 and sixty-four in 2001. His latter total was lost behind Bonds's record-breaking seventy-three homers in 2001, but Sosa's sixty-four bombs made him the first and only player to hit more than sixty three times. Further, Sosa still bested Bonds that year by leading the league in runs scored (146) and RBIs (his career best 160) while batting an impressive .328 (also a career high).[14]

Then came 2002. Sosa hit forty-nine home runs, or fifteen fewer than the year before, yet still he led the National League. McGwire, meanwhile, went from seventy homers in 1998 and sixty-five in 1999 down to thirty-two in 2000 and twenty-nine in 2001. By 2002 he was no longer in the league. Finally, Bonds went from seventy-three jacks in 2001 to forty-six the year after to finish behind Sosa. Bonds did manage to stay competitive with forty-five in both 2003 and 2004 and winning four consecutive MVPs from 2001 to 2004. Bonds only led the league in homers twice (1993 and 2001), but he did lead the league in intentional walks twelve times, including seven of his final eight seasons.[15]

Bonds, Sosa, and McGwire would later be linked to steroid use. Bonds admitted to "accidental" steroid use and McGwire to using a "steroid-like" substance. Sosa kept his mouth shut, but the *New York Times* later reported that Sosa had been one of the 104 players who tested positive for steroids during major-league baseball's supposedly anonymous testing experiment in 2003.[16]

After the 2007 season, Sammy Sosa retired with 1,475 runs scored, 2,408 hits, a .273 lifetime batting average, and a career slugging mark of .534.[17] But the number that stands out is 609, Sosa's career home run total, which placed him in an exclusive club. As of 2012, only eight players had clubbed more than 600 homers, and Alex Rodriguez made it on August 4, 2010, becoming the youngest to achieve that plateau. Jim Thome, who played his first dozen years in Cleveland, reached number 600 on August 15, 2011, wearing a Minnesota uniform. He soon surpassed Sosa, who dropped to eighth on the all-time homer list.[18]

Sosa's long-ball total is impressive by any measure, but it is particularly notable since, during the first six years of his big-league career, he had collected just 95 altogether. Almost all the rest came during the next ten years, and he hit 292—almost half his career total—in only five years (1998–2002), averaging almost 60 per season. When Sosa slammed home run number 600 on June 20, 2007, he did so against his old team, the Cubs. Sosa had been out of baseball for a year before returning with the Texas Rangers and becoming only the fifth player to reach 600 at the time. Video clips of that run reveal an almost regal atmosphere as the fanfare horns from the mythical baseball film *The Natural* were piped through the stadium in Arlington, Texas.[19] Sosa's homer occurred while playing again for his first team, and he hit it against the team where he had achieved his greatest moments, the Chicago Cubs.

In retrospect, the fanfare that lingered after those magical long-ball moments has been overshadowed by the taint of the steroid era—not only because of the connection Sosa might personally have had with performance enhancers but also with the entire league's culpability. After 1998, Todd McFarlane, the creator of the popular *Spawn* comic books, paid more than $3.4 million for ten home run balls hit during the great Sosa-McGwire chase and packaged them as part of a national tour that reportedly drew millions of fans over a three-year stretch.[20] Now those same balls are almost invisible, sitting somewhere in storage. Their purgatory at first evokes images of the mammoth government warehouse depicted in the film *Raiders of the Lost Ark*, but an even truer image might be the ignominious lockers from television's *Storage Wars*.

In January 2010, Mark McGwire began apologizing to his coach, team, fans, Commissioner Bud Selig, and others. At that point, of the top fifteen home run hitters in big-league history, six were linked to performance-enhancing drugs because they had played during the steroid era and evidence linked them to some type of performance enhancer.[21] Eight players on the same top-15 all-time home run list played during a meaningful part of the steroid era, and of those men, only two have escaped accusations to date—Ken Griffey Jr., and Jim Thome. (Frank Thomas, another contemporary who ranked at number 19 on the list before the 2012 season, has to date also avoided links and meaningful accusations to performance enhancers.)

The steroid era will be scrutinized for years to come. Some will deny its impact, and some might try to deny that the era existed at all. In addition to tangible evidence, admissions, and suspect physical traits, however, the existence and impact of the steroid era can be corroborated by a surprising source: the science of comparative zoology, or evolution.

In September 1996 the late Stephen Jay Gould was a professor of geology and zoology at Harvard, as well as curator for invertebrate paleontology at Harvard's Museum of Comparative Zoology. One can safely conclude that he knew something about evolution, natural progression, and related deviations from the norm. Gould, who passed away in 2002, was a baseball fan who appreciated the old days of Ty Cobb and made a detailed mathematical study of Joe DiMaggio's hitting streak. Combining the science of evolution with his affinity for the game of baseball, Gould's work led to some convincing analyses about baseball evolution that strongly suggest the steroid era did occur and did distort baseball.[22] Professor Thomas J. Miceli of the University of Connecticut's Department of Economics confirmed Gould's analysis and mathematical conclusions in a paper titled "Minimum Quality Standards in Baseball and the Paradoxical Disappearance of the .400 Hitter."[23]

As discussed previously, no player has hit .400 since Ted Williams managed his .406 season in 1941. On the one hand, this phenomenon is linked to many plausible factors, such as using more specialty relief pitching, sewing higher seams on the ball in 1930, and putting a greater emphasis on players hitting long balls rather than hitting for average as did Ty Cobb and Nap Lajoie, the .400 hitters of the early twentieth century. On the other hand, baseball banned the spitball in 1920, and today's athletes are bigger, faster, stronger—all factors that make good hitters. Between 1921 and 1930, the .400 season was achieved seven times, and in the 1940s, Williams did so once. Baseball has seen various hitting droughts and surges in the last seven decades.[24] But even with such as stars Willie Mays, Mantle, Pete Rose, George Brett, Wade Boggs, Alex Rodriguez, and the rest, why has baseball not seen any .400 hitters since Williams? According to Gould and Miceli, it may simply be a principle of evolution. To be precise, "Gould's Law" suggests the absence of .400 hitters is the result of better overall play by more players who are skilled—this tends to reduce or eliminate the outliers.

According to the principles of Gould's Law, the more established a competition becomes, the standard deviation among the performances disappears. This correlation helps explain why track and field world records no longer fall very often (five times at the Beijing Olympics in 2008), while the records in swimming, a more recent worldwide competitive sport, are broken frequently (twenty-five in Beijing). It is also why the .400 hitters were outliers, pushing outside of the normal distribution of averages, and why there haven't been any since 1941. Another factor is the openness of the competition. Swimming, which requires elaborate costly facilities and an abundance of water, provides fewer opportunities for competition and thus fosters fewer high-level competitors worldwide than the sport of running, which is available even to third world athletes.[25]

As baseball evolved, first the players became better athletes who could pitch and defend better, and then the competition opened up to African Americans and next to players worldwide. The game became more refined as it welcomed more and better players. Basketball giant Wilt Chamberlain offers a good example. Chamberlain once scored a hundred points in an NBA game in 1962, but more remarkably, he also averaged more than fifty points and forty rebounds per game for the year. Both stats amount to about double what today's superstars can manage. Not even the monstrous, quick, and powerful Dwight Howard can match those numbers. What happened? Wilt was among the first of the true big men in the game, and he was the biggest and strongest of his era. At the time, Chamberlain was unusually tall at seven-foot-one, strong, and rather nasty on the court at a time when typical NBA players were around six-foot-five or shorter, and slender. Even Chamberlain's chief rival, Bill Russell, stood only six-foot-nine. But as the game evolved, it developed more big men to counter Chamberlain, and over time he was no longer such an outlier.

As any sport evolves, similar improvements occur: the quality of overall play goes up, and the deviations from the norm are fewer and less dramatic. Contributing to the phenomenon in baseball, says Miceli, is the sport's development of better scouting, better coaching, advanced equipment, and improved player conditioning. In other words, "the technology of baseball has changed in such a way as to eliminate the lower tail of the talent distribution."[26] Players' abilities relative to the league are becoming more consistent; hence, baseball does not have any .400 hitters because no more freaks of nature appear in the batter's box. Plus, the batters are facing fresher pitchers given today's expanded role of relievers and closers. And pitchers, as a group, are improving, too, since Gould's Law applies to the mound as well.

But wait: did not Sammy Sosa, Mark McGwire, and Barry Bonds suddenly rewrite the baseball record books, reminiscent of Ruth's doing so in the 1920s and of like Chamberlain did the same for the NBA in the 1960s? Such an anomaly makes the point exactly. Baseball is America's oldest, most mature, and most evolved major team sport. Similar to the game's not having any .400 hitters after 1941, it has not had any thirty-game winners on the mound since Denny McLain did it in 1968. Because the relief pitchers, the starters, the hitters—everybody—are all better, they keep the baseball outliers from suddenly appearing out of nowhere. The surprising number of home run hitters who exploded onto the major-league scene from 1998 to 2001 is staggering in the context of the game's history. It does not disprove Gould's Law of baseball evolution; in fact, it substantiates the influence of the steroid era. These kinds of major, outlying leaps do not occur in a mature sport, let alone by three players all at once, unless something else has changed, too.

Did the ball get livelier? Was the pitching mound lowered again? Did the players start using metal bats? No. As noted, all three of those outliers from the late 1990s have been tied to steroids in some manner, but even if they were not, statistics tell the story. Only two men during the entire twentieth century hit sixty or more home runs in a season—Ruth in 1927 and Maris in 1961—and they only did it once each. But then suddenly Sammy Sosa did it three times all by himself. And then Mark McGwire and Barry Bonds almost concurrently smashed through the seventy-homer barrier. Bonds was good, but was he better than Mays? McGwire was good, but was he better than Mantle? And without drugs, were any of the three really better than Ruth, Gehrig, DiMaggio, or Williams was?

Was the steroid era baseball's worst moment? To be fair, it probably ranks second behind the "no Negroes" rule imposed for decades before Jackie Robinson's major-league debut, an egregious mark against baseball that reached so far and for so long. The players who fought for years in World War II may have collectively put forth the game's finest effort, but what will posterity say of the bloated home run records of a half century later—followed, incidentally, by a sharp long-ball drop-off after the implementation of serious drug testing? The seventy-three-homer mark that Bonds attained in 2001 has become a virtual "scarlet number." Those home runs still stand as official records, but few pay homage to that home run season.

★ **17** ★

MEN, MUDVILLE, AND DiMAGGIO

Where have you gone, Joe DiMaggio?
—PAUL SIMON[1]

Modern baseball may have saved itself with the 1998 home run chase that triggered three years of long-ball glory, but it seems that baseball sometimes must be saved *from* itself as well.

Baseball is like America's eldest son, a reliable game with much promise but at the same time privileged and often stubborn. The game should be embarrassed by its continuing antitrust exemption, yet baseball brandishes its exaltation as though it is above the law. For decades baseball also flaunted its sheer whiteness, pretending black players were not good enough. It even continued a subtle racism long after Jackie Robinson's playing days, as when Commissioner Bowie Kuhn missed Hank Aaron's 715th home run, the one that broke Babe Ruth's career mark. Kuhn opted to speak at an Opening Day dinner in Cleveland and sent an emissary to Turner Field instead. Was Kuhn protecting Ruth's venerable image or making a passive statement about Aaron's skin color? Or was he unable to get out of a dinner obligation, weak as that excuse is?

Hank Aaron had his first break almost literally when Bobby Thomson, who remains famous for only one remarkable home run, broke his ankle

259

sliding into second. Aaron was the young outfielder who replaced him.[2] By the time Hank Aaron had passed the Ruth milestone of 714 runs in 1974, Aaron was mentally fatigued. He received many accolades, but he did not gain true recognition until the twenty-fifth anniversary of that home run when the Braves' organization honored him with a forty-five-minute ceremony, which featured a two-minute standing ovation, before a game with Philadelphia.[3] This time the baseball commissioner, Bud Selig, was present. Aaron received a second boost after Barry Bonds pushed the career homer record still further with 762 long balls. Yes, Aaron's career record had been broken, but by that time America knew about the impact of steroids on the game and began reflecting upon the true value of Aaron's achievement.

If there is a single baseball metaphor that reflects America, it is the home run, a four- to five-second-long majestic image of success and power that fans admire and opponents endure. The game's legacy of playing loose with the rules, manipulating and sometimes even rewriting history, may offer some of the real reasons that the home run has become an American icon.

Baseball first discovered the home run was a golden goose when Ruth changed the game forever by turning on the ball as a modern-day slugger does, instead of slapping at it the way Ty Cobb and Nap Lajoie did. Ruth paved the way to long-ball greatness not only with the sheer number of his home runs but also with how he hit them: the technique, the distance, the audacity, and the winning. Baseball was quick to catch on, especially in New York. The Yankees saw the marquee value of home runs and noted Ruth's first career record breaker, which left the Polo Grounds altogether when Ruth was still wearing Red Sox gray in 1919. At the end of that year, New York not only acquired Ruth but also created the "house that Ruth built" with a short right-field line to better exploit the Babe's left-handed power.

Baseball offense sold tickets, and home runs kept the fans coming back. At the time, the game needed more offense, more home runs, and more fans in the wake of the 1919 Black Sox gambling scandal that had left the nation reeling. Ruth supplied plenty of long-ball offense, but he could only be in one place at a time. Baseball thus banned the spitball in 1920, the same year that Ruth debuted in New York, and triggered a subtle but important shift in the balance of power from pitcher to batter.

In 1961 baseball received a boost from the home runs of Mickey Mantle and Roger Maris, and by 1969 baseball exploited the offense again when it lowered the pitching mound. The game lost legions of exasperated fans after the 1994 labor action that canceled the World Series and left many Americans disgusted with the game. Another storm was brewing, however, much as it had done after the Black Sox scandal. By this time many emerging sluggers were eager to make their marks: Mark McGwire, Rafael Palmiero, Jose Canseco, Barry Bonds, Sammy Sosa, Frank Thomas, Jim Thome, Ken Griffey Jr., and others. Most would later be linked to performance-enhancing drugs. At this writing, Thomas, Griffey, and Thome have remained untarnished.

When Bonds unleashed his home run barrage in 2001, many thought it was the product of his maple bat. Harder and more brittle than the usual ash bats, maple was thought to generate home runs. Suddenly maple was the rage among big leaguers, but perhaps all it does is shatter more, and more dangerously, too. When a maple bat shatters, its sharp long shards are propelled across the infield and even into the stands.

In 2003 Barry Bonds found himself in front of a grand jury. He testified that he never knowingly used steroids. The "knowingly" qualifier seems so deceptive that one wonders how Bonds's denial could be taken seriously. How many Americans—not to mention ballplayers of any sort—have *accidentally* been on any drug or any type of contraband, including steroids, for upward of a year or two?

Even so, as surly and disingenuous as Bonds may have seemed by the end of his career, he nonetheless was also a victim of the steroid era. Former senator George Mitchell's investigation of performance-enhancing drugs in baseball and the resulting report, the direct testimony, and common sense have all pointed to the curious paucity of testing by the league offices. Baseball's policy passively enabled, if not tacitly encouraged, steroid abuse. It also generated home runs as never before, as well as the incumbent excitement that necessarily follows. The steroid era, though, does not appear to have been an overt conspiracy. It was a grassroots movement that began with a select few players who discovered the healing powers, strength, and marquee contracts that performance enhancers could deliver. When those players achieved success, their trainers, dealers, and hangers-on became the distribution chain for other players. Eventually steroids found the tipping point where they became more than a clandestine advantage and had become a virtual necessity.

Most of the steroid headlines concern the game's premier stars, but such drugs had achieved epidemic proportions at the big-league level when journeyman players began juicing not for headlines but to keep up with everyone else. According to anecdotal evidence from such players as the late MVP Ken Caminiti, up to half of the league had experimented with steroids. The drugs had become necessary to compete at the major-league level, a phenomenon that circled back to the game's stars. Thus, Barry Bonds also became a victim. Each day that Sosa and McGwire banged home runs into the record books, Bonds's own career was becoming less and less relevant. Unfortunately, as the effect of steroids became more widely known, they had already begun to infiltrate college and high school locker rooms. In 2001, the year of the Bonds's home run explosion, a study from the Centers for Disease Control and Prevention suggested that 5 percent of high school students had used unprescribed steroids during their lifetimes.[4] In prior years, athletes in other sports—notably weightlifters, bodybuilders, and football players—had used steroids, but stringent testing helped curtail the abuse. Not so with baseball, which resisted steroid testing for many years until it implemented various surveys and instituted limited testing programs in 2003.

At the beginning of 2001, Barry Bonds had been in the majors for fifteen seasons. Not once had he managed a fifty-home run season during that span. In 1998, while McGwire and Sosa were gaining long-ball accolades, Bonds was having a very good year by normal standards with thirty-seven home runs, 122 RBIs, twenty-eight stolen bases, and a batting average of .303.[5] But hardly anyone outside San Francisco even noticed. As Sosa and McGwire mounted sixty-plus-home run seasons, one after another, Bonds stayed the course, hitting thirty-four more in 1999. But suddenly in 2000 he had a career best forty-nine homers, followed by seventy-three home runs during his sixteenth season. As suggested previously, Gould's Law indicates in a mature sport like baseball, such leaps are scientifically almost impossible *unless* an outside influence is introduced to the equation.

When Ruth banged out sixty homers in 1927, he had already logged several record seasons, including marks of fifty-four and fifty-nine round-trippers. The sixty-homer plateau was a milestone, but it was not an outlier for Ruth—even though Ruth himself was. At the time baseball was simply beginning to discover the power of the home run. But what about Roger Maris's hitting, decades later? Roger had clubbed thirty-nine in 1960 and only sixteen in 1959. Although he was back down to thirty-three runs in 1962, the year 1961 was his stellar record-setting season.[6] Fate, Ruth, Mickey Mantle, and the Yankees' manager, Ralph Houk, were part of the reason.

Houk originally batted Mantle third and Maris fourth in 1961, but he soon switched. For most of the season, Maris batted third in the lineup, Mantle fourth, Yogi Berra at the five spot, and Moose Skowron sixth.[7] Mantle had already established himself as the most feared hitter of his day. Before 1961 he had already led the league in home runs four times, won the MVP twice, and had one of the greatest years of all time in 1956, his Triple Crown season, with fifty-two homers, 130 RBIs, and a .353 batting average. Mantle hit not only for power but also for average, a lethal combination. He batted over .300 five years in a row, including .365 in 1957. In 1960, Mantle led the league with forty homers, 119 runs scored, and total bases with 294.[8]

Mantle was having a stellar home run year in 1961. Clearly he and Maris pushed each other throughout the season. Moreover, with Mantle batting cleanup, teams did not pitch around Maris. Remarkably, even though Maris was banging out home runs at a blistering pace, not one pitcher intentionally walked him. Managers were determined not to be beaten by the dangerous Mantle, so they took their chances by throwing strikes to Maris—all year long.

In 2002, the year after his all-time homer season, Barry Bonds was intentionally walked a record 68 times. Then, in 2004, he was intentionally walked a whopping 120 times, breaking his own major-league record by 52. Those 120 intentional walks were more than any other *team* had that year—and by a wide margin.[9] Together they are outliers that would seem to defy Gould's Law, but again, they were influenced by outside factors. Bonds was a feared hitter, but somewhat reminiscent of Ty Cobb, he was also largely disliked. Few wanted to see Bonds break the Ruth and Aaron career marks, few wanted him to hit home runs, and no one wanted to be beaten by his bat. Similar to the St. Louis Browns' conspiring in the 1910 season to sway the batting title from Cobb to Lajoie, some of those walks thrown Bonds's way were likely intended to keep him from breaking the record.

Only ten players have been intentionally walked more than thirty times in a single season. Ted Williams and Sammy Sosa did so for one season each, Willie McCovey twice, and Albert Pujols three times. It happened to Barry Bonds ten times. Over his career, Bonds was walked on purpose a total of 688 times. Second place belongs to Hank Aaron, who tallied a distant 293.[10]

In 1961 the pitchers did pitch to Roger Maris, and he obliged, crunching sixty-one balls over the wall. But as Ford Frick pointed out, Maris also had the advantage of a longer season. Beginning in 1961, everyone else did as well, including numerous new record holders and Hall of Famers—even Hank Aaron for sixteen of his twenty-three years in the majors. Maris did have 58 long balls through the 154-game mark in 1961, which would have been remarkable in any era during the 154-game seasons, not to mention the 61 homers he ultimately hit that year. Even the 58 mark was more than Mantle ever hit but still not super-human. Moreover, league home runs were on the upswing. In 1927, American League batters had slugged 439 home runs, and Ruth alone hit 60 of them, or a full 13.6 percent of the entire league's total.[11] If someone had hit the same percentage of homers in 1996, he would have led the league with 373. This output is why Ruth was so revered for so long—and still should be. From 1956 through 1960, batters hit slightly more than 1,000 home runs hit each year, and then suddenly in 1961 the total jumped 50 percent to 1,534.[12] Baseball would not see another comparable jump until the pitcher's mound was lowered for the 1969 season.

One more ironic factor influenced Maris's record season, namely, the ghost of Ruth. Yankee Stadium had been built with a short right field, probably to exploit Ruth's left-handed power. It worked; even the record number 60 was hit, barely fair, to right. Maris was also a lefty, and the friendly right-field porch also helped his 1961 record. After all, Maris's sixty-first home run had also landed in the stands at right.

Roger Maris's achievement remains remarkable. His 1961 threshold season was made possible by a confluence of events—the longer season, the spike in homers overall, the batting order, the pitches that went to Maris instead of to Mantle, the push from Mantle all year, and the short right field at Yankee Stadium—that combined with Maris's own MVP hitting prowess. It was a "perfect storm" of positive factors.

In 2001, no one was competing with Bonds, and few teams challenged him with good pitches, if they pitched to him at all. Yet he destroyed the marks of Ruth and all who followed: Maris, Mantle, Lou Gehrig, Joe DiMaggio, Ted Williams, Hank Aaron, Willie Mays, Hank Greenberg, Ralph Kiner, Harmon Killebrew, Alex Rodriguez, Jim Thome, and many more. But in 2003 Barry Bonds was caught in the federal investigation of steroids and of the Bay Area Laboratory Cooperative (BALCO), the firm that allegedly supplied performance enhancers to numerous ballplayers. He did not cause the steroid era; it had long been under way. That he would have turned to steroids on his own is unlikely, for Bonds did not seem to do so until 1998 and 1999 and the rise of Sosa and McGwire.

Truth lives a tortured life, as famed trial lawyer Clarence Darrow observed. The first casualty of war is truth, according to an axiom U.S. senator Hiram Johnson coined to help express his isolationist views before America entered World War I. Perhaps truth is likewise a casualty of major competition. Baseball, a game that transcends sport as a part of the American experience, is replete with gimmicks, rule changes, spitballs, hidden balls, corked bats, stolen signs, and revisionist history. It resists the use of instant replay not merely to protect the umpires—although they would

look better if they could correct a couple of unfortunate calls each week—
but also to protect a misplaced image of baseball as the perfect game. The
victimization of truth is collateral damage to that folly. (*Note:* Many may
regard baseball as the "perfect game," but any given game might not be
executed flawlessly or umpired perfectly.)

Given the game's predisposition to shenanigans—together with a history of recreational drugs and performance enhancers, which also perme-
ate such major sports as football, cycling, track and field, weightlifting, and
wrestling—baseball was vulnerable to steroids. Their use was ultimately
made inevitable by baseball's curious aversion to truth. Having dropped its
former claim that blacks were not good enough players, the game has stuck
to other falsehoods: baseball is not a business in interstate commerce,
Maris's home runs were tainted by too many games, and baseball did not
have to test for steroids because "there are no steroids in baseball."

With marquee home runs driving ratings, money, fame, and egos, all
while baseball shunned adequate testing, the formula for steroid abuse was
in place. The game pretends to blame the users, but everyone was culpable.
When the league did attempt to test, the players' union resisted—perhaps
becoming the only major union in U.S. history to fight against the health
and welfare of its own members. Had the union fought for testing, Barry
Bonds would be headed to the Hall of Fame. And the game's genuine record
holders would likely still be Maris, Aaron, and Ruth.

The steroid era was a tangled web, with the league, the union, the players, and the fans all complicit to varying degrees. In the end, the fans were
victimized, but even they played a role by showering the home run sluggers
with accolades. Although the fans did not actually know of the steroid epidemic, save for those familiar with Gould's Law, nearly everyone ignored
noticeable clues. The modern players were accountable, to be sure, but
mostly they were victims. Complacent authorities virtually gave them a
home run syringe, then looked the other way and applauded the results.
These players should be in the Hall of Fame, although their role in the
steroid era should not be ignored. Who will ever know with reasonable cer-
tainty who was juiced and who was not? We have many good guesses, and

even a number of admissions from Canseco, Caminiti, Bonds, and McGwire, among others, but arbitrarily punishing some offenders and not others hardly resurrects the real victims of the steroid era: Ruth, Maris, Aaron, and, more important, truth.

Where *has* Joe DiMaggio gone? No, not Joe himself, but all that he represents: excellence on the field, star power, and baseball as America. Even now, after all the havoc baseball's shenanigans have wreaked on the record books, Babe Ruth remains the greatest slugger of all time. His career slugging mark pales the competition, all whom had careers of at least a thousand games: Ruth .690; Bonds .607; McGwire .588; Rodriguez .560; Mantle .557; Mays .557; Aaron .555; Griffey Jr., .538; Sosa .534. DiMaggio, by the way, had a career .579, good enough for tenth all-time as of the 2011 season.[13]

There is room for debate about how pervasive performance enhancers really were. Some point to the relatively low numbers of positive test results, such as the 5–7 percent who flunked a sample testing in 2003 or the 1.5 percent who failed in 2005, but these tests were administered well after the Canseco-McGwire-Sosa-Bonds era from the mid-1990s to 2001. If, hypothetically, 6 percent of airline pilots were found to be on marijuana, the world would be shocked. It would be even more so if that result occurred two years after testing became an issue *and* the pilots knew they would be tested. The bigger picture tells even more and corroborates what was really happening: In 1992 players hit 3,038 total home runs in the majors, a number not atypical for recent decades that saw 3,001 in 1962, 3,102 in 1973, 3,087 in 1980, and a spike to 4,458 in 1987. But the 1998 season amassed 5,064 home runs—hitting the 5,000 plateau for the first time—increasing to 5,528 in 1999 and 5,693 in 2000, or the highest number ever recorded. Those lofty numbers were propelled by many players, not simply two or three or four of them; but by 2007 the total had dropped below 5,000, to 4,957, and reversed the trend.[14]

Regardless of the steroid era, the top three sluggers of all time still stand for much, especially the integrity and history of the game, and perhaps even more so considering the number of home run hitters in recent times: Ruth and his .690 are on top followed by Ted Williams at .634 and Lou Gehrig with his .632 career mark. Ruth was more than a slugger, though. With his attitude, he was a combatant with an insatiable desire to win and not simply to beat the competition but finally to beat it into submission. Two other athletes in the modern world also evoked Ruth's sense of egocentric talent, and these competitors had an unprecedented ability to defeat their opponents often with their sheer wills—Muhammad Ali and Michael Jordan. Ruth the man had his faults—hubris, women, drinking—but Ruth the icon represents much more than a man ever could. He is a legend, the original bigger-than-life idol of American sports. Win or lose, all the sluggers who followed, including those on steroids, shall remain indebted to George Herman Ruth.

NOTES

CHAPTER 1. THE HOME RUN MYSTIQUE

1 "Harmon Killebrew Quotes," *Baseball Almanac*, http://www.baseball-almanac.com /quotes/quobrew.shtml (accessed June 17, 2010).

2 "Ralph Kiner Quotes," *Baseball Almanac*, http://www.baseball-almanac.com /quotes/quokiner.shtml (accessed June 16, 2010).

3 Sport Reference LLC, "Bob Prince," Baseball-Reference.com, August 23, 2005, http://www.baseball-reference.com/bullpen/Bob_Prince (accessed June 17, 2010).

4 "Yogi Berra Quotes," *Baseball Almanac*, http://www.baseball-almanac.com/quotes /quoberra.shtml (accessed June 17, 2010).

5 Burt Solomon, *The Baseball Timeline: The Day-by-Day History of Baseball, from Valley Forge to the Present Day* (New York: Avon Books, 1997), 360.

6 Sports Reference LLC, "Ralph Kiner Player Page," Baseball-Reference.com, http://www.baseball-reference.com/players/k/kinerra01.shtml (accessed June 19, 2010).

7 "A History of the Cadillac," http://www.randomhistory.com/2009/01/21 _cadillac.html (accessed June 19, 2010).

8 William P. Kinsella, *Shoeless Joe* (Boston: Houghton Mifflin, 1982).

9 "New York's World-Beating New Stadium," *Literary Digest*, April 28, 1923, cited from History Matters, http://historymatters.gmu.edu/d/5088/ (accessed May 28, 2011).

10 Shepard C. Long and John Pastier, "Yankee Stadium," BaseballLibrary.com, http://www.baseballlibrary.com/baseballlibrary/ballplayers/S/Stadium _Yankee.stm (accessed August 8, 2006).

11 Munsey & Suppes, "Fenway Park," Ballparks.com, July 2009, http://www.ballparks .com/baseball/american/fenway.htm (access June 19, 2010).

12 Robert K. Adair, *The Physics of Baseball*, 3d ed. (New York: HarperCollins, 2002), 103.

13 Lewis Early, "Mickey Mantle's 10 Longest Home Runs," Mickey Mantle: The American Dream Comes to Life, 2010, http://www.themick.com/10homers .html (accessed June 19, 2010).

14 William J. Jenkinson, "Long Distance Home Runs," *Baseball Almanac*, 1996, http://www.baseball-almanac.com/feats/art_hr.shtml (accessed July 3, 2010).

15 Richard Lally, *Bombers: An Oral History of the New York Yankees* (New York: Crown, 2002), 59.

16 Sports Reference LLC, "Al Kaline Player Page, Baseball-Reference.com, http://www.baseball-reference.com/players/k/kalinal01.shtml (December 17, 2012); and Sports Reference LLC, "Mickey Mantle Player Page," Baseball -Reference.com, http://www.baseball-reference.com/players/m/mantlmi01.shtml (accessed June 19, 2010).

17 Curt Smith, "Bob Wolff—85 Going on 15," *Voices of the The Game* (blog), July 7, 2006, http://curtsmith.mlblogs.com/2006/07/07/bob-wolff-85-going-on-15/ (accessed September 24, 2011).

18 Curt Smith, *The Voice: Mel Allen's Untold Story* (Guilford, CT: Globe Pequot Press, 2007), 104.

19 Sports Reference LLC, "Mickey Mantle Player Page"; and Sports Reference LLC, "Ted Williams Player Page," Baseball-Reference.com, http://www.baseball -reference.com/players/w/willite01.shtml.

20 MLB Advanced Media, L.P., "Rule 6.09," *Official Baseball Rules*, 55–56, http://mlb.mlb.com/mlb/downloads/y2011/Official–Baseball–Rules.pdf, (accessed June 26, 2010).

21 John Thorn, Phil Birnbaum, and Bill Deane, eds., *Total Baseball: The Official Encyclopedia of Major League Baseball*, 8th ed. (Wilmington, DE: Sports Classic Books, 2004), 2668.

22 Brian Applebaum, "How Many Synonyms Are There for 'Home Run?,'" *Old Cardboard* (blog), March 3, 2009, http://bapple2286.wordpress.com/2009 /03/03/how-many-synonyms-are-there-for-home-run/ (accessed June 26, 2010).

23 BookRags Media Network, "Mickey Mantle Quotes," Brainy Quote, http://www.brainyquote.com/quotes/authors/m/mickey_mantle.html (accessed September 24, 2011).

24　"1951 World Series," *Baseball Almanac*, http://www.baseball-almanac.com /ws/yr1951ws.shtml (accessed July 2, 2010).

25　Dave Anderson, "Sports of the Times; on Being Mickey Mantle," *New York Times*, March 16, 1994.

26　Hodgkin's ran in Mantle's family, also taking his grandfather and two uncles. Mickey's son Billy Mantle (named for Yankee player and manager Billy Martin) was also diagnosed with Hodgkin's at age nineteen, and in 1994, at age thirty-six, Billy died of a heart attack, partly due to a lifetime of drug and alcohol addiction traced to his own treatments for the cancer.

27　Merritt Clifton, "Player Profiles: Gil McDougald," BaseballLibrary.com, http://www.baseballlibrary.com/ballplayers/player.php?name=Gil_McDougald _1928 (accessed July 2, 2010).

28　Sports Reference LLC, "Joe DiMaggio Player Page," Baseball-Reference.com, http://www.baseball-reference.com/players/d/dimagjo01.shtml (accessed August 31, 2011).

29　"Gene Geiselmann," *Funny Sports Quotes* (blog), http://funnysportsquotes .blogspot.com/2008/01/funny-sports-quotes-source_5537.html (accessed September 24, 2011).

30　Jack McCallum and Richard O'Brien, "They Said It," SIVault.com, July 18, 1994, http://sportsillustrated.cnn.com/vault/article/magazine/MAG1005411 /index.htm (accessed September 24, 2011).

31　Solomon, *The Baseball Timeline*, 511.

32　Adair, *The Physics of Baseball*, 102–3.

CHAPTER 2. OUR NATIONAL METAPHOR

1　Jeffrey Kluger, "High Point: Alan Shepard Becomes the First American in Space," *Time*, September 27, 2007.

2　"The Flight," Charles Lindbergh: An American Aviator, http://www.charleslindbergh .com/history/paris.asp (accessed November 7, 2010).

3　"50 Greatest Sports Movies of All-Time," *Sports Illustrated*, August 4, 2003.

4　American Film Institute, "AFI's 100 Years . . . 100 Movie Quotes," AFI.com, June 21, 2005, http://www.afi.com/100years/quotes.aspx (accessed November 17, 2010).

5　"Memorable Quotes for Bull Durham (1988)," IMDb.com, http://www.imdb .com/title/tt0094812/quotes (accessed November 14, 2010).

6　Ibid.

7　Jose Canseco, *Juiced: Wild Times, Rampant 'Roids, Smash Hits, and How Baseball Got Big* (New York: Regan Books, 2005).

8 Ibid., 4.

9 Ronald Briley, "Baseball and American Cultural Values," *OAH Magazine of History* 7, no. 1 (Summer 1992).

10 Ernest Hemingway, *The Old Man and the Sea* (New York: Charles Scribner, 1952).

11 Paul Dickson, *Baseball's Greatest Quotations* (New York: HarperCollins, 1991).

12 Christine Kenneally, *The First Word* (New York: Viking Penguin, 2007), 25.

13 David Crystal, *How Language Works: How Babies Babble, Words Change Meaning, and Languages Live or Die* (New York: Overlook Press, 2006), 225.

14 Ibid., 224.

15 Ibid., 224–25.

16 "Brief History of the Radio Industry," Duke University Libraries, http://library .duke.edu/digitalcollections/adaccess/radio-tv.html (accessed November 27, 2010).

17 Tom Lewis, "'A Godlike Presence': The Impact of Radio on the 1920s and 1930s," *OAH Magazine of History* 6, no. 4 (Spring 1992).

18 American Film Institute, "AFI's 100 Years."

19 "Memorable Quotes for Field of Dreams (1989)," IMDb.com, http://www.imdb.com/title/tt0097351/quotes (accessed November 14, 2010).

CHAPTER 3. BASEBALL'S ANTE DIEM

1 Tom Helgesen, "Pre-1845 Baseball: Was Abner Doubleday Really the Originator?," HistoryBuff.com, http://www.historybuff.com/library/refearlybase .html (accessed December 4, 2010).

2 Mary Bellis, "The History of Baseball: Alexander Cartwright," About.com, http://inventors.about.com/library/inventors/blbaseball.htm (accessed December 4, 2010).

3 David Block, *Baseball Before We Knew It: A Search for the Roots of the Game* (Lincoln: University of Nebraska Press, 2005), 1.

4 Helgesen, "Pre-1845 Baseball."

5 "President George Washington Baseball Related Quotations," *Baseball Almanac*, http://www.baseball-almanac.com/prz_qgw.shtml (accessed December 1, 2010).

6 Solomon, *The Baseball Timeline*, 8.

7 "President Abraham Lincoln Baseball Related Quotes," *Baseball Almanac*, http://www.baseball-almanac.com/prz_qal.shtml (accessed December 1, 2010).

8 Solomon, *The Baseball Timeline*, 10–11.

9 Ibid., 29.

10 Ibid., 31.

11 Ibid., 41.

12 "Players: Roger Connor," The Baseball Page LLC, http://www.thebaseballpage
.com/players/connoro01 (accessed September 4, 2011).

13 Solomon, *The Baseball Timeline*, 57.

14 Ibid., 77.

15 Ibid., 92.

16 "Batting Average Records: Single Season Records," *Baseball Almanac*, http://www
.baseball-almanac.com/recbooks/rb_bavg1.shtml (accessed September 4, 2011).

17 Solomon, *The Baseball Timeline*, 128.

18 Ibid., 143.

19 Dickson, *Baseball's Greatest Quotations*, 200.

20 Ibid., 162.

21 Ibid., 189.

22 See "Biography," Babe Ruth Official Website, www.baberuth.com/biography/
(accessed July 12, 2012).

23 "How Did Babe Ruth Get His Name?," Ask.com, http://answers.ask.com
/Sports/Baseball/how_did_babe_ruth_get_his_name (accessed October 1, 2011).

24 Solomon, *The Baseball Timeline*, 190.

25 Ibid., 212.

26 "Frank Home Run Baker Quotes," *Baseball Almanac*, http://www.baseball
-almanac.com/quotes/frank_baker_quotes.shtml (accessed December 1, 2010).

27 Ibid.

28 Ibid.

CHAPTER 4. RUTH: THE QUANTUM LEAP

1 A&E Television Networks LLC, "This Day in History: May 25, 1935: Babe
Ruth Hits Last Home Run," History.com, http://www.history.com/this-day-in
-history/babe-ruth-hits-last-home-run (accessed January 23, 2011).

2 Solomon, *The Baseball Timeline*, 360.

3 Munsey & Suppes "Forbes Field," Ballparks.com, January 2008, http://www
.ballparks.com/baseball/national/forbes.htm (accessed October 1, 2011).

4 Sports Reference LLC, "Babe Ruth Player Page," Baseball-Reference.com,
http://www.baseball-reference.com/players/r/ruthba01.shtml (accessed January
23, 2011).

5   Michael Lamkin, "Gene Tunney vs. Jack Dempsey II," Fight World, http://www.fightbeat.com/judgejake/tunneydempsey2.php (accessed January 23, 2011).

6   Solomon, *The Baseball Timeline*, 226.

7   "Ruth Wallops Out His 28th Home Run," *New York Times*, September 25, 1919.

8   Solomon, *The Baseball Timeline*, 231.

9   Bill Jenkinson, *The Year Babe Ruth Hit 104 Home Runs* (New York: Da Capo Press, 2007), 300–339.

10 Ibid.

11 "Year by Year Leaders for Home Runs," *Baseball Almanac*, http://www.baseball -almanac.com/hitting/hihr5.shtml (accessed May 1, 2011).

12 William Curran, *Big Sticks: The Batting Revolution of the Twenties* (New York: William Morrow, 1990), 28.

13 WGBH, "Radio Transmission: The Early Years of Radio," *A Science Odyssey*, PBS.org, http://www.pbs.org/wgbh/aso/tryit/radio/earlyyears.html (accessed October 1, 2011).

14 "KDKA," Hammond Museum of Radio, http://www.hammondmuseumofradio .org/kdka.html (accessed September 5, 2011).

15 Curt Smith, *Voices of Summer: Ranking Baseball's 101 All-Time Best Announcers* (New York: Da Capo Press, 2005), 6.

16 "Chicago Cubs Attendance Data," Baseball Almanac, http://www.baseball -almanac.com/teams/cubsatte.shtml.

17 Carole E. Scott, "The History of the Radio Industry in the United States to 1940," EH.net Encyclopedia, February 1, 2010, http://eh.net/encyclopedia /article/scott.radio.industry.history (accessed November 27, 2010).

18 Paul Dickson, *Baseball's Greatest Quotations* (New York: HarperCollins, 1991), 137.

19 Jonathan Fraser Light, *The Cultural Encyclopedia of Baseball* (Jefferson, NC: McFarland & Co., 1997), 767.

20 Steve Silverman, "List of Home Run Calls in Baseball," Livestrong.com, April 26, 2011, http://www.livestrong.com/article/160439-list-of-home-run-calls-in -baseball/ (accessed February 5, 2011).

CHAPTER 5. THE MISSILES OF MUDVILLE

1   "Babe Ruth Quotes," *Baseball Almanac,* http://www.baseball-almanac.com /quotes/quoruth.shtml (accessed February 9, 2011).

2   "Memorable Quotes for *The Man Who Shot Liberty Valance*," IMDb.com, http://www.imdb.com/title/tt0056217/quotes (accessed September 5, 2011).

3 "Chicago Cubs History and News," Chicago Cubs History and News—Welcome to Just One Bad Century, http://www.justonebadcentury.com/chicago_cubs_tales_09_43_.asp (accessed September 5, 2011).

4 "Babe Ruth Quotes."

5 "League by League Totals for Batting Average," *Baseball Almanac*, http://www.baseball-almanac.com/hitting/hibavg4.shtml (accessed December 2, 2012).

6 "League by League Totals for Home Runs," *Baseball Almanac*, http://www.baseball-almanac.com/hitting/hihr6.shtml (accessed December 12, 2012).

7 "Year by Year Leaders."

8 Curran, *Big Sticks*, 185.

9 Sports Reference LLC, "1921 Detroit Tigers," Baseball-Reference.com, http://www.baseball-reference.com/teams/DET/1921.shtml (accessed December 2, 2012); and Sports Reference LLC, "1927 New York Yankees," Baseball-Reference.com, http://www.baseball-reference.com/teams/NYY/1927.shtml (accessed December 2, 2012).

10 Sports Reference LLC, "Rogers Hornsby Player Page." Baseball-Reference.com, http://www.baseball-reference.com/players/h/hornsro01.shtml (accessed December 2, 2012).

11 "The House That Ruth Built," Babe Ruth Central, http://baberuthcentral.com/Legacies/the-house-that-ruth-built/ (accessed December 1, 2010).

12 Curran, *Big Sticks*, 55.

13 "Wally Pipp Stats," *Baseball Almanac*, http://www.baseball-almanac.com/players/player.php?p=pippwa01 (accessed February 12, 2010); and Bruce Anderson, "Just a Pipp of a Legend," *Sports Illustrated*, June 29, 1987, http://sportsillustrated.cnn.com/vault/article/magazine/MAG1066131/index.htm (accessed December 2, 2012).

14 Noah Adams, "Timeline: Remembering the Scopes Monkey Trial," NPR, June 5, 2005, http://www.npr.org/templates/story/story.php?storyId=4723956 (accessed February 12, 2011).

15 Light, *Cultural Encyclopedia of Baseball*, 767.

16 MLB Advanced Media, LP, "History of the Game: Doubleday to Present Day—Albert Benjamin 'Happy' Chandler," MLB.com, http://mlb.mlb.com/mlb/history/mlb_history_people.jsp?story=com_bio_2 (accessed December 2, 2012).

17 "Sport: Baseball Slipping," *Time*, January 18, 1926.

18 Robert McG. Thomas, Jr., "Johnny Sylvester, the Inspiration for Babe Ruth Heroics, Is Dead," *New York Times*, January 11, 1990.

19 "Babe's Impact on the Game of Baseball," Babe Ruth Central, http://www.baberuthcentral.com/Legacies/babes-impact-on-the-game-of-baseball/ (accessed October 2, 2011).

20 Ibid.

21 "The House That Ruth Built."

22 "Babe's 1934 Barnstorming Trip to Japan," Babe Ruth Central, http://babruthcentral .com/Legacies/1934-barnstorming-trip-to-japan/ (accessed December 1, 2010).

23 Ibid.

24 James Greenfield, "Year of the Babe," *Sports Illustrated*, November 14, 1955.

25 "50 Greatest Sluggers," *Baseball Almanac*, http://www.baseball-almanac.com /legendary/lisn50s.shtml (accessed December 1, 2010).

26 Brian Schwimmer, "A Definition of Culture," 76.122 Cultural Anthropology, University of Manitoba, 1997, http://www.umanitoba.ca/faculties/arts /anthropology/courses/122/module1/culture.html (accessed December 1, 2010).

27 *Dictionary of Anthropology*, s.v., "Culture," http://www.anthrobase.com/Dic/eng /def/culture.htm (accessed December 1, 2010).

28 "Ruth's Illness and Passing—a Country Mourns," Babe Ruth Central, http://baberuthcentral.com/hero-and-icon/ruths-illness-passing-the-country -mourns/ (accessed December 1, 2010).

CHAPTER 6. THE HOME RUN THAT CHANGED AMERICA

1 "Year in Review: 1927 American League," *Baseball Almanac*, http://www.baseball -almanac.com/yearly/yr1927a.shtml (accessed September 5, 2011).

2 Bruce Lowitt, "Long Count Allows Tunney to Keep Title," *St. Petersburg Times*, November 30, 1999.

3 "Betting on Fight May Set a Record," *New York Times*, September 18, 1927.

4 Solomon, *The Baseball Timeline*, 293.

5 David Kaiser, "Views of Sport: Pete Rose and the Public's Right to Know; the Hearings Should Be Open to the Public," *New York Times*, June 18, 1989, http://www.nytimes.com/1989/06/18/sports/views-sport-pte-rose-public-s -right-know-hearing-should-be-open-public.html?src=pm (December 2, 2012).

6 Solomon, *The Baseball Timeline*, 295.

7 KCET, "Pilots: Charles Lindbergh," *Chasing the Sun*, PBS.org, http://www.pbs .org/kcet/chasingthesun/innovators/clindbergh.html (accessed September 5, 2011).

8 "1926 World Series," *Baseball Almanac*, http://www.baseball-almanac.com /ws/yr1926ws.shtml (accessed September 5, 2011).

9 Solomon, *The Baseball Timeline*, 295.

10 Sports Reference LLC, "1927 American League Batting Leaders," Baseball -Reference.com, http://www.baseball-reference.com/leagues/AL/1927-batting -leaders.shtml (December 2, 2012); and Thorn, Birnbaum, and Deane, eds., *Total Baseball*, 113.

11   Ibid.

12   Ibid.

13   Jeffrey Linkowski, "Babe Ruth's 60 Home Runs in 1927," Angelfire, http://www.angelfire.com/pa/1927/ruth60.html (accessed October 5, 2011).

14   Ibid.

15   Ibid.

16   "Lou Gehrig Grand Slams," Baseball Almanac, http://www.baseball-almanac.com /players/Lou_Gehrig_Grand_Slams.shtml.

17   Solomon, *The Baseball Timeline*, 298.

18   Editors of Publications International, Ltd., "1927 Baseball Season," Howstuffworks.com, http://entertainment.howstuffworks.com/1927-baseball -season.htm (accessed November 6, 2010).

19   "1919 New York Yankees Roster," *Baseball Almanac*, http://www.baseball -almanac.com/teamstats/roster.php?y=1919&t=NYA (accessed October 5, 2011).

20   John Kieran, "Sports of the Times," *New York Times*, October 2, 1927.

21   Ibid.

22   Ibid.

23   Sports Reference LLC, "1927 New York Yankees."

24   Lewis, "A Godlike Presence."

CHAPTER 7. THE IMMACULATE DECEPTION

1   "Gaylord Perry Quotes," *Baseball Almanac*, http://www.baseball-almanac.com /quotes/quoperry.shtml (accessed January 23, 2011).

2   Ibid.

3   Joel Achenbach, "A Brief History of the Spitball," *Achenblog* (blog), *Washington Post*, June 15, 2005, http://voices.washingtonpost.com/achenblog /2005/06/a_brief_history_of_the_spitball.html (accessed February 23, 2011).

4   Adair, *The Physics of Baseball*, 63.

5   During the 2003 season, the author asked slugger Eric Karros, who was playing for the Cubs at the time, when he last saw a spitball in a major-league game. "Yesterday," was the answer. (Interestingly, Karros, a somewhat unsung power hitter, blasted more home runs for the Dodgers [270] during the team's post-Brooklyn era than Reggie Jackson hit for Oakland or than Don Mattingly, Dave Winfield, or even Roger Maris ever hit for the Yankees.)

6   "Unsplendid Splinter: Cubs Rally Past Rays after Sosa's Ignominious Ejection," SI.com, June 3, 20003, http://sportsillustrated.cnn.com/baseball/news/2003 /06/03/sosa_ejected_ap/ (accessed February 26, 2011).

7   Adair, *The Physics of Baseball*, 137.

8   Ibid., 138.

9   Ibid., 119.

10 "Graig Nettles," Wikipedia, http://en.wikipedia.org/wiki/Graig_Nettles
    (accessed March 2, 2011); and Sports Reference LLC, "Graig Nettles Player
    Page," Baseball Reference.com, http://www.baseball-reference.com/players/n
    /nettlgr01.shtml (accessed December 2, 2012).

11 Rick Telander, "Telander: The Inside Story of Sammy Sosa's Corked Bat,"
    Chicago Sun-Times, February 16, 2011.

12 Nick Cafardo, "Perry Cuts to the Chase; Today's 'Cheaters' Will Pass Hall Test,"
    Boston Globe, December 23, 2007.

13 Adair, *The Physics of Baseball*, 50.

14 Ibid.

15 ESPN Internet Ventures, Page 2 Staff, "Biggest Cheaters in Baseball," ESPN
    Page 2, http://espn.go.com/page2/s/list/cheaters/ballplayers.html (accessed
    February 23, 2011).

16 Ibid.

17 Ibid.

18 Sports Reference LLC, "Ty Cobb—BR Bullpen," Baseball-Reference.com,
    http://www.baseball-reference.com/bullpen/Ty_Cobb (accessed October 2, 2012).

19 Ed Walton, "Player Profiles: Ty Cobb," BaseballLibrary.com, http://www
    .baseballlibrary.com/ballplayers/player.php?name=ty_cobb_1886 (accessed
    February 23, 2011).

CHAPTER 8. THE GAME OF INFAMY

1   Rob Ohira, "Moiliili Bank's Motif a Tribute to Honolulu Stadium," *Star-
    Bulletin*, January 18, 1999.

2   Solomon, *The Baseball Timeline*, 411.

3   Ibid., 413.

4   Sports Reference LLC, "Stan Musial Player Page," Baseball-Reference.com,
    http://www.baseball-reference.com/players/m/musiast01.shtml (accessed
    December 5, 2012).

5   Jennifer Rosenberg, "Pearl Harbor Facts," About.com, http://history1900s.about
    .com/od/Pearl-Harbor/a/Pearl-Harbor-Facts.htm?p=1 (accessed September 10,
    2011).

6   "The Army and Navy Benefit All-Star Game of 1942," *Misc. Baseball: Gathering
    Assorted Items of Baseball History and Trivia* (blog), July 6, 2011, http://miscbaseball

.wordpress.com/2011/07/06/the-army-and-navy-benefit-all-star-game-of-1942/ (accessed September 10, 2011).

7 M. L. Shettle Jr., "Californians and the Military: Ted Williams—Baseball Legend, Marine Corps Aviator," The California State Military Museum, http://www.militarymuseum.org/Williams.html (accessed September 10, 2011).

8 Solomon, *The Baseball Timeline*, 427.

9 Ibid., 429.

10 Online Highways LLC, "D-Day, the Battle of Normandy," U-S-History.com, http://www.u-s-history.com/pages/h1749.html (accessed September 10, 2011).

11 "President Dwight D. Eisenhower Baseball Related Quotations," *Baseball Almanac*, http://www.baseball-almanac.com/prz_qde.shtml (accessed December 1, 2010).

12 Solomon, *The Baseball Timeline*, 437.

13 "Pete Gray Stats," *Baseball Almanac*, http://www.baseball-almanac.com/players /player.php?p=graype01 (accessed January 8, 2011).

14 S. Mintz, "Learn about World War II," Digital History, 2007, http://www .digitalhistory.uh.edu/modules/ww2/index.cfm (accessed September 10, 2011).

15 Solomon, *The Baseball Timeline*, 446.

16 Sports Reference LLC, "Hank Greenberg Player Page," Baseball-Reference.com, http://www.baseball-reference.com/players/g/greenha01.shtml.

17 "Jewish Baseball Players," *Baseball Almanac*, http://www.baseball-almanac.com /legendary/Jewish_baseball_players.shtml (accessed January 12, 2011).

18 Nicholas Dawidoff, "Scholar, Lawyer, Catcher, Spy," *Sports Illustrated*, March 23, 1992.

19 Ibid.

20 Ibid.

21 Solomon, *The Baseball Timeline*, 363.

22 Brian Moynahan, "Hank Greenberg: The Player Nobody Wanted," *Baseball Almanac*, http://www.baseball-almanac.com/articles/hank_greenberg _article.shtml (accessed January 5, 2011).

23 Steven R. Bullock, *Playing for Their Nation: Baseball and the American Military during World War II* (Lincoln: University of Nebraska Press, 2004), 2.

24 Ibid., 16.

25 Ibid.

26 Ibid., 22.

27 Gary Bedingfield, "Elmer Gedeon," *Baseball in Wartime*, 2008, http://www .baseballinwartime.com/player_biographies/gedeon_elmer.htm (accessed January 19, 2011).

28 Tim Wolter, *POW Baseball in World War II: The National Pastime behind Barbed Wire* (Jefferson, NC: McFarland, 2002), 1.

29 Ibid., 13.

30 Ibid., 24.

31 Ibid., 85.

32 Ibid., 91.

33 Ibid., 173.

34 Billy Goat Tavern, "The Legend: The Billy Goat Curse," *Billy Goat's Blog,* http://www.billygoattavern.com/legend/curse (accessed October 7, 2011).

35 David Brooks, "The Missing Characters of Page One," *New York Times,* July 6, 2005, http://theunknowncandidate.blogspot.com/2006/07/ghosts-of-billy-goat-tavern.html (accessed January 10, 2011).

36 *Author's note*: I worked as a weekend *Chicago Tribune* copy boy while attending law school in the mid-1970s, and I regularly visited the Billy Goat, relying on its affordable but tasty cheeseburgers for sustenance. So did scores of other *Tribune* personnel, such as national columnist Clarence Page, who was a weekend city editor at the time. Many years later, as one of the lawyers for the late Chicago sportscaster Tim Weigel, I found myself at one of Weigel's famed New Year's Day parties at his home in Evanston, Illinois, where Billy Goat owner Sam Sianis, nephew to Bill, was personally cooking Billy Goat burgers on the Weigel porch, even though it was all of 10 degrees outside.

CHAPTER 9. MANIPULATING HISTORY

1 "Baseball Quotes: Monte Irvin," The Baseball Vault, http://www.baseball-vault.com/baseball-quotes.html (accessed September 10, 2011).

2 Sports Reference LLC, "Monte Irvin Player Page," Baseball-Reference.com, http://www.baseball-reference.com/players/i/irvinmo01.shtml (accessed September 10, 2011).

3 Brown v. Board of Education of Topeka et al., 347 U.S. 483 (1954).

4 Dickson, *Baseball's Greatest Quotations*, 266.

5 Flood v. Kuhn, 407 U.S. 258 (1972).

6 William Grimes, "William S. Stevens, 60, Dies; Wrote Infield Fly Note," *New York Times,* December 11, 2008.

7 Anthony D'Amato, "The Contribution of the Infield Fly Rule to Western Civilization (and Vice Versa)," *Northwestern University Law Review* 100, no. 1 (2006).

8 Kessler v. Pennsylvania National Mutual Casualty Insurance Company, 531 F.2d 248 (1976).

9   Ibid.

10 Grimes, "William S. Stevens."

11 Kevin Baxter, "Despite Brian Sabean's Reaction, Giants Go On without Buster Posey," On Baseball, *Los Angeles Times*, June 11, 2011.

12 Dickson, *Baseball's Greatest Quotations*, 456.

13 "Jackie Robinson Quotes," *Baseball Almanac*, http://www.baseball-almanac.com /quotes/quojckr.shtml (accessed September 10, 2011).

14 *Brown.*

15 Ibid.

16 Ibid.

17 Tom Verducci, "Embarrassing Moments: Owners, Cheaters, Gamblers All Disgrace Baseball," Inside Baseball, August 2, 2006, http://sportsillustrated .cnn.com/2006/writers/tom_verducci/07/13/moments/index.html (accessed September 10, 2001).

18 Ibid.

19 Dave Greenwald, "Alumnus Jackie Robinson Honored by Congress," UCLA Spotlight, February 1, 2005, http://spotlight.ucla.edu/alumni/jackie-robinson/ (accessed September 10, 2011).

20 "Jackie Robinson Quotes."

21 Tom Gallagher, "Player Profiles: Jackie Robinson," BaseballLibrary.com, http://www.baseballlibrary.com/ballplayers/player.php?name=Jackie_Robinson _1919&page=summary (accessed December 2, 2010).

22 Hon. Adam B. Schiff, "Commemorating Black History Month," *Congressional Record* 150, no. 20 (February 24, 2004).

23 Associated Press, "Study: MLB Gets 'A' for Racial Hiring," ESPN.com, April 29, 2010, http://espn.go.com/espn/print?id=5146934&type=story (accessed October 7, 2011).

24 U.S. Census Bureau, "People QuickFacts: Black persons, percent, 2010 (a)," State & County QuickFacts: USA, August 16, 2012 (last revised), http://quickfacts.census.gov/qfd/states/00000.html.

25 William C. Rhoden, "N.F.L. Players Evaluate Their Coaches," *New York Times*, October 25, 2008; and Richard Lapchick, "NBA Diversity Makes for a Pretty Big Picture," ESPN NBA, May 9, 2007, http://sports.espn.go.com/nba/columns /story?columnist=lapchick_richard&id=2865144 (accessed September 10, 2011).

26 "Quotes by Bill Veeck," ESPN Classic, November 19, 2003, http://espn.go.com /classic/s/veeckquotes000816.html.

CHAPTER 10. THE MISSILES OF CAMELOT

1 "Home Run in Last At-Bat," *Baseball Almanac*, http://www.baseball-almanac.com /feats/feats18.shtml (accessed September 14, 2011).

2 Ibid.

3 Ibid.

4 "Home Run in First At-Bat," *Baseball Almanac*, http://www.baseball-almanac .com/feats/feats5.shtml (accessed March 16, 2011).

5 "Home Run Allowed to First Batter Faced," *Baseball Almanac*, http://www .baseball-almanac.com/feats/feats23.shtml (accessed March 16, 2011).

6 MLB Advanced Media, L.P., "Statistics: Sortable Player, Hitting, All-Time Total, AVG," MLB.com, http://mlb.mlb.com/mlb/history/all_time_leaders.jsp (accessed March 16, 2011).

7 MLB Advanced Media, L.P., "Statistics, Sortable Player, Hitting, All-Time totals, OPS," MLB.com, http://mlb.mlb.com/mlb/history/all_time_leaders.jsp (accessed March 16, 2011).

8 Sports Reference LLC, "Switch Hitter," Baseball-Reference.com, http://www .baseball-reference.com/bullpen/Switch_hitter (accessed March 16, 2011).

9 Dave Anderson et al., *The Yankees: The Four Fabulous Eras of Baseball's Most Famous Team* (New York: Random House, 1979), 109.

10 MLB Advanced Media, L.P., "Mickey Mantle Stats," MLB.com, http://mlb .mlb.com/team/player.jsp?player_id=118258 (accessed March 16, 2011).

11 Ibid.

12 "Mickey Mantle Quotes," *Baseball Almanac*, http://www.baseball-almanac.com /quotes/quomant.shtml.

13 "Players: Mickey Mantle Facts," The Baseball Page, http://www.thebaseballpage .com/players/mantlmi01.php (accessed March 19, 2011).

14 Ibid.

15 Ibid.

16 Ibid.

17 Sports Reference LLC, "1961 New York Yankees," Baseball-Reference.com, http://www.baseball-reference.com/teams/NYY/1961.shtml (accessed October 8, 2011).

18 I was nine years old at the time. Even though I was a small-town midwestern kid in the middle of Illinois cornfields, I remember the magic of 1961, the television coverage, and the suspense.

19 "Mickey Mantle Facts"; and "Mickey Mantle Quotes."

20 "Mickey Mantle Facts."

21 Jack Doyle, "Mantle's Griffith Shot, April 1953," The Pop History Dig, February 12, 2010, http://www.pophistorydig.com/?tag=baseball-pop-culture (accessed December 20, 2011).

22 Jenkinson, "Long Distance Home Runs."

23 "70 Single Season Home Runs by Mark McGwire," *Baseball Almanac*, http://www.baseball-almanac.com/feats/feats1.shtml (accessed October 8, 2011); and "66 Single Season Home Runs by Sammy Sosa," *Baseball Almanac*, http://www.baseball-almanac.com/feats/feats12.shtml (accessed October 8, 2011).

24 Early, "Mickey Mantle's 10 Longest Home Runs."

25 Anthony McCarron, "Ex-Outfielder Brian Anderson Gives Majors One Final Pitch with Yankees," *New York Daily News*, February 12, 2011, http://articles .nydailynews.com/2011-02-12/sports/28613061_1 (accessed December 2, 2012).

26 Joi Sigers, "Mickey Mantle: The Man Behind the Legend," *Self Help Daily* (blog), http://www.selfhelpdaily.com/mickey-mantle-inspirational-quotes/ (accessed June 26, 2010).

CHAPTER 11. THE RISE AND FALL OF ROGER MARIS

1 BookRags Media Network, "Roger Maris Quotes," BrainyQuote, http://www .brainyquote.com/quotes/authors/r/roger_maris.html (accessed December 17, 2012).

2 "Person of the Year: 1961," *Time*, January 5, 1962.

3 Joseph Durso, "Roger Maris Is Dead at 51; Set Record Home Runs," *New York Times*, December 15, 1985.

4 Ibid.

5 Ibid.

6 "Person of the Year: 1961."

7 "Cost of Living 1961," The People History, http://www.thepeoplehistory.com /1961.html (accessed November 6, 2010).

8 "Four Home Runs in One Game," *Baseball Almanac*, http://www. baseball -almanac.com/feats/feats4.shtml (accessed December 9, 2012).

9 "Year in Review."

10 Durso, "Roger Maris Is Dead."

11 "Players: Roger Maris," Baseball Page LLC, http://www.thebaseballpage.com /players/marisro01 (accessed March 19, 2011).

12 MLB Advanced Media, L. P., "History: The Hall of Fame Veterans Committee," MLB.com, http://mlb.mlb.com/mlb/history/mlb_history_halloffame .jsp?story=4 (accessed September 14, 2011).

13 "Players: Roger Maris."

14 "Hall of Famers: Club 297," National Baseball Hall of Fame and Museum, http://baseballhall.org/hall-famers (accessed October 12, 2011).

15 Sports Reference LLC, "Roger Maris Player Page," Baseball-Reference.com, http://www.baseball-reference.com/players/m/marisro01.shtml (accessed September 14, 2011).

16 Norman L. Macht and Christopher D. Renino, "Player Profiles: Roger Maris," BaseballLibrary.com, http://www.baseballlibrary.com/ballplayers/player .php?name=roger_maris_1934&page=chronology (accessed April 6, 2011).

17 Sports Reference LLC, "Bill Mazeroski Player Page," Baseball-Reference.com, http://www.baseball-reference.com/players/m/mazerbi01.shtml (accessed September 14, 2011).

18 Maury Allen, *Roger Maris: A Man for All Seasons* (New York: Dutton Adult, 1986), 163.

19 Sports Reference LLC, "Roger Maris Player Page."

20 Allen, *Roger Maris*, 133.

21 Ibid., 155.

22 Ibid., 25.

23 Ibid., 51.

24 Sports Reference LLC, "2013 Hall of Fame Election-BR Bullpen," Baseball -Reference.com, http://www.baseball-reference.com/bullpen/2013_Hall_of_Fame _Election (accessed February 27, 2013).

CHAPTER 12. STEALING HISTORY

1 Adam Liptak, "This Bench Belongs in a Dugout," *New York Times*, May 31, 2010.

2 "Justice John Paul Stevens: A Biography," Justice at Stake Campaign, http://www .justiceatstake.org/resources/justice_john_paul_stevens_a_biography.cfm (accessed April 12, 2011).

3 American Needle, Inc., v. National Football League et al., 130 S. Ct. 2201 (2010).

4 "Presidential Baseball Famous Firsts," *Baseball Almanac*, http://www.baseball -almanac.com/firsts/prz_1st.shtml (accessed April 13, 2011).

5 Federal Base Ball Club of Baltimore, Inc., v. National League of Professional Base Ball Clubs et al., 259 U.S. 200 (1922).

6 "Presidential Baseball Famous Firsts."

7   Ibid.

8   Michael Ariens, "Supreme Court Justices: William Howard Taft (1857–1930)," michaelariens.com (blog), http://www.michaelariens.com/ConLaw/justices /taft.htm (accessed April 17, 2011).

9   I. Grinfeld, letter to the editor, *New York Times*, October 12, 1912.

10 Sherman Antitrust Act, 15 U.S.C. § 1, et seq. (1890).

11 "Standard Oil Company," Ohio Historical Society, July 1, 2005, http://www.ohiohistorycentral.org/entry.php?rec=988 (accessed April 17, 2011).

12 "Oil Trust Fine Is $29,240,000," *New York Times*, August 4, 1907.

13 Clayton Act, 15 U.S.C. § 12, et seq. (1914).

14 Shayna M. Sigman, "The Jurisprudence of Judge Kenesaw Mountain Landis," *Marquette Sports Law Review* 15, no. 2 (Spring 2005), http://scholarship .law.marquette.edu/sportslaw/vol15/iss2/2 (accessed December 12, 2012).

15 Hart v. B. F. Keith Vaudeville Exchange, 262 U.S. 271 (1923).

16 Ibid., 272.

17 "Kenesaw Mountain Landis," U-S-History.com, http://www.u-s-history.com /pages/h2074.html (accessed April 19, 2011).

18 Henry D. Fetter, "How Justice Stevens Changed Baseball," *The Atlantic*, June 29, 2010.

19 *Flood*, 407 U.S. 258 (1972).

20 Plessy v. Ferguson, 163 U.S. 537 (1896); and *Brown*.

21 Richard O'Brien, ed., "Scorecard," *Sports Illustrated*, April 18, 1994.

22 Grimes, "William S. Stevens."

CHAPTER 13. THE DEAD BALL MALAISE

1   Roger Abrams, *Legal Bases: Baseball and the Law* (Philadelphia: Temple University Press, 1998), 130–31.

2   "Year in Review: 1968 American League," Baseball-Almanac, http://www .baseball-almanac.com/yearly/yr1968a.shtml.

3   Sports Reference LLC, "1960 Major League Baseball Batting Leaders," Baseball -Reference.com, http://www.baseball-reference.com/leagues/MLB/1960 -batting-leaders.shtml (accessed April 30, 2011); and Sports Reference LLC, "1968 Major League Baseball Batting Leaders," Baseball-Reference.com, http://www.baseball-reference.com/leagues/MLB/1968-batting-leaders.shtml (accessed April 30, 2011).

4   Sports Reference LLC, "1961 Major League Baseball Batting Leaders," Baseball -Reference.com, http://www.baseball-reference.com/leagues/MLB/1961 -batting-leaders.shtml (accessed April 30, 2011).

5   Sports Reference LLC, "1968 Major League Baseball Batting Leaders."

6   William Leggett, "From Mountain to Molehill," *Sports Illustrated*, March 24, 1969.

7   Ibid.

8   Sports Reference LLC, "1969 Major League Baseball Batting Leaders," Baseball -Reference.com, http://www.baseball-reference.com/leagues/MLB/1969 -batting-leaders.shtml (accessed April 30, 2011).

9   "Year by Year Leaders."

10 ESPN Stats & Information Group, "Highlight Homers: Reggie Jackson, 1971 All-Star Game, Tiger Stadium, July 13," ESPN Home Run Tracker, September 19, 2012, http://www.hittrackeronline.com/historic.php?id=1971_9 (accessed May 1, 2011).

11 Ibid.

12 "Year by Year Leaders."

13 RK559 for Sporcle, "Can You Name the Two Teammates with the Most Home Runs?," Sporcle, April 18, 2010, http://www.sporcle.com/games/rk559 /auckland (accessed May 4, 2011); and http://www.vitalstatistics.info/stat2 .asp?id=8487&cid=9&scid=585.

14 Sports Reference LLC, "2006 Philadelphia Phillies," Baseball-Reference.com, http://www.baseball-reference.com/teams/PHI/2006.shtml.

15 RK559 for Sporcle, "Can You Name?"

16 Ibid.

17 Ibid.

18 "Sport: Charlie Finley: Baseball's Barnum," *Time*, August 18, 1975.

19 Mark Armour, "SABR Baseball Biography Project: Charlie Finley," SABR/Society for American Baseball Research, http://sabr.org/bioproj/person /6ac2ee2f (accessed December 17, 2012).

20 Finley v. Kuhn, 569 F.2d 527 (1978).

21 William Leggett, "The Big Leagues Select a Fan," *Sports Illustrated*, February 17, 1969.

22 Jim Langford, "Player Profiles: Sandy Koufax," BaseballLibrary.com, http://www.baseballlibrary.com/ballplayers/player.php?name=Sandy_Koufax _1935&page=chronology (accessed May 11, 2011); and Tom Gallagher, "Player Profiles: Don Drysdale," BaseballLibrary.com, http://www.baseballlibrary.com /ballplayers/player.php?name=Don_Drysdale_1936 (accessed May 11, 2011).

23 Gallagher, "Player Profiles: Don Drysdale."

24 "History: Peter Ueberroth," TheBaseballPage.com, http://www.thebaseballpage .com/content/peter-ueberroth-biography-baseball-page (accessed May 11, 2011).

25 Paul C. Weiler, Gary R. Roberts, Roger I. Abrams, and Stephen F. Ross, *Sports and the Law: Text, Cases and Problems*, 4th ed. (St. Paul, MN: West, 2011), 267.

26 Ibid., 268.

27 "World Series Television Ratings," *Baseball Almanac*, http://www.baseball -almanac.com/ws/wstv.shtml (accessed April 30, 2011).

28 "The Pine Tar Game: George Brett's Bat Sparks Controversy," MLB.com, July 24, 1983, http://www.mlb.com/mlb/baseballs_best/mlb_bb_gamepage .jsp?story_page=bb_83reg_072483_kcrnyy (accessed April 30, 2011).

29 "1988 World Series/Game 1," MLB.com, October 14, 1988, http://mlb.mlb .com/mlb/baseballs_best/mlb_bb_gamepage.jsp?story_page=bb_88ws_gm1 _oakla (accessed May 14, 2011).

30 "President George Bush Baseball Related Quotations," *Baseball Almanac*, http://www.baseball-almanac.com/prz_qgb.shtml (accessed December 1, 2010).

31 "President Bill Clinton Baseball Related Quotations," *Baseball Almanac*, http://www.baseball-almanac.com/prz_qbc.shtml (accessed December 1, 2010).

32 "President George Bush."

CHAPTER 14. SOSA-McGWIRE: THE SUMMER THAT ROARED

1 "70 Single Season."

2 Ibid.

3 Ibid.

4 Ibid.

5 Sports Reference LLC, "Sammy Sosa: Player Page," Baseball-Reference.com, http://www.baseball-reference.com/players/s/sosasa01.shtml (accessed October 15, 2011).

6 "66 Single Season."

7 "Sammy Sosa Stats," *Baseball Almanac*, http://www.baseball-almanac.com /players/player.php?p=sosasa01 (accessed May 18, 2011).

8 Munsey & Suppes, "Wrigley Field," Ballparks.com, May 2008, http://www .ballparks.com/baseball/national/wrigle.htm (accessed October 25, 2011).

9 MLB Advanced Media, L.P., "Cubs History: Wrigley Field Ballpark Information," MLB.com, http://mlb.mlb.com/chc/ballpark/information /index.jsp?content=history (accessed May 21, 2011).

10 Marc Zarefsky, "Homer in the Gloamin' Most Memorable," Cubs.com, August 8, 2007, http://mlb.mlb.com/content/printer_friendly/chc/y2007/m07 /d20/c2099223.jsp (accessed May 21, 2011).

11 "Sammy Sosa Stats."

12 "66 Single Season."

13 Jim Salisbury, "Phillies Burned by Two Hot Cubs," *Philadelphia Inquirer*, June 21, 1998.

14 "Home Run in a Month Records," *Baseball Almanac*, http://www.baseball-almanac.com/recbooks/rb_hr3.shtml (accessed May 22, 2011).

15 Michael S. Schmidt, "Sosa Is Said to Have Tested Positive in 2003," *New York Times*, June 16, 2009.

16 "70 Single Season."

17 "1998 MLB All-Star Game: One for the Ages: AL's Wacky 13–8 Win Had Something for Everyone," CNN/*Sports Illustrated*, http://sportsillustrated.cnn.com/baseball/mlb/1998/allstar/news/1998/07/08/all_star_game_final/ (accessed May 25, 2011).

18 "Home Run Derby (1990–1999)," *Baseball Almanac*, http://www.baseball-almanac.com/asgbox/hrderby2.shtml (accessed May, 25, 2011).

19 "70 Single Season."

20 "66 Single Season."

21 "70 Single Season."

22 Ibid.

23 Ibid.

24 "66 Single Season."

25 Bill Dedman, "On Bad Day for Cubs, Sosa Ties McGwire at 65," *New York Times*, September 24, 1998.

26 Ibid.

27 "MLB Season History—1998," ESPN, http://espn.go.com/mlb/history/season/_/year/1998 (accessed October 8, 2012).

28 Murray Chass, "No Letup in Home Run Race: 66 and 66, Just Minutes Apart," *New York Times*, September 26, 1998.

29 Ibid.

30 Ibid.

31 "Target: 61, the Home Run Chase: McGwire's Last 10 Home Runs," CNN/*Sports Illustrated*, http://sportsillustrated.cnn.com/baseball/mlb/1998/target61/movies/mac.html (accessed May 15, 2011).

32 Murray Chass, "McGwire's Grand Finale Makes It 70," *New York Times*, September 28, 1998.

33 "Single Season Leaders for Home Runs," *Baseball Almanac*, http://www.baseball-almanac.com/hitting/hihr4.shtml (accessed May 28, 2011).

34 Ibid.

35 Ibid.

CHAPTER 15. NEW YORK, NEW YORK

1   President Franklin Roosevelt, "Green Light Letter—Baseball Can Be Played during the War," *Baseball Almanac*, http://www.baseball-almanac.com /prz_lfr.shtml (accessed June 4, 2011).

2   Ibid.

3   Gerard Bazer and Steven Culbertson, "Baseball during World War II: The Reaction and Encouragement of Franklin Delano Roosevelt and Others," *NINE: A History of Baseball and Culture* 10, no. 1 (Fall 2001): 114–29.

4   Tim Dirks, "The History of Film: The 1940s: Hollywood during the War Years," AMC filmsite.org, http://www.filmsite.org/40sintro.html (accessed June 12, 2011).

5   Ibid.

6   "The Pride of the Yankees (1942)," Reel Classics LLC, March 10, 2011, http://www.reelclassics.com/Movies/Yankees/yankees.htm (accessed June 12, 2011).

7   "The Best of the Century," *Time*, December 31, 1999, http://www.time.com /time/magazine/article/0,9171,993039,00.html (accessed July 9, 2011).

8   David Whitley, "Lou Gehrig's Farewell Speech Still Underrated by American Scholars," *Sporting News MLB*, July 4, 2011, http://aol.sportingnews.com /mlb/story/2011-07-04/gehrigs-farewell-speech-still-underrated-by-american -scholars (accessed July 9, 2011).

9   RVW Foundation, "About Lou: Biography," Lou Gehrig: The Official Website, http://www.lougehrig.com/about/bio/htm (accessed June 15, 2011).

10 Michael E. Eldenmuller, "The Top 100 Speeches of the 20th Century by Rank," American Rhetoric: Top 100 Speeches, www.americanrhetoric.com /top100speechesall.html (accessed July 9, 2011).

11 "Left Field: Legendary: League by League Totals for Home Runs," *Baseball Almanac*, http://www.baseball-almanac.com/hitting/hihr6.shtml.

12 Sports Reference LLC, "The Star Spangled Banner," Baseball-Reference.com, http://www.baseball-reference.com/bullpen/The_Star_Spangled_Banner (accessed July 2, 2011).

13 Gary Bedingfield, "Hall of Fame Player Biographies," *Baseball in Wartime*, 2009, http://www.baseballinwartime.com/player–biographies/player –biographies_hof.htm (accessed July 4, 2011).

14 Rod Beaton, "Baseball Great Ted Williams Dies," *USA Today*, July 22, 2002, http://www.usatoday.com/sports/baseball/williams/ted-obit.htm (accessed July 4, 2011).

15 Solomon, *The Baseball Timeline*, 610.

16 Online Highways LLC, "Jackie Robinson," U-S-History.com, http://www.u-s
-history.com/pages/h2068.html (accessed July 4, 2011).

17 Gary Bedingfield, "Negro Leaguers Who Served With the Armed Forces in
WWII," *Baseball in Wartime*, http://www.baseballinwartime.com/negro.htm
(accessed July 4, 2011).

18 "This Day in Truman History, July 26, 1948: President Truman Issues Executive
Order No. 9981 Desegregating the Military," Harry S. Truman Library &
Museum, http://www.trumanlibrary.org/anniversaries/desegblurb.htm (accessed
July 6, 2011).

19 Filip Bondy, "After 9/11, It Was No Longer 'Just' Sports," NBC Sports,
September 5, 2006, http://nbcsports.msnbc.com/id/14668883/ns/sports
-other_sports/ (accessed December 5, 2009).

20 Anthony Emerson, "After 9/11, Baseball Brought Hope Back to America,"
BleacherReport.com, September 11, 2009, http://bleacherreport.com/articles
/252671-after-911-baseball-brought-hope-back-to-america (accessed July 10,
2011).

21 Ibid.

22 "Baseball Responds to September 11th Attacks: Silenced Stadiums,"
NationalPastime.com, 2010, http://www.nationalpastime.com/stitches
/september11.html (accessed July 16, 2011).

23 Bondy, "After 9/11."

CHAPTER 16. THE SCARLET NUMBER

1 Sports Reference LLC, "Barry Bonds Player Page," Baseball-Reference.com,
http://www.baseball-reference.com/players/b/bondsba01.shtml (accessed July
16, 2011).

2 Ibid.

3 Ibid.

4 Ibid.

5 Lewis Early, "*Big Mac* (Mark McGwire) Takes on *The Mick*," Mickey Mantle:
The American Dream Comes to Life, 2010, http://www.themick.com
/macvsmick.htm (accessed May 18, 2011).

6 Sports Reference LLC, "Mark McGwire Player Page," Baseball-Reference.com,
http://www.baseball-reference.com/players/m/mcgwima01.shtml (accessed July
16, 2011).

7 Ibid.

8 Sports Reference LLC, "Sammy Sosa."

9 Ibid.

10 Ibid.

11 Sports Reference LLC, "George Bell Player Page," Baseball-Reference.com, http://www.baseball-reference.com/players/b/bellge02.shtml (accessed July 16, 2011).

12 Sports Reference LLC, "Sammy Sosa."

13 Ibid.

14 Ibid.

15 Ibid.

16 Greg Bishop, "After Drug Revelations, Redefining '98 Home Run Chase," *New York Times*, July 4, 2009.

17 Sports Reference LLC, "Sammy Sosa."

18 Tim Britton, "A-Rod Youngest in History to 600 Homers," MLB.com, August 4, 2010, http://newyork.yankees.mlb.com/news/article.jsp?c_id=mlb&content _id=13011408&fext=.jsp&vkey=news_mlb&ymd=20100804 (accessed December 15, 2012); Justin Albers, "Thome Passes Sosa on All-Time Home Runs List," MLB.com, July 21, 2012, http://mlb.mlb.com/news/article .jsp?ymd=20120720&content_id=35262770&vkey=news_mlb&c_id=mlb &partnerId=rss_mlb; and "Jim Thome Hits 600th Home Run," ESPN.com, August 15, 2011, http://espn.go.com/mlb/story/_/id/6864854 /minnesota-twins-slugger-jim-thome-clubs-600th-career-homer.

19 Complex Sports, "This Day in Sports History (March 30th)—Sammy Sosa," Total Pro Sports, March 30, 2012, http://www.totalprosports.com/2012/03 /30/this-day-in-sports-history-march/30th-sammy-sosa/ (accessed July 16, 2011).

20 Bishop, "After Drug Revelations."

21 "McGwire Apologizes to La Russa, Selig," ESPN.com, January 12, 2010, http://sports.espn.go.com/mlb/news/story?id=4816607 (accessed May 15, 2011).

22 Stephen Jay Gould, *Full House: The Spread of Excellence from Plato to Darwin* (New York: Three Rivers Press/Crown Publishing Group, 1997).

23 Thomas J. Miceli, "Minimum Quality Standards in Baseball and the Paradoxical Disappearance of the .400 Hitter," *Economics Working Papers*, Paper 200515, 2005, http://digitalcommons.uconn.edu/econ_wpapers/200515 (accessed October 19, 2011).

24 Ibid.

25 Nate Silver, "Which Records Get Shattered?," *New York Times*, July 28, 2012, http://www.nytimes.com/2012/07/29/sunday-review/why-olympic-records -are-broken-or-not.html (accessed August 4, 2012).

26 Miceli, "Minimum Quality Standards."

CHAPTER 17. MEN, MUDVILLE, AND DiMAGGIO

1   "Mrs. Robinson by Simon & Garfunkel," Songfacts LLC, http://www.songfacts .com/detail.php?id=1283 (accessed July 24, 2011).

2   Larry Schwartz, "Hank Aaron: Hammerin' Back at Racism," ESPN.com, http://espn.go.com/sportscentury/features/00006764.html (accessed September 23, 2011).

3   "Hailing the Hammer: Baseball Begins Season-Long Tribute to Hank Aaron," CNN/*Sports Illustrated*, April 8, 1999, http://sportsillustrated.cnn.com/baseball /mlb/news/1999/04/08aaron_tribute/ (accessed September 23, 2011).

4   "All You Need to Know about Teenage Steroid Use," TestCountry.org, http://www.testcountry.org/teenage-steroid-use.htm.

5   Sports Reference LLC, "Barry Bonds."

6   Sports Reference LLC, "Roger Maris."

7   Sports Reference LLC, "1961 New York Yankees Batting Orders," Baseball -Reference.com, http://www.baseball-reference.com/teams/NYY/1961-batting -orders.shtml (accessed July 27, 2011).

8   Sports Reference LLC, "Mickey Mantle."

9   Asher B. Chancey, "Intentional Walks," BaseballEvolution.com, July 23, 2009, http://baseballevolution.com/asher/00025.html (accessed July 27, 2011).

10 Ibid.; and Sports Reference LLC, "Career Leaders & Records for Bases on Balls," Baseball-Reference.com, http://www.baseball-reference.com/leaders/BB _career.shtml.

11 "League by League Totals for Home Runs," *Baseball Almanac*, http://www .baseball-almanac.com/hitting/hihr6.shtml (accessed July 27, 2011).

12 Ibid.

13 "Career Leaders for Slugging Average," *Baseball Almanac*, http://www.baseball -almanac.com/hitting/hislug1.shtml (accessed July 24, 2011).

14 Ibid.; and "League by League Totals."

BIBLIOGRAPHY

BOOKS

Abrams, Roger. *Legal Bases: Baseball and the Law*. Philadelphia: Temple University Press, 1998.

Adair, Robert K. *The Physics of Baseball*. 3rd ed. New York: HarperCollins, 2002.

Allen, Maury. *Roger Maris: A Man for All Seasons*. New York: Dutton Adult, 1986.

Anderson, Dave, Murray Chass, Robert W. Creamer, and Harold Rosenthal. *The Yankees: The Four Fabulous Eras of Baseball's Most Famous Team*. New York: Random House, 1979.

Bouton, Jim. *Ball Four: My Life and Hard Times Throwing the Knuckleball in the Big Leagues*. Edited by Leonard Shecter. New York: World Publishing, 1970. Twentieth-anniversary edition, New York: Collier Books, 1990.

Bullock, Steven R. *Playing for Their Nation: Baseball and the American Military during World War II*. Lincoln: University of Nebraska Press, 2004.

Canseco, Jose. *Juiced: Wild Times, Rampant 'Roids, Smash Hits, and How Baseball Got Big*. New York: Regan Books, 2005.

Crystal, David. *How Language Works: How Babies Babble, Words Change Meaning, and Languages Live or Die.* New York: Overlook Press, 2006.

Curran, William. *Big Sticks: The Batting Revolution of the Twenties.* New York: William Morrow, 1990.

Dickson, Paul. *Baseball's Greatest Quotations.* New York: HarperCollins, 1991.

Gould, Stephen Jay. *Full House: The Spread of Excellence from Plato to Darwin.* New York: Three Rivers Press/Crown Publishing Group, 1997.

Hemingway, Ernest. *The Old Man and the Sea.* New York: Charles Scribner, 1952.

Jenkinson, Bill. *The Year Babe Ruth Hit 104 Home Runs: Recrowning Baseball's Greatest Slugger.* New York: Carroll & Graf Publishers, 2007.

Kenneally, Christine. *The First Word: The Search for the Origins of Language.* New York: Viking Penguin, 2007.

Kinsella, William P. *Shoeless Joe.* Boston: Houghton Mifflin, 1982.

Lally, Richard. *Bombers: An Oral History of the New York Yankees.* New York: Crown, 2002.

Light, Jonathan Fraser. *The Cultural Encyclopedia of Baseball.* Jefferson, NC: McFarland, 1997.

Smith, Curt. *The Voice: Mel Allen's Untold Story.* Guilford, CT: Globe Pequot Press, 2007.

———. *Voices of Summer: Ranking Baseball's 101 All-Time Best Announcers.* New York: Da Capo Press, 2005.

Solomon, Burt. *The Baseball Timeline: The Day-by-Day History of Baseball, from Valley Forge to the Present Day.* New York: Avon Books, 1997.

Thorn, John, Phil Birnbaum, and Bill Deane, eds. *Total Baseball: The Ultimate Baseball Encyclopedia.* 8th ed. Wilmington, DE: Sport Classic Books, 2004.

Weiler, Paul C., Gary R. Roberts, Roger I. Abrams, and Stephen F. Ross. *Sports and the Law: Text, Cases, and Problems.* 4th ed. St. Paul, MN: West, 2011.

Wolter, Tim. *POW Baseball in World War II: The National Pastime behind Barbed Wire*. Jefferson, NC: McFarland, 2002.

LEGAL CASES

American Needle, Inc., v. National Football League et al., 130 S. Ct. 2201 (2010).

Brown v. Board of Education of Topeka et al., 347 U.S. 483 (1954).

Clayton Act, 15 U.S.C. § 12, et seq. (1914).

Federal Base Ball Club of Baltimore, Inc., v. National League of Professional Base Ball Clubs et al., 259 U.S. 200 (1922).

Finley v. Kuhn, 569 F.2d 527 (1978).

Flood v. Kuhn, 407 U.S. 258 (1972).

Hart v. B. F. Keith Vaudeville Exchange, 262 U.S. 271 (1923).

Kessler v. Pennsylvania National Mutual Casualty Insurance Company, 531 F.2d 248 (1976).

Plessy v. Ferguson, 163 U.S. 537 (1896).

Sherman Antitrust Act, 15 U.S.C. § 1, et seq. (1890).

NEWSPAPERS/ARTICLES

Anderson, Bruce. "Just a Pipp of a Legend." *Sports Illustrated*, June 29, 1987. http://sportsillustrated.cnn.com/vault/article/magazine/MAG1066131/index.htm.

Anderson, Dave. "Sports of the Times; on Being Mickey Mantle." *New York Times*, March 16, 1994.

Baxter, Kevin. "Despite Brian Sabean's Reaction, Giants Go On without Buster Posey." *Los Angeles Times*, June 11, 2011.

Bazer, Gerald, and Steven Culbertson. "Baseball during World War II: The Reaction and Encouragement of Franklin Delano Roosevelt and Others." *NINE: A History of Baseball and Culture* 10, no. 1 (Fall 2001). Cited from Project Muse website at http://muse.jhu.edu/journals/nine/toc/nin10.1.html.

Beaton, Rod. "Baseball Great Ted Williams Dies." *USA Today*, July 22, 2002. http://www.usatoday.com/sports/baseball/williams/ted-obit.htm.

"Betting on Fight May Set a Record." *New York Times*, September 18, 1927.

Bishop, Greg. "After Drug Revelations, Redefining '98 Home Run Chase." *New York Times*, July 4, 2009.

Briley, Ronald. "Baseball and American Cultural Values." *OAH Magazine of History* 7, no. 1 (Summer 1992).

Britton, Tim. "A-Rod Youngest in History to 600 Homers." MLB.com, August 4, 2010. http://newyork.yankees.mlb.com/news/article .jsp?c_id=mlb&content_id=13011408&fext=.jsp&vkey=news_mlb &ymd=20100804.

Brooks, David. "The Missing Characters of Page One." *New York Times*, July 6, 2005.

Cafardo, Nick. "Perry Cuts to the Chase; Today's 'Cheaters' Will Pass Hall Test." *Boston Globe*, December 23, 2007.

Chass, Murray. "McGwire's Grand Finale Makes It 70." *New York Times*, September 28, 1998.

———. "No Letup in Home Run Race: 66 and 66, Just Minutes Apart." *New York Times*, September 26, 1998.

D'Amato, Anthony. "The Contribution of the Infield Fly Rule to Western Civilization (and Vice Versa)." *Northwestern University Law Review* 100, no. 1 (2006).

Davies, Ross E. "A Tall Tale of the Brethren." *Journal of Supreme Court History* 33, no. 2 (July 2008).

Dawidoff, Nicholas. "Scholar, Lawyer, Catcher, Spy." *Sports Illustrated*, March 23, 1992.

Dedman, Bill. "One Bad Day for Cubs, Sosa Ties McGwire at 65." *New York Times*, September 24, 1998.

Durso, Joseph. "Roger Maris Is Dead at 51; Set Record Home Runs." *New York Times*, December 15, 1985.

Fetter, Henry D. "How Justice Stevens Changed Baseball." *The Atlantic*, June 29, 2010.

Greenfield, James. "Year of the Babe." *Sports Illustrated*, November 14, 1955.

Grimes, William. "William S. Stevens, 60, Dies; Wrote Infield Fly Note." *New York Times*, December 11, 2008.

Grinfeld, I. Letter to the editor. *New York Times*, October 21, 1912.

Ham, Eldon L. "Aside the Aside: The True Precedent of Baseball in Law: Law the Residue of Luck—or, Who's Not on First?" *Marquette Sports Law Review* 13, no. 2 (2003).

Kaiser, David. "Views of Sport: Pete Rose and the Public's Right to Know; the Hearings Should Be Open to the Public." *New York Times*, June 18, 1989. http://www.nytimes.com/1989/06/18/sports/views-sport-pte-rose-public-s-right-know-hearing-should-be-open-public.html?src=pm.

Kieran, John. "Sports of the Times." *New York Times*, October 2, 1927.

Kluger, Jeffrey. "High Point: Alan Shepard Becomes the First American in Space." *Time*, September 27, 2007.

Leggett, William. "The Big Leagues Select a Fan." *Sports Illustrated*, February 17, 1969.

———. "From Mountain to Molehill." *Sports Illustrated*, March 24, 1969.

Lewis, Tom. "'A Godlike Presence': The Impact of Radio on the 1920s and 1930s." *OAH Magazine of History* 6, no. 4 (Spring 1992).

Liptak, Adam. "This Bench Belongs in a Dugout." *New York Times*, May 31, 2010.

Literary Digest. "New York's World-Beating New Stadium." April 28, 1923. Cited from History Matters, http://historymatters.gmu.edu/d/5088/.

Lowitt, Bruce. "Long Count Allows Tunney to Keep Title." *St. Petersburg Times*, November 30, 1999.

O'Brien, Richard, ed. "Scorecard." *Sports Illustrated*, April 18, 1994.

Ohira, Rod. "Moiliili Bank's Motif a Tribute to Honolulu Stadium." *Star-Bulletin*, January 18, 1999.

"Oil Trust Fine Is $29,240,000." *New York Times*, August 4, 1907.

Rhoden, William C. "N.F.L. Players Evaluate Their Coaches." *New York Times*, October 25, 2008.

"Ruth Wallops out His 28th Home Run." *New York Times*, September 25, 1919.

Salisbury, Jim. "Phillies Burned by Two Hot Cubs." *Philadelphia Inquirer*, June 21, 1998.

Schmidt, Michael S. "Sosa Is Said to Have Tested Positive in 2003." *New York Times*, June 16, 2009.

Sigman, Shayna M. "The Jurisprudence of Judge Kenesaw Mountain Landis." *Marquette Sports Law Review* 15, no. 2 (Spring 2005). http://scholarship.law.marquette.edu/sportslaw/vol15/iss2/2.

Sports Illustrated. "50 Greatest Sports Movies of All Time." August 4, 2003.

Telander, Rick. "Telander: The Inside Story of Sammy Sosa's Corked Bat." *Chicago Sun-Times*, February 16, 2011.

Thomas, Jr., Robert McG. "Johnny Sylvester, the Inspiration for Babe Ruth Heroics, Is Dead." *New York Times*, January 11, 1990.

Time. "The Best of the Century." December 31, 1999. http://www.time.com/time/magazine/article/0,9171,993039,00.html.

———. "Person of the Year: 1961." January 5, 1962.

———. "Sport: Baseball Slipping." January 18, 1926.

———. "Sport: Charlie Finely: Baseball's Barnum." August 18, 1975.

WEBSITES

A&E Television Networks LLC. "This Day in History: May 25, 1935: Babe Ruth Hits Last Home Run." History.com. http://www.history.com/this -day-in-history/babe-ruth-hits-last-home-run.

Achenbach, Joel. "A Brief History of the Spitball." *Achenblog* (blog), *Washington Post*, June 15, 2005. http://voices.washingtonpost.com /achenblog/2005/06/a_brief_history_of_the_spitbal.html.

Adams, Noah. "Timeline: Remembering the Scopes Monkey Trial." NPR, June 5, 2005. http://www.npr.org/templates/story/story.php?storyId =4723956.

Albers, Justin. "Thome Passes Sosa on All-Time Home Runs List." MLB.com, July 21, 2012. http://mlb.mlb.com/news/article.jsp?ymd =20120720&content_id=35262770&vkey=news_mlb&c_id=mlb &partnerId=rss_mlb.

American Film Institute. "AFI's 100 Years . . . 100 Movie Quotes." AFI.com, June 21, 2005. http://www.afi.com/100years/quotes.aspx.

Applebaum, Brian. "How Many Synonyms Are There for 'Home Run'???" *30-Year Old Cardboard* (blog), March 3, 2009. http://bapple2286.wordpress .com/2009/03/03/how-many-synonyms-are-there-for-home-run/.

Ariens, Michael. "Supreme Court Justices: William Howard Taft (1857– 1930)." *michaelariens.com* (blog). http://www.michaelariens.com /ConLaw/justices/taft.htm.

Armour, Mark. "SABR Baseball Biography Project: Charlie Finley." SABR/Society for American Baseball Research. http://sabr.org/bioproj /person/6ac2ee2f.

"The Army and Navy Benefit All-Star Game of 1942," *Misc. Baseball: Gathering Assorted Items of Baseball History and Trivia* (blog). July 6, 2011. http://miscbaseball.wordpress.com/2011/07/06/the-army-and-navy -benefit-all-star-game-of-1942/.

Ask.com. "How Did Babe Ruth Get His Name?" http://answers.ask.com /Sports/Baseball/how_did_babe_ruth_get_his_name.

Associated Press. "Study: MLB Gets 'A' for Racial Hiring." ESPN.com, April 29, 2010. http://espn.go.com/espn/print?id=5146934&type=story.

Babe Ruth. "Biography." www.baberuth.com/biography/.

Babe Ruth Central. "Babe's Impact on the Game of Baseball." http://baberuthcentral.com/Legacies/babes-impact-on-the-game-of -baseball/.

———. "Babe's 1934 Barnstorming Trip to Japan." http://baberuthcentral .com/Legacies/1934-barnstorming-trip-to-japan/.

———. "The House That Ruth Built." Babe Ruth Central. http://baberuthcentral.com/Legacies/the-house-that-ruth-built/.

———. "Ruth's Illness and Passing—a Country Mourns." http://baberuthcentral.com/hero-and-icon/ruths-illness-passing-the-country-mourns/.

Baseball Almanac. "Babe Ruth Quotes." http://www.baseball-almanac.com/quotes/quoruth.shtml.

———. "Batting Average Records: Single Season Records." http://www.baseball-almanac.com/recbooks/rb_bavg1.shtml.

———. "Career Leaders for Slugging Average." http://www.baseball-almanac.com/hitting/hislug1.shtml.

———. "50 Greatest Sluggers." http://www.baseball-almanac.com/legendary/lisn50s.shtml.

———. "Four Home Runs in One Game." http://www.baseball-almanac.com/feats/feats4.shtml.

———. "Frank Home Run Baker Quotes." http://www.baseball-almanac.com/quotes/frank_baker_quotes.shtml.

———. "Gaylord Perry Quotes." http://www.baseball-almanac.com/quotes/quoperry.shtml.

———. "Harmon Killebrew Quotations." http://www.baseball-almanac.com/quotes/quobrew.shtml.

———. "Home Run Allowed to First Batter Faced." http://www.baseball-almanac.com/feats/feats23.shtml.

———. "Home Run Derby (1990–1999)." http://www.baseball-almanac.com/asgbox/hrderby2.shtml.

———. "Home Run in a Month Records." http://www.baseball-almanac.com/recbooks/rb_hr3.shtml.

———. "Home Run in First At-Bat." http://www.baseball-almanac.com/feats/feats5.shtml.

———. "Home Run in Last At-Bat." http://www.baseball-almanac.com/feats/feats18.shtml.

———. "Jackie Robinson Quotes." http://www.baseball-almanac.com /quotes/quojckr.shtml.

———. "Jewish Baseball Players." http://www.baseball-almanac.com /legendary/Jewish_baseball_players.shtml.

———. "League by League Totals for Batting Average." http://www.baseball -almanac.com/hitting/hibavg4.shtml.

———. "League by League Totals for Home Runs." http://www.baseball -almanac.com/hitting/hihr6.shtml.

———. "Left Field: Legendary: League by League Totals for Home Runs." http://www.baseball-almanac.com/hitting/hihr6.shtml.

———. "Lou Gehrig Grand Slams." http://www.baseball-almanac.com /players/Lou_Gehrig_Grand_Slams.shtml.

———. "Lou Gehrig 1939 Game by Game Batting Logs." http://www .baseball-almanac.com/players/hittinglogs.php?p=gehrilo01&y=1939.

———. "Mickey Mantle Quotes." http://www.baseball-almanac.com /quotes/quomant.shtml.

———. "1919 New York Yankees Roster." http://www.baseball-almanac.com /teamstats/roster.php?y=1919&t=NYA.

———. "1926 World Series." http://www.baseball-almanac.com/ws /yr1926ws.shtml.

———. "1951 World Series." http://www.baseball-almanac.com/ws /yr1951ws.shtml.

———. "Pete Gray Stats." http://www.baseball-almanac.com/players /player.php?p=graype01.

———. "President Abraham Lincoln Baseball Related Quotes." http://www.baseball-almanac.com/prz_qal.shtml.

———. "President Bill Clinton Baseball Related Quotations." http://www.baseball-almanac.com/prz_qbc.shtml.

———. "President Dwight D. Eisenhower Baseball Related Quotations." http://www.baseball-almanac.com/prz_qde.shtml.

———. "President Franklin Roosevelt Green Light Letter—Baseball Can Be Played during the War." http://www.baseball-almanac.com/prz_lfr.shtml.

———. "President George Bush Baseball Related Quotations." http://www.baseball-almanac.com/prz_qgb.shtml.

———. "President George Washington Baseball Related Quotations." http://www.baseball-almanac.com/prz_qgw.shtml.

———. "Presidential Baseball Famous Firsts." http://www.baseball-almanac.com/firsts/prz_1st.shtml.

———. "Ralph Kiner Quotes." http://www.baseball-almanac.com/quotes/quokiner.shtml.

———. "Sammy Sosa Stats." http://www.baseball-almanac.com/players/player.php?p=sosasa01.

———. "70 Single Season Home Runs by Mark McGwire." http://www.baseball-almanac.com/feats/feats1.shtml.

———. "Single Season Leaders for Home Runs." http://www.baseball-almanac.com/hitting/hihr4.shtml.

———. "66 Single Season Home Runs by Sammy Sosa." http://www.baseball-almanac.com/feats/feats12.shtml.

———. "Wally Pipp Stats." http://www.baseball-almanac.com/players/player.php?p=pippwa01.

———. "World Series Television Ratings." http://www.baseball-almanac.com/ws/wstv.shtml.

———. "Year by Year Leaders for Home Runs." http://www.baseball-almanac.com/hitting/hihr5.shtml.

———. "Year in Review: 1927 American League." http://www.baseball-almanac.com/yearly/yr1927a.shtml.

———. "Year in Review: 1968 American League." http://www.baseball-almanac.com/yearly/yr1968a.shtml.

———. "Yogi Berra Quotes." http://www.baseball-almanac.com/quotes/quoberra.shtml.

The Baseball Page LLC. "History: Peter Ueberroth." http://www
.thebaseballpage.com/content/peter-ueberroth-biography-baseball-page.

———. "Players: Mickey Mantle Facts." http://www.thebaseballpage
.com/players/mantlmi01.php.

———. "Players: Roger Connor." http://www.thebaseballpage
.com/players/connoro01.

———. "Players: Roger Maris." http://www.thebaseballpage.com
/players/marisro01.

The Baseball Vault. "Baseball Quotes: Monte Irvin." http://www.baseball
-vault.com/baseball-quotes.html#m.

Bedingfield, Gary. "Elmer Gedeon." Baseball in Wartime, 2008. http://www
.baseballinwartime.com/player_biographies/gedeon_elmer.htm.

———. "Hall of Fame Player Biographies." Baseball in Wartime, 2009.
http://www.baseballinwartime.com/player_biographies/player
_biographies_hof.htm.

———. "Negro Leaguers Who Served with the Armed Forces in WWII."
Baseball in Wartime, 2008. http://www.baseballinwartime.com/negro.htm.

Bellis, Mary. "The History of Baseball: Alexander Cartwright." About.com.
http://inventors.about.com/library/inventors/blbaseball.htm.

Billy Goat Tavern. "The Legend: The Billy Goat Curse." *Billy Goat's Blog*.
http://www.billygoattavern.com/legend/curse.

Bondy, Filip. "After 9/11, It Was No Longer 'Just' Sports." NBC Sports,
September 5, 2006. http://nbcsports.msnbc.com/id/14668883/ns
/sports-other_sports/.

BookRags Media Network. "Mickey Mantle Quotes." Brainy Quote.
http://www.brainyquote.com/quotes/authors/m/mickey_mantle.html.

———. "Roger Maris Quotes." Brainy Quote. http://www.brainyquote.com
/quotes/authors/r/roger_maris.html.

Britton, Tim. "A-Rod Youngest in History to 600 Homers." MLB.com, August
4, 2010. http://newyork.yankees.mlb.com/news/article.jsp?c_id=mlb
&content_id=13011408&fext=.jsp&vkey=news_mlb&ymd=20100804.

Chancey, Asher B. "Intentional Walks." BaseballEvolution.com, July 23, 2009. http://baseballevolution.com/asher/00025.html.

CharlesLindbergh.com. "The Flight." Charles Lindbergh: An American Aviator. http://charleslindbergh.com /history/paris.asp.

Clifton, Merritt. "Player Profiles: Gil McDougald." BaseballLibrary.com. http://www.baseballlibrary.com/ballplayers/player.php?name=Gil _McDougald_1928.

CNN/*Sports Illustrated.* "Hailing the Hammer: Baseball Begins Season-Long Tribute to Hank Aaron." April 8, 1999. http://sportsillustrated .cnn.com/baseball/mlb/news/1999/04/08/aaron_tribute/.

———. "1998 MLB All-Star Game: One for the Ages: AL's Wacky 13–8 Win Had Something for Everyone." July 8, 1998. http://sportsillustrated.cnn. com/baseball/mlb/1998/allstar/news/1998/07/08/all_star_game_final/.

———. "Target: 61, the Home Run Chase: McGwire's Last 10 Home Runs." 1999. http://sportsillustrated.cnn.com/baseball/mlb/1998 /target61/movies/mac.html.

———. "Unsplendid Splinter: Cubs Rally Past Rays after Sosa's Ignominious Ejection." June 3, 2003. http://sportsillustrated.cnn.com /baseball/news/2003/06/03/sosa_ejected_ap/.

———. "Video Almanac: Jimmy 'The Greek' Snyder Canned for 'Racist' Remarks." January 16, 1988. http://sportsillustrated.cnn.com/almanac /video/1988/.

Complex Sports. "This Day in Sports History (March 30th)—Sammy Sosa." Total Pro Sports, March 30, 2012. http://www.totalprosports.com /2012/03/30/this-day-in-sports-history-march-30th-sammy-sosa/.

Dirks, Tim. "The History of Film: The 1940s: Hollywood during the War Years." AMC filmsite.org. http://www.filmsite.org/40sintro.html.

Doyle, Jack. "Mantle's Griffith Shot, April 1953." The Pop History Dig, February 12, 2010. http://www.pophistorydig.com/?tag=baseball-pop-culture.

Duke University Libraries. "Brief History of the Radio Industry: Pittsburgh's KDKA and the Growth of Radio in the 1920s." http://library.duke .edu/digitalcollections/adaccess/radio-tv.html.

Early, Lewis. "*Big Mac* (Mark McGwire) Takes on *The Mick*." Mickey Mantle: The American Dream Comes to Life, 2010. http://www.themick.com/macvsmick.htm.

———. "Mickey Mantle's 10 Longest Home Runs." Mickey Mantle: The American Dream Comes to Life, 2010. http://www.themick.com/10homers.html.

Editors of Publications International, Ltd. "1927 Baseball Season." HowStuffWorks.com. http://entertainment.howstuffworks.com/1927-baseball-season.htm.

Eldenmuller, Michael E. "The Top 100 Speeches of the 20th Century by Rank." American Rhetoric: Top 100 Speeches. http://www.americanrhetoric.com/top100speechesall.html.

Emerson, Anthony. "After 9/11, Baseball Brought Hope Back to America." BleacherReport.com, September 11, 2009. http://bleacherreport.com/articles/252671-after-911-baseball-brought-hope-back-to-america.

ESPN Classic. "Quotes by Bill Veeck," November 19, 2003, http://espn.go.com/classic/s/veeckquotes000816.html.

ESPN. "Jim Thome Hits 600th Home Run." ESPN.com, August 15, 2011. http://espn.go.com/mlb/story/_/id/6864854/minnesota-twins-slugger-jim-thome-clubs-600th-career-homer.

———. "MLB Season History—1998." ESPN.com. http://espn.go.com/mlb/history/season/_/year/1998.

ESPN Internet Ventures, Page 2 Staff. "Biggest Cheaters in Baseball." ESPN Page 2. http://espn.go.com/page2/s/list/cheaters/ballplayers.html.

———. "McGwire Apologizes to La Russa, Selig." ESPN.com, January 12, 2010. http://m.espn.go.com/mlb/story?storyId=4816607&wjb=&pg=1.

ESPN Stats & Information Group. "Highlight Homers: Reggie Jackson, 1971 All-Star Game, Tiger Stadium, July 13." ESPN Home Run Tracker, September 19, 2012. http://www.hittrackeronline.com/historic.php?id=1971_9.

Gallagher, Tom. "Player Profiles: Don Drysdale." BaseballLibrary.com. http://www.baseballlibrary.com/ballplayers/player.php?name=Don_Drysdale_1936.

———. "Player Profiles: Jackie Robinson." BaseballLibrary.com,
    http://www.baseballlibrary.com/ballplayers/player.php?name=Jackie
    _Robinson_1919&page=summary.

"Gene Geiselmann." *Funny Sports Quotes* (blog). http://funnysportsquotes
    .blogspot.com/2008/01/funny-sports-quotes-source_5537.html.

Greenwald, Dave. "Alumnus Jackie Robinson Honored by Congress." *UCLA
    Spotlight*, February 1, 2005. http://spotlight.ucla.edu/alumni/jackie
    -robinson/.

Hammond Museum of Radio. "KDKA." http://www.hammondmuseumofradio
    .org/kdka.html.

Harry S. Truman Library & Museum. "This Day in Truman History, July
    26, 1948: President Truman Issues Executive Order No. 9981
    Desegregating the Military." http://www.trumanlibrary.org/anniversaries
    /desegblurb.htm.

Helgesen, Tom. "Pre-1845 Baseball: Was Abner Doubleday Really the
    Originator?" HistoryBuff.com. http://www.historybuff.com/library
    /refearlybase.html.

IMDb.com, Inc. "Memorable Quotes for *Bull Durham* (1988)."
    http://www.imdb.com/title/tt0094812/quotes.

———. "Memorable Quotes for *Field of Dreams* (1989)."
    http://www.imdb.com/title/tt0097351/quotes.

———. "Memorable Quotes for *The Man Who Shot Liberty Valance*
    (1962)." http://www.imdb.com/title/tt0056217/quotes.

Jenkinson, William J. "Long Distance Home Runs." *Baseball Almanac*,
    1996. http://www.baseball-almanac.com/feats/art_hr.shtml.

Justice at Stake Campaign. "Justice John Paul Stevens: A Biography." 2012.
    http://www.justiceatstake.org/resources/justice_john_paul_stevens_a
    _biography.cfm.

Just One Bad Century. "Chicago Cubs History and News." Chicago Cubs
    History and News—Welcome to Just One Bad Century.
    http://www.justonebadcentury.com/Chicago_cubs_tales_09_43.asp.

KCET. "Pilots: Charles Lindbergh." *Chasing the Sun*. PBS.org. http://www.pbs.org/kcet/chasingthesun/innovators/clindbergh.html.

Lamkin, Michael. "Gene Tunney vs. Jack Dempsey II." Fight World. http://mmashare.mmavideoforum.com/boxing-f44/r-r-jack-dempsey-vs-gene-tunney-t54048.html.

Langford, Jim. "Player Profiles: Sandy Koufax." BaseballLibrary.com. http://www.baseballlibrary.com/ballplayers/player.php?name=Sandy_Koufax_1935&page=chronology.

Lapchick, Richard. "NBA Diversity Makes for a Pretty Big Picture." ESPN NBA, May 9, 2007. http://sports.espn.go.com/nba/columns/story?columnist=lapchick_richard&id=2865144.

Linkowski, Jeffrey. "Babe Ruth's 60 Home Runs in 1927." Angelfire. http://www.angelfire.com/pa/1927/ruth60.html.

Long, Shepard C., and John Pastier. "Yankee Stadium." BaseballLibrary.com. http://www.baseballlibrary.com/baseballlibrary/ballplayers/S/Stadium_Yankee.stm.

Macht, Norman L., and Christopher D. Renino. "Player Profiles: Roger Maris." BaseballLibrary.com. http://www.baseballlibrary.com/ballplayers/player.php?name=roger_maris_1934&page=chronology.

Mantle Holdings IP, Ltd. "Mickey's Historic Homer on Trial." Mickey Mantle Insights. http://www.mickeymantle.com/insights.htm.

McCallum, Jack, and Richard O'Brien. "They Said It." SIVault.com, July 18, 1994. http://sportsillustrated.cnn.com/vault/article/magazine/MAG1005411/index.htm.

McCarron, Anthony. "Ex-Outfielder Brian Anderson Gives Majors One Final Pitch with Yankees." New York Daily News, February 12, 2011. http://articles.nydailynews.com/2011-02-12/sports/28613061_1.

Miceli, Thomas J. "Minimum Quality Standards in Baseball and the Paradoxical Disappearance of the .400 Hitter." *Economics Working Papers*, Paper 200515, 2005. http://digitalcommons.uconn.edu/econ_wpapers/200515 (October 19, 2011).

Mintz, S. "Learn about World War II." Digital History, 2007.
http://www.digitalhistory.uh.edu/era.cfm?eraid=15&smtid=1.

MLB Advanced Media, L.P. "Cubs History: Wrigley Field Ballpark
Information." MLB.com. http://mlb.mlb.com/chc/ballpark/information
/index.jsp?content=history.

———. "History: The Hall of Fame Veterans Committee." MLB.com.
http://mlb.mlb.com/mlb/history/mlb_history_halloffame.jsp?story=4.

———. "History of the Game: Doubleday to Present Day—Albert
Benjamin 'Happy' Chandler." MLB.com. http://mlb.mlb.com/mlb/history
/mlb_history_people.jsp?story=com_bio_2.

———. "Mickey Mantle Stats." MLB.com. http://mlb.mlb.com/team
/player.jsp?player_id=118258.

———. "MLB All-Time Leaders." MLB.com. http://mlb.mlb.com
/mlb/history/all_time_leaders.jsp.

———. "1988 World Series/Game 1." MLB.com, October 14, 1988.
http://mlb.mlb.com/mlb/baseballs_best/mlb_bb_gamepage.jsp?story
_page=bb_88ws_gm1_oakla.

———. "The Pine Tar Game: George Brett's Bat Sparks Controversy."
MLB.com, July 24, 1983. http://www.mlb.com/mlb/baseballs_best
/mlb_bb_gamepage.jsp?story_page=bb_83reg_072483_kcrnyy.

———. "Rule 6.09." *Official Baseball Rules.*
http://mlb.mlb.com/mlb/downloads/y2011/Official–Baseball_Rules.pdf.

———. "Statistics: Sortable Player: Hitting, All-Time Totals, AVG."
MLB.com. http://mlb.mlb.com/index.jsp.

———. "Statistics: Sortable Player, Hitting, All-Time Totals, OPS."
MLB.com. http://mlb.mlb.com/index.jsp.

Moynahan, Brian. "Hank Greenberg: The Player Nobody Wanted." *Baseball
Almanac*, 2003. http://www.baseball-almanac.com/articles/hank
_greenberg_article.shtml.

Munsey & Suppes. "Fenway Park." Ballparks.com. July 2009.
http://www.ballparks.com/baseball/american/fenway.htm.

———. "Forbes Field." Ballparks.com, January 2008. http://www.ballparks.com/baseball/national/forbes.htm.

———. "Wrigley Field." Ballparks.com, May 2008. http://www.ballparks.com/baseball/national/wrigle.htm.

National Baseball Hall of Fame and Museum. "Hall of Famers: Club 297." http://baseballhall.org/hall-famers.

NationalPastime.com. "Baseball Responds to September 11th Attacks: Silenced Stadiums." 2010. http://www.nationalpastime.com /stitches/september11.html.

Ohio Historical Society. "Standard Oil Company." Ohio History Central, July 1, 2005. http://www.ohiohistorycentral.org/entry.php?rec=988.

Online Highways LLC. "D-Day, the Battle of Normandy." U-S-History.com. http://www.u-s-history.com/pages/h1749.html.

———. "Jackie Robinson." U-S-History.com. http://www.u-s-history.com /pages/h2068.html.

———. "Kenesaw Mountain Landis." U-S-History.com. http://www.u-s -history.com/pages/h2074.html.

———. "Roaring Twenties: Social Issues, 1920–1929." U-S-History.com. http://www.u-s-history.com/pages/h1564.html.

Partapuoli, Kari Helene, and Finn Sivert Nielsen, eds. "Culture." AnthroBase.com. http://www.anthrobase.com/Dic/eng/def/culture.htm.

The People History. "Cost of Living 1961." http://www.thepeoplehistory.com/1961.html.

QuotationsPage.com. "Quotations by Author: Edward R. Murrow (1908– 1965)." The Quotations Page. http://www.quotationspage.com /quotes/Edward_R. Murrow/.

Random History. "A History of the Cadillac." January 21, 2009. http://www.randomhistory.com/2009/01/21_cadillac.html.

Reel Classics LLC. "The Pride of the Yankees (1942)." March 10, 2011. http://www.reelclassics.com/Movies/Yankees/yankees.htm.

RK559 for Sporcle. "Can You Name the Two Teammates with the Most Home Runs?" Sporcle, April 18, 2010. http://www.sporcle.com /games/rk559/auckland.

Rosenberg, Jennifer. "Pearl Harbor Facts." About.com. http://history1900s .about.com/od/Pearl-Harbor/a/Pearl-Harbor-Facts.htm?p=1.

RVW Foundation. "About Lou: Biography." Lou Gehrig: The Official Website. http://www.lougehrig.com/about/bio.htm.

Schwartz, Larry. "Hank Aaron: Hammerin' Back at Racism." ESPN.com. http://espn.go.com/sportscentury/features/00006764.html.

Schwimmer, Brian. "A Definition of Culture." 76.122 Cultural Anthropology, University of Manitoba, 1997. http://www.umanitoba.ca /faculties/arts/anthropology/courses/122/module1/culture.html.

Scott, Carole E. "The History of the Radio Industry in the United States to 1940." EH.Net Encyclopedia, February 1, 2010. http://eh.net /encyclopedia/article/scott.radio.industry.history.

Shettle, Jr., M. L. "Californians and the Military: Ted Williams—Baseball Legend, Marine Corps Aviator." The California State Military Museum. http://www.militarymuseum.org/Williams.html.

Sigers, Joi. "Mickey Mantle: The Man Behind the Legend." *Self Help Daily* (blog). http://www.selfhelpdaily.com/mickey-mantle-inspirational -quotes/.

Silverman, Steve. "List of Home Run Calls in Baseball." Livestrong.com. http://www.livestrong.com/article/160439-list-of-home-run-calls-in -baseball/.

Smith, Curt. "Bob Wolff—85 Going on 15." *Voices of the Game* (blog), MLBlogs Network, July 7, 2006. http://curtsmith.mlblogs.com /2006/07/07/bob-wolff-85-going-on-15/.

Songfacts LLC. "'Mrs. Robinson by Simon & Garfunkel." http://www.songfacts.com/detail.php?id=1283.

Sports Reference LLC. "Al Kaline Player Page." Baseball-Reference.com. http://www.baseball-reference.com/players/k/kalinal01.shtml.

———. "Babe Ruth Player Page." Baseball-Reference.com. http://www.baseball-reference.com/players/r/ruthba01.shtml.

———. "Barry Bonds Player Page." Baseball-Reference.com. http://www.baseball-reference.com/players/b/bondsba01.shtml.

———. "Bill Mazeroski Player Page." Baseball-Reference.com. http://www.baseball-reference.com/players/m/mazerbi01.shtml.

———. "Bob Prince." Baseball-Reference.com, August 23, 2005. http://www.baseball-reference.com/bullpen/Bob_Prince.

———. "Career Leaders & Records for Bases on Balls." Baseball -Reference.com. http://www/baseball-reference.com/leaders/BB _career.shtml.

———. "George Bell Player Page." Baseball-Reference.com. http://www.baseball-reference.com/players/b/bellge02.shtml.

———. "Graig Nettles Player Page." Baseball-Reference.com. http://www.baseball-reference.com/players/n/nettlgr01.shtml.

———. "Hank Greenberg Player Page." Baseball-Reference.com. http://www.baseball-reference.com/players/g/greenha01.shtml.

———. "Joe DiMaggio Player Page." Baseball-Reference.com. http://www.baseball-reference.com/players/d/dimagjo01.shtml.

———. "Mark McGwire Player Page." Baseball-Reference.com. http://www.baseball-reference.com/players/m/mcgwima01.shtml.

———. "Mickey Mantle Player Page." Baseball-Reference.com. http://www.baseball-reference.com/players/m/mantlmi01.shtml.

———. "Monte Irvin Player Page." Baseball-Reference.com. http://www.baseball-reference.com/players/i/irvinmo01.shtml.

———. "1921 Detroit Tigers." Baseball-Reference.com. http://www.baseball-reference.com/teams/DET/1921.shtml.

———. "1927 American League Batting Leaders." Baseball-Reference.com. http://www.baseball-reference.com/leagues/AL/1927-batting-leaders .shtml .

————. "1927 New York Yankees." Baseball-Reference.com. http://www.baseball-reference.com/teams/NYY/1927.shtml.

————. "1960 Major League Baseball Batting Leaders." Baseball -Reference.com. http://www.baseball-reference.com/leagues/MLB /1960-batting-leaders.shtml.

————. "1961 Major League Baseball Batting Leaders." Baseball -Reference.com. http://www.baseball-reference.com/leagues/MLB/1961 -batting-leaders.shtml.

————. "1961 New York Yankees." Baseball-Reference.com. http://www.baseball-reference.com/teams/NYY/1961.shtml.

————. "1961 New York Yankees Batting Orders." Baseball-Reference .com. http://www.baseball-reference.com/teams/NYY/1961-batting -orders.shtml.

————. "1968 Major League Baseball Batting Leaders." Baseball -Reference.com. http://www.baseball-reference.com/leagues/MLB /1968-batting-leaders.shtml.

————. "1969 Major League Baseball Batting Leaders." Baseball -Reference.com. http://www.baseball-reference.com/leagues/MLB/1969 -batting-leaders.shtml.

————. "Ralph Kiner Player Page." Baseball-Reference.com. Baseball -Reference.com. http://www.baseball-reference.com/players/k/kinerra01 .shtml.

————. "Roger Maris Player Page." Baseball-Reference.com. http://www.baseball-reference.com/players/m/marisro01.shtml.

————. "Rogers Hornsby Player Page." Baseball-Reference.com. http://www.baseball-reference.com/players/h/hornsro01.shtml.

————. "Sammy Sosa Player Page." Baseball-Reference.com. http://www.baseball-reference.com/players/s/sosasa01.shtml.

————. "Stan Musial Player Page." Baseball-Reference.com. http://www.baseball-reference.com/players/m/musiast01.shtml.

————. "The Star Spangled Banner." Baseball-Reference.com. http://www.baseball-reference.com/bullpen/The_Star_Spangled_Banner.

———. "Switch Hitter." Baseball-Reference.com. http://www.baseball-reference.com/bullpen/Switch_hitter.

———. "2006 Philadelphia Phillies." Baseball-Reference.com, http://www.baseball-reference.com/teams/PHI/2006.shtml.

———. "Ty Cobb—BR Bullpen." Baseball-Reference.com. http://www.baseball-reference.com/bullpen/Ty_Cobb.

TestCountry. "All You Need to Know about Teenage Steroid Use." http://www.testcountry.org/teenage-steroid-use.htm .

U.S. Census Bureau. "People QuickFacts: Black Persons, Percent, 2011 (a)." *State & County QuickFacts: USA*, August 16, 2012 (last revised). http://quickfacts.census.gov/qfd/states/00000.html.

Walton, Ed. "Player Profiles: Ty Cobb." BaseballLibrary.com. http://www.baseballlibrary.com/ballplayers/player.php?name=ty_cobb_1886.

WGBH. "Radio Transmission: The Early Years of Radio." *A Science Odyssey*, PBS.org. http://www.pbs.org/wgbh/aso/tryit/radio/earlyyears.html.

Whitley, David. "Lou Gehrig's Farewell Speech Still Underrated by American Scholars." *Sporting News MLB*, July 4, 2011. http://aol.sportingnews.com/mlb/story/2011-07-04/gehrigs-farewell-speech-still-underrated-by-american-scholars.

Vanguard Publications. "Spring Training History Articles: Yankees Go West in 1951." Spring Training Yearbook Online, 1998. http://springtrainingmagazine.com/history.html.

Verducci, Tom. "Embarrassing Moments: Owners, Cheaters, Gamblers All Disgrace Baseball." *Inside Baseball*, August 2, 2006. http://sportsillustrated.cnn.com/2006/writers/tom_verducci/07/13/moments/index.html.

Wikimedia Foundation, Inc. "Graig Nettles." *Wikipedia*. http://en.wikipedia.org/wiki/Graig_Nettles.

———. "USS *Arizona* Memorial." *Wikipedia*. http://en.wikipedia.org/wiki/USS_Arizona_Memorial.

———. "Who's on First?" *Wikipedia*. http://en.wikipedia.org/wiki/Who's_on_First%3F.

Zarefsky, Marc. "'Homer in the Gloamin' Most Memorable." Cubs.com, August 8, 2007. http://mlb.mlb.com/content/printer_friendly/chc /y2007/m07/d20/c2099223.jsp.

INDEX

ABOUT THE AUTHOR

Eldon L. Ham is a member of the faculty at Chicago-Kent College of Law, where he has taught sports, law, and society since 1994 and won the Distinguished Service Award in 2010. He is also the designated legal analyst for WSCR sports radio in Chicago and the three-time past chair of the Chicago Bar Association Law and Literature Committee. Since 1976, he has practiced law in Chicago and represented scores of athletes, agents, and sports entrepreneurs.

Ham is also the author of four previous books on topics of sports history: *Broadcasting Baseball: A History of the National Pastime on Radio and Television* (McFarland, 2011); *Larceny & Old Leather: The Mischievous Legacy of Major League Baseball* (Academy Chicago Publishers, 2005); *The Playmasters: From Sellouts to Lockouts—an Unauthorized History of the NBA* (Contemporary Books, 2000); and *The 100 Greatest Sports Blunders of All Time* (Masters Press, 1997). He has been nationally quoted in the *New York Times, USA Today, Business Week, ESPN.com, Chicago Sun-Times, Washington Post,* and many more; and his articles have been published by the *New York Times, Harvard University Sports Law Journal, Street & Smith Sports Business Journal, Chicago Tribune, Baltimore Sun, St.*

Louis Post-Dispatch, Trial Magazine, Seton Hall Sports Law Journal, Marquette Sports Law Review, and others.

For additional background, please visit www.eldonham.com.